114 927

KU-547-134

English Drama: Restoration and Eighteenth Century

-27

-3.

B.C.H.E. - LIBRARY

00131831

Longman Literature in English Series

General Editors: David Carroll and Michael Wheeler
University of Lancaster

For a complete list of titles see pages x and xi

English Drama: Restoration and Eighteenth Century, 1660–1789

Richard W. Bevis

Longman

London and New York

BATH COLLEGE
OF
HIGHER EDUCATION
NEWTON PARK
LIBRARY
DISCARD

CLASS
No.   822·66
              BEV

ACC
No.   1140270

Longman Group UK Limited
Longman House, Burnt Mill, Harlow
Essex CM20 2JE, England
and Associated companies throughout the world

*Published in the United States of America
by Longman Inc., New York*

© Longman Group UK Limited 1988

All rights reserved; no part of this publication
may be reproduced, stored in a retrieval system,
or transmitted in any form or by any means, electronic,
mechanical, photocopying, recording, or otherwise,
without the prior written permission of the Publishers,
or a licence permitting restricted copying
issued by the Copyright Licensing Agency
Ltd, 33–34 Alfred Place, London, WC1E 7DP

First published 1988

BRITISH LIBRARY CATALOGUING IN PUBLICATION DATA
Bevis, Richard W.
    English drama: Restoration and
    eighteenth century, 1660–1789.
    1. English drama — Restoration, 1660–1700
    — History and criticism 2. English drama —
    18th century — History and criticism
    I. Title
    822'.009   PR691

    ISBN 0-582-49394-3   CSD
    ISBN 0-582-49393-5   PPR

LIBRARY OF CONGRESS CATALOGING IN PUBLICATION DATA
Bevis, Richard W.
    English drama: Restoration and eighteenth century

    (Longman literature in English series)
    Bibliography: p.
    Includes index.
    1. English drama — Restoration, 1660–1700 — History
    and criticism. 2. English drama — 18th century —
    History and criticism. I. Title. II. Series.
    PR691.B48   1988   822'.009   87–4244
    ISBN 0-582-49394-3
    ISBN 0-582-49393-5 (pbk.)

Set in Linotron 202 9½/11pt Bembo
Produced by Longman Singapore Publishers (Pte) Ltd.
Printed in Singapore

Contents

General Bibliographies 284

Individual Authors 293

Index 326

List of Abbreviations

The following abbreviations for learned journals are employed in the Endnotes and the Author Bibliographies.

Durham U. Jour.:	*Durham University Journal*
EC:	*Essays in Criticism*
ECS:	*Eighteenth-Century Studies*
Educ. Theat. Jour.:	*Educational Theatre Journal*
ELH:	*English Literary History*
ELN:	*English Language Notes*
Harvard Lib. Bull.:	*Harvard Library Bulletin*
HL Bull.:	*Huntington Library Bulletin*
HLQ:	*Huntington Library Quarterly*
MLQ:	*Modern Language Quarterly*
MLS:	*Modern Language Studies*
MP:	*Modern Philology*
PMLA:	*Publications of the Modern Language Association*
PQ:	*Philological Quarterly*
RECTR:	*Restoration and Eighteenth-Century Theatre Research*
RES:	*Review of English Studies*
SEL:	*Studies in English Literature*
SP:	*Studies in Philology*
Theat. Jour.:	*Theater Journal*

Editors' Preface

The multi-volume Longman Literature in English Series provides students of literature with a critical introduction to the major genres in their historical and cultural context. Each volume gives a coherent account of a clearly defined area, and the series, when complete, will offer a practical and comprehensive guide to literature written in English from Anglo-Saxon times to the present. The aim of the series as a whole is to show that the most valuable and stimulating approach to literature is that based upon an awareness of the relations between literary forms and their historical context. Thus the areas covered by most of the separate volumes are defined by period and genre. Each volume offers new informed ways of reading literary works, and provides guidance to further reading in an extensive reference section.

As well as studies on all periods of English and American literature, the series includes books on criticism and literary theory, and on the intellectual and cultural context. A comprehensive series of this kind must of course include other literature written in English, and therefore a group of volumes deals with Irish and Scottish literature, and the literatures of India, Africa, the Caribbean, Australia, and Canada. The forty-seven volumes of the series cover the following areas: pre-Renaissance English Literature, English Poetry, English Drama, English Fiction, English Prose, Criticism and Literary Theory, Intellectual and Cultural Context, American Literature, Other Literatures in English.

David Carroll
Michael Wheeler

Longman Literature in English Series
General Editors: David Carroll and Michael Wheeler
University of Lancaster

Pre-Renaissance English Literature

* English Literature before Chaucer *Michael Swanton*
 English Literature in the Age of Chaucer
* English Medieval Romance *W. R. J. Barron*

English Poetry

* English Poetry of the Sixteenth Century *Gary Waller*
* English Poetry of the Seventeenth Century *George Parfitt*
 English Poetry of the Eighteenth Century, 1700–1789
* English Poetry of the Romantic Period, 1789–1830 *J. R. Watson*
* English Poetry of the Victorian Period, 1830–1890 *Bernard Richards*
 English Poetry of the Early Modern Period, 1890–1940
 English Poetry since 1940

English Drama

 English Drama before Shakespeare
* English Drama: Shakespeare to the Restoration, 1590–1660
 Alexander Leggatt
* English Drama: Restoration and Eighteenth Century, 1660–1789
 Richard W. Bevis
 English Drama: Romantic and Victorian, 1789–1890
 English Drama of the Early Modern Period, 1890–1940
 English Drama since 1940

English Fiction

* English Fiction of the Eighteenth Century, 1700–1789
 Clive T. Probyn
 English Fiction of the Romantic Period, 1789–1830
* English Fiction of the Victorian Period, 1830–1890 *Michael Wheeler*
 English Fiction of the Early Modern Period, 1890–1940

English Prose

 English Prose of the Renaissance, 1550–1700
 English Prose of the Eighteenth Century
 English Prose of the Nineteenth Century

Criticism and Literary Theory

Criticism and Literary Theory from Sidney to Johnson
Criticism and Literary Theory from Wordsworth to Arnold
Criticism and Literary Theory from 1890 to the Present

The Intellectual and Cultural Context

The Sixteenth Century
The Seventeenth Century
★ The Eighteenth Century, 1700–1789 *James Sambrook*
The Romantic Period, 1789–1830
The Victorian Period, 1830–1890
The Twentieth Century: 1890 to the Present

American Literature

American Literature before 1865
American Poetry of the Twentieth Century
American Drama of the Twentieth Century
★ American Fiction, 1865–1940 *Brian Lee*
American Fiction since 1940
Twentieth-Century America

Other Literatures

Irish Literature since 1800
Scottish Literature since 1700

Australian Literature
Indian Literature in English
African Literature in English: East and West
South African Literature in English
Caribbean Literature in English
★ Canadian Literature in English *W. J. Keith*

★ *Already published*

Author's Preface

When first presented with the idea of writing this volume, I hesitated: surely the *Revels History* would suffice for a while longer? Those admirable volumes, however, each the work of several hands, reflect the state of theatre research and drama criticism in the early 1970s, and a great deal of scholarly and critical activity – much of it revisionist – has occurred since. A fresh expedition through the territory would give me a chance not only to update the scholarship to the eighties, but to offer a single reader's view of how drama interacted with theatre and society from the Restoration of the French Revolution, a seminal era for our modern entertainment world. For a teacher who has spent twenty years trying to explain the period to students – and to understand it with them – the opportunity to expand and propagate the course was too tempting to resist.

I have tried to produce an account of the 'life of the drama' from Dryden to Holcroft that would be informative and even challenging for the moderately advanced student without being unintelligible to the general reader, and as free from personal idiosyncrasies as possible. The omission of a single, central thesis is deliberate; I think that what we need is a determined effort to describe what happened in the various phases and aspects of Augustan and Georgian theatre, not the imposition of a 'comprehensive' theory that fits here and pinches there.

After a general introduction surveying some pertinent developments in the Jacobean, Caroline and Commonwealth periods, I treat Restoration and eighteenth-century drama in the three broad phases into which it seems naturally to fall: the Restoration itself, which properly ends in 1688, a long period of reforms and retrenchments (1689–1737), and the era dominated by Garrick. Within each section, I sketch the historical, intellectual and theatrical contexts before discussing the principal dramatic genres of the age. An epilogue describes the transitional decade of the 1780s more briefly.

Whatever the shortcomings of this scheme, they are less than those arising from the restricted space in which I had to work. To give a coherent account of 130 years of drama in its social contexts in 100,000 words proved impossible; even with a grant of additional words by my editors, it may be questioned whether the concise does not become terse, and the terse laconic, in the following pages. No one can regret the omissions and the skimpy treatment of interesting plays more than I. No author, no work, escaped cutting. 'The pruning knife!' roars Sheridan's Puff; 'Zounds, the axe!' One way of handling this problem and conveying more information economically was to relegate some of it to Appendices. The main text should be read with reference to the Chronology and the General and Author Bibliographies, which provide a framework for the critical discussions and free them of cluttering (but necessary) factual details.

Dates given for plays refer to first production unless otherwise noted; the New Year is dated from 1 January throughout the period. The citation of texts is handled in two ways. Any modern, edited edition is footnoted on its first occurrence, and referenced parenthetically thereafter. Early, unedited printings are indicated by an act–scene reference without a note.

Like any scholarly author who surveys a large field, I am indebted to friends and colleagues as well as to the critical tradition acknowledged in the endnotes. Professor Robert D. Hume was extremely helpful in sending packets of offprints to my autoexilic study in the Yucatan; Profs Alexander Leggatt, Harold Love and Terence Freeman likewise took the trouble to mail me scholarly materials. The University of British Columbia and the Social Sciences and Humanities Research Council of Canada underwrote the time I needed to complete the work; my colleagues Andrew Parkin and Ian Ross, and Prof. Anne Messenger, helped me obtain this support. Tim Pearson ably researched the Author Bibliographies. I am grateful for the careful editing of David Carroll and Michael Wheeler. And to all those who bore with me through the last three years, my special thanks for their understanding.

Richard W. Bevis
Vancouver, B. C., Canada

To
C. H. O. Scaife
Actor, poet, teacher, friend

Introduction

In seventeenth-century theatres, before the first curtain, an actor or actress stepped forth alone as prologue: to anticipate criticism, perhaps to needle the playwright or the audience, certainly to whip up interest and 'set the stage' with a series of neatly turned couplets. O for a Nell Gywn to warm the audience and introduce Restoration drama, sketching prettily and wittily the context in which it was written and performed! Some such effort is needed, for our habit of chopping literary study into periods causes many readers with some background in Shakespeare and modern drama to leap directly from the Age of Elizabeth into the Restoration, where, landing heavily amid the indoor theatres thronged with courtiers, the exotic hero-plays, the narrowly urban comedies in prose, they suffer cultural shock and dislocation. Whatever became (they wonder) of the forest of Arden, the king on the heath, the Muse of Fire?

Such questions cannot be fully answered within the confines of Restoration drama: they require the contexts of seventeenth-century political and social history, and of Jacobean and Caroline drama, from which it grew. In the Restoration, writers were still apt to be public figures who took an interest in the whole of contemporary life and in at least the recent national past – often in classical and European history as well. Drama being the most social of the arts, dramatists also reflected the prejudices and preferences of their chief patrons, the court circle, and the concerns of the citizens and gentry who frequented the theatres. Restoration plays may slight the cosmos, but they deal extensively with the issues and mores of their age, from fears of Dutch warships and French Catholics through the rise of empirical science to the affectations of returned travellers and the ethics of the sexual revolution. A modern reader or spectator can certainly glean amusement and sometimes edification from this drama, but unless conversant with its background will often be alienated or left wondering what all the fuss is about. Whatever the *general* merits of Leslie Stephen's remark, 'The adequate criticism must be rooted in history', it applies with full force to works so much of their time and place.

Then too, this is the life-story of a drama, and like most stories rests upon a rich narrative past. As 'Once upon a time' is just a point on a continuum, so 'periods' of literature are as a rule deeply rooted in the previous age. Restoration drama is no exception, despite the apparently surgical neatness of its edges. Probably because of the partial break in the native tradition, it reached back in time and outward in space as few English literatures have done. Tudor and Stuart plays were revived, imitated and argued over; French, Spanish, and Italian styles were admired or deplored; classical models and neo-classical critics provoked debate; the new Continental stagecraft had to be absorbed, and so on. Puritan hostility to the theatre began long before 1642, and plays performed during the Commonwealth, defying the official ban, influenced what audiences wanted after 1660. So this, like every biography, must begin with roots.

From Gloriana to the Protector

The salient characteristics of Restoration art can be traced to some troubling fissures that began to open in English life during the apparently brilliant reign of Elizabeth I. These were economic and religious as much as political; in fact Reformation England, like modern Ireland and Lebanon, seldom had one without the others. Conspicuous on the public stage was the double alienation of the established Anglican Church from Rome on one hand (Elizabeth was excommunicated in 1570) and its own Nonconformists (or 'Puritans' or 'Dissenters') on the other.[1] The religious schisms had political overtones from the beginning: Elizabeth made a secret treaty with French Huguenots, and a century later French Catholics returned the favour by intriguing with the Stuart dynasty, whose Catholicism, always its Achilles' heel, was not purged until 1688. To the left, dissenting voices in Parliament and on London's Common Council periodically contradicted court policy on issues ranging from finance and foreign policy to theatre and morals.[2] One or the other of these sectarian estrangements led to sporadic bloodshed in England throughout the seventeenth century and as late as 1745.

Somewhat less obvious at first were the cleavages between social classes caused by the rise of capitalism and the reaction to it of traditional, agricultural England. The enclosure of land and dislocation of people, the gulf between luxury and want, that Hogarth and Goldsmith publicized in the eighteenth century began to fracture English life in Elizabethan times, causing social unrest, especially in London, swollen to three times its 1520 size.[3] As the population shot up, so did the rate of illegitimacy and the cost of government. Gaps and inequities increased: thousands of new gentlemen were bred out of the new wealth, but the new chances also created the worst poverty problem in a century. Prices climbed away from wages after 1550, and the curve steepened in the 1590s, just as real wages were hitting a seven-century low. In fact, between inflation, unemployment, debt, the Essex rebellion (1599–1601), and the succession crisis, the last years of 'Gloriana' the Virgin Queen had a much darker cast than the lyrical age just after the Armada.

The arrival of James I and the Stuart line in 1603, while settling the succession for a time, added the problem of an unpopular monarch to the religious and socio-economic divisions. His fiscal policies and talk of divine right disliked, his foreign adventures distrusted, his selling of knighthoods despised, his favourite Buckingham hated, his personal style, even his accent, derided, James, along with his luxurious Court, soon drifted apart from the mainstream of national life.[4] One crisis followed another, polarizing the country: quarrels with Puritan leaders (1604), the Gunpowder Plot by disaffected Catholics (1605), rioting in the Midlands, Parliament's Petition of Grievances (1610) leading to a ten-year prorogation, disruption of the wool industry (1614) followed by a long depression, and, in the span of 1615–18, the Overbury case, the dismissal of Coke, and the execution of Ralegh.[5] Through it all James struggled, as did every male Stuart to some degree, to find some way to finance the operations of government, but ended by greatly increasing the Crown's debt.

If religion *per se* was less of an issue at this time – James's opponents included many Anglican merchants, entrepreneurs, and gentry – royal prerogative and extravagance became more pressing ones. To many, the King's lavish new Banqueting House at Whitehall and the expensive entertainments there, such as masques, seemed irresponsible.[6] 'Say to the Court it glows/And shines', wrote Sir Walter Ralegh, 'like rotten wood'. As the disparities between the wealthy and the destitute grew more obvious, they generated a satiric literature on the parvenus. A whole school of comedy, led by Ben Jonson, commented on Jacobean social inequities in tones very different from those of 1590s drama; there was never a 'Stuart myth' to succeed the 'Tudor myth'. The mellowness of Shakespeare's last comedies is atypical of the period: Jonson's satires on greed and avarice in *Volpone* (1606) and *The Alchemist* (1610) are much more closely attuned to the mood developing then, which carried over (with the economic depression) into the next reign. The year Charles I acceded (1625), Philip Massinger produced *A New Way to Pay Old Debts*, with its powerful portrait of Sir Giles Overreach, one of the rapacious 'new men'; in Jonson's *The Staple of News* (1625), Miser hails Lady Pecunia as 'The Venus of the time and state'.

Inheriting this legacy of debt and division, Charles, whom many found more attractive than James, immediately negated any personal advantages by marrying Princess Henrietta Maria of France, a devout Catholic. It was a foretaste of his arrogance and insensitivity. ('Remember', he told Parliament with unwitting irony in 1626, 'parliaments are altogether in my power for their calling, sitting and dissolution; therefore as I find the fruits of them good or evil, they are to continue or not to be.') His queen was of some importance to literature, especially drama, through her encouragement of a cult of Platonic love, but the Papist issue would seldom cease to haunt the Stuarts for the next six decades.[7] A court studded with Catholics could only exacerbate Charles's wrangles with his Protestant Parliament over money, policies, and personalities, chiefly Buckingham, who was impeached and assassinated (1628). The repressions of William Laud (Archbishop of Canterbury from 1633) and the Earl of Strafford in the King's name, and the Court's tendency to withdraw into its own European-style world of Platonic theatre, further fragmented the nation in the 1630s.

Of the many clashes – the Petition of Right (1628), leading to the dissolution of Parliament and eleven years of Star Chamber government, the issue of ship-money, the imposition of the Prayer Book on Scotland, bringing on the Scottish National Covenant (1638) – one shows with particular clarity how the lines and forces were arranging themselves as the nation moved towards civil war. William Prynne, a learned Puritan barrister, published an attack on the stage, *Histriomastix* (1632), which Laud held to be libellous of the Queen, a devotee of sumptuous theatricals. In 1634 the Star Chamber – a symbol of Stuart high-handedness – stripped Prynne of his Oxford honours, fined him five thousand pounds, had him pilloried and partly 'eared', and sent him to prison for life. When he continued to write in the Tower he was fined again, completely 'eared', and branded on both cheeks. The Long Parliament did not forget him: when it impeached Laud and Strafford (1640), it released and exonerated Prynne.

By then Royalists and Parliamentarians were on a collision course, and in 1641 the latter accelerated, ordering the execution of Strafford, the dismissal of the Queen's Catholic attendants and the abolition of the Star Chamber. The seemingly inexorable tearing of the social fabric – which would haunt English minds for over a century – proceeded swiftly thereafter; the King's disastrous attempt to arrest Parliamentary leaders and his withdrawal to Oxford, the Queen's departure for Holland, and the raising of battle standards all occurred in 1642. Anarchy and economic breakdown developed apace.[8] In that perspective, the closing of the theatres by Parliament (September) seems a minor matter, though it was symptomatic both of drama's Royalist leanings and the cultural dimension of the conflict. Charles, with too few adherents and too little financial backing, especially in London, lost the major battles to Parliament, which had Laud executed and forced the surrender of Oxford. The Royalists collapsed when the King surrendered to the Scots army (1646) and the Prince of Wales fled to Paris. The first phase of the Civil War had ended.

The *interbellum* was neither long nor placid. Purchased by Parliament and seized by the New Model Army in 1647, the King escaped but was recaptured as a second round of fighting began (1648). Again Parliament ruled the battlefields, but now the Royalists were winning minds and hearts; the execution of Charles I (1649) on scaffolding outside the Banqueting House where he had played in masques – positively his last appearance on any stage – cost Parliament much support in the political centre. Running on momentum, it proclaimed a Commonwealth and turned back a Scots invasion. Charles II, proclaimed in Scotland, went there in 1650 to accept the Crown, but had to flee to France again after the Battle of Worcester (1651).

That was the last of the Royalist military threat (after 100,000 deaths) but not of wars and civil wars. In 1652 the savaging of Ireland gave way to the First Dutch War, which was hardly ended when hostilities broke out with Spain. On the home front, Oliver Cromwell expelled Parliament and established his Protectorate in 1653, while a stream of anti-stage ordinances and arrests of spectators shows that Londoners did not take the prohibition of their amusements lightly. A Royalist uprising in 1655 was the most visible manifestation of growing dissatisfaction with the Protectorate. When Oliver died in 1658, his son Richard was named Lord Protector, but a substantial majority of the nation had become weary of sequestered property, official repressions, and the influence of religious fundamentalists on government and everyday life. General Monk, declaring for Charles Stuart, led his army down from Scotland in 1659; a Convention Parliament assembled and requested Charles II to return as king. It is a telling irony of those turbulent years that one of the Parliamentarians who voted for the King's return was the earless, branded William Prynne.

Most of the defeated Royalists had been exiles between 1646 and 1660. Charles settled in Paris for much of the interregnum, providing a focus for courtiers, loyalist nobility, and thespians; from there many of them travelled or lived in Spain, Italy, Germany, or the Spanish Netherlands. This exposure to Continental culture had marked effects on Restoration life in two areas particularly, the political and the theatrical. As it happened, the years of strife in England coincided with a period of settled strength for France: the minority of Louis XIV. The demoralized English courtiers could not but be struck by the contrast between their own oligarchical shambles and the spectacle of an absolute monarchy in complete control of an obedient nation, as well as by the artistic brilliance and pageantry of a court that patronized some of the finest artists in Europe and made its daily life an elegant ceremony. Thomas Hobbes's *Leviathan* (1651), with its massive argument for the necessity of subjugating individuals – restless, egocentric, disorderly – to a strong central authority, is a crucial document of those formative years; no English book was more influential on the psychology and political theory of the Restoration, or is more basic to understanding it.

Meanwhile the courtiers, formerly patrons of the English stage, had plenty of time for the theatre. Charles maintained a company of actors in Paris, and the exiles also enjoyed the plays of Corneille, Scarron, the early Molière, French and Italian opera and ballet, the *commedia dell'arte* of Italy and the *comedias* of the Spanish *siglo de oro*. A few of them wrote material that would find its way on to the Restoration stage, but most of the Royalists were content to take it all in: the *gloire* of heroic tragedy, the music and spectacular scenery of the operas, the complex bustle of the intrigue comedies, the actresses! And they returned to England in 1660 with some distinct notions of what the theatre should be.

From Shakespeare to Dryden

Restoration theatre was not merely a Gallic transplant, despite the Continental exile of many of its patrons. The tendency of early historians to blame the excesses of the 'Carolean' stage (1660–85) on the French has been chastised; the fundamental Englishness of the Restoration is now generally accepted. Late-seventeenth-century English plays resemble the pre-1642 varieties sufficiently to make 'Stuart drama' a coherent entity, notwithstanding the partial break of the interregnum and a greater European contribution thereafter. Even a cursory look shows this continuity, as well as the changes that occurred as a result of the traumata of social breakdown, civil war, and exile.

Theatres and companies

The general appearance of the Elizabethan public playhouse is familiar to us from reproductions of the Johannes de Witt sketch of the Swan (*c.* 1596) and reconstructions of the Globe and Fortune of the same era: a smallish frame building, square or hexagonal outside, surrounding an unroofed courtyard into which a platform stage projects about half-way. The chief virtues of this arrangement are that the virtual absence of scenery and artificial lighting forced the playwright to use *words* to create his visual effects in the spectator's mind, and that a stage three-quarters surrounded by audience fostered intimacy between actors and their public. For our purposes, however, the crucial point is that this institution was obsolescent even in Shakespeare's later years, during and after which it steadily lost ground to the new indoor theatres.

Shakespeare makes wry reference to this development in *Hamlet*, where the Prince questions the strolling players about 'the boys' who 'carry it away' in their rivalry with the 'common stages' of London (II. 2). A children's company had moved into Blackfriars theatre (a converted monastic refectory) in 1599–1600, attracting crowds that cut into the professionals' audiences. Ben Jonson soon joined the company, where he could write for better educated spectators, including a higher proportion of courtiers and gentry than graced the Fortune or the Globe. Shakespeare's own company took over Blackfriars as their main (winter) theatre in 1608, deriving greater profits from higher charges to the wealthier patrons there.

For theatre-goers, the indoor 'private' (i.e. economically selective) playhouse had several obvious advantages: protection from inclement weather, comfortable seating, 'better' company and illusions. Artificial lighting was necessary, but permitted some striking effects. The stage could be darkened and then lit only by a single torch or candle, for example. Scenery could be used to simulate physical reality – the beginning of the long process by which the poet gave ground to the scene painter – and the scenes tended to grow ever more elaborate and costly. Some of this could be done outdoors on the public stages, but the atmosphere and clientele of the private theatres were more con-ducive to 'scenarism'. A subtler change was the shortening of the plat-form stage, which no longer jutted among the spectators. The actors had begun to retreat from a darker auditorium towards a brighter stage behind a proscenium, though they still had a good way to go.

Altogether seven private theatres (not counting rebuilds), eight public theatres, three court theatres, and seven inns or taverns occasionally produced plays in Jacobean–Caroline times.[9] Not all at once – they came and went, like acting companies – nor were they all full-time playhouses. Probably six theatres regularly offered plays in London in 1625 and also in 1642. The number of acting troupes was five in each of those years, though only the King's Men (Shakespeare's old company) appear on both lists, using two theatres, Blackfriars and Globe. By way of comparison, there had been four theatres – all public

– in 1596; after 1660, in the largest London yet, there were two theatres and two companies.

The names of the troupes – King's Men, Prince Charles's, Queen Henrietta's Men, and so on – remind us that most companies survived under royal patronage, which meant protection from the Puritan outlook on London's Common Council, more playing dates at Court, and an appreciable influence on repertories. Nobility were fond of heroic, genteel, and spectacular forms, such as the masque, in which gorgeously costumed courtiers and even a prince or a queen might join the actors in presenting allegorical tableaux and declaiming formal poetry. Such productions were costly, but when the professional companies played at Court they could use the scenery and machines there and so provide the lavish effects associated with the form. Cheaper and less elegant versions of the masque reached the public stages, usually as a scene in a regular play (e.g. *The Tempest*, IV. 1), a custom that continued after the Restoration.

By the closing of the theatres, private indoor playhouses had achieved a position of rough equality with public stages, and all the momentum – of construction, incentive to perform, prestige – belonged to the former. With three court theatres, and the legal position of the actors as royal servants, pulling drama to Court, the pendulum had swung far towards an aristocratic stage. Six or seven inns – the oldest Tudor playhouses – sometimes presented plays, and their importance would revive during the Commonwealth, but in Stuart times they were the least important venue for drama.

Audiences

Naturally these changes in the physical surroundings of drama were accompanied by changes in the make-up of audiences. Though primary records are fragmentary, there is no serious scholarly dissent from the common-sense conclusion: Jacobean and Caroline audiences were more élite than their Elizabethan counterparts.[10]

In 1600, the typical London audience was still the heterogeneous mixture of groundlings and gallants that the inexpensive admissions at the Globe and Fortune made possible. And Shakespeare's public, besides being a democratic cross-section of London society, was passably well educated on relevant subjects and keen on drama; Shakespeareans generally consider the Bard's audience one of his greatest assets.[11] Very different observers testified to the rich mixture. Edmund Gayton, a pamphleteer, remembered 'Water-men, Shoomakers, Butchers and Apprentices . . . Mechanicks of all professions' at Elizabethan playhouses, while Orazio Busino, Chaplain to the Venetian Embassy, noticed 'much nobility' and 'many very honourable and handsome ladies' at the Fortune (1617) even as he was being solicited by a masked prostitute.[12] Presumably this pot-pourri continued at the public theatres until 1642, with some loss of gentle and noble patrons to the private playhouses.

As soon as Blackfriars began the move indoors, however, filtering its clientele by charging more for its seats, there are adversarial overtones to playwrights' comments on their audiences. The Prologue to John Day's *The Isle of Gulls* (Blackfriars 1606) complains about spectators who demand bawdy or bombast – or walk out. It is a reasonable inference from the repertoire that audience taste grew more extreme in the next decade, though William Archer's contention that Jacobean playgoers demanded violence, crudity, rant, or ribaldry is probably excessive.[13] Henry Fitzgeffrey cast a satirical eye over the Blackfriars audience in 1620, and in addition to a braggart captain and a traveller whom he might have seen at the Globe, limned characters that his descendants would be able to see in Dorset Garden or Drury Lane fifty years later: the fashion-plate in holland shirt and French suit; the 'Musk-ball Milke-sop', a mincing fop who dances in; the 'spruse Coxcomb' in his feather cap and whalebone corset who would not be caught *dead* without his pocket mirror.[14] Such types had once risked attending the Globe, but now they had a world of their own where their nostrils would not be assaulted by garlic, nor their persons by butcher boys.

The scene at the court theatres was the most dazzling of all. When Orazio Busino went to the Royal Banqueting House for a masque in 1618, he divided his attention between 'admiring the beauty and decorations of the house', and the boxes full of 'most noble and richly arrayed ladies, . . . the most delicate plumes over their heads . . .'.[15] When the performance began, with the King in attendance, the dancers included the Marquis of Buckingham and the Prince of Wales, the future Charles I.

The trend towards a courtly theatrical clientele continued into the reign of Charles I. As the gulf between stage-hating Puritan and stage-loving Royalist grew, the players naturally took refuge with the latter. If there was a 'typical' Caroline theatre-goer, it was a somewhat jaded courtier, fond of seeing an idealized version of himself on-stage, and of masques. Though the Cavalier audience was itself shrinking, dramatists, virtually an endangered species, saw no good alternative to being kept in the royal preserve.[16] More and more playwrights were gentlemen, even Cavaliers: a process that had begun with Marston and Fletcher, and continued through Ford, Shirley, and Davenant. With courtiers now established at each level – spectator, playwright, at times actor – a fair proportion of English theatre could by 1640 reasonably be called 'coterie'.

Earlier Stuart drama

One of the first points on which modern dramatic criticism agreed was that the Elizabethan flowering was brief, lapsing into decadence upon Shakespeare's retirement, or a little earlier. Whatever one thinks of the quality of Jacobean–Caroline drama, however, it was a fecund period, whose main outlines can only be sketched here. To do this – and no more – is an impertinence, in view of the importance that T. S. Eliot, Kathleen Lynch, and others have accorded the period; but it is necessary to establish the major trends that led English drama, by a series of gradual transitions, from Shakespearean tragedy and romantic comedy to the heroic plays and satiric wit comedy of the Restoration.

Stuart masques have been denigrated as pompous 'spectacles of state' by critics from Jonson to Allardyce Nicoll, and admired for integrating characters, audience, and media in ways that anticipate modern drama.[17] Both views can be supported from different texts and periods; for my purposes, what is important is the popularity of the masque and its influence on playwrights and spectators. Profound or shallow, native development or foreign import, it became a significant part of seventeenth-century English theatre. Masques devolved from court ritual to reach general audiences as interludes in ordinary plays, and it was probably these entertainments that, resurfacing during the Commonwealth ban, generated Restoration operatic drama.[18]

The true masque was a dramatic form in which courtly and (later) professional maskers representing mythological gods, type characters or qualities such as Reason and Pleasure, spoke, sang, moved rhythmically and performed symbolic actions. Originally masques allowed the Court to heighten its experience, to create the magical world of the *domaine*: the absolute realm apart from time that has fascinated authors from Chrétien de Troyes to John Fowles. By the 1620s, though, the emphasis had shifted to costumes, scenic wonders, music, and dance. When they seemed to offer some scope for serious poetry, serious dramatists – chiefly Ben Jonson – were led to compose masques, but in 1631 Jonson decided that he was simply writing prompts and *libretti* for scene designers and musicians, and vented his 'Expostulation with Inigo Jones', the leading scenarist:

> What is the cause you pomp it so, I ask?
> And all men echo, you have made a masque.
> I chime that too, and I have met with those
> That do cry up the machine and the shows; . . .
> The eloquence of masques! what need of prose,
> Or verse, or sense. . . .

'Painting and carpentry are the soul of masque', charges Jonson. However that may be, all levels of the theatrical audience welcomed the spectacles, which came to be demanded on the public stages. Shakespeare inserted into *Cymbeline* and *The Tempest* masque elements clearly based on the example of the court theatres; James Shirley, the leading Caroline dramatist, also wrote a number of masques for the Court.

Jonson gained considerably more repute by founding a school of satiric 'humours' comedy than by his masques. Though his comedies also have their detractors, his influence on the comedy and comic theory of at least the next century is as undeniable as the vigour of his style and the zest of his characters. The list of Jonsonian innovations adopted by Restoration writers is *sans pareil*. It was he who deflected comedy, even before Elizabeth's death, from the romantic to the satiric–realistic, though it is true his 'realism' wavers. It was Jonson who pointed comic writers in the direction of character *types* based on the old medical theory of the humours – 'choler, melancholy, phlegm and blood' – whose balance or imbalance was held to determine temperament. He explains in the Induction added to *Every Man in His Humour* (1598) in 1616 that the concept may be applied metaphorically to the 'general disposition':

> As when some one peculiar quality
> Doth so possess a man that it doth draw
> All his affects, his spirits and his powers,
> In their confluctions, all to run one way –
> This may be truly said to be a humour.

Some have objected that the fruit of this approach is mere caricature – and it does not adequately describe his own characterizations – but a century after Jonson, playwrights were still using and debating 'humours theory'. In this Induction and in prologues that define comedy as 'an image of the times' wherein the writer tries to 'mix profit with your pleasure', Jonson provided a critical apologue for his own work, setting a precedent for Dryden, Goldsmith, and others. Jonson was also largely responsible for making prose the normal medium of satiric comedy, though his best comedies are in verse. Finally, Jonson showed how a network of interlocking intrigues and colliding characters could serve as a plot. This is somewhat ironic, in view of his devotion to Aristotle (for whom plot was prime) and Coleridge's admiration for the 'perfect' plot of *The Alchemist*, but Restoration writers, admiring the dense texture of Jonson's weave, copied it often, sometimes with lamentable results.

Among the influential texts of the satiric school, Francis Beaumont's

The Knight of the Burning Pestle (1607), besides being a very funny play, is historically important in two ways. It presented (to the Blackfriars audience) a gentle satire on popular, 'citizen' taste at the public theatres, while its 'rehearsal format' – actors impersonate spectators who comment on (and enter) a dramatic performance – prefigured many a Restoration and eighteenth-century burlesque. Philip Massinger's *A New Way to Pay Old Debts* (which remained 'in rep' for two and a half centuries despite a sharp sense of class) satirizes greedy *nouveaux riches* and lawyers with a moral seriousness that gives a premonitory whiff of Georgian didacticism. Richard Brome, an avowed follower of Jonson, wrote a number of lively and original satires, notably *The Antipodes* (1638) and *A Jovial Crew* (1641), on the eve of the war. In print and in revival he affected Restoration comedy.

Another type of early Stuart comedy enormously influential for the next century was that devoted to displays of wit and more or less fashionable conduct or 'manners'. The debt of Etherege, Dryden, Congreve, and their imitators to John Fletcher, Shirley, and Brome, demonstrated at length in the 1920s, has been challenged, and it is true that the more closely one compares earlier with later Stuart comedy the more differences one sees, both of ethos and of individual style.[19] But the whole debate is whether Fletcher and Shirley 'achieved' the comedy of manners – a notoriously slippery term – or only 'anticipated' it in certain scenes.

Certainly Fletcher's *Wit Without Money* (*c.* 1615) and *The Wild-Goose Chase* (*c.* 1621) foreshadow the Restoration comedy built around the marriage-hating rake. A close observer of both theatrical trends and upper-class society, the well-born Fletcher shrewdly gave his genteel audiences what they could regard as a heightened depiction of some aspects of their lives, a beau ideal. Especially interesting is *The Wild-Goose Chase*, a comedy of witty devices showing how Oriana, jilted by her fiancé Mirabel (the wild goose), tricks him into marriage. Set in Paris, it places little emphasis on 'manners', and the witty couple are united purely through trickery, yet it has many features of later manners comedy: spirited young women who outplot the men, *risqué* banter, a shy would-be rake (anticipating Goldsmith's Marlow) and a real one. Mirabel's description to Oriana of rakehood (II. 1) is the play's central and most powerful scene. 'A loose and strong defier of all order', Mirabel may be our first Don Juan (Tirso's *El Burlador de Sevilla*, written about 1615, was not published until 1630); he carries a little book listing all his conquests to show whomever needs disabusing next. Shamelessly misogynist and devoid of conscience, Mirabel shows the rake's dark side – 'Why should I be at charge to keep a wife of my own,/When other honest married men's will ease me?' – that was usually glossed over, prettied up, or (as here) 'reformed', in the Restoration and eighteenth century, but that emerged with *Don Giovanni* to fascinate the nineteenth. Fletcher's reform of Mirabel is technical, perfunctory, and ambiguous; he bequeaths the rake to posterity as a dangerous and interesting figure.

Several of James Shirley's comedies – *The Witty Fair One* (1628), *Hyde Park* (1632), *The Gamester* (1633), and especially *The Lady of Pleasure* (1635) – presage the Restoration mode in portraying upper-class manners and playing with anti-romantic ideas. Some scholars now emphasize the differences, and point to the scarcity of Restoration revivals as evidence of *dis*continuity between the periods, but the plays were in print, and the polite plagiarist prefers not to have the original on-stage. Whatever Shirley's influence on the Restoration comic writers, they were working with very similar materials. *The Lady of Pleasure* exhibits the urban contempt for the country, light satire on aristocratic behaviour (including cultural subservience to France), demolition of worthless gallants, free-spirited ladies, and stretches of witty dialogue frequently found in the Restoration, together with an emphasis on reform prefigurative of early-eighteenth-century plays. Aretina Bornwell is a genteel 'country wife', less delightful than Wycherley's Margery and less witty than Sheridan's Lady Teazle but a progenitor none the less; the scene of a lord dressing at three p.m. is straight out of Etherege. The play's most Caroline features – its emphasis on Platonic love, and its fulsome compliments to 'the two royall luminaries' at Court, 'the onely sphere wherein/True beauty moves' (IV. 3) – reveal the courtly drift of drama, and the artistic price that Shirley paid for his privileged position.

Richard Brome wrote manners as well as satiric comedy; in fact Bonamy Dobree thought *A Mad Couple Well Match'd* (1639?) the first 'Restoration' comedy, and certainly its title might apply to a dozen of them. But Careless and the widow Crosstill hardly give an accurate idea of the debonair couples to come, he being a self-indulgent cad whom Brome treats too leniently, and she having too little time on-stage to be much of anything. The Thrivewells, however, are clever and interesting, especially Lady Thrivewell's witty revenges on her husband and Alicia Saleware for their one-night fling. The absurd ending depends too much on disguise and surprise, yet here and there (e.g. Act II) are passages of delectable dialogue that still please the palate. With a rake, some bawdy, a citizen-cuckold, vignettes of high society and of relations between the classes, *A Mad Couple* has many Restoration ingredients, if not exactly the right recipe.

The preference of audiences in the court and private theatres for 'exalted' forms of drama (such as the masque) created a demand that playwrights quickly supplied. One result was the comedy of aristo-cratic life; another was the love-and-honour tragicomedy developed chiefly by Beaumont and Fletcher. 'A tragicomedy is not so called', Fletcher explained, 'in respect of mirth and killing, but in respect it wants death, which is enough to make it no tragedy, yet brings some near it, which is enough to make it no comedy.'[20] This no-tragi–no-comedy has often been stigmatized as coarse, shallow, extravagant, escapist, sentimental, meaningless, and theatrical, but only the last counted with audiences, who seem to have preferred it to Shakespeare. The other point about Beaumont and Fletcher on which criticism has agreed is that their blend of an intricate and fast-moving (though flimsy) plot out of heroic romance, noble and royal characters liable to sudden surprising shifts of mind, an exotic setting, and balanced contrasts in people and ideas (love/lust), all couched in the high-flown rhetoric of chivalry, points towards the heroic play of the Restoration, during the early part of which they were the most popular of the Stuart playwrights in revivals.[21]

A fair sample of the genre is *Philaster; or, Love Lies A-Bleeding* (1609?). The titular hero, true heir to the Sicilian throne, is kept on a short chain at Court by the usurping King, whose daughter Arethusa loves Philaster, and he her. In Act III, however, Philaster chooses to believe a hearsay charge of inchastity against her, and commences a poor imitation of Othello (a favourite eighteenth-century trope). This sets up a remarkable scene in a woodland grove wherein Philaster wounds Arethusa and her supposed lover 'Bellario'; when a country fellow intervenes, Arethusa rounds on him: 'What ill-bred man art thou, to intrude thyself/Upon our private sports, our recreations?' (IV. 5). It requires a remarkable *volte-face* by the King towards Philaster in Act V – and the revelation that 'Bellario' is a disguised girl, Euphrasia, who wanted to be near Philaster – to save the day. Euphrasia's motivation for preserving her troublesome disguise to the brink of three graves (and Arethusa's dishonour) seems slender, to say the least; yet she is to remain with the newlyweds as a maid: an imprudent arrangement, one would think. *Philaster* appealed to James's troubled Court, and helped create a taste for tragicomedy that lasted well into the Restoration.

The traditional dramatic genres had begun to subdivide. The spirited wit-duels of Shakespearean comedy (e.g. Beatrice and Benedick in *Much Ado About Nothing*) became proto-comedies of manners; their romance contributed to tragicomedy. A similar breakup took place in tragedy, whose loftier, nobler strains passed to tragicomedy, leaving a residue of low cunning, lust, ambition, and diabolical revenge for tragedy itself. Jacobean tragedy has powerfully poetic scenes of psychological insight, but few critics can discuss it without recourse to words such as 'decadent', 'perverted', or 'psychopathic'. The popularity of tragicomedy – the alternative form of serious drama – may have been related to the disturbing excesses of this 'dark tragedy'.

Cyril Tourneur, author of *The Atheist's Tragedy* (1609?) and probably of *The Revenger's Tragedy* (1607?), is a case in point. As the latter opens, Vindici, holding the skull of his dead mistress, vows revenge on her murderer, the old Duke. This he achieves in Act III by inducing the Duke to kiss the poison-smeared skull, which forms part of a grotesque puppet with whom the Duke has a darksome assignation. There are roughly fifteen other murders and executions, which T. S. Eliot thought expressive of Tourneur's own 'loathing and horror of life itself'.[22] In *The Atheist's Tragedy*, by contrast (and despite the title), the hero is exhorted by the ghost of his murdered father to 'leave revenge unto the King of Kings'. It is in good hands. As the villain goes to behead the hero at the end, he awkwardly – to put it mildly – drives the axe into his *own* head, saving hero and playwright at a stroke. Evidently Tourneur thought his audiences too sated for conventional revenge.

Though the powers of John Webster to depict character *in extremis*, to evoke the macabre, and to achieve genuine dramatic poetry are widely recognized, a strain of melodramatic excess is undeniable. *The White Devil* (*c.* 1611) kills off seven characters by means of backstabbings, strangulations, ingenious poisonings, and a broken neck from gymnastics. *The Duchess of Malfi* (*c.* 1613), considered his masterpiece, has ten deaths, four of them in Act IV, where the Duchess, her two children and her maid are strangled on-stage by assassins. What is characteristic of Webster, however, is the prelude. The Duchess is not despatched until she has been given a severed hand and told that it was her husband's, shown wax figures depicting her husband and children as dead, and treated to a song and dance by lunatics from the local asylum. On one level, Webster is a precursor of Grand Guignol. Both plays are set in the Machiavellian Italy of the Elizabethan imagination, whose *Catholic* villainies would resonate anew for the Restoration.

With some of these same features, including a lunatic show, *The Changeling* (1622), by Middleton and Rowley, is a powerful study of how evil infects, and a satire on some notions of sexual honour.[23] A noxious grimness seeps from the play's darker characters. In the authors' source, Deflores is a handsome gallant who commits murder for Beatrice-Joanna in exchange for a few kisses; Middleton's Deflores – a ruined gentleman driven into employment – is hideously ugly, but he wants (and gets) all of Beatrice-Joanna. What follows is the story of her self-conscious and almost self-willed degradation, though the roaming madmen and ominous Piranesi setting create more subrational darkness through tone than the characters actually generate. It is a remarkable, frightening play.

John Ford, the most convincing Caroline tragedian, was a psychologist of the abnormal, rendering forbidden passions with the excessive force of desperate epochs. *'Tis Pity She's a Whore* (pub. 1633) begins as a taut rendering of brother–sister incest – the title slanders Annabella, who requites Giovanni's passionate love – but the fourth and fifth acts (after she disastrously marries Soranzo) become a welter of poisonings and stabbings that leave five dead. You could, of course, say that of *Hamlet*, but the Prince never enters with Ophelia's 'heart upon a dagger', as Giovanni does with Annabella's. *The Broken Heart* (pub. 1633) also cultivates the bizarre. Orgilus traps Ithocles in a mechanical device ('the Chair closes upon him') and, after mutual compliments, stabs him to death; caught and condemned, he cuts open his arm and bleeds to death on-stage. Such devices are aspects of Ford's ardour and poetic force. How they might have been expressed for another age and audience we cannot imagine; it was his doom to express the disintegrating Caroline ethos.

The tragedies of James Shirley show how bankrupt the revenge tradition had become by the closing of the theatres; its conventions are carried to the point of absurdity. *The Cardinal* (1641) pursues *three* revenge plots to bloody conclusions (six dead); in the final scene the Cardinal (based on Richelieu) sets out to rape and then poison a duchess. Prevented by a stab wound, he tricks her into taking the poison anyway before he gloats his last. This portrait of a French churchman foreshadows the Restoration anti-Catholic dramas of Lee and others, though Shirley was probably a Catholic. An earlier scene comes close to summing up the changes in tragedy: as a means of obtaining revenge, one character (who seems conversant with *Hamlet*) substitutes for the intended play at the castle a *masque*, during which masked assassins kill the Duke.

For Restoration dramatists, the Webster–Ford–Shirley strain was the closest living English tragic tradition, the most obvious model. That may help explain their penchant for rant and excess; it may also suggest why Carolean tragic writers soon looked for other models. That they had, within two decades, worked through the heroic play, the influences of tragicomedy and France, and had begun to do homage to Shakespeare, says something for their taste as well as for his greatness.

Two lesser Caroline playwrights survived to contribute to the Restoration as elder statesmen: Thomas Killigrew and William Davenant. Killigrew's comedy *The Parson's Wedding*, written by 1640, revised in 1664, bridged the interregnum neatly, and is said to document the decay of the Court's Platonism, though its carelessness and monotony are conceded.[24] It is a dull, verbose play that subordinates plot and character to crude manners and cruder language. Its four 'leading wits', whose favourite pastime is insulting women to their faces, are difficult to distinguish from self-satisfied boors. Long before the tediously padded discourses are over, one understands why Restoration writers thought of themselves as reforming and refining the barbarisms of the previous age.

Davenant, a more talented and distinguished figure, began as a writer of tragedy, but turned to comedy in the 1630s. *The Wits* (*c.* 1633) shows some young have-nots in London living by their wits off the likes of Sir Tirant Thrift and Sir Mowglay Thwack. Between these humorists and the energy expended on 'gulling the dupes', *The Wits* is vaguely Jonsonian, but frequently tiresome and obscure. Ideas are few, the plot is thin, the dialogue mostly metaphorical ornament. If language is taken as the subject, the play holds together, but the language wavers between rich and over-rich. Davenant anticipates later comedy both in his farcing and in his irrelevant conclusion, where Palatine shakes a moralizing finger at those 'That undertake to live here by their wits'; in fact his younger brother has just witted him out of a manor house, using tricks Palatine admired as 'so ingenious' he 'could wish/To fall in them again' (v. 3). The play rejects itself.

The following year Davenant found his calling, perhaps cynically, as poet-priest to Queen Henrietta Maria's cult of Platonic love, the French *préciosité*, writing four *précieux* plays in the five years before the war. *Love and Honour* (1634), an obvious link between the Beaumont and Fletcher tragicomedy and the Restoration heroic drama, is the most important, though the far-fetched plot strains after heroic conundrums and occasions for chivalric rant. Duke Alvaro, whose love enables him to 'march strong/Through hideous gulfs, through numerous herds/Of angry lions' (II. 1), is one of three knights in love with Princess Evandra. While they are contesting who will die for her (she has a price on her head), she locks up two in a cave and induces the third, Leonel, to guard them while she goes to turn herself in. This leaves Leonel with that durable dilemma, the love/honour conflict. Honour wins; he guards them until Evandra has gone. When they are released, Prospero wants to fight Leonel, but Alvaro reminds him that 'Ladies . . . imitate the upper beauty' (IV. 5), and as they are all co-religionists at the shrine of Evandra, they vow friendship. Fortunately no one has to die. At Court, after a general exchange of noble sentiments and self-sacrificing gestures, the man for whose supposed murder Evandra was to have died turns up healthy. The warring dynasties are united and wedding bells chime.

This knack of snatching comedy from the jaws of tragedy would serve Davenant well in the next quarter-century: he would survive capture and prison to revive his play in the Restoration.

The Commonwealth

In September 1642 Parliament issued an ordinance prohibiting 'publike Stage-plays' as inappropriate to the times; this was followed by sterner measures in 1647–48 that made actors rogues, spectators felons, and theatres sources of firewood. Violators were raided, arrested, fined, harassed. Most professional actors supported the losing side, after which they emigrated or drifted back to London. One by one the old theatres were wrecked or razed: the Globe (1644), the Fortune, Phoenix, and Salisbury Court (1649), the Blackfriars (1655).

Yet the very *succession* of edicts, raids, and theatre-smashings shows that acting never stopped altogether.[25] A nucleus of actors in Cromwellian England organized, persisted, and gradually gained public support. They published *The Actors' Remonstrance . . . for the silencing of their profession* (1643), operated three London theatres in 1647 and began circulating playbills the next year. Parliament hired a special agent to suppress plays, yet there were further raids and demolitions in 1649–50. More performances and repressions culminated in a harsh raid on the Red Bull in 1655, but audiences continued to gather in schools, inns, houses. In 1656 the authorities allowed Davenant to present operatic 'entertainments' at his home in London, and charge admission: the first light of dawn. Surely the lesson is that the dramatic instinct will out. 'By his nature', says Aristotle, 'man delights in imitation.'

But the years of outlawry took their toll, in the form of lives impoverished, marred, or lost, and in the attenuation of the drama itself. As the Parliamentary raiders became more efficient, full-length, full-dress plays proved an encumbrance to quick getaways; what was needed were short, snappy playlets that could travel light. These were called farces ('stuffing') or drolls, as in 'The Droll Humours of the Bouncing Knight', and often came out of larger plays: the Bouncing Knight being Falstaff. This was the form in which Commonwealth audiences had to get *Henry IV, Hamlet*, Beaumont and Fletcher and other favourites. We have a first-hand recollection of such performances at the prime interregnum venue for 'drama':

> all that we could divert ourselves with were these
> humours and pieces of Plays . . . and these being all that
> was permitted us, great was the confluence of the
> Auditors. . . . I have seen the Red Bull Play-House, which
> was a large one, so full, that as many went back for want
> of room as had entered.[26]

What began as a clever dodge of the thought-police continued as a taste in some spectators, and a temptation to dramatists: if enough of the audience were content with the stuffing, why dress the whole bird? Farce (or 'farcicality') became a critical issue in the Restoration, practically no one having a good word to say for it, but many writing it.

The *publication* of plays – not prohibited by Parliament – continued during the Commonwealth, helping to link pre-1642 with post-1660 drama. Davenant, Shirley, and Brome issued plays at intervals (1643–56); a Beaumont and Fletcher folio appeared in 1647, Fletcher's *Wild-Goose Chase* in 1652, *The Changeling* in 1653, and so on. These texts preserved Jacobean–Caroline tastes that could not presently be indulged, and provided the rising generation of playwrights with models for imitation. Musical texts, either suggestive of Italian opera or derived from the masque, began to appear, opening a new avenue of interest.[27] Two versions of *Ariadne Deserted*, one by Lawes and Cartwright (*c.* 1640), the other by Richard Flecknoe (1654), were published.

Musical drama, it turned out, *could* be performed, with the aid of influential music-loving Puritans such as Davenant's friend Sir Bulstrode Whitelock. Through him the resilient Davenant, fresh from prison, arranged to present *The First Day's Entertainment at Rutland House*, his London residence, in May 1656; this collage of 'Declamations and Musick' opened the way for *The Siege of Rhodes* at Rutland in September. Davenant staged both *Rhodes* and a second exotic musical, *The Cruelty of the Spaniards in Peru*, at the rebuilt Cockpit in Drury Lane in 1658, and in 1659 Part II of *Rhodes* and *The History of Sir Francis Drake*, another 'opera'.

With their formal recitatives and arias, choruses and scenic spectacles, these are not plays but proto-operas: 'melo-dramas' would be denotatively accurate. Yet *The Siege of Rhodes* was as epochal as any play in English theatre history. Some of its innovations are technical and subject to qualification: it began the dramatic 'restoration', introduced actresses and movable scenery (emphasizing spectacle to a degree unprecedented outside the Court), and sketched a first draft of English opera for the Restoration to revise.[28] Its *literary* originality – as the 'first light' of the heroic play in England – was noted by Dryden; though it lacks the heroic couplets later considered essential, *The Siege of Rhodes* has 'begun to shadow' the Great Subject: 'Love and Valour'.[29] A noble marital love is placed in the context of the defence of Rhodes against the Turks, and gives occasions for jealousies and conflicts of love and honour, both rather trumped up for effect.

One must, however, admire the shrewdness of Davenant's showmanship, his attunement to time and place. The Grand Priory of the knights who had defended Rhodes was near Rutland House.[30] Eastern Europe was under Turkish threat, Christian Europe riven by religious faction: Davenant presents a story of Christian Rhodes left unaided by squabbling Christian powers against the Turks. The prevailing critical dogma exalted the heroic epic; Davenant informs his readers that 'The story represented . . . is heroical.' *The Siege of Rhodes* tries too hard to generate admiration and grandeur, but it set a fashion for Christian –infidel confrontation in exotic locales, and synthesized (from English and European dramatic and non-dramatic sources) a form that held playwrights and audiences for twenty years.

By 1659, then, the pump was primed. All that remained was to license regular drama for the stage again – and that would have to wait for the King.

Notes

1. J. P. Kenyon 'debunks' Elizabeth I and questions the coherence of the term 'Puritan' in *Stuart England* (Harmondsworth, 1978), pp. 13, 22–23, 48.

2. On the divisiveness of the Reformation in England, see Asa Briggs, *A Social History of England* (London, 1983), p. 121.

3. Briggs, Chapter 5; and L. C. Knights, *Drama and Society in the Age of Jonson* (London, 1937), pp. 36, 173.

4. Thomas M. Parrott and Robert H. Ball, *A Short View of Elizabethan Drama* (New York, 1943), pp. 182–83.

5. For a discussion, see Kenyon, Chapter 2 and pp. 80–81.

6. Briggs, p. 139; p. 138 for following quote.

7. On the Queen, and Charles's Catholic problems, see Kenyon, pp. 28–29, 89, 92, 95, 119, 125, 129; 101 for Charles's statement.

8. For particulars, see Kenyon, pp. 130, 141, 144.

9. G. E. Bentley, *The Jacobean and Caroline Stage*, 7 vols (Oxford, 1941–68), VI (1968), gives details on each venue. This section draws heavily on Bentley's work.

10. Parrott and Ball, p. 183.

11. See Alfred Harbage, *Shakespeare's Audience* (London, 1941); and *Shakespeare: The Complete Works*, edited by G. B. Harrison (New York, 1948), p. 53, a useful summary.

12. Quoted in A. M. Nagler (ed.), *A Source Book in Theatrical History* (New York, 1959), pp. 132–33.

13. See Archer's *The Old Drama and the New* (London, 1923), p. 78.

14. See *Source Book in Theatrical History*, pp. 138–40.

15. Quoted in *Source Book in Theatrical History*, p. 150.

16. The shrinking audience is noted in *Six Caroline Plays*, edited by A. S. Knowland (London, 1962), pp. xi, xiii.

17. See Ben Jonson's 'Expostulation with Inigo Jones' (1631) and Allardyce Nicoll, *British Drama*, fifth edition (London 1962), p. 126, for the negative; contrast Stephen Orgel, *The Jonsonian Masque* (Cambridge, Massachusetts, 1965), *passim*, especially the Conclusion.

18. See the article on 'Masque' in *The Oxford Companion to the Theatre*; and A. H. Scouten, 'Dramatic Opera', in *The Revels History of Drama in English*, edited by T. W. Craik and C. Leech, 8 vols (London, 1975–83), v (1976), 288–89.

19. The similarities are stressed by Kathleen Lynch, *The Social Mode of Restoration Comedy* (New York, 1926), the differences by Norman N. Holland, *The First Modern Comedies* (London, 1959), Chapter 17. Holland perhaps overstates the affirmativeness of Jacobean and the negativeness of Restoration comedy.

20. See his Preface to *The Faithful Shepherdess*.

21. The conclusion of A. C. Sprague, *Beaumont and Fletcher on the Restoration Stage* (Cambridge, Massachusetts, 1926).

22. In his *Essays on Elizabethan Drama* (New York, 1936). p. 120.

23. This paragraph is indebted to Alexander Leggatt's discussion, which he kindly let me see in typescript, in his *English Drama: Shakespeare to the Restoration, 1590–1660* in this series.

24. By Lynch, p. 101.

25. See Leslie Hotson, *The Commonwealth and Restoration Stage* (Cambridge, Massachusetts, 1928), pp. 16–17 and *passim* (on the Red Bull raid, p. 46). My discussion is generally indebted to Hotson.

26. From Francis Kirkman, Preface to *The Wits; or, Sport Upon Sport* (1672 edition). Reprinted in *Source Book in Theatrical History*, p. 157.

27. See Scouten, p. 288; and Eric W. White, *A History of English Opera* (London, 1983), pp. 60–62.

28. White discusses the play, pp. 65–74, especially p. 73.

29. See Dryden's essay 'Of Heroic Plays', in *Of Dramatic Poesy*, edited by George Watson, 2 vols (London, 1962), I, 157. Dryden's statement oddly ignores *Love and Honour* and its brethren.

30. White, p. 65.

Part One:
The
Restoration
1660–1688

Chapter 1
Thespis Redux

King and country

And welcome now (great monarch) to your own;
Behold th'approaching cliffs of Albion;
It is no longer motion cheats your view:
As you meet it, the land approacheth you.

John Dryden, 'Astraea Redux' (1660)

Astraea Redux: 'Justice led back home'. Dryden's lines on Charles II's triumphal return to Dover, 25 May 1660, though extravagant, catch the mood of national euphoria, the widespread sense of relief and renewal. The age's foremost diarist, Samuel Pepys, an excitable but less baroque witness, observed 'Great joy . . . at London, and at night more bonfires than ever, and ringing of bells, and drinking of the King's health' a good three weeks before Charles's arrival; and he described in much the same hues as Dryden the scene at Dover as the King was welcomed by General Monk: 'Infinite the crowd of people and the gallantry of the horsemen, citizens, and noblemen of all sorts. . . . The shouting and joy expressed by all is past imagination.'

Charles began by doing everything right. From Holland he had already proclaimed that 'tender consciences' would be handled with care; his first statements were generous and forgiving. All agreed that Charles (who remarked that he was pleased to be home from his travels) had wit and polish, ease and amiability. As the restored King rode splendidly over flower-strewn streets into London on his thirtieth birthday, accompanied by 20,000 cavalry and infantry, church bells pealed, fountains ran with wine and more shouts of joy were raised.[1] No one shouted louder than the theatre folk, themselves as good as restored, who set out within a few months to create a patriotic theatre that would compliment the King and celebrate his social and monarchical ideals.

It could not last – whatever Charles's personal qualities – because none of the old contentions had been settled: Anglican versus Puritan and Catholic, Royal versus Parliamentary authority, landed squire versus moneyed 'cit'. And if the King was lenient, others were vindictive. Major General Harrison was hanged, drawn, and quartered at Charing Cross; Cromwell and other Puritan leaders were exhumed from the Abbey, hung, and buried under the gallows. Nonconforming ministers were replaced by Anglicans, Dissenters were barred from municipal office, and all the legislation of 'their' Parliaments since 1635 was rescinded. The Act of Uniformity (1662) required that all ministers be ordained by Anglican bishops and that preachers and teachers accept the Anglican Prayer Book. Henceforth the law of the land effectively excluded Puritans from city councils, pulpits, and classrooms.

Nor was all well at Whitehall. As early as 31 August 1661 Pepys noted: 'At Court things are in very ill condition, there being so much emulation, poverty, and the vices of drinking, swearing, and loose amours, that I know not what will be the end of it, but confusion.' There is ample evidence that the amorous (and negligent) royal spendthrift was a large part of the problem.[2] The Great Plague (1665) and Great Fire (1666) could not rationally be held against the King, but the disasters of the Second Dutch War (1665–67) were a different matter. From his vantage point in the Navy Department, Pepys blamed England's unreadiness and humiliation on 'the negligence of our Prince', supposedly supping with a mistress while the Dutch were taking English warships in the Medway. His entry for 12 July 1667 is a requiem for Charles's early promise:

> It is strange how everybody do nowadays reflect upon
> Oliver, and commend him, what brave things he did, and
> made all the neighbour princes fear him; while here a
> prince, come in with all the love and prayers and good
> liking of his people, . . . hath lost all so soon, that it is a
> miracle what way a man could devise to lose so much in
> so little time.

The long decline of Charles's reign was marked by familiar evils: divisive legislation, financial quarrels, corruption, unpopular and unsuccessful wars. He did not pay his sailors in 1667, nor Dryden his laureate's pension after 1677. His policies towards Scottish Dissenters led to uprisings in 1666 and 1679 that his troops put down brutally ('the Killing time'), but his concessions to Catholics and Dissenters enraged Anglicans and caused Parliament to bring in a Test Act. It was said that the King and his ministers were crypto-Catholics, that in a secret clause of the Treaty of Dover (1670) Charles had promised to convert. Then the Third Dutch War (1672–74) proved as costly and indecisive as its predecessors. Still, it was the Merry Monarch's affairs with actresses and duchesses that became legendary. Dryden, a friendly witness engaged in defending the King, still pictured him as one who

> His vigourous warmth did variously impart
> To wives and slaves, and wide as his command
> Scatter'd his Maker's image through the land.[3]

Ironically Charles, with all his getting, begot no legitimate heir, but rather the worst succession crisis in eighty years.

In 1678 rumours began to circulate of a Jesuit plot against Charles in favour of his Catholic brother James, Duke of York. Then one Titus Oates, a motley zealot who had tried most major faiths at least once, came forward with a richly embroidered tale of projected regicide and massacre of Protestants; eventually he accused James of being implicated. This 'Popish Plot', 'the nation's curse,/Bad in itself but represented worse (Dryden), sent aftershocks through England for the next four years. An Exclusion Bill was introduced into Parliament (1679) to exclude James from the succession, while Charles was pressured to declare his Protestant bastard James Scott, Duke of Monmouth, his heir. The country divided into Tory successionists and Whig exclusionists (led by the first Earl of Shaftesbury): divisions dangerously reminiscent of Royalists and Parliamentarians. In the courts, perjured testimony and hysteria led to the condemnation and 'judicial murder' of dozens of people, at least some of them innocent. Charles dissolved his Whiggish Parliament and turned to the Tories, while Shaftesbury encouraged Monmouth to assert his 'right' and save his Church and nation.

The Rye House Plot (1683) and increased persecution of Dissenters marred Charles's last years, but matters did not come to a head until his death in 1685. James duly succeeded his brother, whereupon Monmouth raised a rebellion, was defeated and executed. In this affair the nation seemed united behind James II, who reaffirmed the sanctity of English laws and Anglican prerogatives, and summoned Parliament. But James had already declared himself a Catholic, and religious politics dominated his short reign. Attending mass in state, liberalizing the laws governing non-Anglicans and putting Catholics in high military positions in violation of the Test Act, James alarmed Parliament, which resolved bluntly that it 'did not entirely rely on his royal declaration' to preserve the Anglican Church, 'as by law established, by far dearer and nearer to them than their lives'.[4] The implied threat of a new civil war – and the pleas of fearful Catholics – did not deter James, who henceforth governed without Parliament, but with secret financial aid from Louis XIV. A Jesuit adviser at his side, James appointed a Catholic Lord-Lieutenant of Ireland, engineered a judicial decision placing his prerogatives above Parliamentary power, and issued a Declaration of Indulgence for Dissenters and Catholics.

When James tried to prosecute seven bishops for refusing to promote his Declaration, and his Queen produced a Catholic heir (1688), Parliament cried 'Enough!' It invited the staunchly Protestant William of Orange, husband of James's eldest daughter Mary, to replace James II in the name of Anglicanism and civil liberty. William accepted, and again a Dutch fleet approached England, this time by popular request, to land William's army; James II fled to France in disguise. A Convention Parliament named William and Mary joint monarchs, stipulating the conditions under which power would be exercised. And this 'Glorious Revolution', which changed English politics forever, was accomplished without bloodshed.[5]

The literary and philosophical temper

Corresponding fractures appear in Restoration intellectual life; in fact, the tensions resulting from opposed forces give late-seventeenth-century English thought its most interesting features. At first glance we might be tempted to call it a 'heroic' age, for its resounding issues and high stakes gave its principals a sense of grandeur, of being one of a few crucial epochs in history. In welcoming Charles II home, Dryden (like others) thought of Caesar Augustus establishing himself in Rome after the civil wars:

> Oh, happy age! Oh, times like those alone
> By fate reserv'd for great Augustus' throne!
> When the joint growth of arms and arts foreshew
> The world a monarch, and that monarch You.[6]

Note the scope: back 1700 years, outward to 'the world'. In declaring the Augustan Age open, Dryden provides a clear instance of neo-classicism – the desire to associate oneself culturally with the ancients, to be guided by them, and the willingness to be judged by their standards – which would be one of the most persistent impulses of the next century.

But for the moment 'heroism' was the larger category, subsuming 'Augustanism'. Dryden's first published poem, the 'Heroick Stanzas' on the death of Cromwell, shows that the Protector would do as well as the King whose place he was usurping: Dryden *needed* a hero he could parallel with Pompey and Alexander, one possessing 'such heroic virtue' as 'Heav'n sets out', yet with 'a soul above/The highest acts it could produce'. After the Restoration, as Charles II himself became more difficult to 'heroicize', dramatists developed the 'heroic play': a grandiose type of tragicomedy built around a superhero and conducted in an elevated manner that was part Corneille, part Beaumont and Fletcher. Uncritical admiration was perhaps the most sought-after response in Restoration drama; audiences were asked to admire – in the root sense 'to wonder at' – everything from spectacle down to farce. Restoration tragedy generally sought to arouse admiration, not terror, and later, when heroic drama had passed, its supermen returned as the exemplary heroes of genteel comedy.[7]

It was an Age That Would Be Heroic. Poetry was dominated by Milton's epics, in which the Satan of *Paradise Lost* (1667) and the Samson of *Samson Agonistes* (1671) are drawn as hero-figures. Prose offered not only the stately cadences of its 'Olympians' (Milton, Hobbes, Clarendon), but, on the popular level, John Bunyan's *Pilgrim's Progress* (1678), no less than a guide 'from this World to that which is to come', and Aphra Behn's *Oroonoko* (1688), with a noble savage as hero. Sir Christopher Wren's conception for the new, post-Fire St Paul's was in the grand Italian neoclassical manner, and who has seen the pictures of his dome rising above the blitz-fires of 1940 without feeling its heroic qualities? In music, composers adapted the traditional trumpet fanfare of Court to the new public orchestras as the trumpet concerto. In place of the old consort of equals, these concertos brought forward a soloist who sent his high *clarino* trumpet soaring brilliantly above the other instruments. Declamation, large gestures, and daring flights were everywhere.

Only a blinkered vision, however, would take the Restoration's heroic ideals for its entire reality; not even the Restoration could do that for long. As the 'new Augustus' became the Merry Monarch, heroic drama elicited *The Rehearsal* (1670), which, by burlesquing the absurdities of the form, revealed how close to self-parody the heroic plays operated. Within a few seasons the superheroes began to weaken; soon the heroic couplets were muted to blank verse and the whole genre gave way to regular tragedy with softer protagonists. And far beneath the Miltonic Olympus flourished low-life prose such as Richard Head's cony-catching narrative *The English Rogue* (1665).

Criticism rivalled, then overtook Admiration as the spirit of the age. Prologues complained about the ferocious critics in the pit, though some of the plaintiffs were themselves setting up as theoretical or practical critics, applying rational analysis and historical perspective to problems of literary form and style. Once the spirit of dissection, deflation, and mockery was abroad, it would not stop with *dramatic* absurdities, but spread into other genres and subjects, especially after 1678. The heroic epic was still viable in 1671: ten years later, with Milton and heroic drama equally dead, the talk of the town was Dryden's *mock*-heroics on his literary and political enemies, a form popularized by Samuel Butler's *Hudibras* (1663–78). Mocking, too, are many 'love' poems and some of the 'religious' verse of the Cavaliers and court wits.

The various challenges to the traditional Christian view of the world – the Restoration's most significant debate – appear most clearly in philosophical and scientific writing. Hobbes's *Leviathan* remained the central treatise on man and society, though its materialism, shocking definitions, extreme absolutism, and vision of the state of nature as one of war between power-seeking savages attracted increasingly negative comment, even from fellow Tories like Dryden. A more lasting threat to conventional Christianity was the rise of empirical science. The Royal Society (founded 1660) took over from Bacon, Galileo, and Descartes the annoying habit of accepting nothing as proven until it could be demonstrated; satirists (including Thomas Shadwell) attacked its experiments and its insistence on simple language. Not surprisingly in a time of deeply felt and strongly reasoned but antithetical views, the old philosophy of scepticism found new adherents inclined to distrust all speculative assertions.[8] What was confusing was that some sceptics turned to science, some to Christianity, and some to Hobbes.

The tension between appearance and reality – or the real and the ideal – has been the basic theme of Western literature, though its strength and form have varied. During ages of social and ideological stress, such as the Restoration, a great many cracks in a culture's unity need to be papered over or hidden behind the furniture, or as a last resort absolutely denied. Potentially dangerous conflicts may have to be circumvented rather than confronted. Not only faces but words and intentions must be masked. Of course appearances are proverbially deceiving, and drama generally makes free use of concealment and deception, but the sheer number of masks, veils, fans, screens, aliases, impersonations, ironic colloquies, and feigned appearances on the Restoration stage is impressive: a useful reminder that we are entering what is often called the 'age of irony' or the 'age of disguise'.[9]

Restoration audiences

There is much dispute about the nature of the Restoration audience, but none about the existence of a close connection between drama and the Court. King Charles II, a friend to drama before 1660, remained its premier patron, socializing with playwrights, donating properties to actors and visiting the theatre frequently. When he attended, the house was fuller; when he smiled, the house smiled with him. Many dramatists besides Davenant and Killigrew were on familiar terms with the monarch – John Dryden, Charles Sedley, Samuel Tuke, the Duke of Buckingham, George Etherege, William Wycherley, John Crowne, Roger Boyle, etc. – so his tastes were highly influential. The King's interest in heroic drama prompted Boyle to write *The General* and *The Black Prince*, which helped establish that genre in England, while his fondness for farcical comedy gave a boost to 'Spanish intrigues', eliciting them from Tuke, Dryden, and Crowne.

Along with the King's interest, conversation, and support went those of his courtiers and ladies, who tended to like the same things he did and so reinforced his influence. Dryden attributed the refinement of wit in his day 'to the Court; and, in it, particularly to the King'; ascribed the popularity of rhymed heroic plays to the courtiers; and later blamed the immorality of Restoration drama on its cosiness with the same group.[10] A number of the court wits – Buckingham, Etherege, Sedley, and others – were dramatists, who in addition to their plays contributed smart ad libs to theatrical entertainment. Pepys was both 'vexed' and 'pleased' by Sedley's witty talk throughout a performance of *The Maid's Tragedy* in 1667 whereby he 'lost the pleasure of the play wholly'. But why should Sedley keep his wit to himself? The audience included a number of his fellow wits, their entourages, aristocrats who deferred to them, and gentry who (like Pepys) came partly to see and hear them.

It is difficult to say how much of the audience could accurately be called 'coterie'. The older view was that the Restoration playhouse was an aristocratic playground, with courtiers, wits, gallants, court ladies and courtesans comprising perhaps four-fifths of the audience.[11] In the mid-1960s, however, *The London Stage* published research (accepted by most subsequent scholars) showing a broader range of social classes in the audience than had been thought.[12]

This is not the place to summarize, debate, or reconcile these views. The essential point is that seventeenth-century evidence about audiences is as mixed as critical interpretations of it. The diarist John Evelyn's remark after seeing *Hamlet* in 1667, 'now the old plays began to disgust this refined age', and Killigrew's observation to Pepys (also

1667) that the social tone of the theatre was much improved now with the 'city' audience almost gone, would seem to support the 'élitists'. Yet Sam Vincent's *The Young Gallant's Academy* (1674) asserts that 'The *Play*-house is free for entertainment, allowing Room as well to the *Farmers Son* as to a Templer': part of the evidence suggesting that audiences became more heterogeneous in the early 1670s.[13] Pepys's reports are also quite diverse. Sometimes he is full of anecdotes about 'My Lord' and 'My Lady'; at other times he sniffs that the house is 'full of citizens' (1 January 1663). The problem – common in historiography – is how much weight to give each piece of data. The crucial issue, though, is power and visibility, rather than numbers. The aristocrats are unlikely ever to have had an absolute majority, but they enjoyed a 'high profile', and they were the theatrical opinion-makers of their day. We can be certain, at least, that the upper class made up a higher proportion of the audience in 1670 than in 1600 or 1770.

The behaviour and tastes of the audience are another puzzle. For a long time most scholarship sketched a scene of almost riotous disorder, with quarrelsome, inattentive spectators clamouring for farce and spectacle.[14] From *The London Stage* onward, however, some writers have argued that pandemonium could not have been the regular condition of the theatres nor vulgarity the dominant taste, given the plays that were performed.[15] Again Restoration sources speak on both sides. Pepys frequently reports disruptions in the 1660s, but also routine performances. Sam Vincent dwells on the noisy gallants (1674), yet a French traveller of 1676 states flatly that 'one never hears any noise'.[16] In prologues and epilogues, Dryden, Lee, and other playwrights heaped astonishingly crude insults on audiences for their crudity, but they spoke polemically and represent a vested interest. The truth lies somewhere between their barbs and Evelyn's 'refined age', though the patrons would certainly have seemed boisterous to us. Their modern counterparts are in the opera-houses of Italy and China, where spectacular and stylized performances are popular, yet the spectators' interest takes – by Anglo-American standards – noisy and disorderly forms. There is material for satire, yet the shows go on, and the audiences' love of the theatre is unquestionable.

Of course the Restoration audience was not monolithic. Women of elevated tastes begin to be heard of as a force against sex comedy in the 1670s, and as a lobby for tragedy and more humane comedy in the 1680s.[17] On the other hand, prostitutes were fairly numerous and audible, 'cackling for a Mate' up in the galleries.[18] Then too, satirists distinguished between the various regions of the playhouse: box, pit, and gallery. The galleries, which offered the cheapest seats, drew the sharpest fire, the expensive boxes were sometimes given a kind word, and the pit was middling in valuation as in price.[19] Again the picture is one of diversity: let the generalizer beware.

Companies and theatres

In the summer of 1660 Charles II granted the veteran dramatists Thomas Killigrew and William Davenant – faithful Royalists and fellow exiles – hereditary patents to form acting companies and build theatres. After a brief struggle with some rival claimants, the patentees made good this effective monopoly on legitimate drama in London, and the two 1660 patents remain the legal foundations of today's Theatre Royal, Drury Lane, and Royal Opera House, Covent Garden. Killigrew's King's Men and Davenant's Duke's Men competed until tiny audiences and cancelled performances in 1681 crippled the King's Men; the two companies then merged and played as one until 1695.[20] But two companies and two patent theatres were the norm for much of the period.

After a brief joint tenure at the old Cockpit Theatre, the companies found separate premises. Significantly, neither turned to the old outdoor Fortune Theatre (which survived until 1662): the Caroline playhouse, with its aristocratic associations, was the model chosen. The King's Men remodelled Gibbons's Tennis Court and played there until their new theatre was ready; the Duke's Men developed Lisle's Tennis Court, Lincoln's Inn Fields, which they used for a decade. Both facilities were indoor, but whereas Gibbons's apparently had something like the old platform stage and no scenery, Davenant equipped Lisle's to handle a gala opening production of his *Siege of Rhodes* (June 1661), featuring elaborate scenes. Richard Southern notes that the scenic and non-scenic traditions might have continued side by side in English theatre as in Japanese Noh and Kabuki.[21] In actuality, though, Killigrew felt pressured to follow Davenant's lead, and the race to spectacle was on.

The first significant theatre of the Restoration was Killigrew's Theatre Royal, Bridges Street at Drury Lane (1663), hailed as 'the real beginning of a regularised world of the theatre', marking 'the emergence of Drama from the barn, the inn-yard . . . the small, ill-equipped playhouses, into the dignity of proper equipment and public resort', the first Theatre Royal or Drury Lane.[22] Not all of the initial visitors were duly impressed. Pepys was there a day after the opening and, though on the whole he approved, he noted some faults, including 'the distance from the stage to the boxes, which I am confident cannot hear' (8 May 1663). Doubtless we would have been struck by the *intimacy* of the whole theatre: the distance Pepys refers to has been estimated at thirty feet, and the entire building was nearly the same size as the stage of the present Drury Lane.[23]

The other two Restoration theatres were the work of Christopher Wren, who built Dorset Garden for the Duke's Men in 1671, and the

second Theatre Royal, Drury Lane, for the King's Men in 1674 after
the first one burned. Each building was just under sixty feet wide,
though Dorset Garden was longer by about a third. Its extra length
was in the auditorium, roughly three-fifths of the whole, whereas in
his second theatre Wren reduced the auditorium to only one-third of
the overall measurement. Both buildings had a forestage jutting about
twenty feet into the pit and a proscenium about thirty feet wide by
seventeen high.[24] The central seating area, still called the pit, was now
equipped with backless benches; enclosing it on three sides like a
horseshoe were the boxes, and at the rear rose the galleries. Given the
flexibility of the pit's benches, seating capacity is difficult to specify.
Lincoln's Inn Fields may have held four hundred to six hundred,
Wren's Drury Lane five hundred to one thousand, Dorset Garden
about twelve hundred.[25] We have many contemporary descriptions of
the early days of these theatres; Act iv of Thomas Shadwell's *A True
Widow* (1678) depicts a fractious audience disrupting a performance.
Some popular customs included leaving after one act without paying
(the 'free act'), eluding the ticket-taker altogether, lolling on the forestage between acts, and paying to chat with the actresses backstage.[26]

Scenery became a contentious issue as soon as Davenant's *Siege of
Rhodes* showed what could be done. By 1664 Richard Flecknoe was
warning the public that whereas old theatres had been 'plain and
simple', 'ours now for cost and ornament are arriv'd to the heighth
of Magnificence; but that which makes our Stage the better, makes our
Playes the worse perhaps, they striving now to make them more for
sight, then hearing; whence that solid joy of the interior is lost'.[27] Of
this we shall hear much more. The fuss was over the new scenery and
machinery – adapted from the court masque and Continental opera –
on the deep stage behind the proscenium. Movable painted scene flats
or 'shutters' could be slid on-stage from both sides in three or four
grooves, brought together to form a 'backscene', or removed and
changed. When all were opened they revealed the backcloth, and
perhaps some ground-rows, at the extreme rear. Serried flats with stag-
gered cut-outs gave a rudimentary kind of depth perspective.[28] There
were also side scenes ('wings') and a hanging border at the top. All
of this 'deep-scene' area was rather dimly sidelit by off-stage candles;
the forestage, where most of the acting proceeded, was more brightly
lit by candles in chandeliers and footlights. The auditorium was
illuminated by candle fixtures along its side walls.

In line with the greater scenic appeal were the costumes, more
gorgeous, expensive and historically accurate than ever before; Charles
II's coronation robes became Thomas Betterton's costume in
Davenant's revival of *Love and Honour*. Seen from the auditorium the

effect was impressive, but the costs added to overheads, and Pepys found that a backstage visit spoiled the illusion:

> But to see their clothes . . . and what a mixture of things there was (here a wooden leg, there a ruff, here a hobby-horse, there a crown), would make a man split himself to see with laughing. Again to think how fine they show on the stage by candle-light, and how poor things they are to look at too near hand, is not pleasant at all. (19 March 1666)

Within half a dozen years of the beginning of scenic theatre in England, then, close observers were warning that its illusions were a fragile and dangerous dependency.

There were actresses in London theatres before the end of 1660 (Pepys first reports them on 3 January 1661).[29] Boys had continued to play women's parts in England right up to 1642 on the public stages; at Court, women had participated in masques. Actresses were well established on the French and Italian stages by the middle of the seventeenth century, however, and the attractions of this arrangement were not lost on Charles and his courtiers. Killigrew's patent specifically states that women will be allowed to act, and predicts that this will be not only delightful, but 'useful and instructive'. Considering the King's later relations with actresses, this sounds tongue in cheek; no subsequent commentator has suggested that playhouse morality or moral influence *improved* after 1660. Not that the actresses were so immoral – some were, some were not – but the wits and beaux came flocking backstage as never before. Actresses, mostly from dance and music schools, became fixtures at once; some were stars of the first magnitude within a decade or two, though they were not permitted to full partnership in a company until 1695.[30] Their arrival influenced both the writing of plays, eliciting many fine women's roles from Restoration dramatists, and the choices made daily by managers. Obviously more good parts for women were needed now, and the plays, new or old, that offered them enjoyed an advantage in the repertoire.

Companies operated on the repertory system throughout the Restoration and eighteenth century, rotating a number of stock plays that they had memorized, occasionally introducing a new one, choosing each night or each week what seemed most likely to 'go'. Long runs were thus rare. A new play that survived three performances – to give the author his benefit 'night' (plays started at three thirty) – was at least a minimal success, six was quite a good showing, and nine a hit. Revivals of old plays did well to run a few afternoons, then find a niche in the repertoire. The system was highly flexible, and well suited to a limited clientele who liked to attend frequently, but it made great demands on actors' memories; it is not surprising that we frequently hear of an actor being 'out' in his part.

The repertories of the two theatres were quite different. Killigrew inherited rights to most of the old plays, so Davenant had more incentive to find out new ones, or procure translations or adaptations of Continental plays. The prompter John Downes has left an interesting list of fifteen 'Principal Old Stock Plays' from the early years of Drury Lane. Almost half are by Beaumont and Fletcher, three each by Shakespeare and Jonson, and two by young John Dryden, just beginning to make his mark. At this stage, revivals dominated the 'rep', but soon the proportions were reversed. By 1700, some 120 old plays had been revived, but 440 new ones had been performed.[31] It is to this emergent Restoration drama that we now turn.

Notes

1. For some accessible accounts, see John H. Wilson, *A Preface to Restoration Drama* (Cambridge, Massachusetts, 1965), p. 2; Louis I. Bredvold, *The Literature of the Restoration and Eighteenth Century* (Oxford, 1950), p. 11; and G. R. Cragg, *The Church and the Age of Reason* (Harmondsworth, 1960), p. 50.

2. See Bredvold, *Literature of the Restoration*, p. 12; and George Sherburn, *The Restoration and Eighteenth Century*, in *A Literary History of England*, edited by Albert C. Baugh, second edition (New York, 1967), pp. 699–700.

3. 'Absalom and Achitophel', Part I (1681), ll. 8–10.

4. Quoted by Louis I. Bredvold, *The Intellectual Milieu of John Dryden* (Ann Arbor, Michigan, 1934, 1956), p. 167.

5. For a fuller account, see J. P. Kenyon, *Stuart England* (Harmondsworth, 1978), Chapters 9 and 10.

6. 'Astraea Redux' (1660), ll. 320–23.

7. Bonamy Dobree, *Restoration Tragedy* (Oxford, 1929), p. 19; Eugene M. Waith, lecture on comedy, Bloomington, Indiana, 1972.

8. Bredvold, *Intellectual Milieu of Dryden*, Chapters 1, 3, 5.

9. By Ricardo Quintana, 'Oliver Goldsmith: Ironist to the Georgians', in *Eighteenth-Century Studies in Honor of Donald F. Hyde*, edited by W. H. Bond (New York, 1970), p. 299; and *English Literature in the Age of Disguise*, edited by Maximillian E. Novak (Berkeley, Los Angeles, and London, 1977).

10. See his 'Defence of the Epilogue' (1672), Dedication to *The Indian Emperor* (1665), 'To the Pious Memory of . . . Mrs Anne Killigrew' (1686), and Epilogue to Vanbrugh's *The Pilgrim* (1700).

11. See, for example, Allardyce B. Nicoll, *A History of Restoration Drama*, fourth edition (Cambridge, 1952), pp. 5–19; Norman Holland, *The First Modern Comedies* (Cambridge, Massachusetts, 1959), pp. 9–10; James Sutherland, *English Literature of the Late Seventeenth Century* (Oxford, 1969), p. 36; and Wilson, pp. 6, 31–33.

12. Emmett L. Avery and Arthur H. Scouten, in *The London Stage 1660–1800*, 5 parts (Carbondale, Illinois, 1960–68), Part 1, edited by William Van Lennep (1965), pp. clxii–clxvii; E. L. Avery, 'The Restoration Audience', *PQ*, 45 (1966), 54–61; Peter Holland, *The Ornament of Action* (Cambridge, 1979), pp. 4, 12–14; and Arthur H. Scouten and Robert D. Hume, 'Restoration Comedy and its Audiences', in Hume's *The Rakish Stage* (Carbondale, Illinois, 1983), p. 80.

13. Vincent is quoted in *A Source Book in Theatrical History*, edited by A. M. Nagler (New York, 1952), p. 213. On the audience see R. D. Hume, 'Reading and Misreading *The Man of Mode*', *Criticism*, 14 (1972), 1–11 (p. 5); John Loftis, 'The Social and Literary Context', in *The Revels History of Drama in English*, edited by T. W. Craik and C. Leech, 8 vols (London, 1975–83), v (1976), 3, 17–18; and Harry W. Pedicord, 'The Changing Audience', in *The London Theatre World, 1660–1800*, edited by R. D. Hume (Carbondale, Illinois, 1980), pp. 237–41.

14. For example, Nicoll, pp. 14–19; Sutherland, pp. 36–41.

15. See Avery and Scouten, *London Stage*, I, clxx–clxxi; and *British Dramatists from Dryden to Sheridan*, edited by George Nettleton, Arthur Case, and George Winchester Stone, Jr, second edition (Boston, 1969), p. xiv.

16. Quoted in *Source Book in Theatrical History*, p. 203.

17. See the Prologue to Nathaniel Lee's *Lucius Junius Brutus* (1680); Sutherland, p. 39; and John H. Smith, 'Shadwell, the Ladies, and the Change in Comedy', *MP*, 46 (1948), 22–33.

18. Epilogue to John Crowne's *Sir Courtly Nice* (1685).

19. See Avery and Scouten, *London Stage*, I, clxvii–clxx; *British Dramatists from Dryden to Sheridan*, p. xiii; and Holland, *Ornament of Action*, pp. 14–15.

20. See Judith Milhous, 'Company Management', in *London Theatre World*, pp. 3–4, 30; Avery and Scouten, *London Stage*, I, xxiii; and Richard Southern, 'Theatres and Scenery', in *Revels History*, v, 84, 88.

21. In *Revels History*, v, 117.

22. W. J. MacQueen-Pope, *Theatre Royal, Drury Lane* (London, 1945), pp. 14–15.

23. Wilson, p. 10; MacQueen-Pope, p. 33.

24. Edward Langhans, 'The Theatres', in *London Theatre World*, p. 62.

25. Thus Langhans, p. 62; Southern estimates Drury Lane to have held six hundred to eight hundred: *Revels History*, v, 110.

26. Discussed by Nicoll, pp. 12–14.

27. 'A Short Discourse of the English Stage', attached to *Love's Kingdom*, quoted by George Nettleton, *English Drama of the Restoration and Eighteenth Century* (New York, 1923), p. 40.

28. See *British Dramatists from Dryden to Sheridan*, p. xii.

29. See Avery and Scouten, *London Stage*, I, xxiv.

30. Avery and Scouten, *London Stage*, I, xxv.

31. *British Dramatists from Dryden to Sheridan*, p. xiii.

Entr'acte

As the rusty wheels began to turn, revivals or revisions of Jonson, Shakespeare, Beaumont and Fletcher, Killigrew and Davenant supplied the initial momentum. First, comedies and heroic plays inspired imitation; later the tragedies came into their own. Original playwriting fell into three phases. From 1660 until the hiatus caused by the Great Plague and Fire (June 1665–November 1666) was a period of experiment, marked by the rise of the full-blown heroic play and a variety of comic types: anti-Puritan plays, the farce of manners, the Spanish intrigue, and Etherege's first effort. The stage was then set for Restoration drama's major achievements. In 1667, Dryden became the dominant playwright, comedy the dominant form, and Carolean drama flowered. Between 1668, when Dryden turned professional and became Poet Laureate, and 1677, when he turned to blank-verse tragedy, heroic drama crested and fell, Etherege and Wycherley gave the 'comedy of manners' its first moments of glory, Shadwell revived the comedy of humours, and farce began to flourish. The Popish Plot began a third stage, almost a dramatic interregnum. More tragedies and political plays, but fewer comedies, were presented after 1678; after 1682, fewer new plays of any kind were produced. Then in 1688 the Glorious Revolution altered conditions again. The second and most important of these three phases receives the greatest emphasis in the following chapters.

Chapter 2
The Noble Experiment: Heroic Drama

Honour sits on me like some heavy Armour,
And with its stiff Defence incumbers me.
John Dryden, *The Rival Ladies*

It is easier to understand the programme than to appreciate the plays. 'Heroic drama' was to be a kind of grand opera without music, a splendid artifice in which monarchs, nobles, and generals of astonishing virtue or evil endured momentous conflicts of love and honour while nations quaked and audiences admired the magnificence of the thought, language, scenes, and costumes. Drawing its sentiments from chivalric romance and the etiquette of the most refined courts, it was to lift serious English drama from the muck of blood and revenge into which it had fallen up to a level befitting a nation whose theatrical establishment had recently sojourned in the capitals of Europe. The themes of honour and martial valour would brace the soul, while that of love would soften the heart, and the characters would provide patterns for imitation, ideals in the Platonic sense. If the goals ultimately proved unattainable, they were not ignoble.

John Dryden, who dominated the genre, traced it back to Davenant's *The Siege of Rhodes*, a 1650s 'opera' that stated the heroic theme, 'Love and Valour'.[1] The two-part, ten-act version produced in 1661 adds to the original plan a new character, Solyman's wife Roxolana, creating (with Alphonso and Ianthe) a marriage quartet. This craving for symmetry – Roxolana's jealousy balances Alphonso's – and the formidable length (requiring two days to present) were both prophetic of Dryden's work. The connection between love and valour is clarified by Mustapha's praise of his opponents:

> Those desp'rate English ne'er will fly!
> Their firmness still does hinder others' flight,
> As if their mistresses were by
> To see and praise them while they fight.
>
> (v)

Such an arrangement, idealized in the neoplatonic code of European romance, appealed strongly to English heroic writers. But *The Siege of Rhodes* has the *sound* of heroic drama only sporadically, when it uses heroic couplets. Alphonso, urged to flee to his bride, replies, 'My honour lost, her love would soon decay./Here for my tomb or triumph I will stay' (I). Told of the marvellous powers of Ianthe's beauty, Solyman asks, 'Where are the limits thou would'st set for praise?/Or to what height wilt thou my wonder raise?' (II). Wondrous, too, are the spectacles described by the scene directions: 'The Scene is varied to the prospect of Mount Philermus, artificers appearing at work about that castle which was there, with wonderful expedition, erected by SOLYMAN. His great army is discovered in the plain below' ('End of the Third Entry'). In its operatic magnificence, stirring theme, sentiments, and popularity, *The Siege of Rhodes* invited emulation.

Reflecting on what Davenant had and had not achieved, Dryden concluded that 'an heroic play ought to be an imitation, in little, of an heroic poem'. In particular, it should imitate the Renaissance epic such as Ariosto's *Orlando Furioso*, whose opening, he said, gave him the programme: 'Le donne, i cavalier, l'arme, gli amori./Le cortesie, l'audaci imprese io canto' ('Arms and the men I sing, and ladies fair,/Their loves and courtesy, and what they dare'). Davenant had fallen just short of the full-fledged heroic epic, which would have 'indulged him a farther liberty of fancy, and of drawing all things as far above the ordinary proportion of the stage as that is beyond the common words and actions of human life', adds Dryden, seemingly oblivious to the pitfalls of such a scheme.

Not everyone agrees that the epic poem was the crucial model for the heroic play. Conventionally the genre is seen as the resultant of various literary and critical influences besides the epic: the line of English hero-plays descending from Marlowe through Beaumont and Fletcher; the neoclassical tragedies of France, especially Pierre Corneille's; the French heroic romances of Honoré d'Urfé, the de Scudérys and La Calprenède; and the Italian opera, which (as Dryden points out) influenced Davenant.[2] Neoclassical critical theory – such as Hobbes's *Answer to Mr Davenant's Preface to Gondibert* (1650) – which held the epic to be the noblest literary form, also encouraged plays of chivalry.

Later in 1661 Davenant revived his *Love and Honour* (see Introduction, p. 17) as well. If he did not *create* the early Restoration dramatic mood he was certainly attuned to it; most if not all of the major new plays in the first half-dozen seasons were love-and-honour dramas, either heroic plays or comedies. Courtly and literary circles, responding to the heady winds blowing through politics, society, and art, cultivated the heroic, though it is equally true that heroic drama was a flinching from true tragedy – of which, it was said, the nation had had enough in real life – and an escape into the exotic.[3] The explanation via literary influences such as European romance and opera, or the King's taste, seems comparatively mechanical; since all of these sources and influences were *courtly* tastes, however, a socio-political basis for heroic drama is again indicated. As noted earlier, the solo trumpet was emerging as the 'hero' of the orchestra at this time. Given that musical fashions reflect shifts in society, it is significant that Restoration composers moved from a corporate to a solo concept – from the consort, which subordinates the individual, to virtuosity and personal prowess.[4] If there was ever a *Zeitgeist*, it was the heroic style in the early years of Charles II.

In poetry and in drama that style was widely believed to require the heroic couplet, not merely as ornament but as an integral part of its rhetoric and outlook. Dryden insisted that a high subject needs a formal style, which in 1664 meant to him rhymed, end-stopped iambic pentameter, though he warned that 'if a fit subject ["great and noble"] be not chosen', the virtues of the couplet would be lost.[5] In dialogue, he observed, couplets have 'so particular a grace . . . that the sudden smartness of the answer and the sweetness of the rhyme' complement each other, and they need not be artificial in grammar or unnatural in sound if skilfully composed. (Modern commentators are more ambivalent, judging the couplet powerful and authoritative, but also bombastic and artificial; firm, flexible, and good for argument, yet facile, sophistic, and hopelessly highbrow.[6]) Its popularity owed something to Charles II's outspoken admiration of its use in French tragedy, where its absoluteness mirrored the monarchy's, but Dryden traces its pedigree from Denham, Waller, and Davenant (he might have added Ben Jonson).[7] Aware that his own forte was the couplet, Dryden used precept and example to make it the usual medium of heroic discourse from 1664 to 1677.

The story of heroic drama is, in fact, mainly the story of Dryden's early career, from his co-founding of the genre to his decision to abandon it most of the heroic plays worth reading are his, as is the bulk of supporting theory. Inspired by Davenant, and probably Roger Boyle's *The General*, Dryden and Robert Howard brought together the crucial ingredients – epic plot and characters, love-and-honour theme, uniformly serious treatment, rhymed couplets – in *The Indian Queen* (1664). A year later Dryden produced a sequel, *The Indian Emperor*, establishing both himself and the genre.

The Indian Queen, first of its kind to reach the London stage, patented the formula. The setting is exotic: Mexico a generation before Cortés. The principals, all invaders or defenders of Mexico, are caught in a tangle of conflicting allegiances and passions that involves the destiny of the kingdom as well as their own. The noblest, Montezuma, holds himself above party: his personal worth unrewarded, he changes sides. The code of values understood as 'epic' receives self-conscious emphasis; most of Montezuma's dialogues stress the amplitude of mind, mutual admiration, and generosity of both speakers. Honourable conflicts abound, as when Prince Acacis is trebly torn between duty to his mother, love for a princess, and ties of honour to his friend (III. 1). The spectacular effects that impressed the first audiences also became *de rigueur* in the form: authentic costumes (with feathers from Surinam), an Indian war dance at Queen Zempoalla's triumph, a conjuring in a cave with an epiphany by the dream god and a song by spirits, and a grand finale in the golden Temple of the Sun, where priests in red and white feathers prepare a human sacrifice.[8]

Heroic drama never flinched from exhibiting the extravagant conduct associated with aristocratic pride, the chivalric code, Machiavellian cunning, or operatic gesture. During the prison scene in Act IV, the evil general's sword at the hero's heart is checked by the evil queen's dagger at the heroine's breast; then each weapon-bearer steps before the loved one (a neat bit of ballet popular with later satirists) without ceasing to exchange symmetrical challenges or cajolements. The characteristic artificiality of the action, the asides, and the sentiments shows how little heroic drama cared for 'nature'.

Set twenty years later as Cortés arrives, *The Indian Emperor* (1665) allowed Dryden to recycle his Mexican reading, his epic formula, his superhero, and more. 'The scenes are old, the Habits are the same/We wore last year', admits the Prologue; another spectacular cave scene features necromancy, epiphanies, song, and dance. Montezuma reappears in his careworn middle age, troubled by ghosts from *The Indian Queen*, including the children of his and Zempoalla's marriages, who become romantically involved. He himself falls for one of her daughters. The same system of values and aesthetics again serves. Admiration is the response Dryden wants, conflict between love and a competing code his way of creating it.[9] When Cortés tries to explain why his sense of personal honour and national duty conflict with his love, Princess Cydaria asks, 'What is this Honour which does love controul?' 'A raging fire of vertue in the Soul', replies Cortés, adding modestly, 'A painful burden which great minds must bear' (II. 2).[10] Once more the typical dilemmas and dialectics carry Dryden to the frontiers of absurdity. Cortés's treatment of Orbellan may seem chivalrous or demented, Alibech's reticence with her suitors sly or pointless, but even Dryden came to regret Montezuma's dying simile, and satirists castigated many long debates and metaphoric flights.

In v. 2, Dryden presents a grotesque argument about revealed versus natural religion between a Spanish and a Mexican priest – while the latter is being stretched on a rack: a lamentable or (if ironic) devastating conclusion to the theme of Old World encountering New that runs through both plays. In *The Indian Queen*'s Prologue, an

Indian Boy and Girl evoke the natural idyll of their pre-Conquest Eden and the 'ancient prophecies' that their 'world shall be subdued by one more old'. Look, here they are, says the Boy – and both turn to the audience, suddenly the new Conquistadors. But only Montezuma's 'jungle-boy' speech recalling his Peruvian forest upbringing (v. 1), and his Epilogue craving the New World's indulgence, echo this note. In the short opening scene of the sequel, three Spaniards debate whether the new territory is temperate and fruitful or (except for precious metals) 'naked and bare'. Later, Cortés and Cydaria contrast Indian with Spanish love (nature versus artifice), though since both are conversant with *préciosité*, 'nature' is poorly represented. The 'religious' discussion in the torture chamber, which might have pulled some of this together, falls between black comedy and a crushing comment on, at least, *Spanish* Christianity.

Thus Dryden approached the drama of ideas but pulled up lame: his theatre did not want it, and 'my chief endeavours', he wrote, 'are to delight the age in which I live'.[11] This and other failures and absurdities do not, however, entirely negate the energy or seriousness of the play. The plotting is fuller than in *Queen*, yet remains under control; the larger cast is arranged in neat patterns.[12] If the themes are not well developed they are abundant, from royal versus priestly claims and public versus private motives to the clash of cultures and the poetics of justice. The heroic couplets, despite awkwardnesses, begin to perform as advertised. In grave exchanges Dryden sometimes achieves the formality and stateliness of French neoclassical drama, then employs short lines and shared couplets to get an effect that anticipates his mature satires:

> *Vasquez:* The night comes on: if Fortune bless the bold
> I shall possess the Beauty – *Pizarro*: I the Gold.
>
> (IV. 3)

The Indian Emperor looks immature and vulnerable beside Dryden's best work, but is already heftier than *The Indian Queen*.

Tyrannick Love (1669) comes nearer to the drama of ideas because it has a setting where ideas were important – the Roman Empire in early Christian times – and characters qualified to articulate them. St Catherine of Alexandria and the philosopher Apollonius carry through the religious discussion that Dryden sidesteps in *The Indian Emperor*. Prodded by the tyrannical Emperor Maximin, Apollonius charges that Christianity follows pagan precepts. But *we* reward them, says St Catherine, which is more effective than mere statement.[13] Then, he counters, we are more disinterested. No, secretly you covet praise or enjoy pride, she insists; and our higher morality goes beyond actions to reach the mind. Apollonius yields, converts, and is sent to a baptism of fire by the furious Maximin. This is only the beginning: St Catherine argues Epicurean philosophy with Placidus and free will with Maximin, who clashes with Porphyrius over the claims of conscience; Porphyrius and Berenice balance love and honour, and so on. Many speeches joust with Hobbes's ideas.[14]

How did Dryden make his fractious audiences sit through all this intellectual debate? By giving them excellent theatre with plenty of variety, solid writing, and strong acting. The clash of opposing views in debate is inherently dramatic, especially when, as here, the topics and speakers are diverse and the rhetoric is tight. In II. 1, Porphyrius tries to seduce Berenice away from her husband Maximin; torn between love, fidelity to her vows, and incipient Christianity, she gives him leave only to 'hope, in Heav'n'. 'So Princes cheaply may our wants supply', objects Porphyrius, 'When they give that their Treasurers deny' – an audacious glance at Charles II's exchequer. Many other couplets are equally pithy, but Dryden's real *coup de théâtre* is the conjuring scene (Act IV) wherein pagan spirits descend in a cloud, singing whimsically, to a cave, and assail St Catherine's mind with dreams until driven away by her guardian angel. With Major Mohun as Maximin and Nell Gwyn as his daughter Valeria, *Tyrannick Love* scored a popular triumph.

Admittedly the hastily written play has some glaring weaknesses, including questionable connections between the various themes.[15] The Prologue warns of excesses: Dryden has 'loosed the reins, and bid his Muse run mad'. The centre of excess is Maximin, who holds himself above conscience and morality, claiming, 'Who can do all things, can do nothing ill' (v. 1). Raving, sentencing, and stabbing, he becomes comical, a satire on self-indulgence, but the infection spreads to Porphyrius who, when doomed to beheading, threatens to direct his gush of blood, and throw his head, at Maximin. And, as with most heroic plays, the dilemmas of divided duty seem too neatly contrived, the unrequited loves too perfectly parallel.

Yet if all heroic drama were as entertaining, as multifaceted and as well written as *Tyrannick Love*, the genre would have held the boards longer; even its literary faults could be histrionic strengths. Despite its extravagances, the play seems a balance point in Dryden's heroic phase, before he carried it too far, perhaps took it too seriously, and provoked ridicule. Here, the clever Epilogue shows him keeping his perspective. Nell Gwyn, as the self-slain Valeria, rises to assure the audience, 'I'm what I was'. She needs no stupid poet to write *her* epitaph: 'Here *Nelly* lies, who, though she liv'd a Slater'n,/Yet dy'd a Princess, acting in *S. Cathar'n.*' Tumultuous cheers.

The Conquest of Granada (Part I, 1670; Part II, 1671) has often been used by critics and anthologists to represent the heroic play. Actually it is not 'representative' of anything, but rather the utmost height and bound of heroic drama in England, notoriously the largest and loudest of the genre. A final blast on the trumpet of *gloire*, it reprises many of the earlier themes.[16] Almanzor, like Montezuma, is a military hero of mysterious birth who changes sides, but he has the hyperbolic passions of Maximin; Lyndaraxa outdoes Zempoalla as a caricature of ambition. *Granada* is truer to Dryden's putative models than are his other heroic dramas, with the grand gestures of the Continental epic, and the scale, the situation, sometimes the atmosphere of *The Siege of Rhodes*. Queen Isabella's speech 'Granada is for noble loves renowned' (Part II, I. 1), for example, contains the kind of chivalric sentiment with which Davenant had delighted his audiences. Appropriately, the essay 'Of Heroic Plays' was prefixed to the first edition of *Granada* (1672).

Its most admirable feature is the sweep and significance of the design. On the broad tapestry of the final Christian siege of Moorish Granada, Dryden weaves several linked stories. Prime is the tale of Almanzor, a valiant stranger and free lance who quells feuding factions with a word, props up King Boabdelin against the Spaniards, shifts over to Prince Abdalla's party but comes back to Boabdelin, only to desert him again in Act V – not to mention further changes in Part II. Every defection is caused by royal ingratitude, though since Almanzor's inamorata is the King's fiancée (later wife) Almahide, he is not easy to please. A second love triangle pits Abdalla against Abdelmelech, chief of one Moorish faction, for the favours of the rival chieftain's sister Lyndaraxa, who wants whichever can become king. The same factions provide the star-crossed lovers Ozmyn and Benzayda, a third plot. After ten acts, Boabdelin and all of the second triangle are killed, the surviving true lovers are united, and Almanzor is revealed as the son of the Duke of Arcos, a Spaniard. Once Granada falls, Almanzor becomes a loyal vassal of King Ferdinand, and Queen Isabella takes Almahide under her protection until the days of her mourning shall have been accomplished.

All this is less exotic than it seems. The two factions – one of which finally betrays Granada to its enemies – sound suspiciously like Puritans and Catholics. Each strand in the plot presents a problem in divided allegiance analogous to those faced by many of Dryden's contemporaries; love versus honour is just one way in which private wishes compete with public claims. Not only do Almanzor, Abdalla, Lyndaraxa, Ozmyn, Benzayda, and the factions undergo this conflict; even the two guards assigned to kill Ozmyn are divided when Benzayda begs his life. *Gazul:* 'To disobey our orders is to die. – /I'll do't: who dare oppose it?' *Reduan:* 'That dare I' (IV. 2). They fight, and

Gazul falls, killed by the providential author for making the wrong choice.[17] Usually Dryden plumps for devotion to duty, Ozmyn and Benzayda being a partial and happy exception that shows his moderation. What we have, finally, is a political fable dramatizing the need for rulers to keep their promises and subjects to maintain their loyalty if chaos is to be avoided.

The design, then, is weighty and relevant – not escapist – but the dialogue is badly overwritten. In 1664 Dryden had scorned rhymesters who, trapped into 'inverting the order of their words, constantly close their lines with verbs'.[18] Now he will write 'Fate for each other did not us ordain' and 'It shows my love you as no tie regard'. The ranting Almanzor, 'Rough as a storm, and humourous as wind' (I. 1) is the greatest problem. His vaunts are bad enough, but in love and articulating he is insufferable:

> I'm pleased and pained, since first her eyes I saw,
> As I were stung with some tarantula. . . .
> I'm numbed, and fixed, and scarce my eyeballs move;
> I fear it is the lethargy of love!
>
> (III. 1)

I do not know how this could be handled on-stage, unless translated into Italian and set to a sprightly Mozart aria: 'Contento! Dolente!' etc. down to 'letargia d'amore'. For a long time we can laugh at (or be appalled by) Almanzor, but eventually he is reformed and presented for approval, like the rakes of later comedy. The sinewy arguments of *Tyrannick Love* are conducted as turns of plot here, while the dialogue itself is frequently tortuous and baroque.[19]

Critics have often given *The Conquest of Granada* a rough ride or a lame excuse, from Dr Johnson's nicely balanced 'illustrious depravity' to modern theories that the characters must be parodies or patterns or fragments of ideas, since they are certainly not people.[20] The first critique appeared in December 1671 (only eleven months after Part II opened) in the form of *The Rehearsal*. The Duke of Buckingham, Samuel Butler, Thomas Sprat, and other wits had been tinkering with a riposte to heroic drama since its birth, but Dryden's appointment as Poet Laureate (1668) and then *Granada* inspired its completion. Dryden appears as Bayes, a conceited, oafish dramatist who presents a rehearsal of his new heroic play to Smith and Johnson, our surrogates. The play-within-a-play structure, the outer mocking the inner, may have been suggested by *The Knight of the Burning Pestle*, but Buckingham and friends set the form subsequently used by Fielding, Sheridan, and other satirists. The joke proceeds on two levels simultaneously: the inner play, a burlesque of (here) heroic drama, and the playwright's self-incriminating commentary on it, with the visitors' arch reactions.

The general accusations in the frame play – making tragedy laughable, novelty-mongering, 'transversing' (prose to verse and vice versa), lifting dialogue from the coffee-houses and pilfering the Classics – lack substance; they are easily made, easily dismissed, and not particularly Drydenesque. The satire in the inner play on fantastic plots, impossible characters, and nonsensical rant is much more effective; Dryden's practice, not his theory, was vulnerable. Boabdelin and Abdalla become the Two Kings of Brentford; Almanzor becomes Drawcansir, 'a fierce hero, that frights his mistress, snubs up kings, baffles armies, and does what he will, without regard to numbers, good manners, or justice' (IV. 1). Almanzor's 'Spite of myself I'll stay, fight, love, despair;/And I can do all this because I dare' turns into Drawcansir's 'I drink, I huff, I strut, look big and stare;/And all this I can do, because I dare'. *The Rehearsal* is satisfying (and legitimate) partly because so little exaggeration was required; a line such as 'Stand off; I have not leisure yet to die' might come from either play. Prince Volscius's struggle with his boots (IV. 1), however, could not appear in a love-and-honour drama: it is the unmistakable voice of Augustan irony.

> Sometimes with stubborn honour, like this boot,
> My mind is guarded, and resolved to do't:
> Sometimes, again, that very mind, by love
> Disarmed, like this other leg does prove. . . .
> So does my honour and my love together
> Puzzle me so, I can resolve for neither.
> (*Goes out hopping with one boot on, and the other off.*)

The Rehearsal, produced by Dryden's own company, revised to keep pace with new follies, was revived throughout the next century.

The attacks on *The Conquest of Granada* – especially on the Epilogue to Part II, asserting the superiority of Restoration to Elizabethan wit – and on his 'Defence of the Epilogue' (1672) seem to have shaken Dryden.[21] When he reappears in the heroic lists with *Aureng-Zebe* (1675) a great deal has changed; we have the form without the spirit of heroic drama. Imperial wars still impend, 'vast' and 'great' are favourite adjectives and some emotional tropes are absurd, yet there is a different harmony in the characters and diction. 'I have only represented a practicable virtue mixed with the frailties and imperfections of human life', writes Dryden (almost apologetically) in the Dedication, and Aureng-Zebe is indeed, for a Dryden hero, remarkably restrained and subtle in his relationships with Indamora and his father. The stormier qualities of Almanzor reside in Morat, the villain, and even he is converted to virtue on his death-bed by the appeal of a good woman.[22] A novel aura of softness and domestic pathos emanates from Indamora and Melesinda to touch those around them.

As the harsher features of the heroic ethos relaxed, so did the heroic couplet. Grown 'weary of his long-loved mistress, Rhyme' (says the Prologue), Dryden employs a considerable number of unrhymed two- and three-foot lines to muffle and syncopate the couplets' march. In this new mood ('he has now another taste of wit'), Dryden uses the Prologue to recant his earlier claims: such 'a secret shame/Invades his breast at Shakespeare's sacred name' that he 'would quit the stage' in defeat and despair. 'Let him retire, betwixt two ages cast,/The first of this, and hindmost of the last.' Actually Dryden was not about to retire; he was just spinning a cocoon.

Though Dryden dominated, he was neither the first nor the last in the heroic field. His predecessor and main rival of the 1660s was Roger Boyle, the Earl of Orrery, to whom the King suggested writing rhymed English tragedy in the French manner.[23] Boyle's first such effort, *The General* (or *Altemera*, Dublin, 1662; London, 1664), qualifies as the earliest Restoration drama of any kind, but its awkward exposition and high-strung *préciosité* beg for satire, and are said to have received it, on the spot, from the court wits attending. *Henry the Fifth* (1664) is a better play of the same species; King Harry and Owen Tudor can sustain the weight of the chivalric code without buckling, and the verse, while artificial, has sometimes a formal, operatic elegance. In *Mustapha* (1665), his best work, most of the Turkish cast from *The Siege of Rhodes* trade extravagant gestures and elaborate compliments, but they live in a darker world where tragedy is possible: Rustan and Pyrrhus manipulate Solyman as Iago does Othello. In the end the plotters die, but so, nobly, do both of Solyman's sons. His tragedy is to survive them, and know that his jealousy and credulity caused their deaths. The eagerly awaited *Black Prince* (1667) bored the audience, despite spectacular effects, with its length and absurdities.[24] Everyone gets caught in agonizing moral or emotional dilemmas, is made confidant or go-between to his or her own love, or is required to renounce one sacred tie for another. No English dramatist ever carried the spirit of French romance further than did Boyle.

Elkanah Settle, initially Dryden's disciple in heroic drama, was later promoted by court friends as a rival to him.[25] The success of *Cambyses* (1671?) probably piqued 'Bayes', and the greater popularity of *The Empress of Morocco* (1673?) certainly did: Dryden collaborated on a pamphlet attacking the play. But Settle was just carrying out the Davenant–Dryden programme, albeit uncritically, with heavier emphasis on spectacle and violence. *Empress* exhibits the arrival of the Moroccan navy, firing ceremonial cannon; a coronation fête; a hailstorm with rainbow; a court masque with murder; and finally the villain 'cast down on the Gaunches' [spikes]. *The Conquest of China* (1675) features a tableau showing a 'Number of Murdered Women', either stabbed, strangled, or poisoned, 'with several other forms of death'. Settle's characters are equally extreme. The Empress of Morocco, having killed her husband, son, and daughter-in-law, stabs herself, observing, 'I Scorn to kill less than whole Families' (v. 1). Settle was an egregious eccentric who described *Empress* as 'A Tragedy with Sculptures', and rather refreshingly blamed the 'ill success' of *Conquest* on its being 'faulty'.

The first three plays of Nathaniel Lee are customarily called 'rhymed heroic dramas', but they show the genre in the process of transition to tragedy.[26] His first, a thing of blood, he correctly called *The Tragedy of Nero* (1674), and some of its rants are in blank verse. *Sophonisba; or, Hannibal's Overthrow* (1675) concludes with the Antony and Cleopatra-like love–death of King Massinissa and his wife Sophonisba, leaving the Roman leader Scipio alive but dashed: he vows to make peace with Carthage and retire. Hannibal himself has already faded from view, still fighting, so the final scene is dominated by death, loss, and withdrawal. It is still worth reading, especially for the attractive character of Massinissa and a possible influence on *All for Love*; its language is no more extravagant than Dryden's.[27] *Gloriana* (1676), loosely based on La Calprenède's *Cléopâtre*, combines love and honour in couplets with tragic pathos. Lee's weakness was passionate excess, like his frenzied priestess who 'Cuts her hot flesh, grovels upon the ground,/Sings, Dances, kicks the golden Tripeds round'; he would do better work in tragedy.

A few other rhymed plays of these years exhibit heroic drama in its *Götterdämmerung*. Thomas Otway began heroically enough with *Alcibiades* (1675) and *Don Carlos* (1676), of which the second, especially, has been admired for its relatively (an important qualification) restrained rhetoric.[28] But his *Titus and Berenice* (1676), a compact version of Racine's *Bérénice*, ends quasi-tragically with the final parting of the royal lovers, Titus vowing to become a tyrant. The imperfect opening rhymes – 'here', 'Fair', 'adores', 'hers', 'conceals', 'tells' – suggest a restlessness with the couplet. In *The State of Innocence and Fall of Man* (1677), an 'opera', Dryden reworked *Paradise Lost* in heroic couplets, often with bizarre effect; it did not reach the Restoration stage (see Ch. 6). Neither of these last two plays has a hero, certainly not an Almanzor. The old superhero, like his musical counterpart, the high *clarino* trumpet, had 'shortcomings and limitations' that 'prevented any far-reaching modulations', caused 'great technical difficulties in playing' and 'ultimately led to their disappearance'.[29] Both flourished in a period enamoured of the brilliant solo, but fell victim to an increased awareness of the virtues of co-operation. Let this stand as their epitaph: 'They would not blend.'

Notes

1. Part I, 1656, Part II, 1659, Parts I and II, 1661; see Introduction, p. 19. For Dryden's comments in this and the next paragraph, see his essay 'Of Heroic Plays' (1672), in *Of Dramatic Poesy*, edited by George Watson, 2 vols (London and New York, 1962), I, 156–66 (esp. pp. 157–59); here after cited as Watson.

2. For learned discussions, see Cecil V. Deane, *Dramatic Theory and the Rhymed Heroic Play* (Oxford, 1931), pp. 8–16; Arthur Kirsch, *Dryden's Heroic Drama* (Princeton, 1965), pp. 46–65; and James Sutherland, *English Literature of the Late Seventeenth Century* (Oxford, 1969), p. 51.

3. On the first point, see Laura Brown, *English Dramatic Form, 1660–1760* (New Haven, 1981), p. 18; the second is a commonplace.

4. The argument of E. D. Mackerness, *A Social History of English Music* (London, 1964), p. 85.

5. This and the following quotations are from his Dedication to *The Rival Ladies* (1664), in Watson, I, 1–9 (esp. pp. 6, 8, 9).

6. See George Saintsbury, *A History of English Prosody*, 3 vols (London, 1908), II, 367; Sutherland, p. 51; and Paul Ramsey, *The Art of John Dryden* (Lexington, Kentucky, 1969), pp. 69, 91–94.

7. See Watson, I, 7, for Dryden's comments; W. J. Courthope, *A History of English Poetry*, 6 vols (London, 1895–1910), IV (1903), 403–04; and Arthur H. Scouten, 'Tragedy', in *The Revels History of Drama in English*, edited by T. W. Craik and C. Leech, 8 vols (London, 1975–83), V (1976), 257–58.

8. Marion Jones, 'Actors and Repertory', *Revels History*, V, 145.

9. See his 'Defence of *An Essay of Dramatic Poesy*' (1668), in Watson, I, 114.

10. References to Dryden's plays are to *The Works of John Dryden*, general editors, E. N. Hooker and H. T. Swedenborg, 19 vols (Berkeley, Los Angeles, and London, 1956–). *The Indian Emperor* appears in Volume IX (1966), edited by John Loftis.

11. 'Defence of *An Essay*', in Watson, I, 116. See also Kirsch, pp. 93–96; Scouten, pp. 261–62; and Bruce King, *Dryden's Major Plays* (London and Edinburgh, 1966), pp. 35–36.

12. Discussed by Loftis in *Works of Dryden*, IX, 300.

13. King, p. 50, shows that her ideas come from Archbishop Tillotson's sermons.

14. See Kirsch, pp. 97, 100, 104–5; *Works of Dryden*, edited by Maximillian Novak, X (1970), 384; and King, pp. 19, 38, 50–58.

15. See Dryden's Preface, in Watson, I, 141; and *Works of Dryden*, X, 399. On Maximin, see King, pp. 19, 38, 41.

16. See Kirsch, pp. 106–7; and King, p. 76.

17. See Anne T. Barbeau, *The Intellectual Design of John Dryden's Plays* (New Haven, 1970), pp. 13–14; and Robert D. Hume, *The Development of English Drama in the Late Seventeenth Century* (Oxford, 1976), p. 273.

18. Dedication to *The Rival Ladies*, in Watson, I, 6.

19. *Works of Dryden*, edited by John Loftis and David S. Rodes, xi (1978), 414–17 makes and documents the point.

20. Samuel Johnson, *Lives of the English Poets*, 2 vols (London, 1952), i, 248; Deane, pp. 14–15; Barbeau, pp. 5 ff.; and D. W. Jefferson, 'The Significance of Dryden's Heroic Plays' (1940), in *Restoration Dramatists*, edited by Earl Miner (Englewood, New Jersey, 1966).

21. See *Works of Dryden*, xi, 431–35.

22. I am greatly indebted to Kirsch's discussion, p.121.

23. See Scouten, p. 260.

24. *The Dramatic Works of Roger Boyle*, edited by William S. Clark, 2 vols (Cambridge, Massachusetts, 1937), i, 306–7, narrates the fiasco.

25. Leonard R. N. Ashley, 'Elkanah Settle', in *Restoration and Eighteenth Century Drama*, edited by James Vinson (London, 1980), pp. 125–26. See also Sutherland, p. 64.

26. See Scouten, p. 270.

27. Kirsch, pp. 137–40, argues that all three plays (and *The Rival Queens*) influenced Dryden's tragedy. The quotation from *Sophonisba*, iv. 1, is from *The Works of Nathaniel Lee*, edited by Thomas B. Stroup and Arthur L. Cooke, 2 vols (New Brunswick, New Jersey, 1954–55), Vol. i; the editors discuss Lee's passions, i, 4.

28. See, for examples, George Nettleton, *English Drama of the Restoration and Eighteenth Century* (New York, 1923), p. 99; Allardyce B. Nicoll, *A History of Restoration Drama*, fourth edition (Cambridge, 1952), pp. 120–21; and Scouten, p. 272.

29. From programme notes to 'The Baroque and Classical Trumpet' (Turnabout/Vox, n.d). The closing quotation comes from Reginald Nettel, *The Orchestra in England* (London, 1948), p. 38.

Chapter 3
The Jaws of Defeat: Tragicomedy

Then there are gods, and virtue is their care.
Nahum Tate, *The History of King Lear*

English drama has always been restless with the classical genres. One way of understanding heroic drama is as a kind of tragicomedy, that treats high and potentially tragic material in rhyme, but saves the virtuous from slaughter. The Restoration had prose and blank-verse tragicomedies too, in various shadings of darkness as one parent or the other dominates: thus they are often difficult to define or classify. In this chapter we examine some specimens that partake more closely of tragedy, but pull up short; the lighter kind is discussed under comedy.

Serious tragicomedy in the 1660s was almost a Howard family business. Edward Howard's *The Usurper* (1664) and *The Woman's Conquest* (1670) are interesting now mainly for Prefaces attacking farce and heroic drama, and espousing blank verse. His *Change of Crownes* (1667), a stronger play, was banned by Charles II for references to corruption at Court.[1] Robert Howard gave *The Vestal Virgin* (1665) alternative endings, tragic or happy: its only real distinction.[2] His *The Great Favourite; or, The Duke of Lerna* (1668), however, is noteworthy even apart from the Preface's attack on Dryden's critical dogmatizing. As political as Edward's plays, it traces the intrigues of the Spanish Court at the death of an aged king, providing a plot of studied symmetry that focuses sharply on Lerna's party. In the vividly realized scramble for positions at the 'change of crowns', Lerna uses the young King's interest in his daughter Maria to climb to favour, and has his enemy the Queen Mother poisoned. A faction led by the Duke of Medina counters Lerna's stratagems, and the virtuous Maria turns against her father, warning the King of his danger before withdrawing to a nunnery. But as Medina's party surround Lerna for the *coup de grâce*, he pulls a stunning *coup de théâtre*: entering in his new cardinal's habit, he vaunts at length, and exits to a monastery. Maria consents to delay her final vows to consider the King's ardent marriage proposal. The plot, characters, and staging are more memorable than the dialogue, but while it lacks strong images, Howard's verse is smooth, competent, and usually free of rant. At intense moments the co-founder of heroic drama still shifts into couplets.

Thomas Shadwell's socially and philosophically interesting *The Libertine* (1675) illustrates both how broad a genre tragicomedy was, and how radically an inherited story and character (Don Juan) may vary from one author to another. The Preface admits debts to several European versions, but claims, justifiably, that much of the play is new and the rest altered.[3] Shadwell's Don John is certainly his own – part Hobbesian libertine, part Satan: a rake to shock Restoration London – and his treatment reeks with promiscuous violence. Tirso de Molina's original 'Burlador de Sevilla' (*c.* 1630) was a prankster; Don John is a graceless villain, guilty of 'Some thirty murders, Rapes innumerable . . . Parricide' (I. 1). 'My bus'ness is my pleasure', remarks Don John, 'there is no right or wrong, but what conduces to, or hinders pleasure', and off he goes to 'live the noble life of Sense' (I. 1): 'sense' being here a code for the kind of materialism associated with Hobbes and Rochester. On his way to more rapes and murders, he also advocates polygamy and denies free will.

Yet he and the play are three-dimensional. Don John lacks nobility but not grandeur or courage. When the Stone Guest demands repentance, John retorts coolly, 'Cou'dst thou bestow another heart on me, I might, but with this heart I have, I cannot' (v. 2). Were chaos come, he says, and seas of sulphur flaming round – surely a reminiscence of Milton's Satan –

> I could not fear or feel the least remorse.
> To the last instant I would dare thy power.
> Here I stand firm . . .
> . . . now do thy worst.
>   (v. 2).

Resisting a cheap conversion, Shadwell gives the diehard libertine his due. The servant Jacomo provides some comedy, but his urge to 'sin in private' (I. 1) is just the kind of hypocrisy Don John scorns. Other evidences of irony are the virtuous women's song of freedom ('by Nature wild', Act III), which is close to the rake's ideal, and the shepherds' song in praise of 'Nature'. Thus Shadwell offers a double image – Lucifer and Satan – of the libertine.

Double vision of a different kind mars Dryden's *The Spanish Fryar; or, The Double Discovery* (1680), blurred by the author's inability to keep both his heroic material and a tenuously connected cuckolding plot in focus. The nearly tragic high plot is the more satisfactory of the two. Queen Leonora, daughter of a deceased usurper and captor of the rightful King, is betrothed to Bertran but falls in love with Torrismond. To rid herself of the former she hints at the old King's murder to him; when this is announced, she repudiates him. Torrismond, however, proves to be the former King's son, and avoids his bride's bed – until Bertran produces King Sancho unharmed, a *deus ex machina* in keeping with his wily character. Not trusting this action alone, Dryden alternates it with a comic subplot of Spanish intrigue in which Friar Dominic, a 'Tun of Devotion . . . big enough to be a Pope', pimps for Lorenzo (II. 3). The discovery that Lorenzo and his inamorata Elvira are siblings discredits Dominic, who is hustled off-stage by 'a rabble'. The flagrant anti-Catholicism of the play, welcome in 1680, embarrassed Dryden later, when both he and the King were Catholics.

The famous Dedication (1681) distinguishes between theatrical performance – 'where everything contributes to impose upon the judgment' and the actor can produce 'false beauties . . . no more lasting than a rainbow' – and the published text, which the reader may discover is 'trashy stuff'.[4] Among Dryden's examples of these 'Dalilahs of the theatre' that fade in print are his own Maximin and Almanzor! Sure enough, on the printed page *The Spanish Fryar* shows its flaws: a lack of subtlety, some silliness, and, yes, some Dalilahs of rant.

King Lear becomes a tragicomedy in Nahum Tate's notorious 1681 alteration: Lear and Cordelia are saved, and she marries Edgar. Whereas Shakespeare's tragedy was not being performed, Tate's fascinating mixture of original, revised, and new material remained popular until the nineteenth century. Everything is recast in the Restoration mould: King Lear becomes a humours character, the choleric man; Edgar and Cordelia are heroic lovers whose piety is emphasized (v. 5); Kent is understood as a 'plain dealer' (II. 1) and Edmund as a Hobbesian villain.[5] Minus the Fool, the play becomes a heroic drama, complete with symmetrical plot, parallel scenes, a love versus duty problem, and a good end for virtuous characters. An admirer of Shakespeare and sensitive to his power, Tate (like Dr Johnson) found the original ending too painful, too lacking in poetic justice, to bear; his Cordelia, who has warned the gods, 'Your image suffers when a monarch bleeds' (IV. 5), can finally say, 'Then there are gods, and virtue is their care' (v. 5). Set Tate down as one who loved Shakespeare not wisely but too well.

Nathaniel Lee's *The Princess of Cleve* (1681?) turns Mme de La Fayette's delicate psychological novel into something strange and rough: 'Farce, Comedy, Tragedy, or meer Play'.[6] To satirize the meanness and immorality of his times, Lee transformed the novel's polished libertine hero Nemours into 'a Ruffian'. The most significant of several changes, this makes the play another attack on the rake as Hobbesian villain (Lee's Dedication mentions *The Libertine*). The recent death of the notorious Rochester and the unfolding problems of the royal rake made the subject especially pertinent. Nemours continues to pursue the

Princess after her husband has died of jealousy, but she rejects him because she knows 'You have a sense too nice for long Enjoyment' (v. 3). Nemours predicts that he will 'Bed her eighteen months three weeks hence'; he *knows* women, 'the ingredients just that make 'em up,/All to loose Grains, the subtlest volatile Atoms' (v. 3). His 'reform' some lines later – a ploy to regain an errant mistress – is the most cynical touch of the upper plot which, with its deceit, fornication, and hints of homosexuality, hardly needs the cuckolding underplot to darken it. Crude, compelling, sometimes incoherent, *The Princess of Cleve* is the most piquing and problematical of Restoration tragi-comedies, a world apart from the pieties of Tate's *Lear*.[7]

Notes

1. See *The Change of Crownes*, edited by F. S. Boas (London, 1949). pp. 9, 17.

2. Discussed by James Sutherland, *English Literature of the Late Seventeenth Century* (Oxford, 1969), pp. 45–46; and Arthur H. Scouten, 'Tragedy', in *The Revels History of Drama in English*, edited by T. W. Craik and Clifford Leech, 8 vols (London, 1975–83), v (1976), 261.

3. See *The Complete Works of Thomas Shadwell*, edited by Montague Summers, 5 vols (London, 1927) iii, 21. All of the Shadwell quotations come from this edition.

4. See *On Dramatic Poesy*, edited by George Watson, 2 vols (London and New York, 1962), i, 275 (p. 276 on the following sentence).

5. The changes are admirably summarized by James Black in the introduction to his edition of Tate's *Lear* (Lincoln, Nebraska, 1981), esp. p. 24. My quotations come from this edition.

6. *The Works of Nathaniel Lee*, edited by Thomas B. Stroup and Arthur L. Cooke, 2 vols (New Brunswick, New Jersey, 1954–55), ii, 153. All references are to this edition. On the date, see Robert D. Hume, *The Rakish Stage* (Carbondale, Illinois, 1983), pp. 113–18.

7. For two contrasting interpretations see Hume, pp. 122–23; and Thomas B. Stroup, '*The Princess of Cleve* and Sentimental Comedy', *RES*, 11 (April 1935), 200–3.

Chapter 4
The World Well Lost: Tragedy

In tragedy, where the actions and persons are great, and
the crimes horrid, the laws of justice are more strictly to
be observed; and examples of punishment to be made to
deter mankind from the pursuit of vice.

John Dryden, Preface to *An Evening's Love*

When blank-verse tragedy was rekindled from the ashes of heroic
drama and rhymed heroic tragedy by Lee and Dryden in 1677, the
break in its traditions had reached thirty-five years, twice the length
of the interregnum itself, and the equation was full of new variables.
How would tragedy look in larger, more scenic theatres? What effect
would actresses and a more declamatory acting style have? How should
it respond to direct royal patronage and an audience highly conscious
of European models and theories? Tragic playwrights had intellectual
worries, too. The rising philosophical tide – Bacon, Descartes, Hobbes
– was empirical, emphasizing sense and observation; the leading
theological tendencies, Deism and Latitudinarianism, urged reason and
moderation; Bishop Sprat, in his *History of the Royal Society* (1667),
recommended a 'Mathematical plainness' in language. What should
tragedy, a form rooted in fate and passionate metaphorical excess, do
or be in such a climate?

It was, moreover, an age of criticism. A dramatist was expected to
be conscious of history, of how he fit in, and conversant with tragic
theory, which was a bewildering amalgam of diverse strains.[1] An
influential body of doctrine stemming from Aristotle defined tragedy
as an imitation (mimesis) of a serious, complete, and ample action
whose incidents arouse pity and fear in the audience and then purge
them (catharsis). Horace admonished that all art should delight and
instruct. Shakespeare and English tragedy provided one set of models,
Corneille and French tragedy quite another. Prestigious Italian and
French critics, especially Boileau and Rapin, emphasized the virtues of
restraint, decorum, and the unities (time, place, and action); English
critics ran the gamut. In self-defence, authors themselves turned critic,
penning essays and prefaces that sought to impose their own view of
tragedy, or – like Latitudinarian divines looking for the essence of
Christian belief – to find a lowest common denominator of competing
theories.

The Restoration's important tragedies appeared over a seven-year
span, 1677–84, with Dryden and Nathaniel Lee dominating the first

two seasons. In March of 1677 Lee took the step of moving beyond the rhymed quasi-tragedies of 1674–76 to blank-verse tragedy in *The Rival Queens; or, The Death of Alexander the Great*. In the Epilogue Lee cursed those who taught his 'censorious age' to criticize, and his instincts were sound. Though the play was popular with audiences – in the original or revised versions – for a century and a half, critics have charged it with bombastic extravagance, artificiality, and disorder. William Archer complained that the 'subsidiary episodes' of Alexander's and Clytus's deaths, and the love triangle of the subplot, have 'no essential connection' with the 'main theme' of the rival queens.[2] But the emphasis of the original title may have sprung from a rivalry between actresses; by the eighteenth century the titles had been reversed – *Alexander; or, The Rival Queens* – which clarifies the unity of the plots around the Emperor. The competition between his two queens for Alexander in the main plot is mirrored by the contest between two of his favourites for a princess, while the drunken murder of Clytus is the first warning of the addiction that makes poisoned wine the conspirators' choice of a murder weapon.

Archer's general indictment, however – 'remoteness from life and nature', 'utter vulgarity of feeling' – is harder to refute; most readers are repelled by Lee's intemperance. He was a veritable Icarus of language, as self-indulgent as his own Alexander; open one of his plays anywhere for a definition of 'rant'. When torture is mentioned, Lee inevitably has a character describe in detail the bones laid bare, the veins lanced, the flesh 'With pincers from his manly bosom ripped/Till ye discovered the great heart lie panting'. (I. 1)[3] A Lee hero does not just kill a lion with his bare hands: he tears out 'by th' roots/The foaming, bloody tongue' (IV. 2) and smashes the skull. Alexander, Roxana and Statira (his queens) are terrible ranters.

The Rival Queens is not reducible to the sum of its rants, however; its enduring theatrical success was based on Lee's mastery of stage effect. Consider the fast start: two rivals enter fighting, the old soldier parts them, and as he arbitrates we naturally learn the background of the quarrel. Any craftsman would admire exposition so neatly dove-tailed with action. Lee borrows unashamedly from Shakespeare and heroic drama such passages as Cassander's portents (I. 1), the spectacular aerial omens (II. 1) and the drunken banquet (IV. 2), but his own speciality is passion, and when the passion rises high enough, 'rant' becomes dramatically appropriate, as in the quarrel at the banquet or the death of Statira. An actor who cannot make Alexander's charge to her physicians ('Say she shall live, and I will make you kings', v. 1) or his lament over her body moving to an audience does not deserve the role.

> Tell the gods I'm coming
> To give 'em an account of life and death, . . .
> Oh, she is gone! the talking soul is mute!
> She's hushed – no voice, no music now is heard!
>
> (v. 1)

This mixture of self-importance and abject pathos from a man who has just killed his best veteran in their cups and is rapidly sobering up over the body of his second wife, slain by his first, while poison works in his veins, is masterly: Lee had learned something from Shakespeare. His shortcoming is that he does not work up to this, but sustains a shrill pitch of declamation from first to last. Lee's organ had only one stop, *fff*, which is fine for finales, but wearies the mortal ear in a long piece.

Dryden's *All for Love; or, The World Well Lost* (1677), often called the finest Restoration tragedy, retains traces of 1670s heroic drama.[4] As changeable as Almanzor, Antony is a softer hero, a more feeling (even lachrymose) man; love versus duty, or honour, or ambition, is no longer a contest, as the title tells us. Such changes continue the direction of *Aureng-Zebe*, and of Lee and Otway. Lee's Sophonisba (see p. 50) is Cleopatran, particularly when she dies with her lover in mutual admiration; his Hannibal, who 'for a Mistress gave the world away', has a touch of Antony; his Menander and Clytus both play Ventidius to their lovesick chiefs. The rivalry of Roxana and Statira may have encouraged Dryden to confront Cleopatra with Octavia. *All for Love* is firmly grounded in the theatre of its own decade.

That is not the context Dryden invites, however; his Preface admits to a respectful 'imitation' of Shakespeare's *Antony and Cleopatra*. The comparison has often been made, to Dryden's disadvantage: it is not difficult to show that Shakespeare's poetry is superior.[5] Whether *Antony and Cleopatra* is superior *theatre* is another matter; Dryden went to great lengths to make his play effective on-stage. The sweep and pageantry of Shakespeare's play – thirty-four characters, seven locales, eleven years, forty-two episodes – that flowed easily over the platform stage, were ill-adapted to a theatre that thought of 'episodes' as 'scenes', took scenery and costumes seriously, and was sensitive about the unities. Not surprisingly, *Antony and Cleopatra*, like *King Lear*, was moribund as a stage work.

Dryden's two-part solution is evident in the first few minutes of *All for Love*. Shakespeare's panorama is reduced to one locale (Alexandria), one stage 'day', one scene per act and ten characters. Actium is past, and so is more than half of *Antony and Cleopatra*. What Dryden thus loses in sweep he gains in concentration on the lovers' last hours. These changes undoubtedly have some connection with the 'rage for order' in seventeenth-century science, philosophy, and literary criticism, and with a desire to observe the unities, but they also had the effect of making the play actable on the Restoration stage.

The first scene, which has no Shakespearean counterpart, discloses Dryden's other tactic: to build up a strong sense of Egypt as a cultural entity, and then to show what it means to be an Egyptian or a Roman in that world. Serapion – superstitious, weak, verbally luxuriant, and conscious that '*Ægypt* is doomed to be/A *Roman* Province' if Antony loses – is Dryden's compleat Egyptian. (I. 1)[6] The first seventy lines contain more feeling for Nilotic destiny than does all of *Antony and Cleopatra*. Then Ventidius enters, emanating a strong and sharply contrasted sense of Rome. Egyptians concede his 'plainness, fierceness, rugged virtue' and bravery, and feel his disapproval of their holiday ('Fine pageantry!') and music: 'Let your *Ægyptian* Timbrels play alone,/Nor mix Effeminate Sounds with *Roman* trumpets.' (Shakespeare mixes these instruments indiscriminately.) Both Serapion and Ventidius are roles that Dryden developed.

The whole play moves between these cultural polarities. What was for Shakespeare a passing touch – e.g., 'A Roman thought hath struck him' (I. 2) – becomes for Dryden a schema, an organizing principle that subsumes the old love/honour dichotomy. Egyptian Cleopatra stands for love and Roman Ventidius for duty, but 'Egypt' and 'Rome' stand for much more: private/public, emotion/reason, hedonism/stoicism, disease/health, sycophancy/bluntness, etc. In this Augustan play, Roman values naturally seem superior – '*Rome* has conquer'd *Ægypt*' (v. 1), says the despairing Antony – but at the level of character and action the play is finally a marriage of Roman and Egyptian. Those who identify wholly with one side (Serapion, Ventidius, Octavia) are two-dimensional and secondary. The early Cleopatra, who loved with 'noble madness', soaring 'quite out of Reasons view' (II. 1), sounds wholly Egyptian, yet her final act of matronly duty and stoical self-sacrifice moves her into the cultural middle ground occupied throughout by Antony, whose half-heroic, half-domestic soul is torn between 'Rome' and 'Egypt'.

Dryden's careful categorizing owes something to his researches in Appian and Dio Cassius and contemporary travellers (where Shakespeare drew mostly on Plutarch), and to his period's increasingly acute sense of temporal and regional differences. Again, however, there is a solid histrionic rationale: the play moves to the sense-rhythms of 'Rome' and 'Egypt'. The second act, like the first, curves from Egyptian to Roman; then it swings back to a point where Antony feels his love and honour are reconcilable. Consequently the opening of Act III (the structural centre) is a moment of Roman–Egyptian equipoise.

From one side enter Antony and Romans with trumpets, fresh from victory; from the other, Cleopatra and dancing Egyptians with timbrels: sensory equivalents of 'Rome' and 'Egypt' that (with others) can be used throughout. Cleopatra then crowns Antony with laurel. She does so again at the only other such point of balance, the end, where Rome and Egypt wed and die united. The comparable passage in Shakespeare is the end of *Romeo and Juliet*, where the *Liebestod* becomes the means of reconciling Montague and Capulet.

Dryden's Preface to the first edition (1678) argues that what attracts writers to this story is 'the excellency of the Moral': the protagonists 'were famous patterns of unlawful love; and their end accordingly was unfortunate'. This makes nonsense of the subtitle and the magnificent scene in which the reconciled lovers die in each others' arms. 'Grieve not', urges Antony,

> My last disastrous times:
> Think we have had a clear and glorious day;
> And Heav'n did kindly to delay the storm
> Just till our close of evening. Ten years love,
> And not a moment lost, but all improv'd
> To th'utmost joys: What Ages have we liv'd!
> And now to die each others. . . .
>   (v. 1)

If there is a moral here against unlawful love, it is lost on Antony, and probably on most readers and spectators, for in the lovers' *éclaircissement* (after the misunderstandings of Act IV) and in this splendid affirmation of a life lived to the full, we achieve catharsis. Dryden also states that his lovers' crimes 'were not occasion'd by any necessity, or fatal ignorance, but were wholly voluntary; since our passions are, or ought to be, within our power'. The latter clause begs a vital question, undermining the former. And if the protagonists' 'crimes' *were* 'wholly voluntary', what becomes of 'tragic fate', and pity, or what replaces them? The whole passage reveals the tension that was developing between the tragic and rationalistic views of man, muddying tragic theory and starting to erode tragedy itself, but it is more a problem of the Preface than of the play. Trust the tale, not the teller.

Nathaniel Lee used hints from classical authors plus his own feverish imagination to produce the popular *Mithridates* (1678). He termed it his 'Fairest Child': an attempt to combine Shakespeare's strengths with Fletcher's, but refine them for his age.[7] It is difficult to imagine what notion of 'refinement' could include the extravagant horrors of this plot and the characters of Mithridates, who resembles Maximin in his passionate self-indulgence, and his son Pharnaces. Mithridates favours his other son Ziphares while he covets Pharnaces's beloved, then switches his favour when he sees Ziphares's love, Semandra. Though she rejects him, he marries her by force and rapes her. To this point Mithridates is Shadwell's libertine; subsequently, however, 'a Thorn, call'd Conscience' (IV. 1) and the spectacle of his dishevelled victim combine to destroy him. He repents, gains insight, and dies ranting, crushed by his own errors.

Semandra begins as the heroine of chivalric romance, lifting Mithridates (temporarily) above his lawless passion and inspiring Ziphares to fight the Romans. You are the 'bus'ness of the war' who 'draws every sword', he tells her (II. 1). Acts IV and V become almost a 'she-tragedy' (as the coming mode of Otway and Rowe would be called), which the Prologue implies Lee originally intended. He botches her ending, however: Semandra is not allowed to clear her name and commit suicide with her lover until Ziphares has accidently stabbed her in the dark. The incident is symptomatic of Lee's lack of finesse. *Mithridates* has the defects of *The Rival Queens* without most of its merits; the symmetrical situations, love versus duty dilemmas, rants and exaggerated personalities are a reversion to early heroic drama. So many of Lee's characters are excessive in word and deed that eventually you realize they *are* Lee. The rage of Pharnaces – 'every Nerve thin as a Spider's Thread,/ . . . I swell almost to bursting' (I. 1) – is the incipient madness of his Bedlam-bound creator.

Mithridates was the last considerable tragedy written before the Popish Plot; *Oedipus*, a joint venture of Dryden and Lee (November 1678), already bears the impress of that trauma. Sophocles's Creon becomes an ugly, evil agitator – a cross between Richard III and Shaftesbury – who stirs up the Theban mob to rebellion in Oedipus's absence. Oedipus suppresses two outbreaks in remarkably anti-populist terms, addressing his subjects as a 'wild herd', 'barbarians', 'vile souls', and 'brutes'. The Tory note returns in the anti-regicide moral:

> How sacred ought
> Kings lives be held, when but the death of one
> Demands an Empire's blood for Expiation?
>
> (V. 1)[8]

These speeches were Lee's, but Dryden claimed responsibility for the overall scenario, so the political theme was presumably his idea. The Epilogue even jokes about the 'burning of a Pope'.

One of the first English plays with a Greek source, *Oedipus* illustrates the vast gulf between Classical Athens and Restoration London. The Preface admits that English custom forced the authors to add a subplot. The extensive use of ghosts, the on-stage gore, the prodigies in the night sky, Tireisias's echo of the blinded Gloucester (I. 1) and Oedipus sleepwalking with dagger and candle betray a strong Elizabethan influence. The symmetry of the subplot – where Creon contends for his niece Eurydice (incest again) against Adrastus – and Adrastus's dilemmas of love versus honour revive the heroic idiom. Oedipus's recurrent fears of incest and parricide, and of his and Jocasta's mother–son feelings, are un-Sophoclean in their heaviness.

The fifth act works through madness and violence to exhausted resolution. Predictably, Lee's Oedipus plucks out his eyes and his Jocasta describes the disfigurement, goes insane, hangs her daughters, and stabs her sons and herself before dying on-stage; but Dryden probably designed the slaughter of the whole subplot triangle and Oedipus's suicide leap from a tower to the stage. A popular success, the play has some effective speeches. Oedipus sometimes strikes sparks, but Dryden's Creon has more hard-edged lines, especially in III. 1: his 'heroes are fools' speech, his attack on Adrastus, and his description of his conscience: 'my Slave, my Drudge, my supple Glove'.

Lee and Thomas Otway dominated tragedy for the next two seasons. Their plays, despite severe limitations, are interesting reflections of the troubled times and prefigure the new tragic style. Lee's increasingly violent anti-Catholic feelings began to hurt his career. After *The Massacre of Paris* (1679) was prohibited, Lee angrily wrote another bloody anti-Papist play, *Caesar Borgia* (1679–80), which was unsuccessful. Plots and mob politics link this and Lee's *Lucius Junius Brutus* (1680) with Otway's *Caius Marius* (1679–80). All three of them, and Lee's *Theodosius* (1680), use Shakespearean motifs; all four, and Otway's *The Orphan* (1680), had strong casts headed by Thomas Betterton, usually paired with Elizabeth Barry. Themes such as deception, violence, and the breakdown of communication keep resurfacing, and the pathetic note becomes stronger.

Otway's *Caius Marius*, an unlikely hybrid of *Romeo and Juliet*, *As You Like It*, and a Roman history play, bloomed in this heated atmosphere. Two political enemies, Caius Marius and Metullus, try to keep their son and daughter apart amid a welter of steals from Shakespeare: the balcony and *aubade* scenes, the Queen Mab speech, the garrulous old nurse. When the Marii are defeated and exiled to the country, though, 'Juliet' (Lavinia) turns Rosalind to follow her Orlando in disguise. Otway adds some original twists: two herdsmen discussing the civil strife do a lovely parody of tragic omens – the heifer knocked down a fence, the swallows' nest fell in the porridge – and in the tomb scene Lavinia awakes before her lover dies, taxes Caius Marius with his cruelty, and falls on his sword, leaving him a broken man. But overall it is a garbled dream of Coriolanus and Juliet, with a 1680 emphasis on mob scenes.

The stolen-marriage motif recurs in *The Orphan*, which, though deeply flawed, established pathetic tragedy. Twin brothers who admire each other both love the orphan Monimia (Mrs Barry). Castalio, a *précieux*, promises Polydore he will not wed her and even forwards Polydore's suit; then marries her secretly. Polydore, rejected by Monimia and convinced that she has yielded to his brother, contrives to supplant him on the wedding night. At last the secret comes out, destroying the guilt-ridden trio. The first of many to complain of Castalio's poorly motivated lack of candour was Polydore: 'Hadst thou, Castalio, used me like a friend/This ne'er had happened'. (v. 1)[9] *The Orphan* could have been a study in deceit and uncommunicativeness, but frequent absurdities of plot and character, incoherence, luxurious rhetoric, and downright prurience undermine its credibility. Even Betterton and Mrs Barry could not initially make it a success; that came later, when its drawn-out pathos had grown fashionable.

Lee's *Theodosius* also builds a plot around a *précieux* gesture and then criticizes it. Theodosius falls madly for Athenais and their marriage is arranged; but when he learns that his friend Varanes has also loved her, he insists that Athenais, despite her protests, hear Varanes's suit. The interview is so intense and unsettling that Athenais drinks a slow poison before the wedding, while Varanes runs on his sword and has his body carried to the ceremony, dampening the festivities. As Athenais collapses on the corpse, Theodosius complains:

> Thou mightest have made
> Thy choice without this cruel act of Death.
> I left thee to thy will, and in requital
> Thou hast murder'd all my fame. (v. 4)[10]

This seems reasonable, though she reminds him, 'I beg'd you would not let me see the Prince' (v. 4). None of the principals is quite rational, and again Lee contemns restraint, yet the play's popularity is understandable. The pagan–Christian clash is absorbing, the father–daughter scene in Act II and the Pulcheria–Marcian relationship are well handed, and the situations, though overdrawn, possess dramatic interest.

Lee warned that *Lucius Junius Brutus* required him to 'elevate his fancy with the mightiest imagination'.[11] The story is that of the republican revolution, led by Brutus, that overthrew the Tarquins after the rape of Lucrece; Brutus then spoke for executing two of his sons who had joined the royalists. Lee assures us that 'nothing ever presented itself to my fancy with that solid pleasure as Brutus did in sacrificing

his sons' (p. 4), but after a few performances the Lord Chamberlain
suppressed the play for its anti-monarchical tendencies.

With a plot, pathos, deception, sexual violation, anti-Catholicism,
and Shakespearean borrowings, *Brutus* recapitulates much of recent
tragedy, but is rife with aesthetic problems revolving around Brutus.
Is he admirable, or 'more tyrannical than any Tarquin' (v. 1), as
Tiberius says? Addison's *Cato* repels many readers by greeting his
son's battlefield death so stoically, but Lee's *Brutus* goes much further,
insisting – against all pleas – on scourging and executing Tiberius *and*
Titus, who was forced to side with the royalists by their threats against
his bride. Titus, torn between love for his Tarquin wife and love for
his republican father, seems the hero, or at least the centre of
sympathy; we too cannot choose between the absurdly bloody royalists
and the republicans led by Brutus, who gives a long Whiggish speech
on the glories of commerce while his sons' bodies are cooling. Whatever Lee's intentions, both parties are offensive, leaving our emotions
nowhere to settle except on Titus. Perhaps this difficulty reflects
Lee's own political vacillation between Whig and Tory during the
crisis.[12]

The most distinguished tragedy of the 'political eighties', Otway's
Venice Preserved; or, A Plot Discovered (1682), preserves the mood of
1680; civil strife, deceit, and severed communications rend private
lives. As political as Lee's *Brutus*, it was accepted by the authorities as
supporting 'the right side': the plot against the state is crushed, the
Epilogue speaks out for the King and the Duke of York, and the Whig
leader Shaftesbury is mocked. Behind this Tory façade, though, the
play is somewhat equivocal. The only senators we meet are a cruel
father and a doting, idiotic pervert; the senate itself breaks a solemn
oath to treat the betrayed conspirators honourably. Those conspirators
are a mixed lot, with flashes of nobility and heroism among the fractious anarchists, the soundness of whose case against the state is never
determined. A caricature of Shaftesbury appears on *each* side.[13] In any
case, the play's long-term success and the persistent idea that it placed
Otway 'next to Shakespeare' rest on solider grounds than topicality.

The first 300 lines are brilliant. Aggrieved and impoverished, Jaffeir
confronts his obdurate father-in-law Priuli with his and Belvidera's
sufferings, but Priuli has a grievance too: Jaffeir, trusted 'like an open
friend', eloped with Belvidera, an only child, 'like a thief . . . at dead
of night'. (I. 4)[14] Jaffeir responds 'to me you owe her' – he once saved
her from drowning – 'and I have ruined myself maintaining her as befits
a senator's daughter'. Unimpressed, Priuli directs him to 'retrench': 'to
some suburb cottage both retire;/Drudge, to feed loathsome life, get
brats, and starve'. His resentment, originally legitimate, has been
sustained for three years against the couple and their child. Thus

Brabantio, Othello, and Desdemona might have become, had the Moor stayed in Venice and declined.

But Jaffeir is only the husband-half of Othello. The soldier-half now appears: Pierre, a foreign mercenary who has done the state some service, but has become a cynic and political malcontent. His personal hatred of a lecherous old senator who stole his courtesan has combined with a sense of social injustice to produce a revolutionary; now he works to create the same reaction in Jaffeir, another senatorial victim. To achieve critical mass, he must make the public and private causes coincide, so Pierre informs him that his family and possessions have just been evicted, on Priuli's order. The light breaks with, 'Priuli – is – a senator!' We have a revenge tragedy.

With the entrance of Belvidera (Mrs Barry), however, everything changes. She enters distraught, emanating the new desideratum in tragic emotion, domestic pathos, for which Otway and the play were prized until sentimental indulgences palled. Her mood is infectious: Jaffeir cannot be sensible with or about her. As a couple they pendulate between emotional extremes. Part of the problem may have been auto-biographical: Otway's Jaffeir-like poverty and hopeless love for Mrs Barry. Nevertheless the couple are responsible for most of the play's nonsense. Why should Jaffeir lodge his beloved wife in the courtesan's house where the conspirators meet? Deliver her to them at midnight – along with a dagger to kill *her* if *he* breaks faith – without a word of explanation to her? Expect her to approve his participation in the plot, which includes the murder of her father? Rational communication between them seems impossible.

The Jaffeir–Belvidera–Pierre triangle is central to the play's structure and movement. Belvidera represents love, pity, soft emotions, private cares; Pierre is honour, friendship, duty, a public role. When Jaffeir delivers Belvidera as a pledge to the conspirators, he pawns love for honour. When the conspirator Renault propositions her, love and honour divide. Betraying the conspiracy for Belvidera's sake, Jaffeir gives up honour for love, but then he forsakes his love to give Pierre and himself honourable deaths. Belvidera is imaged as angelic, Pierre as satanic, but the play's morality is more subtle than that.[15] Belvidera at the last is anything but beatific, and Jaffeir's decision to die with Pierre is less a choice of hell than a reconciliation with what had been estranged of himself.

The dagger with which Jaffeir 'pledges' Belvidera comes to symbolize his honour. It turns up in Renault's hands as 'proof' of Jaffeir's scant regard for his wife, and is returned contemptuously to Jaffeir after the betrayal. Jaffeir threatens Belvidera and stabs Pierre with it, then sends it to Belvidera as a 'token' of his last blessing. 'Objective correlative' and theatrical prop, the dagger helps pull the major actions of the play together, reminding us that Jaffeir, having given love for honour, then honour for love, finally had to give all for honour.

Venice Preserved is not a traditional tragedy. Who is the hero? Jaffeir is too weak and foolish and, after the betrayal, abject, 'whining' and 'crawling' to Pierre, offering to kill his wife and child 't'appease thee' (v. 3). Pierre is strong and consistent, rising as Jaffeir declines, yet lacks inner struggle, being spared the main moral conflict. Belvidera has a divided soul, but does not convince us that she understands the implications for Jaffeir of what she persuades him to do. Of the traditional tragic emotions, pity abounds – the text begs for it – while fear has become detached from the principals. The last word, by a reformed Priuli, is not 'remember fallen greatness', but 'bid all cruel fathers dread my fate': apprehension connects us (didactically) with the suffering of the pathetic survivor. Though *All for Love* also has more pity than fear, Otway, with lower characters and softer emotions, has moved further than Dryden from classical tragedy, towards the genre's future.

The years preceding Monmouth's Rebellion were difficult ones for drama. Political distractions hurt theatrical attendance; the two companies merged into one (1682), constricting the market for new plays. A number of tragedies were suppressed: Dryden and Lee's *The Duke of Guise* (1682), and John Banks's *Cyrus the Great* (c. 1681), *The Innocent Usurper* (c. 1683), and *The Island Queens* (1684). Contemporary politics did provide material for Thomas Southerne's first tragedy, *The Loyal Brothers* (1682) and Nathaniel Lee's last, *Constantine the Great* (1683), but that risky arena rarely produced good work. Tragic dramatists fell away: Dryden was preoccupied with polemics, Otway turned to dark comedy, Lee was admitted to Bedlam.

The career of Banks, whose historical importance is well established, brightens this gloomy picture somewhat. Beginning as a writer of forgettable heroic plays and exotic tragedies, he found himself in a series of blank-verse tragedies on Elizabethan subjects featuring strong women: *The Unhappy Favourite* (1681; Elizabeth and Essex), *Virtue Betrayed* (1682; Anne Boleyn), *The Innocent Usurper* (Lady Jane Grey), and *The Island Queens* (Elizabeth and Mary, Queen of Scots). The first two were popular, but collectively they were smeared as 'she-tragedies', despite Otway's recent precedents and Lee's announcement in 1680 that henceforth 'women shall rule' the theatre.[16] (In fact, women did make notable gains – as actresses, dramatists, subjects of drama, and arbiters of taste – in the next few decades.) Banks's influence on Southerne and Rowe was only less than that of Shakespeare, and he brought tragedy closer to home and nature than any playwright since the Bard.

But Banks has been labelled a 'bad poet' since Steele – a questionable judge – remarked that there is not a good line of poetry in *The Unhappy Favourite*.[17] This is unfair, *Unhappy Favourite* being his weakest play. The Countess of Nottingham is bombastic ('You torture me with this excess', says Burleigh), the idea that Elizabeth accepts *her* evidence against Essex strains belief, and the pathos of Essex's last interview with his wife is overextended. Yet even here the charge is inaccurate. Banks is a dramatic poet, all right – his verse is competent and flexible, the occasional metaphors surprise and please – and though he is constantly wrought up to the highest pitch, his images are less strained and violent than Lee's.

It is by his later plays, and there not by his verse alone, that Banks should be judged; focus on the confrontations of a few strong characters is his forte. In *Virtue Betrayed*, Cardinal Wolsey's interview with Lady Blunt and Anne's with Diana, Wolsey's playing Iago to Henry VIII's Othello, and Henry's stormy accusation of Anne show what Banks could do. The thought is not profound, but feeling is intense, language meaty, and personality vivid. Often a passionate character is pitted against a cooler one. When Wolsey suggests that Anne has been unfaithful, Henry storms, 'there's thunder in that word;/The bolt ran thro', and shiver'd me to pieces' (II. 1) before he realizes the potential usefulness of the news. But, he warns his tempter, 'All hell shall be too little for thy carcase;/New hells shall be created' unless the accusation is proved: 'Speak how thou know'st it – Quick.' Wolsey explains that it is just a rumour, a report.

> Reported, saidst thou? Is not that enough?
> Report! Why, she's damned, if she's but thought
> A whore,

rages Henry. This is shrewd, and characteristic. It may seem derivative, but the best Restoration tragedy was written under the shadow and tutelage of Shakespeare.

With *The Island Queens* we have the complication of a revised text (*The Albion Queens*, 1704), but in either version the shifting fortunes of Norfolk and Morton as they battle for Elizabeth's mind (Act I), and Mary's encounter with her mirror and Norfolk (Act II) are well worth reading or acting. Sitting on the floor among her maids, unable to believe she looks so good after the years of captivity, Mary asks, 'Who is behind me? who lookt in the glass?' When Norfolk enters and avows his love, though, she disclaims any beauty. Elizabeth's reflections on the agonies of rule – 'where's the Quiet? where's the Freedom here?' (V. 1) – with parallel speeches in *The Unhappy Favourite* and *Vertue Betrayed* rang true for the 1680s. By 1704, though, Elizabeth's moving lament for Mary's blood ('*England*'s stain'd, its Maiden Monarch stain'd') had to be cut: with Anne regnant, it sounded tactless.

The banning of this play in 1684 – the third of his tragedies to be suppressed in four years – caused Banks to join the defectors from the genre. He would resurface after the Revolution, along with Dryden and Southerne, but with *The Island Queens* tragedy was effectively 'Closed for the Duration'.

Notes

1. In Chapter 1 of *Restoration Tragedy* (Madison, Wisconsin, 1967), Eric Rothstein argues that stable doctrines did emerge.

2. *The Old Drama and the New* (London, 1923), p. 153.

3. Quotations in the text follow *The Rival Queens*, edited by P. F. Vernon (Lincoln, Nebraska, 1970).

4. Eugene Waith, *The Herculean Hero* (London and New York, 1962), and Arthur Kirsch, *Dryden's Heroic Drama* (Princeton, 1965), dispute the size of these traces; I tend to follow Kirsch. On the next two sentences, see Kirsch, pp. 133–40; and Robert D. Hume, *The Development of English Drama in the Late Seventeenth Century* (Oxford, 1976), with whose conclusion I disagree.

5. See F. R. Leavis, '*Antony and Cleopatra* and *All for Love*: a critical exercise', *Scrutiny*, 5, no. 2 (1936), 158–69 (p. 165).

6. Quotations from Dryden's plays follow *The Works of John Dryden*, edited by E. N. Hooker and H. T. Swedenborg, 19 vols (Berkeley, Los Angeles, and London, 1956–). *All for Love* appears in Volume XIII (1984, edited by Maximillian Novak). See also my 'Rome Has Conquered Egypt', *Transactions of the Samuel Johnson Society of the Northwest*, 13 (1982), 1–9.

7. From Lee's Dedication. See *The Works of Nathaniel Lee*, edited by Thomas B. Stroup and Arthur L. Cooke, 2 vols (New Brunswick, New Jersey, 1954–55), I, 291–92. Further citations appear in the text. On the parallels between lust and power in superheroes, see Margaret Ann Doody, *Natural Passion* (Oxford, 1974), pp. 108–9.

8. *Works of Dryden*, XIII. On the authors' division of labour, see Dryden's 'Vindication of *The Duke of Guise*' (1683).

9. Quotations follow *The Orphan*, edited by Aline M. Taylor (Lincoln, Nebraska, 1976). For interpretation see her Introduction, pp. xviii and xxiv–xxx; Clifford Leech, 'Restoration Tragedy: a Reconsideration', *Durham U. Jour.*, 11 (1950), 106–15 (pp. 112–13); and Arthur H. Scouten, 'Tragedy', in *The Revels History of Drama in English*, edited by T. W. Craik and C. Leech, 8 vols (London, 1975–83), V (1976), 273.

10. In *Works of Lee*, II.

11. See *Lucius Junius Brutus*, edited by John Loftis (Lincoln, Nebraska, 1967), p. 3. Citations in the text refer to this edition.

12. On this point see *Lucius Junius Brutus*, p. xviii; and Robert D. Hume, *The Rakish Stage* (Carbondale, Illinois, 1983), pp. 136–37. On the character of Titus, see *Lucius Junius Brutus*, pp. xxi–xxiii.

13. John Loftis, 'Political and Social Thought in the Drama', in *The London Theatre World 1660–1800*, edited by R. D. Hume (Carbondale, Illinois, 1980), pp. 261–63. Antonio's extraneous subplot was often omitted in the eighteenth century. Otway's contemporaries coined the phrase 'next to Shakespeare', used by Aline M. Taylor for the title of her book (Durham, North Carolina, 1950).

14. I. 1. Quotations follow Malcolm Kelsall's edition (Lincoln, Nebraska, 1969); further references appear in the text.

15. See D. R. Hauser, 'Otway Preserved: Theme and Form in *Venice Preserved*', *SP*, 55 (1958), 481–93 (pp. 486–89, 493).

16. In the Prologue to *Lucius Junius Brutus*.

17. Cited by Scouten (p. 276), who concurs.

Chapter 5
Mask and Veil: Comedy

When the house began to fill she put on her vizard, and so
kept it on all the play; which of late is become a great
fashion among the ladies, which hides their whole face. So
to the Exchange to buy things for my wife, among other
things a vizard for herself.

Samuel Pepys, 12 June 1663

Why does anyone don a mask? To achieve anonymity and thereby gain
freedom of action, for one thing. With her vizard, Mrs Pepys could
visit the naughty playhouse without sullying her reputation. The
'dominoes' and 'shepherdesses' of Stuart and Georgian masquerades
could carry on intrigues incognito, as Tom Jones discovered. Lady
Mary Wortley Montagu, visiting Istanbul in 1717, concluded that
Europeans misjudged the Muslim veil: far from being a symbol of
servitude, it gave Turkish women an enviable freedom to behave as
they pleased, to masquerade the year round. In England, playhouse
prostitutes soon adopted the vizard, achieving at a stroke social
equality with Mrs Pepys and an elegant badge of office. But, since any
'mask' was then apt to be propositioned, respectable women had
henceforth to attend bare-faced: the vizard had acquired its own
identity.

   Passing from life to art, the mask became a central symbol of
Restoration theatre. The atmosphere of Carolean comedy resembled
that of the pre-Lenten carnival in Europe: a time of masks, sexual
pursuits, kidnapping and release.[1] Masking takes many forms, either
cloaking a harsh reality in an acceptable appearance, or protecting a
truth from inconvenient or premature disclosure. Sometimes it is a
disguise indicating a need for anonymity, sometimes a deceit indicating
hypocrisy – 'women are least masked when they have the velvet vizard
on', says Wycherley's Mrs Fidget – sometimes the façade of urbane
manners and wit behind which the clever individual manipulates
society for personal ends. Or the mask may be the 'moral tag', the
solemn closing couplets that give the completed action a didactic
veneer – beneath which lurks the unregenerate satyr of the real play.

The earliest Restoration comedies were satires lashing the 'Roundheads'. John Tatham's *The Rump* (1660), a kind of 'instant journalism',
has more than timeliness to recommend it: the committee meeting of
venal Puritan pretenders to power (Act III) and the night of disorder

in which soldiers desert and apprentices run wild (Act IV) make exciting theatre. Lively but bitter, the play exists to spew venom on the Cromwellians, who are seen as grave threats to social order – 'We are in a chaos, a confusion', says one character (I. 1) – while their moment lasts. At the end, crushed and scattered, they survive as street vendors. Abraham Cowley's *Cutter of Coleman Street* (1661), a revision of *The Guardian* (1642), is more even-handed; both sides accept the dictum of Tatham's Lockwhite: 'he that will live in this world' must employ 'dissimulation, equivocation and mental reservation'(I. 1). A Royalist poses as a Roundhead, Cutter (who is neither) poses as both, two brides conceal their identities behind veils, four spies jockey for position, and two sets of disguises impersonate the same identity. But Cowley equivocated too well: the play was blamed for satirizing the King's cause.[2]

Robert Howard's *The Committee* (1662) also shows Royalists surviving by their wits in Commonwealth England. A Puritan couple specialize in parasitizing orphaned heiresses from sequestered Cavalier estates, but one of these girls steals their keys, deeds, and some incriminating letters, and bribes them into accepting two good Royalist marriages – a tenuous formal link to comedy. Despite rough dialogue and a crude plot, its patriotism, the comical outfoxing of the Puritans, and the shenanigans of the Irish servant Teague kept it on-stage until the nineteenth century. The deceits and disguises of these three plays convey the social tensions that led one critic to call Restoration comedy 'part of the literature of the Civil War'.[3]

The great success of 1663, a romantic intrigue of Spanish inspiration, was also rooted in royalism. Charles II suggested to Sir Samuel Tuke that he adapt *Los Empeños de Seis Horas* (authorship uncertain), which he did, reductively, as *The Adventures of Five Hours*. It is instructive to see what so pleased the royal palate, made *Othello* seem to Pepys 'a mean thing' by comparison, and launched 'Spanish intrigues' (the period's first new genre) down their popular ways.[4] The salient feature of *Adventures* – and of the type – is a situation of daunting complexity. Don Henrique is a jealous guardian of his sister Porcia, while Don Carlos treats *his* sister, Camilla, more casually. Henrique pines for Camilla, who has refused him; she loves Don Antonio, who, however, is meant for Porcia, who loves Don Octavio, who killed a friend of Henrique, who thinks Octavio is his rival for Camilla. So much for Act I. The whole interest being situational, Tuke is not anxious to untie these knots quickly, so Acts II to IV deepen the confusion and complicate the errors, resolved in Act V by bringing everyone together. As text *Adventures* is pure froth, all mistaken identities, with hardly a memorable character or line, nor an idea except a comic version of love and honour; but the brisk farcing was irresistible, while the bristling caballero pride, couched in heroic couplets, lent a touch of class. It is noteworthy that a Restoration comedy could be clean *and* successful in 1663: the women are virtuous, the men decent, in word and deed. Henceforth, 'intrigue' was a powerful and sustained influence on comedies of all kinds.

Tuke's hit outshone everything else in the first significant season of Restoration playwriting: Richard Rhodes's *Flora's Vagaries*, a more readable intrigue comedy and Nell Gwyn's first triumph; John Wilson's *The Cheats*, another attack on Puritans, treated as 'humourists'; Dryden's unsuccessful first play *The Wild Gallant* (not extant in this version); and *The English Monsieur* by James Howard. An anticipation of Etherege and the wit-duelling 'gay couple', Howard's play has other handles as well.[5] In Frenchlove, the title-character, we see the satiric focus shifting from the Puritans to the French; given a prepared entrance, he bows and struts while others describe him, draw him out – as Etherege's wits do his fops – and savage his foibles after he leaves. In the top plot, Wellbred courts Lady Wealthy, who uses witty tests to distance him until she hears him tell his friend Comely he loves her. Comely adores a country girl, Elsbeth, engaged to William, a 'Wiltshire clown'. Their verbal contest for Elsbeth is the play's comic centre. 'I could eat thy lips', drools William. 'I could lick thee all over. . . . I could tear thy Cloaths off thy back, Smock and all, my heart does leap and caper when I do see this leg and thy Coats tuck't up . . .' (v. 1). Comely counters with the standard *précieux* neoplatonic imagery, shrewdly criticized by William – 'there's no tongue in the Eyes . . . the man's a Papist' – and rejected by Elsbeth. The pro-country slant did not prevail in Restoration comedy, but racy language, satire on Gallic affectations, multiple interwoven plots, and wit-duels all became characteristic.

Short speeches, graceless prose, and undeveloped characters make *The English Monsieur*, which contains the seed of the comedy of manners, only a *farce* of manners. Despite many English precedents, farce was generally regarded as a French import. The word was applied to comedy that was broad, low, or extravagant; it still connotes 'crude' and 'improbable'.

The man who would bring 'genteel comedy' (as comedy of manners was then called) to its first peak, George Etherege, made a successful debut in 1664. With four plots on three distinct levels worked into each act, *The Comical Revenge; or, Love in a Tub* has variety and energy, though Etherege's control is questionable.[6] There is even a love-and-honour plot written in heroic couplets. Like most Restoration comedies this is set in London, but during the late Commonwealth, when issues of great moment teetered in the balance. A gallant Cavalier colonel and a noble lord compete for Graciana, whose father promised her to the colonel, for whom her sister yearns. Eventually, after a duel, a wound, and a convalescent courtship, the girls obtain their true loves and the men are reconciled.

This is not the main plot, only the highest. It is contrasted chiefly with a 'gulling' story in which two confidence men swindle a 'half-witted fellow' knighted by Cromwell. First they make him buy his way out of a duel of 'honour' – just before the aristocrats, also actuated by 'honour', confront and challenge (III. 5–6).[7] Then they try to match him with a wench named Grace, tendentiously juxtaposed with Graciana (I. 2). Deadpanned within his high plot, Etherege winks at it obliquely. Lowest of all is the title-plot about a French servant named Dufoy with venereal disease, which was treated in a sweat bath. Early prints show him walking about in his tub while English servants mock him.

In the main plot – widely praised for originality and realism – Sir Frederic Frollick courts Widow Rich. Frollick is certainly crucial, serving as a sensible second in the aristocrats' duel, breaking up the swindle, distributing justice and marrying Graciana's aunt. Whether he represents a 'realistic but golden mean' is more debatable: there are dark shades to his character that Etherege does not resolve.[8] His 'frolics' are drunken riots. We meet him the morning after a debauch, suavely excusing his drunkenness on the grounds that he always repents; but Jenny sees it differently: 'You have made such an uproar . . . we must be forced to change our lodgings . . . you and your rude ranting companions hooped and hollowed like madmen. . . . These were not all your heroic actions; . . . you marched bravely at the rear of an army of linkboys; . . . committed a general massacre on the glass-windows; are not these most honourable achievements . . .'? (I. 2). Frollick, Restoration comedy's first significant rake, is an *anti*-heroic roisterer: a few years later his conduct would qualify him as the boor, not the lead. Once, the widow invites him to look at a drunken intruder and see himself: 'he has challenged you at your own weapons . . . shake off these lousy companions' (V. 2). Frollick does *not* reform; he wins a wit-contest and is given the lady and the last word. But it is difficult to buy him at Etherege's valuation: as comic material he needs refining. Frollick is wittier than the low-plot trio and more sensible than the heroic lovers, for what that is worth, yet his only competition in the reasonable middle, Widow Rich, is more humane. This was not the last time that Etherege would excuse a protagonist more easily than posterity has, which is why Dobree called this 'Free [i.e. amoral] Comedy'.

What is conspicuously missing from this ambitious and diverse play is manners comedy; not a single scene works that vein. Frollick is a wit, he and the widow are a gay couple, but he is too crude and their relationship too primitive and too minor an interest for the comedy of manners. This is not really a limitation: the play's vitality will just not confine itself to the manners key, modulating all around it. *The Comical Revenge* gave a new lead to social comedy, and its success produced a number of imitations, though not of comparable quality.

Of the other early Restoration comedies worth mentioning, John Lacy's *The Old Troop* (1664?) is a lively romp through the wartime countryside and refreshingly frank about the Royalists' failings, though plot and characters operate at farcical levels. Dryden's *The Rival Ladies* (1664) attempts to combine heroics with apparent mock-heroics.[9] The result is a predictably schizoid and frequently silly play that would have received less attention had its author been less famous. Dryden's 1667 revision of *The Wild Gallant* fell short of all expectations. The 1669 text is defensive: the first Epilogue calls it 'a wretched play', and the second a 'motley garniture of Fool and Farce'. Trice, Loveby, Bibber, and Isabelle are all amusing characters, but the plot *is* as improbable as a farce. Dryden and Newcastle's *Sir Martin Mar-All* (1667), one of the era's most successful plays, is unabashedly farcical, especially in the incredible stupidity of the title character, who makes Sir Andrew Aguecheek look like Agent 007. Yet his witlessness has nearly mock-epic magnitude, like the apotheosis of Dulness in *The Dunciad*, and the play could be entertaining on-stage with a good Sir Martin.

In *Secret Love* (1667), an unusual and diverting 'tragicomedy', Dryden moved closer to the manners mode. Celadon and Florimell descend from Benedick and Beatrice, and their bantering bargains ('*Item*, I will have the liberty to sleep all night') foreshadow Mirabell and Millamant. Like *The Comical Revenge*, however, the play is encumbered by sections in heroic couplets that belong elsewhere. Also in 1667, Lacy adapted *Taming of the Shrew* to Restoration London as *Sauny the Scot*. Kate's 'rebellion' upon reaching 'town' is an original touch, but Lacy – having no idea how to proceed once he had left Shakespeare – quickly dropped the idea. Collectively these plays, besides setting off Etherege's achievement, indicate that playwrights were still searching for the 'right' comic style.

There was no agreed-upon 'theory of comedy' as there was a theory of heroic drama. Many playwrights had instead an admiration for, say, Fletcherian tragicomedy or Jonsonian humours, and a general desire to continue their style. Everyone knew that comedies ended happily (i.e. maritally), including anyone not downright evil or Puritan in a final embrace. No one talked about rites of spring. Romantic love existed, even in the city, but its language was *précieux* or witty or blunt, not lyrical. Shakespearean romance had almost no followers: recent arrivals such as the Spanish intrigue seemed more interesting.

Restoration comedy hit its stride in 1668. Etherege's second play, *She Wou'd If She Cou'd*, is widely accepted as the first true comedy of manners, though it missed the popularity of *The Comical Revenge*. It departed from the prevailing norms, which were more heterogeneous and/or boisterous, by restricting itself to one plot and a smallish cast of upper-middle-class characters: in effect a *selection* of certain scenes and modes in recent comedies.[10]

Our attention centres on 'two country knights', one's wife, the other's two young kinswomen, and two young 'gentlemen of the town'. The manners of the gentry are occasionally described: by Mrs Gazette in a conversation that amusingly parodies *précieux* jargon (III. 1), and by Lady Cockwood, listing 'blameless recreations' she has denied herself (III. 3). We learn that male gossip about women's reputations was a sensitive issue, and are regaled with witty repartee between young lovers. We may not think much of the society, yet it is coherent and vividly realized, partly through its distinctive language. The talk, mostly of sex, love, and marriage, is highly metaphorical. Courtship is like hunting, fishing, horse-racing, falconry, gambling, piracy, and war; sex is like commerce. Says Ariana sarcastically: 'Every one in their way; a huntsman talks of his dogs, a falconer of his hawks, a jockey of his horse, and a gallant of his mistress' (IV. 2).[11] The pattern is obviously animalistic, but the airiness of the imagery suits the high spirits of the courting couples.

Most of Etherege's characters are more interesting and diverting than attractive. Sir Oliver Cockwood, a philanderer, and Sir Joslin Jolly seem boorish alongside the urban men, whose freedom they envy and heavily emulate. The sophisticated young rakes are idle rather than vicious: fodder for Marxists, not moralists. Courtall, a coolly skilful plotter, contrives to get his woman despite Lady Cockwood's machinations, even winning her gratitude by preserving her reputation, though personally he retreats from what he perceives as an 'old haggard' (Freeman thinks otherwise). Her exact value remains uncertain: Etherege characteristically withholds final condemnation, yet she is called 'Madam Machiavel' by Freeman, and plays Iago in lying to her husband about Courtall's advances. 'Cockwood' denotes libidinousness ('she would is she could') and suggests Lady Wishfort as a descendant. In Lady Cockwood – and in the sharper, Rakehell – is a subtler sense of evil (as frustration) than in Restoration serious drama; if she cannot have beaux, neither shall the girls.

Ariana and Gatty, 'Sly-girl and Mad-cap', are the most enjoyable characters, for their wit and mettle and yearning after a season of privilege within the bounds of virtue. Precocious and well informed of the hazards of the route, they will kick up their heels before accepting the yoke of marital subordination. 'Slife', exclaims Freeman, alarmed by the prey he and Courtall have cornered in Mulberry Garden, 'their tongues are as nimble as their heels' (II. 1).

The girls' quest for liberty requires their masks, which allow them to encounter young gentlemen in the park without loss of reputation. Later, however, they (and Lady Cockwood) mask as the whores Sir Oliver and Sir Joslin are expecting, to balk an immoral project and to protect themselves. The play is full of such concealments and deceptions: Courtall's feigned interest in Lady Cockwood, their rival stratagems, the 'screen scene' where both rakes hide from Sir Oliver (V. 1), and the well established hypocrisies of the Cockwood marriage.

> Sir Oliver: . . . farewell, my virtuous dear. [Exit.]
> Lady C: Farewell my dearest dear. I know he has not
> courage enough to question Courtall.
>
> (IV. 1)

The play's own mask is its saturnalian close, sardonic in the Cockwoods' case. 'Give me thy hand, my virtuous, my dear', says Sir Oliver. 'Henceforwards may our mutual loves increase' (V. 1). But Courtall has just suggested that she employ an 'able chaplain' in her rural retirement. This and the other anti-matrimonial jibes furnish a dark context for the young couples; only Wycherley would carry the hint further.

All these pretences relate to tensions felt by 'divided man' between 'artificial and real values' or 'social requirements and "natural" desires'.[12] (This, let it be noted, is the period for which T. S. Eliot posited a 'dissociation of sensibilities' severing thought from feeling.) And Sir Oliver, determined to achieve 'Christian liberty' even if it makes him a 'wild man', is a fair (though not flattering) representative of the Restoration emerging from the enforced rustication of the Commonwealth years.

Thomas Shadwell hailed She Wou'd as the best comedy written since the Restoration.[13] His own promising debut, The Sullen Lovers (1668), though less substantial, was entertaining enough to succeed. The Preface quarrels with Dryden, eulogizes Ben Jonson, and minimizes Shadwell's debt to Molière's Les Fâcheux; the spirit of Le Misanthrope, however, is strong. The sullen Stanford finds that the whole world grates on his nerves, while his friend Lovel skims easily over the surface of things. 'Where's the trouble?' he asks. 'You are too Satyricall' (I. 1). To these humours come three more: a conceited poet, a familiar coxcomb, and the foolish knight Sir Positive-at-All. A popular caricature of Robert Howard, Sir Positive must know everything. His new courant (which he sings) must be admired. Stanford mentioning Flanders, 'Flanders!' snorts the knight. 'If any man gives you that

account of *Flanders* that I do, I'le suffer Death.' Stanford alludes to
mankind. 'Mankind! Dost thou know what thou say'st now? Do'st
thou talk of Mankind? . . . I will give Dogs leave to piss upon me,
if any Man understands Mankind better than my self. . . . I have
consider'd all Mankind, I have thought of nothing else but Mankind
this Moneth . . . let me tell you, we are all Mortal', etc. (I. 1).

The plotless first act simply exhibits these humours. In Act II Emilia
and Carolina, who correspond to Stanford and Lovel, initiate a love-
interest, but the focus remains on humours. Criticized for showing
'the same thing over and over', Shadwell replied that he had presented
'variety of Humours' (Preface). One can see both sides. There are too
many humours – Huffe, Roger, Father, Country Gentleman, Scribble,
and Dash besides the above – and each goes on too long; being static,
they *could* perform at any length. On the other hand, Shadwell does
give different examples of the same humour, some of which are
amusing (pimps being mentioned, Sir Positive must affirm that he
knows more of pimping than any man). But Shadwell's indiscriminate
enthusiasm for his humours disserves the interesting love plot and
limits the play to a stage vehicle for character actors.

The other comedies of 1668 do not challenge Etherege. Sir Charles
Sedley's eagerly awaited *The Mulberry Garden* was a disappointment
though not a failure. Like *The Comical Revenge*, it mixed heroical
romance with realistic scenes, but as the former are set in the 1650s,
the latter in the 1660s, it suffers from disjunction as well as the clash
of modes.[14] More damaging are the sometimes farcical conduct of the
low scenes and the occasionally nonsensical ideas of the high. Wildish
is the most interesting character; despite his rakish name and wild talk,
he is new to the salon warfare and quickly falls for Olivia. Their evenly
matched wit-duels are among the earliest, and the scene where, as skit-
tish as mating horses, they make provisos and agree to marry is good
theatre, but Sedley dilutes their strength. Dryden's *An Evening's Love*
is, he conceded, a farce (Preface), and a dreary, hustle-bustle Spanish
intrigue farce at that. Written to please, it pleased in the theatre, but
only the Preface retains interest in print, and it admits that the author
did not believe in what he was doing.

Robert Howard's recently discovered *The Country Gentleman* is
extraordinary, if the 1690s manuscript represents the play as acted in
1669.[15] The implied values are Georgian. Sir Richard Plainbred and his
clever daughters prefer the country and rural suitors to anything the
city can offer; he is an amiable, almost exemplary father; and Trim's
daughters would prefer 'honest Tradesmen' to the knights they get.
The play was banned because of a scene contributed by Buckingham
satirizing Sir William Coventry as Sir Cautious Trouble-All. Ironically,
in his 'oyster table adapted for business', which is supposed to be

absurd, Trouble-All has invented the plot board of the modern war room, which displays friends' and enemies' positions and will 'tell you how the whole world is dispos'd' (III. 1). Despite an almost Shadwellian preference for humorous talk over action, Howard reveals himself in the remarkable symmetry of some scenes and actions, which are as artificial as his heroic dramas.

In 1670 Etherege's style was still not dominant. Shadwell's *The Humorists* of course genuflects to Jonsonian humours, though the Preface also lauds *She Wou'd*. The title is a fair description of its texture: the action *seems* more intense and complex than in *The Sullen Lovers*, but it is all a humourous froth. Actually the early scenes, when the humourists are flourishing, are the most pleasing; when Shadwell turns to farce, intrigue, and confusion in the dark, his play thins and palls. None of the eccentrics is as memorably zany as Sir Positive, though several are amusing, and Crazy, full of pox, love, and debt, seems centuries ahead of his time as he moans, 'I have spilt my bottle of Diet-drink in my Pocket, and spoil'd all my Almonds and Raisins'. (v. 1)[16]

In his Preface, Shadwell champions Jonson, Horace, and the moral utilitarian view of comedy against farce and frippery and, one suspects, Dryden. The Epilogue offers a definition of humours worth comparing with Jonson's (see Introduction, p. 11):

> A Humor is the Byas of the Mind,
> By which with violence 'tis one way inclin'd:
> It makes our Actions lean on one side still,
> And in all Changes that way bends the Will.

This biological determinism jars with the talk of correcting vice and folly through satire, itself a strange attachment to the play's rough picture of manners and vapid stage business.

In outline, Thomas Betterton's *The Amorous Widow* (1670?), adapted from Molière's *George Dandin*, may seem Etheregean: Lady Laycock is a superannuated belle; she would if she could with Cuningham and/or Lovemore, who make sham addresses to her. But the spirit is neither Etheregean nor Molièresque. Betterton conducts the action as a rough sex farce, and introduces class tensions (between Sir Peter Pride and Barnaby Brittle) that are unusual before 1690. The plot to have a servant court Lady Laycock as the 'Viscount Sans Terre' (which Betterton garbles badly) sounds like the 'Sir Roland' scheme in *The Way of the World*, and – if the 1710 text represents the 1670 play – some impact on Congreve is likely, given *The Amorous Widow*'s popularity.[17] At this point Etherege's isolation appeared total.

Dryden's first comedy in three years provided reinforcements of a sort. Having been occupied with heroic drama, he retained that interest in *Marriage à la Mode*, but added realistic scenes of manners comedy. In 1671 this combination seemed rather old-fashioned, plays with its structure having flourished from 1664 to 1667. Though it was designated 'tragicomedy' in the Fletcherian sense (see Introduction, p. 14) Dryden had been employing for years, it is usually called a comedy now, following Dryden's own judgement, 'perhaps . . . the best of my comedies' (Preface).

The high plot is a far-fetched heroical romance (reminiscent of *Philaster*) about a Sicilian usurper, Polydamas, who has lost track of both his family and his enemies. One day an old peasant turns up with two beautiful youths, Leonidas and Palmyra, clearly in love with each other. First he says Leonidas is Polydamas's son and Palmyra his own daughter; later he reverses the lineages. But Leonidas turns out to be the son of the deposed King, hence Polydamas's (and Palmyra's) enemy. After a love–duty struggle, Leonidas gains the throne *and* Palmyra, whose father he treats leniently. Some long sections, especially those in heroic couplets, make tedious reading, though Leonidas's soliloquy. 'Tis true, I am alone;/So was the Godhead ere he made the world', captures attention, while the lovers' evocation of their youthful passion is a charming pastoral idyll. (III. 1)[18] The romance's main function, however, is to provide a foil, artificial and idealistic about love, to the manners comedy.

The 'lower' main plot concerns a young married couple and an engaged one who flirt with a *ménage à quatre* before backing away. Rhodophil and Doralice have been married for three years; Palamede has been engaged to Melantha *in absentia*. Rhodophil has been gallanting Melantha, however, and Palamede becomes a 'servant' to Doralice. The men are almost at swordpoint when *Realpolitik* and increased self-knowledge convince them to stay with their own:

> *Rhod*: Gad . . . *Palamede* has wit, and if he loves you,
> there's something more in ye then I have found. . . .
> *Pal*: 'Slife, what's this? here's an argument for me to love
> *Melantha*; for he has lov'd her, and he has wit too.
>
> (v. 1)

This plot is everything the other is not: realistic, local – the lovers are as Sicilian as Hyde Park – contemporary and serious; it dissects the libertine ideal and the fashionable boredom with marriage. The first scene of adulterous courtship and its famous song, which have been taken as summing up Restoration comedy, are only Dryden's starting-point. The song's opening question,

Why should a foolish Marriage Vow,
Which long ago was made,
Oblige us to each other now,
When Passion is decay'd?

is not rhetorical: the play answers that marriage is imperfect but the
alternatives are emotionally unworkable. The song is ironic, as is the
Dedication to Rochester, the age's foremost libertine.

What one remembers of the play, though, are flighty Melantha,
sharp-witted Doralice, and the two couples in the grotto (III. 2), one
of the best short scenes in Restoration (or any) comedy. Melantha's
daily list of French terms ('They began at *Sottises*, and ended *en Ridicule*'), her purchase of words from Philotis at a gown apiece, and her
imagined dialogue with Rhodophil ('What do you mean to throw me
down thus? Ah me! ah, ah, ah') are *exquise*. This whole plot, with its
startlingly bawdy songs and dialogue, masquerade, and fashionable
railing at marriage and the country, is very much *à la mode* Etherege;
yet the mode is undercut, and half the play ignores it.

William Wycherley's first comedy, *Love in a Wood; or, St James's
Park* (1671), bows in various directions. Lady Flippant, an 'amorous
widow', Mrs Joyner, a city matchmaker trying to help her to Sir
Simon Addleplot, and the inter-class rivalry of Alderman Gripe and
the gentleman poet Dapperwit over Martha Gripe and Lucy Crossbite
all seem echoes of Betterton's comedy. As these plots develop,
however, especially when Sir Simon poses as Gripe's clerk to gain
access to his daughter, and the Crossbites extort money from Gripe,
the grubbing for sex and cash recalls Middleton's 'cit coms'.[19] Similarly
in the high plot, the wits' conversations and the park scenes suggest
the influence of Etherege, Dryden, and Sedley; yet the dependence on
confusion arising from darkness, masks, and mistaken identities is
redolent of intrigue comedy (it is adapted from one of Calderón's), and
the crude wit in mixed company smacks of Killigrew. In summary the
play seems a pastiche of literary thefts, as if Wycherley had determined
to be indebted to everyone.

Yet the feeling and tone of *Love in a Wood* set it apart from anyone
else's work. One has to go back to *Volpone* to find a nastier lot of
knaves and fools, forward to *The Alexandria Quartet* to parallel a situation like Dapperwit's, whose mistress Lucy becomes his mother-in-law
by marrying Gripe when Dapperwit marries Martha Gripe, pregnant by someone else.[20] The nocturnal intrigues in the park (v. 1),
where Ranger, addressing Lydia as Christina, and Christina, addressing
Valentine as Ranger, accidentally clear themselves by delivering the
right speech to the wrong person, are worked out with a fiendish

cleverness and a balletic complexity that make Tuke's *Adventures* look simple. The same kind of choreography occurs when Ranger and Christina meet at Vincent's (IV. 3). Valentine is pushed off-stage just in time to miss Lydia's half-entrance/exit and Dapperwit's arrival, which would have clarified all, while Ranger (who had no good reason to order 'Christina' brought there) is left confused and foolish. What formidable energy! Bonamy Dobree's impression of Wycherley as 'a being all angles and unwieldy muscular lumps, shot with unexpected streaks of grace' comes to mind.[21] All is rough brilliance, *vis comica* without discipline. At times the author seems, like love, 'in a wood', i.e. confused, but the histrionic gift that made him famous is unmistakable.[22]

His second play, however, *The Gentleman Dancing-Master* (1672), is an astonishing turnabout from his first. A Thameside Spanish intrigue drawn from Calderón and Molière, it satirizes the mindless affectation of French and Spanish manners in such a simple-minded and repetitive way that one asks if this obvious thing can be by the author of *Love in a Wood*? Though Nokes scored a triumph as Monsieur de Paris, Wycherley's farce was unsuccessful, nor does the text offer food to readers.

In 1672 Edward Ravenscroft, the Restoration's principal *farceur*, made his debut with *The Citizen Turned Gentleman*, lifted from Molière, and Dryden contributed another double-plot 'tragicomedy', *The Assignation*. Though hastily written and a failure, it is more interesting than some of his better known works, to some extent substituting realistic psychology for conventional notions of decorum.[23] The treatment of the high characters violated audiences' expectations and the use of a nun as pimp gave unnecessary offence, but there is some new wine in the old intrigue bottles, and a few scenes rise above farce, which was gaining ground on all other modes.

Shadwell did the best comic work of the year. *The Miser* (1672), a thorough reworking of Molière's *L'Avare*, interprets avarice as a humour: the usurer Goldingham would join a conspiracy against the King merely for gain. In a cynical ending, his son blackmails him and (unlike Molière's Cléante) keeps the money. Shadwell increased the number of settings and enlarged the cast in the belief that *L'Avare* had 'too little Action for an English Theater' – a comment and practice that soon became standard with adapters.[24] *Epsom-Wells* (1672), which Shadwell was 'more fond of than of any thing I have ever wrote' (Dedication), also pleased royalty and critics. Its appeal is not mysterious. The trio of cuckolds – two of whom witness their dishonour during the play – exemplify the advent of the sex comedy that was soon to flourish; the many minute complications of the plot add the pleasures of intrigue. Comedy of humours it is not, nor manners comedy of the drawing-room variety, nor wit comedy, despite its pair of gay couples and some repartee.[25] Virtually devoid of ideas, *Epsom-Wells* is tiresome to read, and the moralizing Shadwell of 1668–70 would have difficulty proving that these very broad characters and events could 'instruct' us.

But Shadwell created a sturdy theatrical vehicle, and in the great Betterton (as Bevil) and the comical Nokes (Bisket) he had the riders he needed. The complex texture of Act I shows Shadwell hitting his stride; it is the method of *Bartholomew Fair* updated to a Restoration spa. Ten or so people enter, babbling and drinking the waters: couples, servants, bullies. As we get to know them, we imbibe the scene and the beginnings of their intrigues. It is a scene that Southerne, Sheridan, and the Georgian novelists may have learned from. Though it is not all this masterful, the London-hating Justice Clodpate was an inspired creation, the fifth act nearly unites all the strands, and the ending, with the gay couples agreeing to remain single and the Woodleys to divorce, came as a surprise. *Epsom-Wells* treats of freedom, but not cerebrally; vivacious and stagey, it lived in the theatre, and scarcely breathes out of it.

During the Third Dutch War (1672–74) there was almost a comic hiatus; politics or other genres preoccupied dramatists. Only a few undistinguished romps appeared, such as Aphra Behn's *The Dutch Lover*, a sex intrigue, and the Duke of Newcastle's *The Triumphant Widow*, a musical farce. Then, between 1675 and 1678, comedy not only reappeared but reached a peak that was not regained until the 1690s.

Without a premonitory rumble, Wycherley's *The Country Wife* exploded on the stage of Drury Lane in January 1675. Though it succeeded and continues to be revived as one of Restoration drama's major achievements, people have been arguing about it ever since. Actually, for a long time there was only one-sided moral denunciation. Our century has gradually progressed to arguments over whether it is satirical or farcical, rebellious or conservative.[26] These divisions arise chiefly from Wycherley's inclusion of several different Restoration comic modes and the way he handles them.

The Country Wife is a good illustration of 'comic economy': good things are never discarded. Horner's pretence that venereal disease has rendered him impotent is a version of Terence's *Eunuchus* (161 BC), while the Pinchwife plot uses material from Molière's *L'École des maris* (1661) and *L'École des femmes* (1662). Each source is significantly altered, however. Whereas Terence's 'eunuch' raped his victim, Horner simply spreads the rumour and waits for 'victims' to break cover. And nothing in Molière's comedies prepares us for the dark violence of

Pinchwife's 'I will write "whore" with this penknife in your face' or the cunning promiscuity of Margery. (IV. 2)[27] The third plot-strand, involving Alithea, Harcourt, and Sparkish, apparently Wycherley's own invention, is an attempt to solve the persistent problem of who can marry a rake. His answer is Alithea, the slandered (and erring) but virtuous town-woman who (like Christina in *Love in a Wood*) is so anomalous she seems to have wandered in from another theatre or planet.

Wycherley controls these disparate materials admirably. The Terence and Molière plots dovetail as Horner pursues Margery, Pinchwife's journey to town for his sister Alithea's wedding links Molière to Wycherley's plot, Horner and Harcourt are cronies (Terence/Wycherley), and all three plots touch when Pinchwife brings the disguised Margery to Horner, thinking she is Alithea. Each story is interesting in its own right and generates effective theatre: Horner has his 'china scene', the Pinchwifes their letter-writing scene, Alithea and her beaux the wonderful *double entendres* of III. 2. These scenes and plots also function in complementary thematic ways: each is concerned with sexual choices, illustrates the centrality of wit, and satirizes vice or folly. No wonder *The Country Wife* has been called sex comedy, wit comedy, and satire, as well as comedy of manners. We see and hear a lot of society manners, but as a social weapon mere knowledge of manners is always beaten by wit.

In the main plot, Horner pays early tribute to the combination of mental sharpness and verbal quickness that his age called 'wit': 'methinks wit is more necessary than beauty; and I think no young woman ugly that has it, and no handsome woman agreeable without it' (I. 1). Intelligence is the most potent aphrodisiac. He proves that *he* has it at the beginning of the notorious china scene (IV. 3), when Sir Jasper Fidget surprises his wife with her arms around Horner. 'But is this your buying china?' asks the knight. 'I thought you had been at the china-house.' 'China-house!' says Horner, aside. 'That's my cue, I must take it'. Lady Fidget, a worthy partner, announces that since Horner 'knows china very well, and has himself very good', she will 'have what I came for yet'. Sir Jasper is left at the starting gate, chuckling while his horns grow. China was new, china-houses were places of assignation: a piece of 'manners' Wycherley turns to brilliant account as Lady Fidget re-enters 'with a piece of china in her hand', simpering, 'I have been toiling and moiling for the prettiest piece of china'.

This scene, which provoked a moral reaction leading to revisions and a long eclipse, is the centre of the interpretation of the play as a 'sex comedy'.[28] But the metaphorical use of 'china' is only the most glaring instance of the pervasive word-play. The metaphors begin early, helping to create the play's world – 'there are quacks in love as well as physic' (I. 1) – and redefinitions of such terms as 'virtue', 'modesty', and 'honour' are central to Wycherley's purposes. Lady Fidget, who has 'still so much honour in [her] mouth – /That she has none elsewhere' (II. 1), harps on it so incongruously (e.g. the end of the china scene) that the word begins to satirize itself. Horner gives horns, but his name also pronounces much like 'honour'.

In sex comedy proper, sex is entertainment, an end in itself, whereas Horner uses his disguise not only to obtain sexual favours but to reveal hypocrisy, an activity he enjoys as keenly as seduction. 'Affectation is [nature's] greatest monster', he observes (I. 1). The heart of his exposé (v. 4) begins with a literal unmasking and proceeds through wine to truth, with Horner prompting the ladies like an investigative reporter: 'Han't I heard you all declaim against wild men?' 'But why that mighty pretence to honour?' 'And you so seemingly honest.' He receives a number of satisfying admissions – 'we women make use of our reputation, as you men of yours, only to deceive the world', and 'women are least masked when they have the velvet vizard on' – culminating in Lady Fidget's reaction when it comes out that Horner has bedded them all. 'Sister sharers', she counsels, 'let us . . . have a care of our honour, . . . the jewel of most value and use, which shines yet to the world unsuspected, though it be counterfeit'. Horner agrees, 'for honour, like beauty now, only depends on the opinion of others'. Behind the masks appears relativism: as the world judges, the 'jewel' of honour is no worse for being fake. Horner's own sins do not invalidate a moral comment by a serious satirist.

As in most problem comedies, the aesthetic difficulties of *The Country Wife* cluster around the conclusion. Are Alithea and Harcourt – the only satisfactory match-up in the play and the only comic feature of the ending – sufficient to overcome the anti-matrimonial rhetoric of the last scene? Dorilant and Sparkish vow never to marry, Horner the cuckold-maker gets off scot-free, the Pinchwife marriage endures, and the play ends with a 'Dance of Cuckolds'. Not content to *omit* saturnalia, Wycherley parodies the usual rites in a black mass celebrating marital union gone wrong: an edifying spectacle for Alithea and Harcourt. One can hardly imagine a more purely *anti*-comic ending.

As a dramatic satire on hypocrisy and affectation, however, the play has already achieved its object: a saturnalian frosting would be a formal hypocrisy. And a work of satire can certainly have a moral argument beneath an immoral surface. But what do we do with Horner, who is never brought to book? The first critics to wrestle with such a character were the Old Testament prophets, who called him the Rod or Scourge of God. 'O Assyrian', cries Isaiah's God, 'the rod of mine anger . . . I will send him against a hypocritical nation . . .' (Isaiah

10. 5–6). Horner is the satiric counterpart of the Scourge of God: the bad man used for moral ends by a higher power. Though no merit attaches to him, his evil is turned to good, like Satan's in Calvinist theology. Whether or not Wycherley conceived Horner in this way – and three religious conversions suggest some spiritual life – it helps in understanding Horner's role. No more a 'hero' than Satan or the Assyrian, Horner is the nasty agent of a higher satirist.

The Plain Dealer (1676), 'one of the most bold, most general, and most useful satires which has ever been presented on the English theatre', proves that the indictment of social hypocrisy in The Country Wife sprang from deep personal feelings.[29] The two plays make their statements in sharply different ways, however. Horner, who knows himself as well as his victims, assumes no airs of moral superiority or self-justification. He does not denounce, but exposes. He fools only his victims: not himself, his friends, or us. And though Wycherley lets him off at the end, he does not presume to reward him. Manly, however, believes that he is one of only three sincere ('plain-dealing') people in the world, the others being his beloved and his friend, whom he trusts absolutely. He is wrong about them and himself: they are villains, he is pathologically idealistic. At the end, he has only transferred his idealism to new objects, yet Wycherley – who seems unaware that his satirist has become satirizable – concludes 'comically', reconciling Manly with the world and awarding him a beautiful heiress. And if Alithea seemed far-fetched, Fidelia is simply incredible.

The relationship between Wycherley and Manly has always been controversial. For years students were warned not to mistake Manly for a projection or ideal of Wycherley.[30] But the author initiated the confusion by dedicating the first edition to a well-known madam as his 'fittest patroness', flinging some Manleian insults at the public, and signing himself 'The Plain Dealer'. His contemporary admirers called him 'manly Wycherley', and in the next generation Congreve and Farquhar referred to him as 'the Plain-Dealer'. Associating the author with this character, then, is not a schoolboy error, but it would be simple-minded to identify them totally. Manly is not all of Wycherley – not Wycherley the artist or the warm friend – but he is part of him, the side that hates social hypocrisy too passionately to be always the artist or the friend. He is not the part of Wycherley that could create The Country Wife, but the part that could be hurt by its prudish reception in some quarters and respond pettishly. The long discussion of The Country Wife (II. 1) is an artistic blemish, a measure of Wycherley's loss of aesthetic distance.

The Plain Dealer did not succeed on-stage and, despite critical encomiums, does not get revived. The reasons are obvious enough: it is too long; the Widow Blackacre plot – though occasionally amusing

– is not well integrated with the plain-dealer action; and there is a lack of scenes with histrionic appeal, previously Wycherley's forte. He gives us instead extremes of character – Manly swinging wildly from Olivia to the angelic Fidelia – and farcical action such as the three of them prowling a darkened bedroom. His extremism is especially noticeable when the play is compared with its sources. Manly is more violent, more sinned against, less rational and perceptive than Molière's Alceste, and the skewed translation of *le misanthrope* reveals an inability to subject the character to Molière's dispassionate analysis. Célimène is disfigured into the vicious Olivia. Fidelia, given Viola's role in *Twelfth Night*, finds herself pimping, propositioned, and fondled. If what Wycherley sought was shock value, he succeeded. Dobree's Wycherley, 'tinged with a deep pessimism, a fierce hatred, the *saeva indignatio* of Swift . . . suspiciously like self-flagellation . . . as though he needed to expiate', is the Plain Dealer.[31]

'Etherege and Wycherley' form one of the oddest couples in literary history. Nothing dramatizes the disparities more strikingly than the concurrence of *The Plain Dealer* and *The Man of Mode* – the final play of each man – in 1676. It is simple to find 'Brawny' Wycherley in his Manly, but we are still looking for 'Easy' Etherege in or above his play. His very easiness, willing to leave so much in ambiguous shadow, has led to three centuries of argument over the meaning of the action and the human value of the protagonists. Is Dorimant a barnyard cock, the flower of Restoration art, or radically ambiguous?[32] Is *The Man of Mode* a courageous analysis of Restoration sexuality, witty light entertainment, or a shocking portrait of empty lives? Every reader confronts these questions.

Our reaction to the 'gay couple', Dorimant and Harriet, is crucial, but Etherege veils his; the camera rolls, recording without apparent comment. Again we meet Etherege's hero as he dresses to meet his world. Dorimant pens a suave note to Mrs Loveit, recites verses, banters with tradespeople, his servant, and his friend Medley, receives Young Bellair, and arranges his social calendar. Do we find these people idle post-adolescents or leisured sophisticates? Perhaps that depends on our social views; certainly no one works for a living. Is Dorimant debonair and cultured, or rude and foppish? Etherege's pen seems dipped in an equal mixture of acid and cologne: 'next to the coming to a good understanding with a new mistress, I love a quarrel with an old one', says Dorimant, planning to abandon Loveit for her friend Bellinda (I. 1).[33] His language to his social inferiors is casually insulting, though it could be delivered affectionately. In the discussion of Dorimant's clothes that leads to the first mention of Sir Fopling Flutter, Etherege may be needling Dorimant – Handy's manner suggests that his master is ordinarily fastidious – or may be

distinguishing the gentleman from the fop. Later, Dorimant is discom-
fited by Loveit (III. 3) and nonplussed by her and Bellinda (v. 1), but
eventually he outmanoeuvres them both. What is incontrovertible is
the hypocrisy of his comments about Young Bellair (I. 1) and Bellinda
(IV. 2) when their backs are turned, and his cold cruelty to Loveit's face
(II. 2, v. 1): that seems to be the distinction he makes between friends
and enemies.

Dorimant's ultimate 'fate' is to win the love of and right to court
Harriet. Is this punishment or reward? By rakish lights, a country
courtship followed by marriage is at least a come-uppance; yet Harriet
is beautiful, rich, and witty: a match for Dorimant in every sense. We
first see her with her woman (III. 1; compare Dorimant and Handy,
I. 1) in a scene emphasizing her wildness; in fifty lines she shows that
she can be tart and nasty. With Young Bellair she is a sharp and
malicious observer of manners. She twits Dorimant on his affectation
(III. 3; IV. 1), trades satirical broadsides with him, plays cool water on
his declarations, and turns a knife in the beaten Loveit (v. 2). Perhaps
the fine edge of Etherege's satire, which 'separates the head from the
body, and leaves it standing in its place', is that Harriet and Dorimant
deserve each other, and no one else.[34]

This action is smoothly melded into a second plot, in which Young
Bellair avoids a proposed match with Harriet and weds Emilia, for
whom his father drools. Old Bellair, a *senex amans*, is the key to both
plots; if he has his way, Dorimant will miss Harriet. Assisted by the
sensible Lady Townley, the young people agree on the right match-ups
and use their wit and mastery of manners to manipulate their elders.
Harriet and Young Bellair give such a convincing imitation of a
courting 'gay couple' (III. 1) that they gain time for him to wed Emilia
secretly, while Dorimant's bravura performance as 'Courtage' deceives
Lady Woodvil and gives him access to Harriet.

The most 'mannered' character, Sir Fopling Flutter, is outside the
action (though Dorimant and Loveit both use him as a pawn), but not
outside the meaning. His first entrance is preceded by a statement of
his social function: 'we should love wit, ·but for variety, be able to
divert ourselves with the extravagancies of those who want it' (III. 2).
Sir Fopling is better entertainment if the company play their roles as
actors/dramatists to draw him out; Dorimant warns Medley not to
'snub him. Soothe him up in his extravagance! he will show the better.'
Sniffs Medley: 'You know I have a natural indulgence for fools, and
need not this caution, sir!' Sir Fopling's absurdity does not disappoint
them or us. With him, manners have taken over, manipulating the
character instead of vice versa; they do not screen the man's purposes
but replace them.[35] Yet he does not fare badly in the plot: nothing
invested, nothing lost. The big loser – the only person ejected in the

finale – is Loveit, because she cannot control her passions: a telling comment on the values of the play's society. Caring too much, she loses her composure, and that is the unforgivable sin. Yet Loveit understands Dorimant (widely regarded as a portrait of Rochester) better than anyone, and captures his ambivalence: 'Exquisite fiend!' Etherege leaves it there.

In the bountiful year of 1676 Shadwell's *The Virtuoso* offered something for almost every palate: 'humor, wit, and satire', the author claims, chiefly the first.[36] Redefining humours as 'the artificial folly of those who are not coxcombs by nature but with great art and industry make themselves so', Shadwell advertises four 'entirely new' ones. These are the virtuoso (amateur scientist) Sir Nicholas Gimcrack; his parasite Sir Formal Trifle, a 'Ciceronian coxcomb'; Snarl, a railer against modern times; and Sir Samuel Hearty, a foolish amorous adventurer. Shadwell treats them as a composer does musical themes, with reprises *con variazioni* and counterpoint, e.g. the florid orator Trifle versus the sullen Snarl (I. 2). Again it is a humourist too many, though most can be defended. Gimcrack carries the topical satire, Hearty the farcical intrigue: dressed as a footman, he gets tossed in a blanket; disguised as a woman, he is assaulted by Trifle, etc. Hearty represents the coarser, populist side of Shadwell, the side furthest from Etherege. While Snarl's function is more obscure, his character is interesting and subtle: the old railer, 'in sadness' more than in anger and 'sometimes in the right', yet undercut by his envy and his vices. Shadwell might have dispensed with Trifle, but that was not his style, and the speeches are witty.

A romantic quartet provides more wit, and manners comedy. Initially devotees of Lucretian aloofness, Longvil and Bruce declare their loves to Miranda and Clarinda in III. 1, an entertaining, symmetrical scene. But, in an original parody of the usual patness of these quartets, the women decide the men have got it wrong: Miranda should have Bruce, and Clarinda, Longvil. In III. 4 they pull the switch, enabling each actress to play to a different actor. Later the men accept the change, and Longvil faces what most rakes must come to: "twill be necessary after all our rambles to fix our unsettled lives to be grave, formal, very wise, and serve our country, and propagate our species . . .' (IV. 3). This plot is juxtaposed with a number of low loves. In a lively sexual sextet (IV. 2), Snarl and his whore Figgup, then Lady Gimcrack and her gigolo Hazard, then Sir Nicholas and Flirt, arrive concurrently to use a 'convenient' room. All perceive the truth, but the Gimcracks decide to accept each other's flimsy pretences.

The Virtuoso was and is best known, however, for satirizing the experiments of the Royal Society, particularly Robert Hooke's. Gimcrack is first seen learning to swim upon a table, linked by a thread to a frog paddling in a jar of water. When questioned about the usefulness of this activity, Gimcrack replies, 'I content myself with the speculative part of swimming; I care not for the practic. I seldom bring anything to use . . .' (II. 2). Thus the traditionalists attacked the new science from Shadwell to Swift; when a mob of weavers comes to chastise Gimcrack for allegedly inventing the engine loom and threatening their livelihood, he protests, 'I never invented anything of use in my life' (v. 2).

This moment of realism – the *weavers* did not think uselessness was the problem – reminds us how Shadwell has slanted the evidence. Among Gimcrack's 'ridiculous' experiments (based on actual Society projects) are blood transfusion, close observation of ants and bacteria, weighing of air, moon flight, and the 'speaking trumpet' with which 'you may make 'em talk from one nation to another' (v. 1). The joke backfires, of course; the future – and the last laugh – lay with the scientists. Though Gimcrack is made absurd, the urbane Bruce now seems a complacent prig: 'What does it concern a man to know the nature of an ant?' (III. 3). Evidently Shadwell considered the question crushingly unanswerable. *The Virtuoso*'s humour and wit have lasted well, but the satire has one more edge than the author intended.

Even in 1675–76, comedy of manners did not rule. With Shadwell it was only a tangential interest, *The Plain Dealer* has other concerns, and farcical intrigue was gaining adherents. Otway's three-act farce *The Cheats of Scapin* (1676), translated from Molière, made English theatre history as the first of many 'afterpieces': short plays performed after the 'mainpiece'. Brisk stage business and easy laughs also characterized the intrigue comedies of Thomas Durfey and Aphra Behn.

It is easy to condescend to Behn's texts, forgetting their theatrical appeal. *The Town-Fopp; or, Sir Timothy Tawdry* (1676) seems mighty silly in print: an assault on common sense throughout. A potentially significant story of forced marriage is overshadowed by disguises, cross-purposes dialogue, and absurd intrigues that Behn takes so seriously as to employ verse on occasion. By the preposterous conclusion one asks if she can have been a sensible person. *The Rover; or, The Banished Cavaliers* (1677) is a better sample of her skills. Based on Killigrew's closet drama about exiled Royalists, *Thomaso; or, the Wanderer* (1664?), it pleased Charles II and lasted until 1750 on-stage.[37] Again we have the threat of forced marriage, vividly described by Hellena (I. 1) but this time prevented. Again there are masked intrigues and nocturnal confusion; still, it *is* 'Mardi Gras' in Naples. Again Behn rises to verse, though here are some characters who can (just) sustain it: Angellica Bianca, the great courtesan, and Willmore the rover, proud though impoverished by the Puritans. He is nicely ambivalent as he rails at her for being so fair and foul:

Though I admire you strangely for your beauty,
Yet I contemn your mind.
And yet I would at any rate enjoy you;
At your own rate; but cannot.

(II. 2)

Apparently a lover of rough verse, she gives him a free pass, but it is the spirited, virtuous Hellena who, after a number of wit-duels, induces him to give up roving for marriage.

Behn can weave as densely textured a scene as Shadwell, making three couples talk and cross-talk complexly, with numerous asides and interventions (III. 1). This relatively sophisticated dramaturgy is balanced against the simpler pleasures of farce: Blunt goes whoring, gets tumbled into a sewer, and comes 'creeping out of a common shore', cursing (III. 4). Such low Neapolitan realism notwithstanding, the play as a whole is set in the Cloud-cuckoo-land of European carnival comedy. If any Restoration drama merits Lamb's epithet 'the Utopia of gallantry', it is *The Rover*.

As dramatic literature, Tom Durfey's early sex intrigues are near the bottom of the barrel, though they were theatrical successes esteemed by Charles II. Both *Madame Fickle* (1676) and *A Fond Husband* (1677) blend humours with low farce and rely heavily on 'witty' strat-agems that fool credulous characters in darkened rooms. *Madame Fickle* is the stronger of the two. Though the dialogue is flat and the contriv-ances are thin, the situations had stage appeal, there are good comic roles (Jollyman, Toby, Zechiel, and Madame Fickle), and a sprinkling of Durfey songs helped the gaiety. Some of the country bumpkin material is broad without being verbally indecent. *A Fond Husband* is broader, lower, and coarser, but the *double entendres* (mostly slang terms for the genitals and intercourse) do not make the language inter-esting. There is little to relieve the grossness and paucity of invention here; in the 1690s Durfey would do more interesting work.

The King's admiration for *A Fond Husband* led Dryden to write *The Kind Keeper; or, Mr Limberham* (1678), a sex farce that out-trashes Durfey. A father and son, the former not recognizing the latter but serving as 'a kind of Deputy-Fumbler' to him, work as a team to seduce various women in a boarding-house.[38] There is much hiding in chests, in and under beds, and *seductio interruptus*. It is all bustle and libido without redeeming virtues. Several whores appear, including Pru, whose first maidenhead brought thirty guineas, her second ten, etc. The father offers to keep her himself: 'thou shalt do my little busi-ness; and I'll find thee an able young Fellow to do thine' (IV. 1). Attacked for bawdy, the play failed after three performances, so, Dryden said, he expunged the offensive material from the quarto (the

only text we have). He called the play a satire on *'Keeping'* (Dedication), and lamented the decline of comedy, 'sunk to Trick and Pun'
(Prologue). There are few more melancholy spectacles in English
literature than Durfey and Charles Stuart inducing Dryden to follow
All for Love with *Limberham*. The real immorality of Restoration
comedy is here: not in the play, but in the prostitution of talent. Later
Dryden would blame Whitehall, and recant his profanation of poesy.

Only Shadwell was writing traditional comedy in 1678, and *A True
Widow*, an entertaining if diffuse play, was damned. He wanted 'to
expose the Style and Plot of Farce-Writers, to the utter confusion of
damnable farce', which had obviously become a threat to comedy.[39]
As usual, Shadwell's first priority is to display his humourists, including
Widow Cheatly's godly brother Lump, a kind of methodist who has
his life planned out (in his journal) fifty years ahead. On 6 May 1728,
for example, he will 'take Physick, and shave'. 'What, sick or well',
asks Lady Cheatly, 'Beard or no Beard?' ''Tis all one for that', replies
Lump: 'I never break my method' (I. 2). Lump grows tiresome, but
Selfish continues to surprise and delight. His dialogue with Young
Maggot (II. 1), really two monologues, with each talking past the other
about himself, is wonderfully non-communicative. When Bellamour
disarms Selfish in a duel and throws him down, Selfish protests this
brutal way of fighting that has dirtied his clothes; and when the
matches are finally made up, he excuses himself to 'put on a very delicate, neat, convenient Suit, to dance with the Brides in here'.

The comedy is valued chiefly, though, for the pimping scene (Act
II) and the play within a play (Act IV). Shadwell was justly proud of
Lady Cheatly's and Lady Busy's attempt to persuade lsabella to be kept
by a lord. The hypocritical Busy, attacking Isabella's moral idealism,
serves to satirize society: 'Madam, you are under a great mistake, for
do not Ladies of Wit and Honour, keep dayly Company with those
things as you call them?' (II. 1). It is momentarily the spirit of *The
Country Wife*, but Shadwell has other causes, such as farce. The playhouse scene presents a Durfeyesque cuckolding intrigue, while fractious spectators roar for even lower stuff. (Ironically, the actual
audiences wanted more of this.) Though its wit is interspersed with
vapid passages, *A True Widow* provides energetic comedy for long
stretches. The women are unusually strong, particularly Theodosia as
a hold-out even against the man she loves, and Lady Cheatly as a
former victim eager to victimize.

These 1678 plays already bear traces of the Popish Plot. Dryden
apologized for printing *Limberham* 'at so unseasonable a time when the
Great Plot of the Nation' has devoured stage plots (Dedication). Shadwell speculated that 'the Calamity of the Time' doomed *A True Widow*,
and his Prologue to *The Woman-Captain* (1679) urged the 'Idle Youth'

who 'forsake our Plays': 'To them whose Right it is, leave Government,/And come to us, we'll give you all content.'[40] The 'political eighties' were beginning, but that is not the problem with *The Woman-Captain*, a rough, funny, titillating farce from the great defender of instructive comedy. The Epilogue explains that the author 'found by's last, you would not like what's good'; thus 'He made this Low, so to your Level fit;/Plenty of Noise, and scarcity of Wit.' Once more audiences are condemned for vulgarity, although in the play Shadwell has something to say about male misbehaviour and women's liberation.

In these years of comic dearth, when farce and politics devoured most of the nourishment, one man was writing hard-times comedy: Thomas Otway. *Friendship in Fashion* (1678) depicts sexual betrayals and deceptions of 'friends' in London society, foreshadowing the perfidies of *Venice Preserved*. *The Souldiers Fortune* (1680), his most popular comedy, takes a serious view of veterans' poverty and forced marriages; its jolliest character is a voyeuristic pimp who likes to squeeze men's legs. A sequel, *The Atheist* (1683), follows the 'gay couple' home from the altar, and finds they soon sunder. Except for *The Souldiers Fortune*, audiences did not welcome these dark plays, nor have we heard much of them since.[41] This is not surprising – their bleak outlook is metacomic – but they have force and originality.

A better representative of early 1680s comedy is Edward Ravenscroft's *The London Cuckolds* (1681), which turns adultery and class divisions into a romp. Three cits have different schemes to avoid cuckoldry. Alderman Wiseacre, at fifty, is marrying a fourteen-year-old orphan, Peggy, whom he has had raised in country ignorance. A sort of sleazy Pygmalion, he expects to 'make her do what I will' (I. 1). Alderman Doodle thinks that a witty wife, like his Arabella, is better surety, while the scrivener Dashwell trusts to his Eugenia's godliness. The cuckold-makers are two rakes, Townley and Ramble, and a young merchant, Loveday. Four adulteries later, the three cuckolds are laughing nervously at each other and trying to maintain appearances.

The London Cuckolds is replete with smutty dialogue and compromising situations: 'completely concerned with sex', as the film censors say. Like Dryden's *Limberham* it is a bedroom farce, but Ravenscroft's farcing is superior. The nine principals are carefully differentiated. Townley, a careless, boozing rake who always succeeds, achieves Eugenia accidentally, then frames the right questions to bed Arabella, who must answer 'No' to everything. Ramble, a mighty intriguer who usually fails, is often a comic butt – beaten, chamber-potted, etc. – but finally teaches Peggy 'the Whole Duty of a Wife' some 'two or three times' (v. 1). Loveday, a former beau of Eugenia, wittily rescues her and circumvents Dashwell. Woven from various plot-sources, the play is diverting as a cuckolder's fantasy; the intrigues (especially Eugenia's) are clever, and the abundant consummations contrast refreshingly with Dryden's teasing.

The numerous farces of the 1680s covered a broad range of types, from the sex intrigues of Ravenscroft to the magical fairy-tale atmosphere of Nahum Tate's *A Duke and No Duke* (1684), based on the *commedia dell'arte* and close to pantomime.[42] Scaramouche and Harlequin from the *commedia* also figure in Mrs Behn's *The Emperor in the Moon* (1687). Some of these pieces are skilful and entertaining, although (by definition) none attempts to present real life and manners. Comedy, meanwhile, laboured through a severe recession. Shadwell claimed that *The Lancashire Witches* (1681) was an alternative to political satire, yet its harsh anti-Catholicism brought down the censor.[43] Durfey was writing intrigues, political comedies, and adaptations. Thomas Southerne's first comedy, *The Disappointment* (1684), too contrived to take seriously, gives little hint of Southerne's future powers; its verse passages and romantic emphasis on honour seem anachronistic. The best comedies of the mid-1680s were John Crowne's, and even his work is limited, if not marred, by farcical intrigues and allusions to political minutiae.

City Politiques (1683) has the feel of the early 1660s, with Puritans replaced by knavish or foolish Whigs. The setting is Naples, *c.* 1620, but Crowne's audiences recognized numerous parallels with the Popish Plot – Dr Sanchy as Titus Oates, Florio as Shaftesbury Buckingham, etc. – that now require footnotes.[44] Much energy is expended on jarring topical allusions of the schoolboy revue type: Neapolitans who call each other Whig and Tory, a poetaster who is 'writing an answer to *Absalom and Achitophel*' (II. 1), and the like. (Imagine Dryden having Achitophel refer to the Exclusion Bill, or King David sing a Durfey ballad.) The Tory propaganda is so blatant and pervasive that the censor delayed the play for six months, yet Crowne boasts of his discretion, and thanks Heaven that 'the frenzy of the nation/Begins to cure' (Prologue).

Crowne's dialogue is so lively, however, that the play can still be read with pleasure; open almost anywhere and you find crisp, colourful exchanges. The speeches of Rosaura and the Podesta in II. 1 are witty and characteristic: 'well carved', as he says of her adage, 'Give me greatness and do you keep policy'. The joke is that she is plotting to cuckold him with Florio, who is posing Hornerlike as 'no man' and as one of the 'dull lewd saints' (Whigs), to gain access to her (I. 1). Their contrivances succeed, and when they are finally caught ('arm in arm'), Florio claims her on Whig principles:

he is not to be regarded who has a right to govern, but he
who can best serve the ends of government. I can better

serve the ends of your lady than you can, so I lay claim to
your lady.
Rosaura: And you have my consent.
Florio: So, I have the voice of the subject too.

(v. 3)

City Politiques is an odd coupling of licentious comedy with political
satire: *Absalom and Achitophel* crossed with *The Country Wife*.

Sir Courtly Nice; or, It Cannot Be (1685), less overtly political, is still
a Tory play: the last of those suggested to Restoration dramatists by
Charles II, who gave Crowne a copy of Moreto's *No puede ser*. The
Prologue flatters James II, and attacks Whig plotters as 'the sawciest,
lewdest, Protestants alive'. One of the heroine's guardians is a canting
fanatic, Testimony, eventually exposed (as one who 'loves a pretty bit
sometimes'), beaten, and kicked off-stage.[45] If the nation's frenzy *was*
abating, Crowne was not one of the healers.

The Spanish origin is evident in the immuring of women, the
schemes, and disguises. Lord Belguard, who distrusts women, means
to keep his sister Leonora locked up until she marries the foolish Sir
Courtly Nice. Violante likes Belguard, but not this plan; Leonora loves
Farewel, though their families are old enemies. Belguard surrounds her
with spies, including Hothead, a 'Zealot against Fanaticks', and his
opposite, Testimony. For the defence, Violante sends her morose
suitor Surley to disgust Sir Courtly. Crowne (like Shadwell) gives
these antithetical characters ample time to clash. Finally Sir Courtly
challenges Surley, though 'If his filthy sword should touch me,
'twould make me sick as a Dog' (iv. 1). Farewel employs Crack, a
'subtle intriguing fellow' and consummate pimp; posing as a tailor and
a nabob, he outfoxes Belguard and brings the lovers to a chaplain.
When the marriage is revealed, Belguard must admit that 'Vertue
is a Womans only guard' (v. 4). Maybe Violante will have him
now.

Masks, real or figurative, pervade the play. Leonora's vizard
encourages Testimony to drop the hypocritical cloak of his saintliness;
on the other hand, the Epilogue notes, 'Audacious Vizards' do not
guarantee virtue. Surley believes that love and lust are 'the same thing.
The word love is a figleaf to cover the naked sense.' Vizarded, an
ancient aunt contrives to marry Sir Courtly, and her *un*masking finally
cracks his façade of manners: 'a Passion for an old Woman?' he
exclaims. 'Ill-bred fop', she retorts, and he withdraws, snuffed out.
Masks elicit or conceal the truth; Crack, a man all masks, makes false
appearances serve comedy's social verity: young love will have its way.
Sir Courtly and Crack are stellar roles, Farewel and Leonora almost
as good. Probability aside, *Sir Courtly Nice* is an excellent acting

comedy, with tasty dialogue throughout, and its maskings reflect the subterfuges and divisions of the time.

Most readers think Charles Sedley's *Bellamira* (1687) superior to his *Mulberry Garden*; one has ranked it with Etherege and Wycherley.[46] Sedley did use one of Wycherley's sources, Terence's *Eunuchus*, retaining the rape and then marrying the rapist to his victim: a course of events unparalleled on the Cavalier stage. When a friend remonstrates, the rapist claims, 'No Woman ever heartily fell out with a Man about that Business' (III. 5). Here at last, at the end of the era, is a comedy as cynical and libertine as the clichés propound. Merryman, adapting Hobbes, avows that 'in the matter of women, we are all in a state of nature, every man is hard against every man' (III. 4). The female libertine/liberationist, Bellamira, prefers courtesanship to marriage: time enough for a husband 'when Love's Feast is over. Who would begin a Meal with Cheese?' (I. 3). But Sedley had o'erstayed his time; there was a sharp moral protest, causing the author to ask why 'the Ice that has borne so many Coaches and Carts, shou'd break with my Wheel barrow'. (Answer: thinner ice.) The objections were also to callousness, and to the lack of redeeming features; *Bellamira* cannot claim to be satire. It is 'adult' and has some good scenes, but never on a par with the best of Etherege and Wycherley. The silly denouement – a duel and *deus ex machina* – reveals how little Sedley had to say.

Whereas Sedley was late with his hedonism, Shadwell was early with the didacticism of *The Squire of Alsatia* (1688), every part of which oozes moral concern. Shadwell wants to enlighten our notions of child-raising, reform a rake, lecture young women, and eliminate the venerable status of Whitefriars – 'Alsatia' – as a legal sanctuary. Paradoxically, Alsatia provides most of the fun and colour in the play, which is a romp as well as a lesson. The romp accounted for its long stage success, while the lesson provides most of the problems and current interest.

From Terence's *Adelphi*, a favourite of the period, Shadwell took the idea of brothers educating and educated on different principles. Sir William Belfond raises his elder son, Tim, strictly and narrowly in the country; brother Ned receives a gentleman's education in London and Europe from his genial uncle Sir Edward Belfond. When the educators meet in the city they argue for their respective principles and point to their charges as support, though Shadwell has already shown us that Tim has run away to London and fallen into the hands of Alsatia's sharpers, among whom he is in the happy state of being well deceived, so we know that Sir William's boasts are hollow. Then we meet Ned, who having just seduced the virgin Lucia is embarrassed by a visit from his cast-off mistress Termagant, demanding more money for their child (II. 1), so we wonder about Sir Edward's prize exhibit too. But the plot vindicates him. While the foolish Tim snaps at every lure, turns against his father, and has to be saved from marrying Termagant, Ned disencumbers himself of both mistresses, bravely rescues father and brother from the Alsatian mob, and marries the virtuous, wealthy Isabella, while remaining a model of filial piety to both fathers. Q.E.D.

Does Shadwell present Sir Edward's achievement as exemplary or take a compromise position?[47] If Ned's portrait is ironic, it is subtly so, yet he can scarcely be a model. His philosophizing with Truman about 'the farce of life' rings false, and his defence of his fornication is unimaginative: 'a young Fellow carries that about him that will make him a Knave now and then, in spite of his Teeth' (II. 1). Several times he equivocates with his father and uncle about his two women. He accepts Sir Edward's counsel to leave off wenching and twice vows to reform, but what we *see* are his cavalier treatment of Lucia (IV. 1), his palliation of the Termagant affair to Isabella and confession of frailty (v. 1), and his lies to Lucia and her father ('*I* must Marry *I* cannot help it . . . she's innocent': v. 3), the last excused by generosity of motive. It is possible to view *Alsatia* as a social problem play (Lucia) or a reform comedy (Ned, Sir William, Alsatia), but difficult to take it as 'exemplary'; Ned being unexemplary weakens Sir Edward's claims. Arguably their *relationship* is idealized for its warmth and openness.

In general, Shadwell's moralizing presents difficulties. The ostensible lessons are: (1) abolish Alsatian privileges; (2) raise children liberally and kindly – Sir William is twice made to admit he was wrong. But a number of unintended conclusions can equally well be drawn. For repressed sons: revolt, and be rewarded with sufficient funds to go 'whoring and drinking', as Tim is. For indulged sons: sow wild oats free of charge, as Ned does. For parents: repression is cheaper. Tim will cost Sir William only five hundred pounds per annum maintenance, whereas Ned's bill to Sir Edward includes fifteen hundred pounds to Lucia's father, one hundred pounds per annum to Termagant, fifteen hundred pounds per annum for Isabella's jointure, and whatever it costs to raise the love-child 'like a Gentlewoman'. The case for the liberal approach is kept afloat only by money, callousness, and a short memory (Ned's 'Sacrifice without a blemish').[48] Shadwell cannot have missed what is so clear to us, but neither does he show us a way out of the muddle.

The pervasive emphasis on money was novel. Besides their pay-offs, the fathers bet one hundred pounds on their charges, and Sir William is buying Isabella (as cheaply as possible) from Scrape, who is selling Teresia too. This mercenariness is only one aspect of what amounts to a new comic world. The merchant Sir Edward exists not to be cuckolded (he is unmarried), but to propound the better of the two educational theories and to have the last word. The emphasis on good nature in Ned and Sir Edward was ahead of its time, and Isabella's remark that 'True Religion must make one cheerful' (III. 1) anticipates Shaftesbury. The serious, almost sentimental treatment of Lucia's plight (IV. 1) and of Sir William's crisis (V. 3) was unprecedented in comedy. Fresh winds blow through this play, and its success indicates that the social weathervane was beginning to swing.

Bonamy Dobree condescended to Shadwell as a country squire whose fare was heavy and plain though ample.[49] This is true, as far as it goes. Shadwell laboured under the banner of Jonson for twenty years without writing a *Man of Mode* or a *Country Wife*, but he kept on producing comedy after more brilliant writers fell off, and his resistance to the threat of farce was stout. Overall his comic work is more substantial than that of Dryden, who pinned the label 'dull' on him for political reasons. The countryman's hospitality deserves better than a sneer.

Afterword

Most readers come to Restoration comedy having previously been bombarded with critical opinions about this controversial literature. To read late-seventeenth-century comedy freshly and fairly – on its own terms – is difficult, since it deviates (how far is debatable) from the main line of European comedy. This deviation, whether admirable or deplorable, makes it fit poorly into most general notions of comic history and theory.

A detailed account of the critical debate is beyond the scope of this book, but its main outlines can be grasped quickly. Early assaults on the licentiousness of Restoration comedy reached a first peak in Jeremy Collier's *Short View of the Immorality and Profaneness of the Restoration Stage* (1698), seconded by some of Steele's writings. These having been answered by Congreve, Vanbrugh, Dennis, and others, comedy was duly moralized and the issue was shelved until the nineteenth century, when Lamb's attempt to defend the comedies (in *Essays of Elia*, 1821) provoked Macauley's denunciation of Restoration comic dramatists ('Leigh Hunt', 1841). A reaction against moralistic criticism began with John Palmer's *The Comedy of Manners* (1913) and continued with various scholars of the 1920s who found the comedy worthy of serious study, but in 1937 L. C. Knights opened a fresh offensive, labelling

Restoration comic texts 'trivial, gross and dull'. He has been opposed and defended; moral critiques, however, virtually ceased about 1960, and the interest shown by subsequent scholars confirms the attitude (if not the conclusions) of Palmer.

It is possible to summarize the various modern debates as follows:
1. Was Restoration comedy 'artificial', or a realistic picture of its society?
2. Was 'comedy of manners' the dominant type?
3. Were the comedies moral, immoral, or amoral?
4. Were they trivial or serious, gross or subtle, dull or lively?
5. Do they indicate social and literary health, or sickness?
6. Were they primarily conservative, or rebellious?

Whatever its faults (some questions overlap), this list shows how fundamental the disagreements have been, and in some cases remain. On questions 5 and 6 there is no consensus yet; on questions 3 and 4 the only consensus is that the answer depends on which plays you mean. On questions 1 and 2, most scholars agree that the comedies were heightened but roughly realistic pictures of life in a part of London society, not totally artificial; and that 'comedy of manners' is a slippery term that does not accurately describe a large number of Restoration comedies. The scholarship of the last twenty years sounds a caveat against generalizing about types of comedy in this mercurial period. Single plays are elusive enough; all typologies are perilous.

Notes

1. See Harold Love, 'Dryden, Durfey, and the Standard of Comedy', *SEL*, 13 (1973), 422–36 (pp. 422–23).

2. Samuel Johnson, 'Life of Cowley', in *Lives of the English Poets* (1779–81), 2 vols (London, 1952), I, 9–10.

3. John Wain, 'Restoration Comedy and its Modern Critics', *EC*, 6, no. 4 (1956), 367–85 (p. 371).

4. John Loftis, *The Spanish Plays of Neoclassical England* (New Haven, 1973), p. 67; see also Arthur H. Scouten, 'Notes Towards a History of Restoration Comedy', *PQ*, 45 (1966), 62–70 (p. 63).

5. See Robert D. Hume, 'Diversity and Development in Restoration Comedy, 1660–79', *ECS*, 5 (1972), 365–97 (p. 372).

6. See Clifford Leech, 'Restoration Comedy: The Earlier Phase', *EC*, 1 (1951), 165–84 (pp. 171–72).

7. Quotations and references follow Michael Cordner's edition of *The Plays of George Etherege* (Cambridge, 1982).

8. Norman Holland, *The First Modern Comedies* (Cambridge, Massachusetts, 1959), p. 21. Louis Kronenberger's discussion is worth reading: *The Thread of Laughter* (New York, 1952), pp. 43–44.

9. See *The Works of John Dryden*, general editors E. N. Hooker and H. T. Swedenborg, 19 vols (Berkeley, Los Angeles, and London, 1956–   ), VIII, edited by J. H. Smith and D. MacMillan (1962), 268, 269, and the Prologue.

10. Hume, 'Diversity', pp. 384–85; and Kathleen M. Lynch, *The Social Mode of Restoration Comedy* (New York, 1926), p. 149.

11. IV. 2. Quotations and scenes follow Cordner's edition.

12. Lynch, p. 152; N. Holland, pp. 28, 29, 37. Only L. C. Knights could not see this.

13. Preface to *The Humorists* (1671). References to Shadwell's plays are to *The Complete Works of Thomas Shadwell*, edited by Montague Summers, 5 vols (London, 1927). *The Sullen Lovers* appears in Volume I. Michael Alssid's discussion of the play in *Thomas Shadwell* (New York, 1967) is interesting.

14. Possibly reflecting stages of composition. See Vivian de Sola Pinto, *Sir Charles Sedley* (London, 1927), pp. 104, 252. Pinto thinks this play contains the earliest of the wit-duels: p. 261.

15. See the edition of A. H. Scouten and R. D. Hume, the source of my quotations (Philadelphia, 1976), pp. 23, 32–35, 38–39. The original title may have been *The Country Gentlemen*.

16. In *Works of Shadwell*, I. See Alssid's serious interpretation of the play: pp. 48–49.

17. See A. H. Scouten, 'Plays and Playwrights', in *The Revels History of Drama in English*, edited by T. W. Craik and C. Leech, 8 vols (London, 1975–83), V (1976), 165; and Hume, 'Diversity', p. 394.

18. Quotations and scenes follow *Works of Dryden*, XI, edited by John Loftis and David S. Rodes (1978). On the preciosity of the main plot, see D. S. Berkeley, '*Préciosité* and the Restoration Comedy of Manners', *HLQ*, 18 (1955), 109–28 (pp. 112–13); on its relation to libertinism and marital fashions, see Kronenberger, pp. 89–90; and R. D. Hume, *The Rakish Stage* (Carbondale, Illinois, 1983), pp. 143, 160–61, 164, 208–9. For discussion of the first song, see L. C. Knights, 'Restoration Comedy: The Reality and the Myth', *Scrutiny*, 6 (1937), 122–43 (p. 138), answering Dobree.

19. The observation of Kenneth Muir, *The Comedy of Manners* (London, 1970), p. 69.

20. Kronenberger, p. 57, captures the mood.

21. See *Restoration Comedy* (Oxford, 1924), p. 78.

22. Given the proverbial meaning of 'in a wood', Gerald Weales is right to criticize Rose Zimbardo's pastoral reading in her *Wycherley's Drama* (New Haven, 1965), Chapter 2. See his *Complete Plays of William Wycherley* (New York, 1966), p. 118, n. 11. On stage effect, see Scouten, *Revels History*, V, 194–95.

23. See *Works of Dryden*, XI, 512–13.

24. Dedication (1672); see *Works of Shadwell*, II. My discussion is indebted to Alssid, pp. 51–53.

25. See Alssid, pp. 58–59.

26. There is not room to trace them here, but see R. D. Hume, 'William Wycherley: Text, Life, Interpretation', *MP*, 78, no. 4 (1981), 399–415, for an admirable summary.

27. IV. 2. Quotations and scenes follow Peter Holland's edition of *The Plays of William Wycherley* (Cambridge, 1981).

28. See especially John H. Smith, *The Gay Couple in Restoration Comedy* (Cambridge, Massachusetts, 1948), p. 132; and A. H. Scouten and R. D. Hume, in Hume's *Rakish Stage*, p. 58.

29. The tribute is Dryden's, in 'The Author's Apology for Heroic Poetry and Poetic Licence', prefixed to *The State of Innocence: an Opera* (1677), in *Of Dramatic Poesy*, edited by George Watson, 2 vols (London and New York, 1962), I, 199.

30. See Lynch, p. 172; Zimbardo, p. 80ff.; and Thomas H. Fujimura, *The Restoration Comedy of Wit* (Princeton, 1952), p. 146. The controversy is summarized by Muir, p. 81, who takes the 'persona' view. Congreve's and Farquhar's comments are in the Prologues to *Love for Love* and *The Beaux' Stratagem*. My discussion of Manly and Wycherley is indebted to Kronenberger, pp. 71, 76–80.

31. *Restoration Comedy*, pp. 78–81 passim.

32. For varying interpretations, see Knights, p. 131; Lynch, p. 177; R. D. Hume, 'Theory of Comedy in the Restoration', *MP*, 70 (1973), 302–18 (p. 307) and 'Reading and Misreading *The Man of Mode*', *Criticism*, 14 (1972), 1–11; Wain, p. 378; and Jocelyn Powell, 'George Etherege and the Form of a Comedy', in *Restoration Theatre*, edited by J. R. Brown and B. Harris (London, 1965), pp. 61–65, among others.

33. Quotations and scenes follow Cordner's edition.

34. The quotation is from Dryden's 'Discourse Concerning the Original and Progress of Satire', in *Of Dramatic Poesy*, II, 93.

35. The sentence is indebted to Jocelyn Powell's enlightening essay, 'George Etherege and the Form of a Comedy'.

36. From the Dedication. Reference is made to the edition of Marjorie H. Nicolson and David S. Rodes (Lincoln, Nebraska, 1966). For the play's satire on the Royal Society, see their introduction, pp. xv–xvii, xxi; and on real-life parallels to the labour uprising, pp. xxv–xxvi.

37. See the edition of Frederick M. Link (Lincoln, Nebraska, 1967), pp. xi–xiii. All references in the text are to this edition.

38. I. 1. References are to *Dryden: The Dramatic Works*, edited by Montague Summers, 6 vols (London, 1932), IV. For background and interpretation, see Love, p. 432; James R. Sutherland, 'The Impact of Charles II on Restoration Literature,' in *Restoration and Eighteenth-Century Literature*, edited by Charles C. Camden (Chicago, 1963), p. 258; and R. D. Hume, 'The Change in Comedy . . .', *Essays in Theatre*, 1, no. 2 (1983), 101–18 (p. 107).

39. 'To the Reader', in *Works of Shadwell*, III. Alssid discusses the play's interesting women, pp. 78–79.

40. Dedication to *A True Widow*, in *Works of Shadwell*, III. References to *The Woman-Captain* are to *Works of Shadwell*, IV.

41. One exception: R. D. Hume, 'Otway and the Comic Muse', in *The Rakish Stage*. See especially pp. 90, 109.

42. See *Ten English Farces*, edited by Leo Hughes and A. H. Scouten (Austin, Texas, 1948), p. 4. On the popularity of farce, see Hume, 'Change in Comedy', p. 112.

43. To the Reader', in *Works of Shadwell*, IV. See Alssid, p. 90.

44. See the edition of J. H. Wilson (Lincoln, Nebraska, 1967), pp. xiii–xviii. Quotations and scene divisions follow this edition.

45. v. 4. Quotations and scenes refer to the edition of Charlotte B. Hughes (The Hague, 1966).

46. Pinto, p. 266. My quotations and scene divisions are those of Pinto's edition of *The Works of Sir Charles Sedley*, 2 vols (London, 1928), II. On the relation of the play to its Restoration context, see Hume, *Rakish Stage*, p. 164, and 'Change in Comedy', p. 111. Joseph W. Krutch views the play as satire: *Comedy and Conscience After the Restoration*, 1924 (New York, 1961), p. 200.

47. Compare Muir, pp. 60–61; and R. D. Hume, 'Formal Intention in *The Brothers* and *The Squire of Alsatia*', *ELN*, 6 (1969), 176–84. Kronenberger has a useful general discussion: pp. 94–98. I have used the text of *Works of Shadwell*, IV.

48. See Scouten, *Revels History*, v, 190, for discussion.

49. In *Restoration Comedy*, p. 116.

Chapter 6
Scenes and Machines: Operatic Drama

In February 1673. The long expected Opera of *Psyche*,
came forth in all her Ornaments; new Scenes, new
Machines, new Cloaths, new *French* Dances: This Opera
was Splendi[d]ly set out, especially the Scenes.

John Downes, *Roscius Anglicanus*

The borderers of the classical dramatic genres are tragicomedy, farce,
burlesque; beyond them, further from the literary or textual centre,
live masque and opera. The Restoration usage of the term 'opera' is
confusing: it does not tally closely with our own, and was only
tangentially related to Continental examples. Any full-length *mélange*
of drama, spectacle, dance, and music was apt to be labelled 'opera'
(if shorter, it was called a masque).[1] As Downes's remarks suggest,
music was not the prime consideration. The English were conversant
with the Italian meaning – John Evelyn described a Roman 'opera' in
1644; Richard Flecknoe and William Davenant, who applied the term
to works of their own in the 1650s, knew European opera – but they
considered that an alien, partially separate tradition. Davenant called
the recitative in his *Siege of Rhodes* (1656; see pp. 19, 40) 'unpractised
here, though of great reputation amongst other nations' ('Address to
the Reader'). English opera owed as much to native forms – exotic
tragedy and Caroline theatre masques such as Thomas Heywood's
Love's Mistress (1634) – as to Continental models. The important
difference was that English operas generally had spoken dialogue (not
recitative) as well as music, spectacle, and dance; this combination
came to be called 'dramatic opera', 'semi-opera', or just 'English
opera'.[2]

At the beginning of the Restoration, Thomas Blount's *Glossographia*
(1661) provided a clear definition of Italian opera as a dramatization
'performed by voices in that way, which the Italians term *Recitative*,
being likewise adorned with Scenes by Perspective, and extraordinary
advantages by Musick'. The spectacular revival of *The Siege of Rhodes*
(1661) afforded an English example, although now that Davenant no
longer needed 'opera' as a cloak for drama, it was probably more of
a 'musical play' than in 1656.[3] Even so, no other playwright evinced
an immediate interest in Davenant's recitative-and-aria approach to
opera: it was too extreme, too European. Instead, heroic drama appro-
priated certain 'operatic elements': masque-like spectacle, the inclusion
of music and dance, and the penchant for formal patterns of language

and behaviour (e.g. heroic couplets, symmetrical plots, stylized gestures based on an artificial code of conduct). Few scholars have examined heroic drama (or French neoclassical tragedy, which exhibits the same features) without resorting to the term 'operatic': natural enough, since heroic plays are one ancestor of modern opera.

When English operas finally appeared in 1673, the impulse came not from *The Siege of Rhodes* (though Davenant probably altered the operatic *Macbeth* in that year), but from the rage for refurbishing old plays and from the French stage. The triumph of the Corneille–Molière–Quinault *Psyché* (1671) in Paris led Betterton to produce the ground-breaking *Psyche* described by Downes, with music by Matthew Locke and libretto by Shadwell.[4] The same team 'operatized' the Dryden–Davenant alteration of *The Tempest* (1667), one of the most controversial and diverting Restoration operas, in 1674. Both versions are studies in Restoration taste. The 1667 version cuts Sebastian and reduces Prospero, introduces Hippolito as a 'natural man', gives Miranda and Caliban sisters, simplifies the plot but adds more low comedy and sex, and modernizes the dialogue.[5] For example, II. 1 is cut from 330 to 110 lines: without Sebastian, there is no mockery of Gonzalo or plot with Antonio; Gonzalo's commonwealth is also missing. Instead, Antonio and Alonzo accept the shipwreck as retribution for their sins against Prospero, and a new song and masque dramatize their offences – the first of several 'operatic' touches. In III. 2 (now only fifty-three lines long) there is a feast set by 'eight fat spirits', but no rebuke; and in III. 4, as Ferdinand follows Ariel they sing antiphonally. Of course it is no substitute for the original, and signals a drift towards a merely clever, or precious, or prurient, handling of serious themes. But it is also an entertaining play (Hippolito and Dorinda are delightful: see II. 5) that acknowledges the power of Shakespeare's myth by trying to extend it.

Estimates of Shadwell's alterations range all the way from 'the operatic *Tempest* . . . is a myth' to a flat 'revised by Shadwell'.[6] To Downes it seemed 'all New': i.e. 'Scenes, Machines; particularly, one Scene Painted with *Myriads* of *Ariel* Spirits; and another flying away, with a Table Furnisht out with Fruits, Sweet meats, and all sorts of Viands'.[7] This version held the stage until 1838.

Dryden seems to have kept a hostile distance from the operatic *Tempest*, though his own heroic plays use music, dance, and spectacle, and he called *The State of Innocence and Fall of Man* (1677; see p. 50) 'an Opera'. Since this curio never reached the Restoration stage there is no justification for discussing it in detail, but it does help to clarify the Restoration meaning of 'opera'. Dryden's first assault is audio-visual: chaos on a dark stage, warlike music, bright angels above, angels falling to fire and brimstone. The only music indicated thereafter is the devils' song in the entr'acte. What he emphasizes is spectacle: the sun and moon with Lucifer riding on a dark cloud; paradise, with fruit trees 'cut out on each side' and a 'prospect' terminating in walks; and Raphael's apocalyptic vision of war and death, culminating in the descent of heaven, 'full of Angels and blessed Spirits'.[8] Too ambitious for the Restoration theatre, it should make a stunning film.

In 1685, Dryden's opera *Albion and Albanius*, a political allegory, failed partly because Charles II's death necessitated revisions, partly because of lacklustre music. By then Dryden could define 'opera' with seeming confidence as 'a Poetical Tale, or Fiction, represented by Vocal and Instrumental Musick, adorn'd with Scenes, Machines and Dancing. The suppos'd Persons of this Musical *Drama*, are generally Supernatural' (Preface). This could equally well describe a masque, however, and at least one historian wants to call John Blow's finely crafted *Venus and Adonis* (*c.* 1683?) an opera rather than a masque.[9] The frontiers were ill defined. Charles Davenant's *Circe* (1677) was the only other opera produced in the Restoration proper. Thus far the composers involved were not distinguished – Matthew Locke was probably the best – and the dramatists were still experimenting. With the genius of Blow's pupil Henry Purcell just around the corner, the best was yet to come.

Notes

1. See Arthur H. Scouten, in *The Revels History of Drama in English*, edited by T. W. Craik and C. Leech, 8 vols (London, 1975–83), v (1976), 288–95, esp. p. 293.

2. See Allardyce Nicoll, *British Drama*, fifth edition (London, 1962), p. 151; and Robert D. Hume, 'Opera in London, 1695–1706', in *British Theatre and the Other Arts, 1660–1800*, edited by Shirley S. Kenny (Washington, 1984), pp. 67–91 (p. 69).

3. Edward J. Dent, *Foundations of English Opera* (New York, 1965), pp. 65–66.

4. Curtis A. Price calls it 'archetypal', a better synthesis of music and drama than any later semi-opera: *Henry Purcell and the London Stage* (Cambridge, 1984), pp. 296–97.

5. The changes are summarized in *The Works of John Dryden*, general editors E. N. Hooker and H. T. Swedenborg, 19 vols (Berkeley, Los Angeles, and London, 1956–), x (1970, edited by Maximillian E. Novak), 329–42.

6. *Works of Dryden*, x, 326; compare Judith Milhous and R. D. Hume, 'Attribution Problems in English Drama, 1660–1700', *Harvard Lib. Bull.*, 31, no. 1 (1983), 32–33; and Scouten, p. 290.

7. John Downes, *Roscius Anglicanus* (1708), edited by Montague Summers (London, 1928), p. 34. On the stage history, see *Works of Dryden*, x, 322.

8. In *Dryden: The Dramatic Works*, edited by M. Summers, 6 vols (London, 1932), III, 461.

9. Dent, p. 172; contrast Eugene Haun, *But Hark! More Harmony* (Ypsilanti, Michigan, 1971), p. 132.

Part Two:

Reform, Retrenchment and Control 1689–1737

Chapter 7
From Revolution to Robinocracy

Government and society

> Great Britain is of all countries the most proper for trade,
> as well from its situation as an island as from the freedom
> and excellency of its constitution.
>   Edward Chamberlayne, *Magnae Britanniae Notitia* (1708)

We tend to oversimplify the events of 1688–89 and their consequences
for England. The quantity of patriotic and mercantile euphoria, for
example, might lead one to believe that the transition from Royalist
to Parliamentary England and the 'nation of small shopkeepers' was
rapid and thorough. 'Parliament had asserted its own supremacy, and
the Court-centred society which (except during the Commonwealth)
prevailed up to 1688 yielded to . . . Parliamentary predominance.'[1]
These and other important changes certainly occurred during the
period, but not right away. It is possible to speak of peace, prosperity,
and political consensus after about 1715; before that date, however, the
overall picture is rather of foreign wars and domestic unrest on the
social, political, religious, and financial fronts.

When 'William in pudding-time came o'er', few Englishmen –
including the Parliamentarians who invited him – knew what they
were getting, beyond a dour Dutch general and his wife (James II's
daughter Mary), both Protestants. England had traded her male Catholic Stuart rulers for a collateral line, but the legality of this exchange
and the relationship between the branches were questions that lingered
until 1745, for James had fled with the infant Prince of Wales. The first
answers were roughed out amid swiftly moving events in 1689. The
Convention Parliament that William had convoked declared that James
II had 'abdicated', ignored Prince James, and bestowed the Crown on
William and Mary jointly; it also passed a Bill of Rights and a Toler-
ation Bill granting Dissenters limited freedom of worship. These

actions initiated a fresh round of troubles: there was still a Tory Jacobite party, hostile to all dissent, and some bishops, having sworn fealty to James II, would not swear anew ('Non-Jurors') to William. Meanwhile James II, with French help, had invaded Ireland and incited a rebellion. War was declared on France, and William led an army to Ireland.

Despite William's great victory in the Battle of the Boyne, the War of the League of Augsburg dragged on until 1697, requiring the King to take the field annually and creating a large military establishment in London.[2] It also necessitated new financial expedients. Though Parliament was generous, the King's ministers had to negotiate long-term loans with bankers in the City of London, who organized themselves into the Bank of England (1694) and the loans into a National Debt. This Whig scheme, disliked by the Tories, signalled the new prominence of the moneyed middle classes, chiefly merchants, in the political equation. It proved itself by paying off the Flanders army (1696), but taxes to service the debt soon became a source of grievance and concern. In the same year a Jacobite attempt to assassinate William caused Parliament to pass an act that would keep it in session when a monarch died: an unprecedented power.

By the Treaty of Ryswick (1697), England obtained a truce and Louis's recognition of William, but not domestic peace. The Commons waged a campaign against the standing army and the National Debt; the Whig 'Junto' who had formed the war ministry yielded to Tories, though both parties were undisciplined and ill-defined, being cross-cut by court, city and country alignments. William made two secret treaties with France: a show of independence (reminiscent of Charles II) that infuriated Parliament when it became known in 1701.[3] Louis soon contravened Ryswick by occupying fortresses and recognizing 'James III' as King of England on James II's death; Parliament responded by fixing the Crown on the House of Hanover if Princess Anne died childless, while William – and Anne's favourite, Marlborough – negotiated an alliance with Holland and Austria that set a collision course with France (1701).

But William's death (1702) made the War of the Spanish Succession Queen Anne's – it occupied virtually her whole reign – and Marlborough's. He was, like William, both diplomat and general, but a bolder tactician whose decisive victories checked Louis XIV's ambitions. The partisan strife of these years, however, did not spare even him. The Tories, lukewarm in prosecuting the war, gave way to another Whig war ministry, which was slow to make peace when opportunity offered; national war-weariness brought the Tories back in 1710, and Marlborough's fall followed the Whigs'. During their season in the sun, the Tories negotiated the Treaty of Utrecht (1713), ending English involvement in European land wars for twenty-five years, but Anne's death sent them into an arctic winter of opposition, for the Whigs were the staunch Hanoverians.

Although the most notable undertakings of Anne's reign – the defiance of Louis and the Union with Scotland (1707) – were the work of Whig–Tory coalitions, the party divisions were now real, and went deeper than politics. In a major realignment of social forces, 'the Whigs, largely Chapel and trading, gradually overcame the Tories, mainly Church and land'.[4] Dissenters and merchants, who fared better in the Revolution Settlement and war years than did the landed aristocracy, supported the Whig emphasis on trade and a Protestant succession. The Tories, less buoyant economically, were smeared as Jacobites, which some of them were; High-Church Tories still saw dissent as a greater threat than popery. Steele's Sir Roger de Coverley is a neat dissection of the Tory country squire: loveable, harmless, and hopelessly obsolete. The religious, social, and political questions were all vexed and entangled in Anne's time, during which voting along party lines became established, and the bitter invectives of wrangling factions periodically alarmed monarchs and disgusted citizens.

Yet beneath the turbulence there was solidity. Britons were free from tyranny, free to make and spend money.[5] Whigs and Tories could bicker and recriminate, but the Constitution and the rule of law remained intact. Upon Anne's death the Regency Council and the Lords Justices named the Elector of Hanover King of England, just as Acts of 1701 and 1705 said they should, and George I took the throne unopposed. The Whigs, winners of the general election, did not get a free ride: taxes on the debt, post-war readjustment, and political hatreds led to mob violence in London in 1714–15, and a Jacobite rebellion in Scotland lasted through the autumn of 1715.[6] But the government were equal to each challenge, passing the Riot Act, establishing a Sinking Fund and despatching an army to check the rebellion, which had little support in England. The involvement of several prominent Tories with the Pretender further discredited their party; henceforth the Whigs had only themselves to fear.

With the passing of the Septennial Act (1716) – extending the normal life of a Parliament to seven years – the Whigs took possession of their Augustan inheritance. The Revolution and Constitution have now become historical facts; 'the political system is in harmony with the great political forces, and the nation has settled . . . in a position of stable equilibrium'.[7] Most problems could be dealt with legally. The Bangorian controversy over church authority led to the repeal of two acts aimed at Dissenters (1717–18); the South Sea Bubble, a huge speculation fraud with political repercussions, brought on the 'Bubble Act' (1720–21). A network of alliances kept English armies at home, while the Royal Navy handled a desultory war with Spain. Foreigners such as Voltaire joined English poets, philosophers, and dramatists in praising the achievements and effects of British liberty; at a time when most of Europe was still subject to autocracy, the first Hanoverians were conceding to the people's representatives such ancient royal prerogatives as forming ministries, dissolving Parliament, and distributing patronage. The isle was thriving.

One man's stable equilibrium, however, strikes another as a 'deadness of all serious political controversy'.[8] Both are right: for with stability came stagnancy. Under the long prime ministry of Robert Walpole (1721–42), England had in effect a one-party system (Tory participation in another Jacobite plot renewed the Whigs' lease in 1723). Walpole, a skilled Parliamentary and financial manager, stood for peace and mercantile prosperity when colleagues wanted to involve England in expensive wars; he was instrumental in establishing such fundamentals of modern British government as the common responsibility of the Cabinet and the leading role of the Prime Minister. But he also became increasingly identified with the corruption that kept Parliament a Whig gentleman's club and himself in office. 'Every man has his price' was his motto, according to numerous articulate critics. Under Walpole, the famous 'liberties of England' were compromised by rigged elections, bribery, votes bought, and places sold.

Walpole adroitly survived the accession of George II and became a close friend of the new King and Queen Caroline, whose support he needed: some fellow Whigs ('Patriots') were opposing his 'peace and trade' policy. The Secretary of State, Lord Townshend, had by various alliances pushed England towards war with Spain; Walpole, with the King's help, made treaties with Spain and Austria and got rid of Townshend. Undeterred thus far by opposition in or out of Parliament, Walpole sustained his greatest reverse in the area where he had been most successful – excise taxes – withdrawing the Excise Bill of 1733 (which would have taxed tobacco) under tremendous pressure. Though his skill in damage control saved his ministry, he was left in a weaker position, worsened by a quarrel between George and the Prince of Wales that gave the opposition a focus. The death of Queen Caroline (1737) deprived Walpole of an important ally at a time of rioting in Scotland and war debates in Parliament, yet he was still sufficiently strong to force passage of the Stage Licensing Act of 1737, thus muzzling some of his noisiest critics.

Only at a comfortable distance is it possible to take A. R. Humphreys's view of the age as a halcyon interval of poise and peace between seventeenth-century political and religious crises and the wars and industrial unrest of the Regency.[9] At the time it must have seemed lively enough, despite the settled Whiggery.

Intellectual culture

> We shall not have much reason to complain of the
> narrowness of our minds, if we will but employ them
> about what may be of use to us. . . . Our business here is
> not to know all things, but those which concern our conduct.
> John Locke, *An Essay Concerning Human Understanding*
> (1690)

If the diverse energies of Augustan thinkers have a common denominator, it is their keen sense of limits. Seventeenth-century Englishmen,
like a nation of Hamlets, had multiplied their troubles by trying to play
God, ran the argument; the antidote was reduced presumption, a level
of aspiration commensurate with our modest capacities. As Alexander
Pope put it, versifying Locke for the ages: 'Know then thyself,
presume not God to scan;/The proper study of Mankind is Man'. So
Augustan poets, operating in Milton's shadow, settled for what they
could do well: the anti-epic satirizing dullness or triviality, the polite
or self-mocking pastoral, the conversation poem, the moral essay in
verse. Prose satire, dominated by Jonathan Swift, mocked man as a
Gulliver, reduced him to a Lilliputian, or magnified his Brobding-
nagian grossness. Addison and Steele packaged philosophy and literary
criticism for the middle-class tea-table in *The Spectator*; Defoe made the
ordinary man and woman the subject of prose fictions such as *Robinson
Crusoe* and *Moll Flanders*. It was an era of familiar, mid-level prose in
the journalistic essay, the proto-novel, drama, satire, even philosophy.

Various readings can be given to this trend. One author, a church
historian, sees it as a reaction to Restoration conflicts: 'The prevailing
exhaustion demanded an interval of peace, and the eighteenth century
provided it. The Hanoverian Age was content with an unheroic
temper'.[10] He is thinking of Anglicanism's subservience to Walpole and
the squirearchy, and the rise of Deism, a religious philosophy that
sought Christianity's doctrinal essence or minimum. But a historian
of ideas finds the absence of heroic gestures suitable to a less bellicose
age, and most modern historians welcome the more relaxed humanism
of the eighteenth century.[11] Although Englishmen of this period were
still, by and large, believers, they held back from taking controversial
positions on abstract matters:

> For forms of government let fools contest;
> Whate'er is best administer'd is best:
> For modes of Faith, let graceless zealots fight;
> His can't be wrong whose life is in the right.

Pope's sensible if unheroic lines represent a profound recoil from seventeenth-century excesses, disguised as an urbane wave of dismissal.

Another area of backlash was 'wit'. The reaction, beginning around 1690, came from two different angles. The moral reform movement attacked wit as vicious, senseless, and irreligious. 'Who can see his native land undone by wit?' asked Richard Blackmore:

> The mob of wit is up to storm the town,
> And pull all virtue and right reason down.
> Quite to subvert religion's sacred fence
> To set up wit, and pull down common sense.
>
> ('A Satyr Against Wit', 1700)

No mental reflex is more characteristic of the period than this appeal against 'wit' in the name of 'right reason' and 'common sense' – rarely defined – and reformers such as Blackmore now enjoyed royal support.

At the same time, philosophy was undercutting wit as intellectually irresponsible. In his *Essay Concerning Human Understanding*, Locke undertakes to explain why 'men who have a great deal of wit . . . have not always the clearest judgement or deepest reason'. Wit for Locke is a 'quickness and variety' in throwing together similar ideas for 'entertainment and pleasantry': a *synthetic* quality. Not only does appreciating wit require 'no labour of thought'; it is actually an 'affront' to examine wit 'by the severe rules of truth and good reason', since it is 'not perfectly conformable to them'. Besides, this examination would necessarily be conducted by the diametrically opposed *analytic* faculty, judgement, which is careful 'to avoid being misled by similitude' (Book II, Ch. 11, no. 2). To Locke, and Pope, wit is a risk limited by judgement: ''Tis more to guide than spur the Muse's Steed;/Restrain his Fury, than provoke his speed'. Addison had to discriminate between true and false wit in order to salvage anything from the category.

Locke's was the premier achievement in Augustan letters. His *Treatises of Civil Government* (1690), by deriving all legitimate authority from the consent of the governed, provided not only an answer to Hobbes's argument for absolutism and a rationale for the English Revolution, but a platform for the American and French Revolutions. 'Man being born . . . with a title to perfect freedom and uncontrolled enjoyment of all the rights and privileges of the law of nature', reasons Locke, 'no one can be put out of this estate and subjected to the political power of another, without his own consent'.[12] The version of the 'state of nature', as different from Hobbes's as could be imagined or desired, led of course to opposite political conclusions: rulers needed subjects, not the reverse.

Locke's *Essay Concerning Human Understanding* gave eighteenth-century psychology its starting-point, demolishing 'innate ideas' in favour of an empirical model in which ideas and knowledge derive from sensory experience; this opened the way to Hume's scepticism, once Bishop Berkeley had shown the unreliability of sense data. Similarly, the treatment of faith and revelation in Book IV (and in *The Reasonableness of Christianity*, 1695), by stressing reason, played into the Deists' hands.[13] Locke's influence remained enormous in several fields, including literature, for over a century; Addison and Pope circulated many of his ideas to the general reader between 1710 and 1735. If Locke was an 'intellectual middleweight', as detraction charges, perhaps that was what the Augustans wanted. He himself was deferent to the heavyweights: 'everyone must not hope to be a Boyle . . .; and in an age that produces such masters as the great Huygenius and the incomparable Mr *Newton* . . . it is ambition enough to be employed as an under-labourer in . . . removing some of the rubbish that lies in the way to knowledge' (Epistle to the Reader). A 'philosopher' would still write on politics, psychology, and religion, but accepted pure science as a separate and superior discipline.

Was it an Age of Reason? Often enough, reading Locke, Pope's or Addison's essays, Newton's *Principia* or *Opticks*, one is inclined to think so. 'Reason must be our last guide and judge in everything', wrote Locke; reason must even judge whether an alleged revelation is truly divine, and whether it conforms to empirical reason. Though divine and 'natural revelation' (i.e. reason) may reveal 'the same truths', the latter 'will always be certainer to us'.[14] Yet Locke demonstrated how frail reason's empire is, how 'imperfect' words are, how easily our ideas become 'obscure', 'confused', 'fantastical', and falsely associated with unrelated ideas.[15] The same ambiguity occurs in Pope's *Essay on Man*. Judgement in literature and reason in life are recommended precisely because 'wit' and emotion are so strong: 'The action of the stronger to suspend/Reason still use, to Reason still attend'. Pope was a realist, however – 'Thicker than arguments, temptations throng' – and inclined to pessimism on this score: 'What Reason weaves, by Passion is undone' (II. 77–78). Against his famous epitaph on Newton, 'Nature, and Nature's Law lay hid in Night./God said, *Let Newton be!* and All was *Light*', must be set his question here: 'Could he, whose rules the rapid comet bind,/ Describe or fix one movement of his mind?' (II. 35–36).

Reason, then, while much discussed and prescribed, was understood to be weaker than 'the passions'. The 'Age of Reason' label is further challenged by the century's roster of mad or eccentric intellectuals, and by the school of philosophy known as Optimism. Reacting partly against Hobbes (as too materialistic), partly against Locke (too rational), the Optimists posited a 'moral sense' analogous to common sense. Their Bible was the Third Earl of Shaftesbury's *Characteristicks* . . . (1711). Shaftesbury had been tutored by Locke, who, Shaftesbury wrote, 'struck at all fundamentals, threw all *Order* and *Virtue* out of the World'.[16] Shaftesbury discovered that a 'Sense of right and wrong' is our 'first principle'; Nature inclines us to good, and God may be understood as 'the best-natur'd one in the World'. This doctrine was widely embodied in literature. Pope, who borrowed Locke's psychology for the *Essay on Man*, based his cosmology on Shaftesbury's idea that 'everything is govern'd, order'd or regulated *for the best*, by a designing Principle, or Mind, necessarily good and permanent'. Dramatists found that the 'moral sense' made the reform of any character credible. Other prominent Optimists were Bolingbroke, Richard Steele, and Francis Hutcheson, who wrote equations to measure benevolent actions, based on 'the *greatest Happiness* for the greatest Numbers'.[17]

Underpinning most philosophy and criticism in the period was the multifarious concept of NATURE, sometimes invoked as a deity. Apostrophized by Shaftesbury as the source of the Good, the Beautiful and the True, defined by Pope as the body whose soul is God, NATURE included the natural world, human nature, and the divine scheme that animates them: i.e. the way things are, plus why they are that way. One corollary was Deism: looking through Nature up to Nature's God. Another was neoclassicism: following the ancients, whose 'Rules' are but 'Nature Methodiz'd' (Pope). NATURE was exciting because it was 'still the same', uniform throughout time, uniting past with present and serving as 'the *Source*, and *End*, and *Test* of *Art*'. Pope (and Locke) urged readers to 'follow NATURE'; so had the Delphic Oracle counselled Cicero.

In the eighteenth century, however, the network of verities implied by NATURE was breaking down. Nature poetry passed from the conventional artificialities of Pope's pastorals to the greater realism of Gay's *Shepherd's Week* (1714), a burlesque, and James Thomson's *Winter* (1726), where direct description supplants pastoral devices. More and more critics had trouble reconciling the rules with their love of Shakespeare, while an enlarged reading public – one of the period's most significant developments – cared little for the rules; they wanted something entertaining and 'novel'. Dramatic innovations, from Rich's pantomimes to Fielding's political burlesques, rivalled the traditional genres; in poetry, blank verse began to challenge the heroic couplet. Music and architecture developed somewhat differently, but the Georgian world of letters began to evince more interest in the 'many-coloured glass' of contemporary life, as opposed to the 'white radiance' of Nature's 'Universal Light'.

Theatre and society

Many of the new plays acted by . . . his Maj^s Comedians
are scandalously lewd and Prophane, and contain
Reflections against his Maj^s Government . . . do not
presume to Act any new Play till you shall have first
brought it to my Secretary, and Receive my Directions
from him . . . you shall answer the Contrary att your
Perill.

> Robert Spencer, Lord Chamberlain (1697)

The pendulum of social tolerance that had swung so far right with
Cromwell and left with Charles II sliced back through the centre
during the 1690s, catching drama off-stride. Encouraged by sovereigns
who sporadically issued proclamations against immorality and whose
lord chamberlains were trying to regulate drama, moralists founded
societies to suppress vice and reform manners, and attacked the stage
as a sink of wit, Hobbism, and Restoration excess. Robert Gould's
'The Playhouse: a Satire' (1689) was the first salvo; three more attacks
in 1694–95 preceded Jeremy Collier's *Short View of the Immorality and
Profaneness of the English Stage* (1698), a famous and effective sum-
mation of Puritan objections to drama.

Despite some notoriety as a non-juror and an absolver of Jacobite
traitors, Reverend Collier in the prevailing climate felt free to lash the
dramatists' 'smuttiness of expression; their swearing, profaneness, and
lewd applications of Scripture; their abuse of the clergy; their making
their top characters libertines, and giving them success in their
debauchery'. His first sentence defines the function of drama as moral
instruction: 'The business of plays is to recommend virtue, and
discountenance vice'. If one accepts this premiss, the rest follows
logically; the stage has failed in its mission and must be reformed. By
1700 many dramatists could have accepted this end, but not Collier's
means: he understood 'instruction' as giving examples to follow,
whereas comedy had traditionally shown vices and follies to avoid. No
critic but a shrewd polemicist, Collier understood as well as any
modern demagogue what can be achieved by maintaining a simple
position forcefully enough. Moreover, he documented his charges
exhaustively from post-Restoration plays, and must be allowed, on
occasion, an almost rakish wit: 'The modern poets seem to use smut
as the old ones did machines, to relieve a fainting invention. When
Pegasus is jaded, and would stand still, he is apt, like other tits, to run
into every puddle' (Ch. 1).

Answered by several dramatists and critics, Collier defended his work and was seconded by other reformers. Generally, the moralists had the better of it. Congreve and Vanbrugh proved ineffective as pamphleteers; Dryden – from whom a major critical statement might have been expected – admitted the fault but passed on the blame: 'a banisht Court, with Lewdness fraught,/The Seeds of open Vice returning brought'.[18] John Dennis's *The Usefulness of the Stage* (1698) was the most substantial reply, but twenty-eight years later he had to answer William Law's *Absolute Unlawfulness of the Stage-Entertainment*. Between 1695 and 1710 especially, the reformers had the support of monarchs, a good segment of public opinion, and the Anglican establishment, including the Archbishop of Canterbury.[19]

Moral pressure also came from the audiences, which from the 1670s became more heterogeneous, i.e. less courtly. After 1689 the social norm was middle to upper-middle class: a group more likely to reflect prevailing (or developing) moral standards in the community than were courtiers.[20] Our best witness to this shift is John Dennis, who in 1702 noted that the courtiers and gentry of Carolean theatres had given place to *nouveaux riches*, foreigners, and business men.[21] As he recalls, 'that was an age of Pleasure', of 'Ease and Plenty', whereas 'there are ten times more Gentlemen now in business than there were', and what with war, taxes, and political factions, they 'come to a Play-house full of some business', 'meerly . . . to unbend'. The tired business man has arrived, and with him, thinks Dennis, a lower standard of taste in drama. While the educated Carolean audiences conversed of 'the Manners and Humours of Men' and were thus 'qualified . . . to judge of Comedy' at least, the playgoers of 1702 discuss 'Interest', politics, and property, and lacking education are 'not qualify'd' patrons. Nor could their taste be refined by courtiers, for 'the Court of *England* at present has other things to mind than' drama.

Details of Dennis's analysis, and his conclusion that 'the English were never sunk so miserably low in their taste, as they are at present', can be questioned. The 'due application' he attributes to Carolean audiences sounds like selective memory, and the tastes of these 'qualified' judges we know often ran to boorish, ragtag entertainment. Theatre patrons are still described as fashion-conscious socialites in 1705, and as 'affluent' in the 1720s.[22] But even scholars who reject the 'courtier stereotype' of Restoration audiences accept Dennis's basic assertion that more playgoers were bourgeois by 1700. Nor did the return of some royal patronage to Hanoverian theatres reverse the social broadening of their clientele.

It is at least arguable that post-1690 audiences, being more democratic, more representative of London (perhaps English) life, encouraged or forced dramatists to break Restoration stereotypes and search for new, more humane formulas, but the traditional view sees a decline in public taste and 'a period of confused and mediocre writing'.[23] What is clear is that drama's attempt to 'internalize' the moral reform movement – in Steele, for example – while it did clean up the plays, was on the whole a costly failure. The effort to *humanize* drama is another story, owing more to Optimism than to Collier.[24]

As conditions changed, the theatres endured a period of retrenchment. Control of patents passed from courtiers (Davenant, Killigrew) to entrepreneurs (the Richs) or actors (Betterton, Cibber), seldom in an orderly manner. The 'United Company' (1682–95) fell apart when Thomas Betterton led a revolt of veteran actors to Lincoln's Inn Fields, leaving Christopher Rich at Drury Lane with a rump of young or second-rate players including Colley Cibber, whose autobiography remains our best primary source on the period. After various struggles, Betterton's company moved to the Queen's Theatre in the Haymarket built by John Vanbrugh (1705), who (along with Congreve) received a new patent from Queen Anne. At least, in the tumultuous years that followed, London was again supporting two acting companies. The Queen's, an opera-house, proved acoustically unsuited to spoken drama; Vanbrugh and Congreve departed within a year; their successor acquired disgruntled actors from Drury Lane, which was drifting into variety shows; and Rich was 'silenced' by the Lord Chamberlain, who agreed to let the actors have Drury Lane and the opera singers the Queen's.[25] Ultimately, after more shuffles, Rich was expelled from Drury Lane, the actors (now led by Cibber) returned (1710), and a 'triumvirate' of actor-managers ran the theatre successfully for some years under a licence.

The deaths of Queen Anne and Rich necessitated fresh arrangements in 1714. Richard Steele was made 'governor' of Drury Lane, then given a new patent. Cibber and other actors, however, continued to manage the theatre, even after Steele's virtual exclusion (1720), and received a fresh twenty-one-year patent in 1732. The sale of the theatre (1733) led to a change of managers, another actors' secession, and a turbulent decade. Meanwhile Rich's son John, only twenty-two, got the Davenant patent renewed and moved into the theatre his father had just remodelled in Lincoln's Inn Fields (1714), where he specialized in pantomime and opera. In 1732 he opened a new theatre in Covent Garden, and bought the Killigrew patent, dormant since 1682. The hegemony of these 'official' theatres was, however, challenged by the new 'illegitimate' playhouses: the Little Theatre in the Haymarket (1720) and Goodman's Fields (1729). The King's (formerly the Queen's) Theatre remained an opera house, primarily the preserve of foreign singers and dancers.

Through all these readjustments the repertory and benefit systems continued and the physical theatres changed little: pit, boxes, and galleries still faced a candlelit proscenium stage. The 'apron' was shortening – Rich cut back Drury's forestage by four feet in 1696, much to Cibber's disgust – yet the proportions and dimensions of Edward Shepherd's 1732 Covent Garden were nearly those of Wren's Drury Lane (as altered by Rich). The stage was shallower and the auditorium longer, the proscenium arch narrower and higher, and the seating capacity increased from under a thousand to about fourteen hundred, but the designs remained close kin. Goodman's Fields was a smaller version of the same plan, seating (by 1732) about 750, with a mere nub of a forestage. The use of 'scenes and machines' increased slowly, yet, except for novelties such as the transparent scene, lighting and scenery hardly progressed. For a sense of life in these and the provincial theatres, one goes to contemporary memoirs such as Charlotte Charke's (Cibber's zany daughter), who describes performing before drunks, and teaming up with another actress to interweave dialogue from three different tragedies in one performance, just for fun.[26]

Early-eighteenth-century drama survived the moral reform movement by adopting much of its programme, and effected a compromise with the Lord Chamberlain over censorship for a while; but after 1715 the arrangement collapsed. Under the 'Steele patent' at Drury Lane, Cibber managed to defy the licensing authority of the Master of the Revels. In fact, the government did little to regulate drama from 1715 to the 1730s, with celebrated exceptions in 1719–20 and 1729.[27] Rarely were plays censored before production, and the patent monopoly was broken by new playhouses. One of them, the Little Theatre in the Haymarket, became in the 1730s a strident mouthpiece of the political opposition to Walpole, and eventually, through the Stage Licensing Act of 1737, the Prime Minister obtained the strict pre-censorship of plays and closure of the non-patent theatres he had been seeking. The Act has been defended as well as attacked from that day to this, but it certainly restricted the outlets for drama in London, and narrowed the range of what could be said or suggested on-stage. Ironically, the muzzle that the reformers had long wanted on drama was finally attached by Robert ('I am no Saint, no Spartan, no Reformer') Walpole in order to protect his political position.

Notes

1. A. R. Humphreys, 'The Social Setting', in *From Dryden to Johnson*, edited by Boris Ford (Harmondsworth, 1965), p. 30.

2. J. P. Kenyon, *Stuart England* (Harmondsworth, 1978), p. 274.

3. See Kenyon, pp. 282–88; and George M. Trevelyan, *A Shortened History of England* (Harmondsworth, 1959), p. 373.

4. Bonamy Dobree, *English Literature in the Early Eighteenth Century* (Oxford, 1959), p. 9.

5. Humphreys, p. 32, elaborates the point.

6. See J. H. Plumb, *England in the Eighteenth Century* (Harmondsworth, 1950), p. 53.

7. Leslie Stephen, *English Literature and Society in the Eighteenth Century* (1904; London, 1963), p. 20.

8. Trevelyan, p. 381.

9. Humphreys, p. 29.

10. Gerald R. Cragg, *The Church and the Age of Reason* (Harmondsworth, 1960), p. 117.

11. See Basil Willey, *The Seventeenth-Century Background* (1934; New York, 1955), p. 269.

12. Willey, p. 265, quoting John Locke, *Treatise of Civil Government*, II, 87 and 95.

13. George Sherburn argues that Locke's work eventually undermined both reason and faith. See *The Restoration and Eighteenth Century*, second edition (London, 1967), p. 704.

14. See *An Essay Concerning Human Understanding*, Book IV, Chapter 18, nos 4–6, 8, 10; and Book IV, Chapter 19, no. 14. See also Willey, pp. 278–79.

15. From *Essay*, Book II, 19–23: Laurence Sterne's favourite chapters.

16. Dobree, p. 259, quoting Locke, *Several Letters* (1716). The following quotations are from Shaftesbury's *Characteristicks of Men, Manners, Opinions, Times* (1711).

17. *An Inquiry into the Original of Our Ideas of Beauty and Virtue*, Treatise II, Section III, quoted by Dobree, p. 261.

18. Epilogue to Vanbrugh's adaptation of Fletcher's *The Pilgrim* (1700). See also Dryden's Preface to *The Fables* (1700) and 'Cymon and Iphigenia' therein.

19. See Calhoun Winton, 'The London Stage Embattled: 1695–1710', *Tennessee Studies in Literature*, 19 (1974), 9–19.

20. See John Loftis, 'The Social and Literary Context', in *The Revels History of Drama in English*, edited by T. W. Craik and C. Leech, 8 vols (London, 1975–83), v (1976), 18; and Harry W. Pedicord, 'The Changing Audience', in *The London Theatre World, 1660–1800*, edited by Robert D. Hume (Carbondale, Illinois, 1980), pp. 239–41, 242–46.

21. In his 'Large Account of the Taste in Poetry'. See *The Critical Works of John Dennis*, edited by Edward N. Hooker, 2 vols (Baltimore, 1939–43), I, 287–97.

22. Richard Steele, Prologue to Vanbrugh's *The Mistake* (1705); and Loftis, p. 24.

23. Sherburn, p. 884; see also Dobree, pp. 13, 223, 229.

24. See Frederick W. Bateson, *English Comic Drama 1700–1750* (Oxford, 1929), pp. 8–11; and Calhoun Winton, 'Sentimentalism and Theater Reform in the Early Eighteenth Century', in *Quick Springs of Sense*, edited by L. S. Champions (Athens, Georgia, 1974), pp. 97–112, especially p. 99.

25. See Marion Jones, 'Actors and Repertory', in *Revels History*, V, 123–25; and Judith Milhous and R. D. Hume, 'The Silencing of Drury Lane in 1709', *Theat. Jour.*, 32, no. 4 (1980), 427–47.

26. See *A Narrative of the Life of Mrs Charlotte Charke*, edited by L. R. N. Ashley (Gainesville, Florida, 1969), pp. 204–5.

27. See Loftis, p. 30; and Cibber, *An Apology for the Life of Colley Cibber, Comedian* (1740), Chapters 7 and 16.

Chapter 8
Sorrows Like Your Own: Augustan Tragedy

Then crush'd by Rules, and weaken'd as refin'd,
For years the Pow'r of Tragedy declin'd;
From Bard, to Bard, the frigid Caution crept,
Till Declamation roar'd, while Passion slept.
          Dr Johnson, Prologue for Drury Lane (1747)

Though Dr Johnson's famous lines are not the whole truth about early-eighteenth-century tragedy, they are a part of it. His couplets describe the type of Augustan tragedy known as 'neoclassical' or 'Franco-Roman': deferent to 'the unities' and other rules of the ancients and the French, mindful of decorum, simplicity, and reason yet indulgent of rhetoric, seeking to achieve intensity and evoke admiration through a few concentrated effects. Addison's *Cato* exemplifies the kind.

Yet the neoclassical style was just one of several types; plays like *Cato* had to compete with heroic, pathetic, and neo-Shakespearean tragedies. Most successful plays blended these modes, but only the neoclassical and pathetic approaches maintained genuinely independent existences: while one finds an occasional heroic or Shakespearean effort (all sides paid lip-homage to Shakespeare), more often these are passing chords in a play fundamentally Classical or pathetic. To be sure, significant changes occurred over these forty-eight years. Most of the tragedies cluster in four periods: 1694–1701, dominated by the pathetic and heroic styles; 1712–15, when vaguely Shakespearean pathos vies with neoclassicism; 1719–21, a time of general confusion; and 1730–36, when pathetic bourgeois tragedy gains a decisive advantage. Johnson's Prologue deals with the neoclassical and heroic modes, but not with pathetic tragedy, by 1737 the preferred tragic idiom, and the genre's most significant innovation in this age. It signified the erosion of the older tragic vision wherein nobility was possible, and its replacement by a limited democratic perspective in which middle-class protagonists made edifying mistakes, and suffered (as Nicholas Rowe put it) 'sorrows like your own'.

As the traditional genres fragmented, the critical sense of them grew softer. *The Mourning Bride* (1697), customarily called 'Congreve's only tragedy', turns out to be a tragicomedy. Not only does the disguised hero Alphonso (long presumed dead) reappear and gladden his 'mourning bride' Almeria, but their friends are triumphantly preserved and their enemies slain. At the level of plot, it *seems* tragic because the slain include Almeria's father, the villainous King Manuel, and Queen Zara, whose only sin is her passionate love for Alphonso. Moreover, one has the *impression* of tragic events from the accumulating weight of captives, prison cells, murders planned and executed, setbacks for the good and power for the bad, gloomy tomb scenes and the grave-yard poetry so admired by Dr Johnson:

> How reverend is the face of this tall pile;
> Whose ancient pillars rear their marble heads,
> To bear aloft its arch'd and ponderous roof,
> By its own weight made stedfast and immoveable,
> Looking tranquillity! etc.
>
> (II. 1)[1]

In praising this speech as 'the finest poetical passage he had ever read', Johnson was talking for victory, defending his authority and his position, which he later qualified to an appreciation of a twelve-line 'description of material objects'.[2] Though dramatically effective, the speech is part of a pattern of verbiage, especially noticeable in the static first act, with its long, ranting speeches, and in the third. The women are especially fond of extended description, for which Congreve will usually stop the show; Almeria is 'too much upon the whine', and sufficiently boring to justify Knights's calling the play dull.[3] There are some chestnuts − 'Music hath charms to soothe a savage breast'; 'Heaven has no rage/Nor hell a fury, like a woman scorned' − yet much of the poetry is strained, as if Congreve (three years in writing the play) were uncomfortable with serious blank verse.

The Mourning Bride needs only rhyme to make it a full heroic drama, complete with love, honour, operatic artifice, success for the princi-pals, and even a conquest of Granada; but the heroic mode continues to soften. Congreve emphasizes the pathos of his heroine's plight in several prolonged scenes, and his hero weeps for 'ill-fated Zara' amid the almost Jacobean bloodiness of Act v. The Dedication boasts 'a moral whose end is to recommend and to encourage virtue': a reference to the last scene, where Manuel's conscientious son Garcia is required to note the justice of Heaven, 'For blessings ever wait on virtuous deeds' − this a year *before* Collier. Despite a plot that strains belief, the Prologue invokes Nature, because 'only nature can affect the heart'. Congreve calculated well, and his play became one of the eighteenth century's favourite 'tragedies'.[4]

Certainly it is the most considerable of the age's tragicomedies. Dryden's *Love Triumphant* (1694) was an anticlimax to a mighty career; Mrs Centlivre's two negligible attempts failed; Rowe's *Tamerlane* (1701?) and *Ulysses* (1705?), called tragicomedies by Addison, have little intrinsic interest.[5] John Dennis's *Iphigenia* (1699) was a spectacular failure, but his *Liberty Asserted* (1704) enjoyed a modest run and stands apart from the pack. Set in Canada, it is an unusually *outdoor* play by eighteenth-century standards, recounting Indian and European wars in the snowy forests. The 'noble savage' Ulamar, leading the pro-British Iroquois against the Hurons and French, proves to be the half-breed son of a French noble. When they meet, Ulamar eloquently convinces his father to leave the service of France and fight for British Canada. Dennis's heavy-handed patriotic rants let slip the possibilities inherent in this experimental concoction, but it has entertaining moments and a fresh scent.

Addison's attack on tragicomedy as a 'monstrous invention' (*Spectator*, no. 40, 1711) may help account for a drop in its popularity. One other worth mentioning is John Gay's *The Captives* (1723?), which calls itself 'a tragedy'. A drama of intrigue during the Persian Wars, it is told straightforwardly, in moderate language. Gay's style is understated, almost perfunctory, as when the Median King hears that his wife has committed suicide after the failure of her assassination plot: 'Her foul treachery/My soul detests. But love will force a tear'. (v)[6] The restraint may be a bow to decorum, or Gay's dry mock of the age's rhetorical inclinations. Reading the play at Court, he 'stumbled at a stool' and 'threw down a weighty Japanese screen', frightening the ladies, reports Johnson.

Tragedy proper enjoyed something of a renaissance after its suspension in James II's reign. The rally was led by John Dryden, forced back to the stage after a four-year absence by his losses in 1689. *Don Sebastian* (1689) has divided critics sharply. Walter Scott pronounced it Dryden's masterpiece, not a surprising preference in the Romantic era; the high estimates of some recent writers, after a period of disfavour, are more impressive.[7] *Don Sebastian* reverts to the diverse, abundant material and free-wheeling treatment of early heroic plays, without sacrificing artistic discipline. Dryden weaves a complex tale of dynastic intrigue and high-born incest, concealed identities and cuckolding schemes, murder and mob violence, against a backdrop of Moorish–Portuguese warfare. Instead of the neo-Classical simplicity and emotive emphasis of *Aureng-Zebe* and *All for Love*, we have the atmosphere of double-plot 'tragicomedies' such as *The Spanish Friar*, in which comic and serious plots compete with each other.

Johnson analysed the mixture with his usual impartiality: 'sallies of frantic dignity . . . more noise than meaning . . . makes approaches to the possibilities of real life . . . passages of excellence universally acknowledged'.[8] One of these, the clash of Sebastian and Dorax (IV. 3), is justly famous; the speeches (as in most of the serious scenes) are strong, sensible, and not bombastic. But the wit-duels, *double entendres*, cuckolding farce, and satire on crowds that precede them constitute poor preparation. It is doubtful that *Oedipus Rex* itself, to which *Don Sebastian* has been compared, could survive such treatment. The basis for this comparison, the fifth-act discovery that the newlyweds Sebastian and Almeyda are half-siblings, is flimsy. Though hints of the relationship have been dropped, nothing in the play drives towards the discovery; when it occurs old Alvarez says that if someone had only told him they were already married he would have kept quiet; and the principals part to religious retirements. The mood is sombre but not tragic, no atmosphere of fatality having been generated.[9]

In his Preface, Dryden defended the 'under-parts of mirth' as 'depending on the serious part', but added that he was yielding to the power of the pit: since English audiences 'will not bear a thorough tragedy' any more than they will 'too regular a play', he could follow the unities 'only at a distance'. He also yielded to the notion of 'poetical justice' popularized by Thomas Rymer in meting out punishments, rather than insisting on probability. Dryden admitted that the play was too long, requiring the removal of 1200 lines to be actable: posterity agreed, and acting editions printed the shorter text.

Dryden returned to the classic simplicity (and Egyptian material) of *All for Love* in *Cleomenes; or, the Spartan Heroe* (1692), a better play than its reputation suggests. The defeated European general rusting in Alexandria is Cleomenes; his Egyptian siren is Cassandra; his 'Ventidius' is Cleanthes, an Egyptian ('Misplanted in this base degenerate soil') who is Egypt's harshest critic: 'O Aegypt! Aegypt! Thou are grown the lees/Of all the World; the Slime of thine own Nile'.[10] The family ties here are more complicated: Cleomenes has in tow a wife whom he loves, a Hotspur of a son, and a mother who breathes Spartanism; Cassandra is Ptolemy's mistress; and Cleanthes is the son of a state minister, Sosybius. Yet for three acts Dryden keeps the lines clean and strong. The scene in which Sosybius sounds Cleanthes's loyalty (III. 1) has a mature frankness, while that in the Temple of Apis (III. 2), amusingly censured by Collier, is a *coup de théâtre*.

In the last two acts, however, the action degenerates into mazy court intrigues, melodramatic devices (black veil, unknown benefactor), and sensationalism (a nursing mother so starved her milk is blood). Cleomenes too quickly distrusts Cleanthes in one of those contrived scenes where friends quarrel that they may be touchingly reconciled (v. 2). In a lame conclusion, these friends, having driven off attackers, give each other mutual death wounds and die embracing. Noting that 'our little band is lost/For want of these defenders', the surviving officer kills himself. Possibly Dryden's illness – Southerne had to write half of Act v for him – caused these shortcomings, which damage the play at its climax and weaken a hero not overly strong. Still, for long stretches, especially in Acts II and III, the writing is as good and the drama as vivid as anything Dryden had done since *All for Love*. He did not come up to this level again.

The bias Dryden imparted to post-Revolution tragedy was a neo-classical approach to heroic romance, still potent as an influence and strong in the repertoire. Thomas Southerne also used romance – heroic or domestic – but his bias tends to be pathetic. *The Fatal Marriage; or, the Innocent Adultery* (1694) has roughly the plot of Tennyson's *Enoch Arden*, with the burden of pathos shifted to the long-suffering female, and the additions of a villain, a violent resolution, and a comic plot not in the source, Aphra Behn's *The Fair Vow-Breaker*. The end-product is lumpy; Southerne knew he 'had no Occasion for the Comedy . . . but the present Humour of the Town' forced him, like Dryden, to compromise (Dedication). From the cracks between the prose comic scenes that dominate the first three acts grows real, passionate tragedy in blank verse. Isabella, her husband Biron, who disappeared three years ago, and Villeroy, the rich older man who finally induces her to remarry, are not problematical: never comic, they simply receive more emphasis in the second half. But Biron's younger brother Carlos seems to be playing at comic love-intrigues in the early acts, and when he proves to have been evil all along – intercepting Biron's letters to their father and forging cold answers, pressing Villeroy to marry Isabella, even hiring ruffians and attacking Biron when he returns – it is quite jarring.

The play was long a stock piece in versions that reduced the comic portions and changed the title to *Isabella*: a significant re-emphasis, but not a distortion of Southerne. The distresses of Isabella as she begs Biron's father to pity her poverty, reluctantly yields to Villeroy's addresses while the creditors bay, and raves her way to suicide after Biron's murder, constitute the play's *raison d'être*, and link Otway's Monimia and Belvidera to Rowe's 'she-tragedies'. Southerne acknowledged that Mrs Barry as Isabella 'made the Play' (Dedication).

Pathos also fuels *Oroonoko* (1695), another borrowing from a romantic novella by Mrs Behn. Again Southerne added a comic under-plot (this one quite licentious), for which the audience is blamed: 'Your different tastes divide our poet's cares:/One foot the sock, t'other the buskin wears'.[11] Again the comic relief was excised in the eighteenth century and the alteration endured. Oroonoko's distress, however, is more heroic than domestic, for he is a prince of Angola, tricked into slavery by an English sea captain (whom he later kills) and taken to Surinam. Reunited with his wife Imoinda and befriended by some

English, Oroonoko is feared and mistreated by other planters, especially after he heads a slave rebellion. At this point Behn's hero is captured and cruelly executed, but Southerne allows his to kill the treacherous governor and commit suicide, as Imoinda has done. The novella is one of the earliest manifestations of anti-slavery sentiment, some of which survives in the play.

Despite its pot-boiler tendencies, *Oroonoko* is a genuine tragedy whose exotic trappings half concealed a theme of indubitable relevance to Stuart England: the human cost of the imperial drive. Even well-disposed English cannot save Oroonoko from their system; while they exclaim at the procession of slaves ('O miserable fortune!'), the captain remarks, 'There's nothing to be done without it, boys. I have made my fortune this way' (I. 2). Compared to most tragedies of the age, this is a bold leap into real, if distant, issues. Oroonoko himself, given certain conventions, is an adequate protagonist. Many have criticized his rants and his ability to speak good blank verse – the first in the play – as he arrives from Africa, but his poetry is the customary stage symbol of his rank, and his bombast is at least strongly provoked. Oroonoko is comfortably ensconced when a former servant urges him to lead a rebellion of their people to free them all (including Imoinda's unborn child) from the label 'slave'. The Prince is caught in a clash of codes more complex than love versus honour: a desire to live peacefully, and gratitude to some English friends, versus *noblesse oblige* and lingering resentment. But Oroonoko's unwillingness to slay the traitor Hottman – his *hamartia* – brings the planters' militia down on the slaves, who 'fall upon their faces crying out for pardon' (IV. 2). A disillusioned Oroonoko, persuaded by emotional appeals to submit, is betrayed to torture.

The play resists categorization. Southerne combines heroic, pathetic, and romantic tragedy with humanitarian sentiment; Oroonoko's speeches run the gamut from natural religion and ethics through righteous rant to satire, pathos, love, and honour. To all this Southerne felt compelled to add sex comedy. It is one drama that might have profited from an editing by Jeremy Collier.

The persistence of the heroic mode – even after Dryden's Preface to *Don Sebastian* pronounced love and honour 'the mistaken Topicks of Tragedy' – is noteworthy. The exploits of the hero-king William III could be adduced, but the tragedies were not rich in heroic kings. The Prince of Libardian in Mary Manley's *The Royal Mischief* (1696) is almost a comic butt – the old man married to a beautiful and passionate young wife – and though he gains sympathy by his resourcefulness in surviving the villains' machinations against him, his final mood is religious resignation. Manley's extravagant characters and plot are reminiscent of Lee and Settle, but the language is awkward rather than ranting. Similar efforts include Robert Gould's *The Rival Sisters* (1695) in heroic couplets, and Lord Lansdowne's moderately successful *Heroic Love* (1697).

Tom Durfey, whose two-part, ten-act *Rise and Fall of Massaniello* (1699) pretends to heroic scope and characters, was also among those attracted to Shakespeare. With heroic figures like the 'fisherman prince' Massaniello and flashy ones like Blowzabella, Dick Pimpwell, and Rock Brazile, a musical dialogue, heavenly visions, rape, and bloody spectacle, this is a motley production, chronicling a Neapolitan revolt as an Elizabethan might, and satirizing Jesuit plots in the Restoration manner. The play builds up a certain amount of power at this length; its exposé of arrogant patricians and revolting rabble, and its vision of the mob in command, stabling their horses in the cathedral, are compelling. Durfey evinces no gift for dialogue or emotion, and his ragged, turbulent, tedious play failed, but *Massaniello* shows how open to suggestions the genre was at century's end, and its flat prose foreshadows the language of eighteenth-century tragedy.

Divided allegiances were the rule at this time. Adapters sought to reduce Shakespeare to symmetry or melodrama (e.g. Colley Cibber's *Richard III*, 1699). John Dennis, theoretically a neoclassicist, produced startling *mélanges*. Catherine Trotter sought to emulate Otway and Southerne in *The Fatal Friendship* (1698), a domestic tragedy that wrings pathos from its unlucky hero's poorly motivated bigamy; but Gramont's genius for the wrong action at the wrong time ranks with Sir Martin Mar-All's. Then Castalio becomes 'conscious of [Gramont's] superior virtue' and filled with 'awful admiration': suddenly Gramont seems exemplary, an anticipation of Steele. (v. 1)[12] A moment later, however, he accidentally stabs Castalio to death. Like most young writers – she was nineteen – and her era, Trotter was an anthology of styles. It would have been risky to predict in 1699 what the eighteenth-century tragic mode would be; certainly the ascendancy of the pathetic was not obvious.

With the appearance of Nicholas Rowe, however, tragic pathos acquired a new apostle and Augustan tragedy its chief ornament. Indeed, Rowe is frequently termed the premier tragedian of the eighteenth century, although the competition is admittedly sparse. Often his success was both popular and critical, immediate and lasting: three of the top-performing Restoration and eighteenth-century tragedies were Rowe's, and they survived well into the nineteenth.[13] Generations of actresses welcomed the roles of Arpasia, Calista, Jane Shore, and Jane Grey. Even the implacable William Archer saw in Rowe 'a return to sanity . . . a born dramatist . . . an eye for character . . . a note of real pathos'. And though pathos was his forte, Rowe also respected the neoclassical restraints (more as time went on), sounded the heroical trumpet early in his career, and echoed Shakespearean tragedy later, especially after his critical edition of Shakespeare (1709). Perhaps he owed his mastery of blank verse to that discipleship; 'No living Englishman could write blank verse more beautifully than Mr Rowe', which is doubtless why generations heard and read him with pleasure.[14]

Rowe's earliest plays, essays in the heroic–pathetic, are little esteemed today except as harbingers of his later work. *The Ambitious Step-Mother*, an oriental palace intrigue, grows from the theatre of Lee and Settle, yet the Dedication reveals that Rowe wanted to follow Otway and perhaps Southerne. 'Terror' is subordinated to 'Pity . . . an uneasiness . . . not altogether disagreeable' that derives from 'Good-nature': the rhetoric of benevolist philosophy from the Latitudinarians and Cambridge Platonists to Shaftesbury and beyond. The deaths of Amestris and Cleone are attempts to achieve this tragic pity.[15] Rowe himself preferred *Tamerlane* to all his other plays, and it was his most frequently performed, thanks to its political associations.[16] Tamerlane – of all people – represents King William and delivers Whiggish homilies on freedom, power, moderation, virtue, etc.; Bajazet is a ferocious caricature of Louis XIV as tyrant and megalomaniac. So pure and unadulterated are Tamerlane's good and Bajazet's evil that the play has been read as a struggle between godly and satanic champions.

In *The Fair Penitent* (1703) Rowe found his true *métier*, which he explained in the Prologue, a manifesto for domestic tragedy: 'Long has the fate of kings and empires been/The common business of the tragic scene.'[17] Though such stories are wondrous, 'We ne'er can pity what we ne'er can share'; and exciting a 'generous pity' is 'one of the main designs of tragedy' (Dedication). 'Therefore an humbler theme our author chose,/A melancholy tale of private woes': here you will find 'sorrows like your own'.

His chosen vehicle was Massinger and Field's *The Fatal Dowry* (1619), which he simplified by focusing on the penitent girl and her villainous seducer, Calista and 'gay Lothario', rather than on the avenging hero. Imagine Juliet, seduced and jilted by Romeo, marrying Paris and being found out by his best friend: you have the structure of *The Fair Penitent*. A skilful blend of character, emotionalism, and edification, it became – after a slow start – one of Rowe's enduring successes. Lothario, another Don Juan, is a dangerously attractive rake who, thought Johnson, 'retains too much of the spectator's kindness'[18] Without submitting his resignation to comedy, the rake has become tragic material, ready for Richardson's Lovelace. Calista, whose sincerity has been debated, is almost equally enigmatic.

Rowe manipulates our emotions heavily, systematically. Calista's maid issues the first call for pity to Lothario –

> Have you put off
> All sense of human nature? Keep a little,
> A little pity to distinguish manhood –

in the opening scene, and serves as chief lamentor of her mistress's woes (II. 1). Horatio pities his friend, the groom Altamont (I. 1); when they fall out, they are reconciled via pity (IV. 1). Calista asks pity of her father (IV. 1). The fifth act is an emotional bath, as the wronged groom and crushed father are brought to forgive the dying penitent Calista. Rowe's structure highlights this pathos: the wedding occurs in II. 1, Lothario's death in IV. 1, leaving the survivors over six hundred lines in which to express strong feelings. Inevitably, Rowe sometimes overreaches. When Altamont soliloquizes on his swift descent from 'past joy' to 'anguish' (IV. 1), we are too aware of the playwright, laboriously engineering the contrast; and the opening of Act V – Calista in black by Lothario's bier, Faust-like rejecting the consolations of religion after a dismal song – seems hopelessly melo-dramatic now, although there is no evidence that eighteenth-century audiences found it overdone.

If pathos was the *dulce*, moral improvement was the *utile* of Rowe's tragedy. Horatio is an unflagging didact, warning the 'fair' to be 'cautious whom ye trust' (II. 2), and reminding us, 'to be good is to be happy', for 'Guilt is the source of sorrow' (III. 1). He gets the last cautionary word as Altamont is borne away: 'By such examples are we taught to prove,/The sorrows that attend unlawful love'. Collier-esque reformers take note: Augustan drama had accepted the burden of moral preachment.

After three unsuccessful plays, Rowe returned to domestic pathos in *Jane Shore* (1714), another 'she-tragedy' – he uses the term slight-ingly in the Epilogue – about a fair penitent. If the sincerity of Calista's repentance can be doubted, Jane Shore's cannot. Physically and mentally she has paid, and throughout the tragedy continues to pay, for having left her husband to be Edward IV's 'minion'; now that his brother Gloster – soon to be Richard III – is in power her days are numbered. The quality, the extent, and some of the details of her suffering make her a figure of sin and atonement like Mary Magdalene, or even – in her public penance (V. 1) – like Jesus, while the Virgilian epigraph likens her to Dido, comforted by her husband in the shades. Shore is in fact almost constantly at Jane's side, as 'Dumont', in their London hell. The incognito observer is a sentimental refinement, which Rowe uses well: Shore can assist his wife, and their reconciliation scene (v. 1) provides a catharsis of pity and forgiveness, though not of terror. Alicia provides a second she-tragedy, and the confrontation of the two women, one mad, one broken (v. 1), is a theatrical *tour de force*.

Jane Shore, like *All for Love*, is 'written in imitation of Shakespeare's style'; the Prologue also reverences (and envies) the Bard. Rowe's story is a kind of entr'acte or subplot to *Richard III*, and when characters such as Gloster, Catesby, Ratcliffe, and Hastings meet, Rowe evidently tries to be 'Shakespearean'. 'The state is out of tune', proclaims Gloster. (III. 1)[19] But Rowe falls well short of his model – the exposition is awkward (Catesby and Ratcliffe should be hung for redundancy), the counsellors are flat, melodramatic villains – and his focus is on minor figures in Shakespeare and Holinshed. Whereas a modern would take such a course for purposes of philosophical satire, Rowe is carrying out his programme of domestic tragedy, and dramatizing the ballad he extols in the Prologue: two aspects of the democratic movement in Georgian literature that also includes the novel and Gray's 'Elegy'. Rowe's 'Shakespeareanism' is of the Augustan variety from the parallel of Gloster with Cromwell (I. 1) to the moral tag: 'Let those who view this sad example know/What fate attends the broken marriage vow' (v. 1). Rowe ends on this flat note, and it is difficult to find uplift in a tragedy where the good fall while the bad thrive, but the century's greatest players, from Anne Oldfield to David Garrick, made it a vehicle for moving performances.

Lady Jane Grey (1715), another 'lady in distress' tragedy, culminates in Queen Mary the Bloody's execution of the heroine and her husband as Protestant martyrs, but the heroine is 'Beauteous Saint' rather than fair penitent, and Rowe's emphasis falls less on private agony than on patriotic and religious concerns. The Prologue invokes William III's 'Great Hand', while Jane Grey's dying call for a redeemer,

> a Monarch of the Royal Blood
> Brave, Pious, Equitable, Wise and Good
> In due season let the hero come,

was a clear reference to George I, whose son is complimented too.[20] Thus the play's whole movement is from 1688 to 1714. Rowe had reason to be grateful to the Hanovers, who had just given him the Laureateship and other emoluments, but neither his timely Protestantism nor his pitch for the 'silent Tears' of the 'Fair Judges' sufficed to establish the play in audiences' favour.

Lady Jane Grey may be Rowe's supreme expression of the trials of the virtuous; in other areas, though, it falls off. His blank verse, while still competent and smooth, has lost warmth and tension, become poor

in images, less capable of eloquence. Bishop Gardinar and the Earl of
Pembroke are strong parts, but Guildford – the chief male role – is not.
His attempt at profundity is painful as he wonders

> Where all this mazy Error will have end. . . .
> There is but one End certain, that is – Death:
> Yet ev'n that Certainty is still uncertain.
>
> (I. 1)

Arranging his hasty marriage with Lady Jane, who is in mourning,
Guildford sensitively agrees to forgo a groom's usual pleasures, 'And
sleep far from thee'. Fine: but when he adds, 'on the unwholsom
Earth/Where Damps arise, and whistling Winds blow loud' (II. 1), he
strays from the point. Then he worries lest their joys be blighted by
'Some Evil terrible and unforeseen'. 'Unforeseen'! Where has he been
during the first two acts? Nonsensical moments like these do much to
undermine, without entirely destroying, the impact of Lady Jane, who,
when invited to regal greatness, responds like a Banks heroine: 'Is it
not rather, to be greatly wretched?' (III. 1).

Rowe's favourite word, after 'pity', is 'fatal'. It recurs frequently
in his tragedies, especially *Fair Penitent* and *Jane Shore*, and was also
common in comtemporary tragic titles, from *Fatal Marriage* and *Fatal
Friendship* to Aaron Hill's *Fatal Vision* (1716) and *Fatal Extravagance*
(1721). 'Fatal' became a cant word, substituting for a *belief* in fate that
writers thought tragedy should embody. In Rowe (at least), 'fatal'
usually means 'mortal' or 'disastrous', not 'destined'. He conveys no
sense of 'tragic fate', which is larger than his chosen canvas. Rowe's
humbler approach to tragedy lies entirely through the affective
domain, in which we sympathize with affliction and pity suffering.

Although the various Augustan tragic styles are mixed in Rowe's
plays, his pathetic and Shakespearean proclivities increasingly
outweighed the heroic and neoclassical elements as time passed; he
grew casual about the unities. On his right, however, some dramatists
of a more formal persuasion cultivated not only the unities but
decorum and polish. Technically, their line extended from Dennis's
Appius and Virginia (1709) to Lewis Theobald's *Electra* (1714), but their
'moment' was 1712–13: the last time the practitioners of neoclassical
tragedy were able to cluster their successes and dominate a period.

The tragedy that made neoclassicism fashionable was Ambrose
Philips's *The Distrest Mother* (1712), an adaptation of Racine's *Andro-
maque* (1667) and one of the high-water marks of French influence on
English drama. Some of his fellow Whigs supported the play, Steele
touting its 'superior Thoughts and Maxims of Conduct' in *Spectator*,

no. 290 and donating the Prologue, Addison perhaps working on the Epilogue. Despite this claquery, and the heavy dependence on Racine, the play pleased critics, remained in repertoire throughout the century, and still repays reading.

'Neoclassical' here means several things: sharp focus on a few characters; a tightly woven, symmetrical plot from the classics; an emphasis on decorum; the unities. The protagonist, Hector's widow Andromache (the distressed mother), is held captive by Pyrrhus, King of Epirus, despoiler of Troy and son of her husband's murderer Achilles; her goal in life is to protect her son by Hector, Astyanax, also a captive, from the Greeks. Pyrrhus is willing to shield Astyanax *if* Andromache will return his love, although this would offend the Greeks, who have sent Hermione (daughter of Menelaus and Helen) as a bride for him, and Orestes (son of Agamemnon) to demand Astyanax. Orestes, however, is carrying the torch for Hermione, who has fallen for Pyrrhus. In the Preface, Philips explains why he (like Racine) suppressed a son that Andromache is said to have had by Pyrrhus: 'it is more conformable to the general notion we form of that princess . . . to represent her as the disconsolate widow of *Hector*, and to suppose her the mother only of *Astyanax*. Considered in this light . . . she moves our compassion much more effectually'.[21] Given our received 'image' of Andromache (from Homer, Virgil, etc.), to have encumbered her with the son of her captivity instead of Hector's would have been indecorous, less productive of 'compassion', which, here as in Rowe, is *the* tragic emotion.

From Andromache and her dilemma – marry the son of her husband's murderer or lose her son – Philips draws considerable pathos and creates a psychological portrait of duress. Her maternal love, ultimately triumphant, is contrasted with the tumultuous erotic love – ultimately punished – that rushes Pyrrhus, Hermione, and Orestes into madness or violent death. During a lucid interval, Pyrrhus fondly imagines himself cured of his love for Andromache in a metaphor from Lucretius sometimes used to explain how we can enjoy witnessing a tragedy.[22]

> The merchant thus, in dreadful tempests tost,
> Thrown by the waves on some unlook'd for coast,
> Oft turns, and sees, with a delighted eye,
> Midst rocks and shelves the broken billows fly!
>
> (II. 1)

Orestes's plight is similar, though simpler: he is mad for a woman whose only use for him is tactical. The two women are also paralleled, each having to make a terrible decision respecting her love.

But the plot's most neoclassical quality is its *stasis*, seen in Pylades's word-portrait of Pyrrhus's abiding dilemma (I. 1) and in the notion of repeating cycles: Orestes as another Paris, and seeing the Furies again. Although a descent into Momism (not in Racine) weakens the ending, overall the play provides interesting characters with good speeches, and handles dramatic situations with artful restraint. In *The Distrest Mother* the precepts of neoclassicism look workable.

Philips's success encouraged Addison to complete a tragedy he had started years earlier and bring it on-stage as a rallying-point for Whig patriots concerned about liberty under Anne's Tory ministers. Alexander Pope supplied a patriotic Prologue, though he had advised against production. But Pope was wrong: *Cato* was tremendously popular, until declamation went out of style. The set speeches that now seem dead were effective claptraps when intoned by a Booth or a Quin. Both Whigs and Tories applauded the rousing appeals:

> Do thou, great Liberty, inspire our souls,
> And make our lives in thy possession happy,
> Or our deaths glorious in thy just defence.[23]

Both parties gave Barton Booth (Cato) a purse: the Tories for resisting Caesar, whom they read as Marlborough, the Whigs for *representing* Marlborough! *Cato* was a political–theatrical event.

Critics were coeval with admirers, however. John Dennis denounced the love plot (among other things) as absurd, Cato as too virtuous for a tragic hero, his suicide as dramatically unwarranted ('Is this . . . his boasted firmness?'), and Addison's application of 'the rules' as inconsistent. For Dennis, *Cato*'s popularity was a sinister omen: 'the very Tragick Stage appears to be sinking, since the great Success of one very faulty Play prognosticates its Ruin more than the Miscarriage of twenty good ones' (the latter covering his own case).[24] Dr Johnson pronounced many of Dennis's arguments unanswerable. Most Georgian admirers limited themselves to praise of Addison's 'noble sentiments' and the 'spirit of liberty and patriotism'.

Today the contravention of poetic justice and the old Stoic's suicide are less disturbing than his lack of any emotion other than patriotism, especially when his son Marcus's body is brought to him:

> Welcome, my son! here lay him down, my friends,
> Full in my sight, that I may view at leisure
> The bloody corse, and count those glorious wounds.
> How beautiful is death, when earned by virtue!

(IV. 4)

One looks for the recoil against *dulce et decorum est*, some realization that *my son is dead*, as in Pirandello's 'War', but it never comes. Juba's rhetorical question, 'Was ever man like this?' is worth careful consideration. Only if this lack of passion for life constitutes Cato's *hamartia* is the play a Classical tragedy; if Cato is wholly good, as Addison seems to think, the action is disgusting, not tragic. And the two love stories, a sop to the public, are extraneous and distracting.

Whatever *Cato*'s faults, as stage tragedy or text, Addison's purpose is clear. In the Prologue – amid some dubious redefinitions of tragedy – Pope makes a significant connection:

> He bids your breasts with ancient ardor rise,
> And calls forth Roman drops from British eyes. . . .
> Britons, attend: be worth like this approved,
> And show you have the virtue to be moved.

Cato is made a test of the national response to patriotism: the first link between Rome and Britain. The Numidian Prince Juba lectures his countryman Syphax on Rome's *mission civilisatrice*:

> To civilize the rude, unpolished world,
> And lay it under the restraint of laws;
> To make man mild and sociable to man;
> To cultivate the wild, licentious savage. . . .
> Make human nature shine, reform the soul,
> And break our fierce barbarians into men.
>
> (I. 4)

The reference here is to Augustan Rome, not Cato's or Caesar's, and by extension to 'Augustan' England. *Cato* is an advertisement for 'Augustanism': the cultural effort to reform the factious English into worthy heirs of Virgil, Horace, Ovid, and the best institutions of imperial Rome. Dryden's satires on the 'headstrong, moody, murmuring' mobs of 1680 and his translation of *The Aeneid*, Locke's redesign of Hobbesian man, Shaftesbury's discovery of a moral sense, Swift's defence of the ancients, Pope's imitations of Horace, Addison's and Steele's dissemination of learning in their periodicals – also seek to pacify 'barbarians into men', to fit unruly Britons for the City of Good Sense. As in *All for Love*, Addison's Romans possess the qualities that English intellectuals wanted their countrymen to strive for; *Cato* could be subtitled *All for Rome*, with the understanding that 'Rome' stands for (Whig) England. Fielding's Parson Adams was right: *Cato* is a sermon, and the text is Augustanism.

The mediocre tragedies of the following years reflect a general
uncertainty over the relative value of the various styles. Susannah
Centlivre, a successful comedian, essayed tragicomedy. Two supposed
neoclassicists moved in opposite directions: Theobald into domestic
drama, Dennis into 'improving' Shakespeare; *The Invader of His
Country* (1719) undertakes to make *Coriolanus* ('Where Master-strokes
in wild Confusion lye') more regular. And the popular tragedies around
1720 suggest, if anything, a resurgence of interest in heroic themes.

Edward Young – the poet of *Night Thoughts* (1742) – used the
eastern hero-play as a vehicle for pathos in *Busiris, King of Egypt* (1719).
Listening to Busiris hurl heroic couplets at treason, or vaunt about his
valour, his bloodthirstiness, and his pedigree, one might think that
Maximin has returned. Some of the young men are also of this kind:
especially Prince Myron, with his love versus duty conflict (Act III).
The extravagant heroics (parodied by Fielding) are the play's weakest
aspect, however, and Young's real interest is elsewhere. Behind the
rants and the gaudy screen of orientalism is an inner sanctum of
sensibility: 'Memnon leaning on his father's tomb', voicing night
thoughts (I); Myron fainting at Mandane's rejection (II) and Memnon
at the news of her rape; the emotional auto-flagellation of Act IV ('See
how they writhe . . . hear them groan!'). The Prologue is forthright
about Young's aim:

> To touch the soul is our peculiar care;
> By just distress soft pity to impart,
> And mend your nature, while we move your heart.

Pleading for the ladies' tears ("tis your virtue swells into your eyes'),
Young aligns himself with Hutcheson's benevolist philosophy: 'By
your afflictions you compute your gain,/And rise in pleasure as you
rise in pain'. The rampant emotionalism recalls Otway, some gestures
towards Shakespeare and Dryden notwithstanding. Unfortunately
Busiris is pathetic in both senses: affective and inept. Young knows
what he wants but not how to obtain it; he is 'saying, not showing'
passion. Yet the overthrow of Busiris as a consequence of the rape –
'The tyrant falls, Mandane strikes the blow' – is neatly managed. The
weakness is language rather than plot.

In *The Revenge* (1721), Young's Shakespearean ambitions are clearer
and the heroic note is muted. Zanga the Moor plays Iago to General
Alonzo's Othello and Leonora's Desdemona. Despite the switch of
'Moorishness' from hero to villain, the latter's view of things is
brought forward into a half-light. He seeks revenge for a father slain
and an angry blow that Alonzo once gave him; he expresses compunc-

tion, yet proceeds with his machinations; at the last he feels regret. Alonzo, on the other hand *is* darkened: he appropriates Leonora from his friend Don Carlos (Cassio), becomes jealous and has him murdered. It is almost as if *Othello* were rewritten as *Iago*. Unsubtle intensity gives *The Revenge* some power, and it was performed for a century, but much of its radiance is reflected.

John Hughes's *The Siege of Damascus* (1720) also lasted until century's end, though the playwright did not outlive opening night. His early death (at forty-three) is a shame, for the quality of tragic writing in *Damascus* is often high; Hughes commanded a more genuine language of passion, with less rant, than did his contemporaries. The play belongs primarily to the heroic tradition, from the title's invocation of Davenant's 'opera' to the Epilogue's quotation of 'all for love'. The lovers, whom Hughes calls 'Heroic maid' and 'unhappy hero', conflate love and war in the style of chivalric romance. 'Welcome, thou brave, thou best deserving lover!' exclaims Eudocia; ''Twas love of thee first sent me forth in arms', Phocyas admits (Act I). His rejection as suitor to Eudocia by her father Governor Eumenes is straight out of *The Indian Queen*. This idiom prevails over the essays in Shakespearean soliloquy, the humane sympathy of the 'good Arab' Adudah for some Christians, and the prolonged pathos of the lovers' last meetings. Despite the limitations of this obsolescent mode, Hughes invests the confrontation of the lovers (after Phocyas has betrayed Damascus to spare lives) with strong and eloquent feeling.[25]

If the next seasons show any pattern, it is a drift towards pathos. Aaron Hill's *The Fatal Extravagance* (1721) has been called 'the first play of its time which deals with middle-class English characters in a "tragic" manner'; Elijah Fenton's *Mariamne* (1723), an oriental palace tragedy emphasizing the feelings of a distressed mother, was successful enough to draw Fielding's satiric fire.[26] Hill's version of *Henry V* also emphasizes the softer emotions. The pathetic, along with the other styles, however, lay fallow in the general dearth of tragedy for the rest of the 1720s.

The 1730s did not begin as if they would be characterized by domestic tragedy. Attention was initially focused on *Sophonisba* (1730), the first tragedy by James Thomson, already famous as a nature poet. Limiting the cast to seven characters, concentrating the action on one day at Cirtha, acknowledging Corneille (but not Lee) among his predecessors, Thomson chose the neoclassical approach to heroic action, with Dryden and Addison as his gurus. Sophonisba's patriotism is as fervent as Cato's, though it is for Carthage; Scipio, who belatedly issues a call to *Roman* duty, is not a sympathetic figure. Given the passionate warmth of the principals, the overall effect is that of an *All for Love* where Cleopatra turns patriotic. Masinissa plays Antony, torn between loyalty to Rome and love for a foreign queen, concluding that 'love is more than all'; without it, 'life were vile,/A sickly circle of revolving days' (III. 1). Sophonisba, however, marries Syphax and later Masinissa solely for political reasons: 'All love, but that of Carthage, I despise' (IV. 2). She is stronger than Lee's Sophonisba, but Masinissa makes a weak partner; his exclamation, 'Oh! Sophonisba! Sophonisba! oh!' was immortalized by Fielding's parody. Few of the long speeches possess histrionic appeal, and the ending is diffuse.

David Mallet's *Eurydice* (1731) also moves in heroic realms: Queen Eurydice of Corinth struggles against the tyrant Proclus for freedom and reputation in the absence of her husband Periander. Mallet is chiefly interested in wringing pathos from Eurydice's plight; the Prologue, advertising love, affliction, fear, and pity, pleads for the ladies' tears. Eurydice's position is that of Philips's Andromache: forced to agree to submit to a man she detests to protect a loved one, meanwhile planning suicide. The play's chief weakness is that the 'good' characters are either ineffectual or unfair, while Proclus is clever enough to make Periander take *his* word against Eurydice's. When Periander returns and expresses suspicion about Eurydice and Proclus, Leonidas – who has been at Court all along – is evasive: I haven't seen her much lately, she was in dire straits, I weep for your wrongs, etc. Finally he vouches for her, but Periander ignores him. Faced with her husband's stubborn distrust, Eurydice can only beg him to flee. Periander must hear his enemies confess that they slandered Eurydice before he believes her, and by then she has taken poison; he goes mad and dies raving. This demented conclusion, the credulity of Periander, the blandness of the blank verse, and an almost Senecan stiffness cripple the play.

George Lillo's *The London Merchant; or, The History of George Barnwell* (1731) shows that a strong enough demand will overlook the poor quality of the supply; the theatrical public must have been ready for bourgeois tragedy in prose. The classical variety was floundering, early domestic dramas such as *A Yorkshire Tragedy* (1606) and *Arden of Feversham* (1591?) were being reworked (the latter by Lillo himself), and recent approaches to 'private tragedy' by Otway, Southerne, and Rowe remained popular offerings. Lillo's actual source, however, was not a play but an old ballad about a naïve apprentice seduced by a courtesan and driven to steal and murder. Accepting the reformers' logic, Lillo declared that 'Plays founded on moral tales in private life may be of admirable use', and 'the more extensively useful the moral', 'the more excellent' the tragedy (Dedication). Lillo's originality lay in eliminating verse and aristocracy from tragedy (female villains were also rare); *The London Merchant* is in those respects a generic breakthrough.

Understanding Lillo's aims is one thing, appreciating his play quite another. Most modern readers find his prose heavy, his action and characters melodramatic, his glorification of commerce tedious, and his moralizing shallow. The obections and problems tend to cluster around Barnwell: young, innocent (Lillo cleaned up the ballad hero a bit), and initially passive, neither interesting, sensitive, nor profound, he makes an unimpressive tragic protagonist. Despite some far-fetched attempts to parallel his career with Satan's (see II. 2), Barnwell seems to the courtesan Millwood merely a 'whining . . . canting villain' (IV. 2), which is closer to the truth.

None of Lillo's 'good' characters is satisfactory; he does not know them well enough. They live in two dimensions, as their type-names reveal. Thorowgood the merchant is too righteous for Barnwell to approach: had he let him confess instead of cutting him short (II. 1), he could have helped. His priggish daughter Maria belatedly professes affection for Barnwell (V. 2): had she been more open earlier, he might have resisted Millwood. Barnwell's fellow-apprentice Trueman – potentially his rival for Maria's and Thorowgood's favours – is sus-piciously apt at rigging accounts ('Nothing more easy': III. 1); his unctuous manners and tactlessness with Barnwell suggest Uriah Heep and Austen's Mr Collins as descendants. The powerful figure of Mill-wood – cunning, ruined, beautiful, man-hating – dominates the play, but Lillo can see only the villainess.[27]

All such objections quarrel with stage success, however. *The London Merchant* won over sceptical audiences, including Pope and Fielding, and secured a regular place in the repertoire: Boxing Day, when apprentices were sent to ponder its lessons. Although Lillo had few followers in Georgian England – even abandoning the form himself – he found admirers and imitators on the Continent, notably Diderot and Lessing, whose *bürgerliches Trauerspiel* returned to England as melodrama about 1800.[28] Lillo had invented the problem play, 150 years early. Miscast as tragic protagonists, Barnwell and Millwood belong with the losers and victims of serious drama from Robertson, Ibsen, and Shaw onwards. But their play does not: cluttered with shopworn theatrics and superfluous baggage from Georgian commerce, it could not be revived without radical cutting of the turgid language. (It was no accident that the play succeeded best in translation.) In its present form it is too often, as Charles Lamb said, 'a nauseous sermon'.

Lillo impressed Germany again with *Fatal Curiosity* (1736), which begat the *Schicksaltragödie* (tragedy of fate). He drew material from an old pamphlet telling how a poor elderly couple murdered a 'stranger' for his jewels, only to discover he was their long-lost son. The play achieved a modest success at the Little Theatre in the Haymarket – though not equal to *The London Merchant*'s – and was revived or adapted throughout the eighteenth century. Some modern critics have ranked it above *The London Merchant* and even compared it to *Oedipus*.[29]

The first claim is dubious and the second overwrought: neither the language (blank verse) nor the plot will stand close scrutiny. If the diction is preferable to the earlier play's, it is still ponderous and image-poor, the metaphors in the occasional heightened passage seeming strained and self-conscious. Granting Lillo some strength of feeling and characterization – Old Wilmot is on a par with Millwood – his plot is defective. True, he sidesteps his first difficulty neatly: why does Young Wilmot not reveal himself to his parents at once? Because he 'would fain/Refine on Happiness. Why may I not/Indulge my curiosity', he wonders, 'to improve/Their pleasure by surprise?' (II. 1). 'It may, indeed,/Enhance your own', remarks the old servant Randal, adding, 'You grow luxurious in your mental pleasures'. Sentimental refinement is here both a tragic flaw and a plot device.

But why do his faithful sweetheart Charlot and his parents not recognize him? By shortening his absence from the pamphlet's fifteen years to seven, Lillo makes this point even stickier. He also has Young Wilmot present his parents with a forged letter of introduction supposedly from Charlot – yet it never crosses their minds that their faithful friend might come enquiring after the chap she sent round. In the pamphlet there is no such letter. Thus Lillo weakened the credibility of a story that already strained belief. *Fatal Curiosity*, despite its vivid depiction of grinding poverty, is melodramatic, and finally a less considerable play than *The London Merchant*, whose main action can at least be accepted.

Domestic tragedy in prose was continued by Charles Johnson in *Caelia; or, The Perjur'd Lover* (1732), a social problem play condemned for a 'low' scene in a brothel. The 'problem' is society's double standard: gentlemen find loopholes in their code of honour where women are concerned. Wronglove seduces Caelia, installs her in a brothel (remarking, 'I am so cool and yawning, and indifferent, and sick, and surfeited'), then goes off to marriage and more wenching (I. 2). Bellamy, a family friend, asks Wronglove how he reconciles his pretensions to gentility and conscience with his treatment of Caelia. But this is *love*, protests the rake. 'Are Women then excluded from all moral Right and Justice?' asks Bellamy (II. 1). After Caelia is imprisoned and falls ill, Bellamy confronts Wronglove again: 'Does this not concern you? does it not concern me? does it not concern Humanity?' (IV. 3). Fatally wounded by Bellamy in a duel, Wronglove finally acknowledges Caelia as his wife and beneficiary. Though earlier inclined to a Millwood-like bitterness – 'He is as all Men are' – she now blames herself and, murmuring of 'the Waste', dies in her father's arms. The old steward points the moral: 'Blush, blush, ye Libertines'. Unabashedly sentimental, *Caelia* strikes a now familiar note:

> He [Johnson] would his humble Sentiments impart,
> In Words that flow directly from the Heart. . . .
> Encourage and reward him with your Tears. (Prologue)

Johnson's pathos and his excesses vitiate his art, but do not destroy his social vision; the overflowing emotions are not inappropriate to the situation presented. There are some resemblances to *Clarissa*, and Fielding's Epilogue only pretends to mock Johnson's concern. Intrinsically, *Caelia* is as good an example of prose domestic tragedy and the embryonic problem play as early Georgian drama affords.

Domestic or courtly, most other tragedies of the 1730s use sympathetic pity as their emotional cornerstone. Even Aaron Hill's translations from Voltaire – usually dismissed as neoclassically dull – rely as much on pathos as on heroism or Shakespeare; the prologues to both *Zara* (1735) and *Alzira* (1736) stress the copious weeping of Parisian audiences over the originals. Hill wrote, 'When tragedies are strong in sentiment' ('love of pity, and of liberty' is specified), 'they will be touchstones to their hearer's hearts' (Dedication to *Alzira*). In *Zara*, the more popular and readable of the two, we are exhorted to pity, first, old King Lusignan and the other Christian captives, including Zara; and then Sultan Osman, whose groundless jealousy of Zara leads him, Othello-like, to kill her and himself on-stage. *Alzira* asks sympathy for the crushed Peruvians, especially Alzira and her heroic lover Zamor, but also for Don Carlos, the cruel Spanish governor, as he learns to pity his subjects. Although both are interesting for the play of Voltaire's intelligence over religious and social ideas, their pathos is symptomatic of tragedy's drift into emotionalism.

Why the subversion of tragedy from terrible nobility to maudlin sympathy occurred at this time has occupied some good minds. Most agree that the Georgian *Zeitgeist* was inimical to the form. 'A society in which common sense is regarded as the cardinal intellectual virtue does not naturally suggest the great tragic themes'; 'grandeur was not to be counterfeited when the belief in its possibility was dead', so, 'turning from the hero to the common man, we inaugurated the era of realism'.[30] As the phrasing implies, this was not just a Georgian problem, but the birth of the modern condition. The question, 'How indeed should the exalted art of tragedy, which has traditionally dealt with the fate of singular individuals, flourish in the age of the common man?' was as pertinent then as now.[31] What makes early Georgian tragedy so awkward is that not everyone had abandoned the classical derelict, and 'realism' was still in the ways. 'The best that we can achieve is pathos', wrote Krutch in 1957; Lillo, Charles Johnson, and Hill could have said the same in 1737.

Notes

1. References are to *William Congreve, Complete Plays*, edited by A. C. Ewald (New York, 1956).

2. See James Boswell's *Life of Johnson*, edited by R. W. Chapman (London, 1957), p. 412 (16 October 1769); and Samuel Johnson, 'The Life of Congreve', in *Lives of the English Poets*, 2 vols (London, 1952), II, 25–26, 31.

3. [Francis Gentleman], *The Dramatic Censor*, 2 vols (London, 1770), II, 415; and L. C. Knights, 'Restoration Comedy: The Reality and the Myth', *Scrutiny*, 6 (1937), 122–43 (p. 122).

4. Emmett L. Avery, *Congreve's Plays on the Eighteenth-Century Stage* (New York, 1951), pp. 75, 100, 156. See also Maximillian E. Novak, *William Congreve* (New York, 1971), p. 122; but compare *Dramatic Censor*, II, 417.

5. On Centlivre's plays, see F. P. Lock, *Susanna Centlivre* (Boston, 1979), pp. 32–35, 39–42; and J. W. Bowyer, *The Celebrated Mrs Centlivre* (Durham, North Carolina, 1952), pp. 33–40, 47–51. On Rowe's, see J. Douglas Canfield, *Nicholas Rowe and Christian Tragedy* (Gainesville, Florida, 1977), pp. 46, 70–73; and Annibel Jenkins, *Nicholas Rowe* (Boston, 1977), pp. 37–51.

6. The text is that of *John Gay: Dramatic Works*, edited by John Fuller, 2 vols (Oxford, 1983), I. The anecdote below is recorded by Johnson, 'Life of Gay', *Lives*, II, 64.

7. Compare George Nettleton, *English Drama of the Restoration and Eighteenth Century* (New York, 1923), p. 93; and Allardyce B. Nicoll, *British Drama*, fifth edition (London, 1962), p. 148; with Eric Rothstein, *Restoration Tragedy* (Madison, Wisconsin, 1967), pp. 148–49; Earl Miner, in *Restoration and Eighteenth Century Drama*, edited by James Vinson (London, 1980), p. 61; and Bruce King, *Dryden's Major Plays* (London, 1966), pp. 165–77. Textual citations follow *The Works of John Dryden*, edited by E. N. Hooker and H. T. Swedenberg, Jr, 19 vols (Berkeley, Los Angeles, and London, 1956–   ) XV (1976, edited by Earl Miner).

8. 'Life of Dryden', *Lives*, I, 257.

9. Compare Arthur H. Scouten, 'Tragedy', in *The Revels History of Drama in English*, edited by T. W. Craik and C. Leech, 8 vols (London, 1975–83), V (1976), 267.

10. Quotations follow *The Dramatic Works of John Dryden*, edited by Montague Summers, 6 vols (London, 1931–32), VI.

11. Epilogue. Quotations and scene indications follow *Oroonoko*, edited by M. E. Novak and David S. Rodes (Lincoln, Nebraska, 1976).

12. Quotations come from *The Female Wits*, edited by Fidelis Morgan (London, 1981).

13. See E. L. Avery, 'The Popularity of *The Mourning Bride*', *Research Studies, State College of Washington*, 9 (1941), 115–16; and Jenkins, p. 145. For some high estimates, see Canfield, p. 1; and Bonamy Dobree, *English Literature in the Early Eighteenth Century* (Oxford, 1959), p. 245. On Rowe's gift to future actresses, see Charles Macready's *Reminiscences* (1875), Chapter 13. Archer's comments are in *The Old Drama and the New* (London, 1923), p. 167.

14. *Three Plays by Nicholas Rowe*, edited by James Sutherland (London, 1929), p. 27.

15. See Canfield, p. 13; and Archer, pp. 167, 230.

16. See Avery, 'Popularity'. From 1714 to 1815 *Tamerlane* was given in William III's honour on November 4 (his birthday) or 5 (the anniversary of his landing in England). For varying interpretations, see Jenkins, pp. 39–46, 148; John Loftis, *The Politics of Drama in Augustan England* (Oxford, 1963), pp. 31–36; and, opposing this, Canfield, p. 46.

17. Quotations and act/scene divisions follow Malcolm Goldstein's Regents Restoration Drama Series edition (Lincoln, Nebraska, 1969).

18. 'Life of Rowe', in *Lives*, I, 391. Lothario's appetite for women and aversion to marriage recall Mirabel in Fletcher's *The Wild-Goose Chase*. See also Margaret A. Doody, *Natural Passion* (Oxford, 1974), p. 113. On Calista, compare Nettleton, p. 175; and Canfield, pp. 129–30.

19. References to *Jane Shore* are to Harry W. Pedicord's Regents Restoration Drama Series edition (Lincoln, Nebraska, 1974). The suggested influences on the play include Banks's tragedies; see Dobree, p. 247; and Canfield, p. 146.

20. The Dedication parallels the Princess of Wales with Lady Jane as defenders of the faith. Quotations are from *The Dramatic Works of Nicholas Rowe*, third edition, 2 vols (London, 1720).

21. *The Distrest Mother* (London, 1776), p. vi; all quotations come from this edition. In general Philips follows Racine closely, but breaks up long speeches, adds something at the end of each act, and emphasizes extremes of pathos, violence, and madness. One scene is transposed from early to late Act IV.

22. See Baxter Hathaway, 'The Lucretian "Return Upon Ourselves" in Eighteenth-Century Theories of Tragedy', *PMLA*, 62 (1947), 672–89 (pp. 672, 675–76, 678). Dennis and Addison were among those espousing the theory.

23. Quotations and scene divisions from Q1, in *British Dramatists from Dryden to Sheridan*, edited by George H. Nettleton, Arthur E. Case, and George W. Stone, Jr, second edition (Boston, 1969). See their Introduction (pp. 473–74) for stage history.

24. See 'Remarks Upon *Cato*, a Tragedy', in *The Critical Works of John Dennis*, edited by Edward N. Hooker, 2 vols (Baltimore, 1939–43), II, 41–80 (pp. 43, 45, 52). Johnson's reaction is in his 'Life of Addison', *Lives*, I, 414. Thomas Wilkes praised the play in *A General View of the Stage* (London, 1759), pp. 31–33.

25. Johnson says that Hughes originally planned for Phocyas to apostatize, but the players forced him to settle for desertion. 'Life of Hughes', *Lives*, I, 453.

26. Nicoll, p. 195. On Fenton's play, see Scouten, p. 284.

27. Here I disagree with Cleanth Brooks and Robert Heilman, who think Lillo 'gives too much attention' to her: *Understanding Drama* (New York, 1945), pp. 183. Overall, however, their analysis is provocative.

28. *The Christian Hero* (1735), a spectacular heroic drama, and *Fatal Curiosity* are in verse. See C. F. Burgess, 'Lillo Sans Barnwell', *MP*, 66 (1968), 5–29 (pp. 11–12). On the dramatic history of the form see George Sherburn, *The Restoration and Eighteenth Century*, second edition (London, 1967), p. 897; Dobree, p. 255; and Peter Lewis, in *Restoration and Eighteenth Century Drama*, p. 105.

29. See *Fatal Curiosity*, edited by William H. McBurney (Lincoln, Nebraska, 1966), pp. x–xxiv; and Burgess, 'Lillo', pp. 6, 15. My quotations are from McBurney's Regents Restoration Drama Series edition.

30. Leslie Stephen, *English Literature and Society in the Eighteenth Century* (1904; London, 1963), p. 51; and Joseph W. Krutch, 'The Tragic Fallacy', in *The Modern Temper* (1957), reprinted in *Tragedy*, edited by Robert W. Corrigan (San Francisco, 1965), p. 280. See also Corrigan's Preface, p. ix.

31. John Gassner, 'The Possibilities and Perils of Modern Tragedy' (1957), in *Tragedy*, p. 405.

Chapter 9

Anything Goes: The Diversity of Comic Drama

The rules of English comedy don't lie in the compass of
Aristotle or his followers but in the pit, box and galleries.
George Farquhar, *A Discourse Upon Comedy* (1702)

Comedy laboured under fewer philosophical and cultural disadvantages
than did tragedy. The age of common sense and the common man was
attuned to the levelling tendencies of the comic spirit: three times as
many comedies as tragedies were written and produced. But quality
– except for a few gems in the first two decades – is another matter.
The pressures for moral reform, the hostility to wit, and the exhaustion of the Restoration style combined with the vigour of the comic
impulse itself to splinter the genre into a multiplicity of forms we can
call 'comic drama'. The 'genteel' type subdivided into 'manners' and
'reform' varieties; lower down, intrigues were popular and 'humours'
lived on. Farce flourished, as did burlesque. Late in the period, musical
entertainments and topical revues burgeoned. Augustan and early
Georgian comedy thrived but seldom excelled; we are impressed by
its energy and breadth, rarely by its depth.

The Old Guard

The first post-Revolution comedies came from familiar hands. In *Bury
Fair* (1689), Thomas Shadwell offered an old/new play as pivotal as its
date. The Prologue's talk of humours and 'general' satire, the play's
ridicule of French affectation, and the use of St Edmundsbury fair as
a microcosm of a hard-bargaining world reveal Jonson's continuing
influence.[1] The wit comedy, the banter about masks, and the use of
realistic detail to illumine character all continue Shadwell's Carolean
style. As in *The Squire of Alsatia*, characters both represent and discuss
ideas: Wilding debates libertinism and rural retirement with Bellamy;
Gertrude and the Fantast ladies argue about 'right conversation'.

In other respects, however, chiefly in being innocent and didactic,
Bury Fair has a new tone. Lord Bellamy is not ridiculed for telling
young Wildish that 'the immorality of [wenching] gave me anxiety of

mind', and waxing sententious about it. Bellamy joins Edward Belfond in *The Squire of Alsatia*, Rant in *The Scowrers* (1690), and Blunt in *The Volunteers* (1691) as teacher-figures; Shadwell in 1690 described 'the Education of Youth' as 'the most important business of this world' (Dedication to *The Amorous Bigotte*). Not that *Bury Fair* is heavy: there is a lot of country horseplay – inane reading but lively on-stage – and the disguise of La Roch as 'le Comte de Cheveux' (like the Fantasts, derived from Molière) also plays well. It was the most popular of Shadwell's post-Revolution comedies – for a dozen years.

Aphra Behn's *The Widow Ranter* (1689) mixes a serious plot (from a pamphlet) with an invented romantic farce in the manner of Elizabethan history plays or heroic drama.[2] General Bacon is a sort of Almanzor who falls for an Indian queen, but both finally die, leaving the stage to the Widow's comic world. Produced posthumously (and badly), it failed.

Dryden, who contributed the Prologue, scored a success with *Amphitryon* (1690), an elegant, energetic, luscious farce based on the classical legend and dramatizations by Plautus and Molière.[3] In his last comic work, Dryden brings the Olympian myth down to earth through such devices as Bromia's vulgarity and a proviso scene between Phaedra and Mercury.

The Restoration *farceur*, Edward Ravenscroft, thought *The Anatomist* (1696) 'the most trivial of any' of his plays: 'Yet it has stood the Test of the Stage'; and, reduced from three acts to one, it survived the eighteenth century.[4] As usual, Ravenscroft rifled French comedy (here, Hauteroche) for a *commedia*-based plot of witty servants helping young men keep young women away from dotards, and added touches of his own: more pratfalls, cruder bawdy, musical entertainments between the acts. Flat in print, *The Anatomist* has obvious stage appeal.

Tom Durfey turned to writing social comedies whose seriousness and originality have been gaining admirers.[5] *Love for Money* (1691) counterpoints bawdy Betty Jiltall, who counsels 'Love for Money ever whilst you live' (I. 1), with a hero and a dispossessed heiress both too proud to marry money. Durfey's style can still be boring, prolix, and farcical, but his plots are no longer contemptible, nor quite incredible; he is writing about a real world of mercenary intrigue and Jacobitism in Chelsea.

The Richmond Heiress (1693) also turns on the pursuit of a young woman's fortune, but is more satirical and hard-boiled: fortune-hunters, stock-jobbing cits, courtiers, dissenting preachers, and playhouse sparks all feel the lash. Even Frederick, the hero apparent, is finally judged mercenary, so the heiress Fulvia says 'no' to marriage and comedy. 'Since such a general defect of honesty governs the Age', she announces, 'I'll no more trust Mankind' (v. 5). This turn is well prepared by Fulvia's nightmare about Frederick, by his abandonment of Sophronia for a richer prize and his admission that Fulvia's fortune is crucial, and by a masque in which Love, Youth, Desire, and Avarice court Pecunia. Fulvia closes by quoting Sophronia (a 'female plain-dealer'): 'Interest governs all'. What distinguishes the play is the way echoes of Wycherley and Jonson coexist with a sudden crescendo of feminism. On-stage, it was a vehicle for actresses.

Both comedies are worlds removed from the inanities of *Madame Fickle* – perhaps Durfey had learned from Shadwell and Southerne – but the coarseness of some scenes in *Love for Money* and the earthiness and anticlericalism of *The Comical History of Don Quixote* (3 parts, 1693–94) brought down Jeremy Collier's wrath. *Don Quixote* is a hotch-potch of farce, song, sentiment, and various plots, some left dangling. Durfey's attitude towards Quixote wavers between indulgence and scorn, when the age was ready to take a mellower view of Cervantes's hero. Besides, the obscenities, Durfey admitted, offended some of the ladies. Taste was moving away from the old entertainer.

Of these veteran dramatists, Thomas Southerne made the most estimable contribution. Audiences enjoyed *Sir Anthony Love* (1690), a lively comedy with a 'breeches' part for the attractive comedienne Mrs Mountfort, but modern critics – deprived of this stimulus – have seen more to *The Wives Excuse; or, Cuckolds Make Themselves* (1691), a stage failure.[6] Beneath a familiar veneer of sexual intrigues, manners, and masks, the plays conducts a sympathetic enquiry into the plight of Mrs Friendall, who tries to live honourably with her philandering coward of a husband while fending off the advances of his friend Lovemore. In two fine scenes (IV. 1, v. 3), Lovemore propositions and Mrs Friendall rejects: eloquently and sensibly, without cant.

The quasi-cinematic flow of the first scene is technically sophisticated: servants waiting outside a concert discuss (and mimic) their masters and mistresses until a curtain lifts and the gentry advance, talking generally. Various tête-à-têtes and plot-lines emerge at intervals, one and another exchange between different combinations being highlighted as groups divide and re-form like primitive cells under a microscope. Stage directions give all the information necessary to organize this movement. Wycherley, Behn, and Shadwell approach this effect in some of their group scenes, but never achieve it so fully. The scene in St James's Park (III. 2) has this same mimetic complexity, full of quick shifts and brief surfacings. The final masquerade (v. 3) is another virtuoso display: successive actions move upstage until a 'Scene draws' to reveal Friendall with his 'mask' upon a couch. Theme and stagecraft come together here; we see the affair through the wife's eyes.

Whether audiences could not follow the crowd scenes, or disliked the wife's resistance or the couple's public agreement to separate, they received it coldly; a disappointed Southerne wrote only one more unsuccessful intrigue comedy before abandoning the genre. *The Wives Excuse*, however, influenced the treatment of marriage in subsequent comedy, and reveals Southerne's essential seriousness before he turned to tragedy.

New voices

Few literary careers have started as brilliantly as William Congreve's: his first play polished and praised by leading dramatists and loved by audiences, his second produced within a year. He was twenty-three, and already known as a poet, translator, and author of a 'Spanish intrigue' novel. *Incognita* (1692) 'imitate[s] dramatick writing' in its plot (said Congreve); it also, however, provides ironic comments by a Fieldingesque narrator – and this was a voice audiences would need, and miss, in some of his plays.

Although Dryden and Southerne immediately hailed Congreve as a champion of high comedy, a worthy successor of Etherege and Wycherley, and one whose plays combined *utile* with *dulce*, it is not immediately apparent why *The Old Batchelor* (1693) aroused such excitement.[7] Several well-worn plots fail to yield anything striking. Heartwell (the plain-dealing old bachelor) is surly to women yet falls for Sylvia (Vainlove's ex-mistress) and secretly 'marries' her; later, vastly relieved to find that the 'parson' was his friend Bellmour, Heartwell swears off marriage. Bellmour, after seducing Laetitia, wife of a city banker, Alderman Fondlewife, engages to marry the affected Belinda; her cousin Araminta, though, will make Vainlove wait. In the underplot, a sharper and a pimp trick a fool and a braggart into marrying Sylvia and her maid. Verbal froth is abundant, and there was enough anticlerical talk to offend Collier. With Betterton as Heartwell, Mrs Barry as Laetitia, and Doggett as Fondlewife, its popularity is no mystery, but why the intellectuals' excitement?

Language, chiefly: much of that 'froth' is wit. Asked by Vainlove, 'Could you be content to go to Heaven?' Bellmour replies, 'Hum, not immediately, in my conscience, not heartily. I'd do a little more good in my generation first, in order to deserve it.' (III. 1)[8] Congreve's style was the most elegant since Etherege's; echoes of the old music are everywhere, with masked women and satire on manners and matrimony underlining the continuity. Congreve has not yet found his own voice: he rummages through early wit comedy, finding scraps of humours, Wycherley, Etherege, even Davenant, so that the play seems pre-Revolution. But for Dryden and Southerne, whose praises admit the extent of the comic drought since 1676, the heavens had opened.

The Double Dealer (1693), a more original and interesting comedy, pleased literati but not audiences, and remained the least popular of Congreve's plays.[9] Its liabilities included licentiousness of speech and situation (to which moralists and some ladies objected), the gulf between the darkness of the conspirators and the lightness of the Froths and Plyants, and the demanding complexity of the rival intrigues. Maskwell generates both energy and problems as he manoeuvres to supplant his 'friend' Mellefont in Cynthia's affections and Lord Touchwood's will, while intriguing (and sleeping) with Lady Touchwood. His genius for duping people by telling them almost the whole truth, and his final quietism, are reminiscent of Iago; his appetite for a virtuous woman suggests Blifil. But Shakespeare was writing tragedy, and Fielding keeps Blifil's villainies shadowy until their final exposure, whereas Congreve gives Maskwell two long, self-disclosing soliloquies that make us feel dangerously superior to his victims. The second soliloquy (v. 1) stands condemned by Congreve's own Dedication: 'if he supposes anyone to be by, when he talks to himself, it is monstrous and ridiculous to the last degree'. Congreve also had to defend Mellefont, who ignores an early warning against Maskwell, from charges of credulity. Finally both Mellefont and the equally unsuspecting Lord Touchwood learn to 'mask well', disguising themselves as parsons to trap the conspirators.

The other plot is unproblematical, unless Sir Paul Plyant's tears of frustration (iii. 1) are taken seriously; the names Brisk, Froth, and Plyant reveal its character. Despite some awkward contrivances, Congreve seems to find himself in this 'school for scandal' underplot, yet the titular half of the play produces the closing moral – let villainy beware exposure! – which Congreve says the action was invented to illustrate (Dedication). Here he sounds uncomfortable. The overall effect is schizophrenic, as if a young Agatha Christie and a mature Noel Coward had contributed alternate scenes to a country-house play. Congreve claims to have followed the unities, but the unity of *action* is tenuous indeed, and though the Touchwoods may recall the Cockwoods, *The Double Dealer* lacks the coherence of *She Wou'd If She Cou'd*. Congreve's sense of evil is more artificial than Etherege's; compared to Lady Touchwood, Maskwell is a plaster toad in an imaginary garden.

After this misadventure, Congreve went back to the larger cast, rollicking humourists and free, almost farcical action of his first play in *Love for Love* (1695): his greatest, most lasting theatrical success.[10] The title, alluding to both *All for Love* and *Love for Money*, inducts us into a world at once familiar and fresh. A gallery of 'types' clusters around the wastrel rake-hero Valentine, who (being comic) does not have to give All, but must (after trying everything else) give Love for the Love of Angelica. Villainy creates no aesthetic problems here: the role is shared between the *senex amans* Sir Sampson, Valentine's heavy father, and the featherweight traitor Tattle.

Wit abounds on every level, cloying some palates: Tattle informs the country girl, Miss Prue, 'All well-bred Persons Lie. . . . Your words must contradict your thoughts; but your Actions may contradict your words' (II. 1). *Eros*, irreverence, and slurs on marriage are rampant enough to please unreconstructed Restoration tastes, but Collier was furious at Valentine's saying 'I am Truth' and at the marriage of Tattle and Mrs Frail as 'monk and nun'. The 'Wycherley connection' is stronger: both Scandal and Sailor Ben recall Manly. 'Since the *Plain-Dealer*'s Scenes of Manly Rage', says the Prologue, 'Not one has dar'd to lash this Crying Age'. Congreve does not *lash* – indeed he promises 'no ill-manners'! – but through Scandal, Valentine (in his mad phase) and Ben ('You don't think I'm false-hearted, like a land-man'), he hits a dozen targets glancing blows.

Congreve is most nearly original in Ben's character and Valentine's madness. The first of the stage's bluff tars, and an outsider who gives perspective on society, Ben brings a breath of salt air and a more spacious sense of life to comedy, which had become not only urban but indoor.[11] Similarly, the madness feigned by Valentine not only gives satire wider scope, but, like its Shakespearean analogues, enables the author to convey us from one level to another. Only a mad Valentine could (or would) tell Angelica, 'You are the reflection of Heav'n in a Pond, and he that leaps at you is sunk' (IV. 1). This is so different from the usual Augustan stage prose that one reader has posited an allegory built around the name Angelica and some religious images.[12] Scandal asks, 'Who would die a Martyr to Sense in a Country where the Religion is Folly?' (I. 1) and Valentine tells Tattle, 'you would have interposed between me and Heav'n [Angelica]; but Providence laid Purgatory [Mrs Frail] in your way' (V. 1). Religious imagery is thus applied to love and other subjects for purposes of wit and satire, not to lift *Love for Love* to metaphysical heights.

Congreve's only approaches to comedy in the next five years were theoretical. His 'letter' to John Dennis 'Concerning Humour in Comedy' (1695) shows how influential Jonson's concept still was in a refined form. A humour is now a 'singular . . . manner . . . Peculiar and Natural to one Man only', distinguishable from wit, folly, or affectation; oddly, it does not occur in women.[13] He reminded Jeremy Collier (1698) that comedy portrays the vices and follies of 'the looser sort of livers', not the manners of ideal humans. Yet Congreve remarked of stage fools, 'I can never care for seeing things, that force me to entertain low thoughts of my Nature'. He was not wholly comfortable with his age, his public, or his chosen genre.

In *The Way of the World* (1700) he *seems* to accept the conventions of his time and style, while pursuing a private course that criticizes or subverts them. The result is an ambiguous play that initially confused audiences and still divides critics, who call it everything from a masterpiece that 'justifies all Restoration drama' to a 'miserably limited' and 'merely verbal' set of conventions, alternately obvious and obscure.[14] The value of the characters, the function of the wit, and the meaning of the action remain debatable topics.

The question of 'morality' is typically tricky. Congreve publicly refuted Collier – and put a copy of his *Short View* among the Puritan tracts on Lady Wishfort's bookshelf – yet *The Way of the World* was cleaner than most recent comedies, including Congreve's. Of the two rakes, Mirabell, the 'good' one who succeeds, has reformed, putting his affairs behind him and seeking a well-dowered love-marriage; Fainall, the 'bad' rake who is carrying on adulterously with Marwood, fails, as Collier wanted.[15] The dialogue, though full of witty innuendoes, is never outrageously smutty. The play is also moral in the other sense – which Congreve doubtless valued more highly – of being serious about values, about right and wrong, without being patly moralistic. Is Mirabell's treatment of Mrs Fainall right? Is he any better than Fainall? Such moral quandaries are left for us.

The old legend that Congreve went on-stage after the première to chastise the audience for its plebeian taste and to announce his retirement is untrustworthy, yet it has emotional validity. His Dedication calls the public insensitive, the Prologue sneers at their manners, and the play attacks wits such as Petulant: 'hast not thou then Sense enough to know that thou ought'st to be most asham'd thyself, when thou hast put another out of Countenance?' (I. 1). Mirabell is preaching reformation of manners; *The Way of the World* is Congreve's most unflattering portrait of 'the town', and this did not help its reception.

The plot is as complicated as a Spanish intrigue's, and Congreve's structure increases the difficulty; like a sophisticated novelist, he alludes to events that have not been presented. In the first two acts, most characters are discussing occurrences that have already taken place off-stage. How can we understand Fainall's probing, 'What should provoke her to be your Enemy?' (I. 1) at first hearing? How could the uninitiated know that Mirabell's remark to Mrs Fainall, 'When you are weary of him, you know your Remedy' (II. 1) refers not to cuckoldry but to 'the writings', the *deus ex machina* that resolves the plot? Congreve demands a great deal of his audience, and many first-timers have problems following the action.

The basic idea, however, is simple: Mirabell and Millamant wish to marry, and to enjoy the six thousand pounds legacy that she receives only if she marries with her aunt Lady Wishfort's consent. What complicates it is the way of the world. Mirabell has offended Lady Wishfort, and is opposed by Fainall and his mistress Marwood, who hope to cut out Millamant and have the money descend to Mrs Fainall, Lady Wishfort's widowed daughter, where they can reach it. They undertake five schemes, from exposing Mirabell's courtship of Lady Wishfort as a sham to blackmailing her by threatening to expose Mrs Fainall's former affair with Mirabell and drag them through the divorce courts, a messy procedure.[16] Mirabell and Mrs Fainall devise four stratagems of their own, ranging from Waitwell's imposture of 'Sir Rowland' to the revelation that Mrs Fainall's own estate is entrusted to Mirabell; she and Lady Wishfort are not in Fainall's power. Mirabell is given Millamant, and the great legacy hunt is over.

If plot images an author's world, then this one (which I have simplified) depicts Congreve's society as very complex, demanding great skill and caution, and very mercenary. *Radix actionium est cupiditas*: nearly all of the action revolves around the six thousand pounds, and this money-drive gives a hard edge to the plot and a brittleness to many of the relationships that make it difficult to accept the idea of Congreve as a 'sentimentalist'.[17] That the play is moral – in either sense – and treats a love affair does not make it sentimental (indulgent of feeling) or romantic. Mirabell, like Dorimant, wants the woman *and* the money; he and Millamant love, but not blindly. Underlying their famous proviso-scene (IV. 1) is the realization that love alone cannot ensure matrimonial success, that there are no ready-made couples. Intelligent people will approach marriage pragmatically, seeking a *modus vivendi*. It plays so well because it is both a love scene, full of sexual tension, and a marriage-contract bargaining session. The new ethos of moral reform required the rake's marriage, but Congreve insists that his characters negotiate the commercial treaty first. It is a compromise – like the couple's – between Congreve and his audience, between the Restoration and the eighteenth century.

Nor is the rest more 'sentimental'. Lady Wishfort is treated as cruelly as most superannuated belles in comedy. The ending, always 'soft' in a sentimental play, features sharp exchanges of "tis the Way of the World, Sir!' and the ejection of villains. In the unkindest cut of all, the Fainalls' marriage is left intact, with a pious hope that they may 'live easily together' – after all this! When comedy became genuinely humane, such couples were parted, as Southerne had already done.

The Way of the World lives at the edge of a style and a set of conventions. Its seriousness about marital, legal, and financial issues is characteristic of the 1690s, yet nowhere before Mirabell and Millamant do they receive such a frank premarital airing. No other cast of characters is so witty, yet this is less a comedy of wit than of prudence. Mirabell triumphs through foresight, not through quickness of mind, like his predecessors; his epithet is 'cautious'. The characters are individualized types. Mirabell *was* a rake, but his present value floats between gentleman and cad; Lady Wishfort partakes of both flat and round styles; Millamant, everyone's delight, is 'only' a heightening of the conventional coquette.[18] Congreve does not sort his people into good and evil categories, but represents the world as he finds it: confusing despite its terrible clarity, a place where values are not given but worked for, where the boor of one scene may be the stout fellow of the next, and where the cues for laughter or tears are not so different. It was a vision audiences were not ready for.

Congreve's career, then, shows the pattern 'one for them, one for me'. *The Old Batchelor* and *Love for Love*, lighter, racier, more sprawling plays, had the popular touch and succeeded accordingly. *The Double Dealer* and *The Way of the World* – darker, more complex 'unities' plays – were less esteemed. The cycle says something about both audience taste and Congreve, who decided after *The Way of the World* that he was 'out of tune with his time' and stopped marketing his wares.

The dialectics of reform

For a decade around 1700, four of London's most prominent playwrights held a remarkable dramatic dialogue about the nature of comedy, of comic reform, even of man. In the assumptions it debated about human nature, this was the theatrical counterpart of the writings of the Cambridge Platonists, the Latitudinarians, Locke, Shaftesbury, and Mandeville, while the distinction it finally made parallels the analyses of Pope and Addison.

Not that Colley Cibber spent hours poring over Cudworth, More, and Tillotson before writing his first play, *Love's Last Shift* (1696); he just wanted a good part for himself.[19] That was Sir Novelty Fashion, the first of his line of fops, but the historically important plot is the one in which an errant husband (Loveless) is reclaimed by his virtuous, long-suffering wife (Amanda), using the old bed trick of Elizabethan drama. The play was a great success, moving the first-night audience, entering the regular repertoire, and gaining a niche as the first 'sentimental comedy'.

Whatever this means, or meant, most readers now find the play hypocritical and prurient rather than sentimental.[20] Cibber, nosing the winds of change, scented both concern with marriage and ambivalence about the rake. Reforming him was no longer new; Cibber's angle was to let a married philanderer (and deserter) be 'lew'd for above four Acts' (Epilogue) and then reform him fulsomely, with mighty pretences to a triumph of 'virtuous love'. The effect is that of *All's Well That Ends Well* rewritten for a scandal magazine. Young Worthy, proposing the bed trick to Amanda, remarks aside, 'she'll have the Pleasure of knowing the difference between a Husband and a Lover, without the Scandal of the former' (I. 1). Amanda's 'Inclination to it' conquers her momentary scruples, and in the seduction scene she acts the female libertine remarkably well. Shortly after Loveless's histrionic 'reform', his servant Snap is caught meddling with Amanda's maid and paid to marry her. 'I can repent', he remarks, 'when I have no more Opportunities of being wicked' (v. 4). The parallel is flagrant: Cibber knew exactly what he was doing, as did Jeremy Collier, who tossed it into the hopper with everything else. So did the French, though they could not preserve the pun: it played in Paris as *La Dernière chemise de l'amour*.

Cibber used the erring-spouse-reclaimed formula repeatedly. *The Careless Husband* (1704), perhaps his best play, moves in higher society: Sir Novelty is now Lord Foppington. The action transpires at Windsor, on the perimeter of the court circle, among such people of 'birth and education' as would shortly enact *The Rape of the Lock*; Lady Betty Modish 'does not know how to turn such a Trifle as a pair of Shoes or an Heart, upon a Fellow's Hands again' (II. 1). Cibber wants to satirize the idle rich, 'Slaves to a vile tainted Mind', preoccupied with social mischief and late adolescent sex-play. After four acts of fashionable intrigue, Lady Easy finds her bareheaded husband and her maid 'asleep in two Easy Chairs': an eighteenth-century sex scene. She leaves her neckcloth on Sir Charles's head – lest he catch cold, she says, though moments later she is full of 'secret Pride' and 'superior Innocence' (v. 6). Awaking, Sir Charles also thinks her conduct 'superior'; their effusive reconciliation, too glib to believe, follows shortly.

The Lady's Last Stake (1707) is also fashionable, occasionally licentious, and usually gay and witty, but again there is one sentimental scene: the *éclaircissement* of the quarrelsome Mr and Mrs Wronglove ('What means this soft Effusion in my Breast! an aching Tenderness ne'er felt before!'). Their problems are treated seriously throughout, and require the attention of Sir Friendly Moral, a boring but original character, almost a *raisonneur*.[22] He also helps to reclaim Lady Gentle from her dangerous penchant for gambling in the title-plot, which moralizes without becoming sentimental. Gaming was then a recognized social problem, also treated by Cibber in *The Careless Husband*, by Centlivre in *The Basset Table* and *The Gamester* (both 1705), and by Vanbrugh in *The Confederacy* (1705).

(Interspersed with Cibber's comedies of reclamation were others whose penchant for farcical intrigue links them to Restoration successes such as *Martin Mar-All*. *Woman's Wit* (1697), which offers manners as well as stratagems, failed, but *Love Makes a Man* (1700), an intrigue made from two of Fletcher's comedies, was one of his longest-running successes. Its humorous dialogue, brisk tempo, and the fop Clodio outweighed critical objections. Louisa's 'reform', while symptomatic of the comic climate, is handled unemotionally. The reconciliation of Hypolita and Don Philip in *She Wou'd and She Wou'd Not* (1702), another intrigue comedy, is 'softer', but does not disturb the basic emotional cycle: confusion, anguish, clarification, resolution. It too was long popular. More risible intrigue, and three impersonations, enliven *The Double Gallant* (1707), in which Atall actually gallants three ladies. These plays show that Cibber's only ideology or programme was success.)

John Vanbrugh began his dramatic career by pouncing on *Love's Last Shift* as Fielding pounced on *Pamela*: worldly realists setting the record straight. *The Relapse* (1696), produced eleven months after Cibber's première, is both sequel and riposte. Doubting the stability of the new-model Loveless, Vanbrugh allows the reunited couple one scene of metrical happiness in the country before returning them to London temptations and prose. During a performance of (apparently) *The Relapse*, Loveless falls for Amanda's cousin Berenthia, whom he seduces, she calling out '(*very softly*)' for help. In the subtitle-plot, *Virtue in Danger*, however, Vanbrugh declines to complete the pattern. Amanda, though persuaded of Loveless's infidelity and solicited warmly by Worthy, refuses him in such exalted terms that he renounces lust for adoration – a Cibberian denouement.[23] On a lower, more boisterous level, Vanbrugh reverses the direction of movement of the main plot, sending Young Fashion and his brother Sir Novelty (now Lord Foppington) out into the country to court Sir Tunbelly Clumsey's daughter Miss Hoyden. The unsinkable Cibber was 'honoured' to play Foppington.

One might, on the basis of a quick reading of *The Relapse*, mistake Vanbrugh for a mere scoffer, but his underlying seriousness appears in *The Provoked Wife* (1697). The plight of wronged wives is now central; Sir John Brute is an urban Tunbelly Clumsey, whose boorishness throws Lady Brute into the arms, and nearly the bed, of Constant. Here Vanbrugh catches the feminist drift of the theatre from Banks, Otway, Shadwell, and Southerne to Rowe and Farquhar; under a veneer of wit and manners, the male aristocratic ethos of Restoration comedy is disintegrating.[24] There is no libertine hero or wit-lord here: the men are either respectable and not very witty (Constant), or have gone to pieces (Sir John). Women can still be libidinous or foolish (Lady Fanciful), but in the top roles are strong women more sinned against than sinning. 'I wish I did but know how I might please you', Lady Brute tells her spouse (i. 1). She is the play's wit, informing her niece, who reminds her 'we must return good for evil', 'That may be a mistake in the translation' (i. 1), and best manipulator of appearances. Despite inept satire and a diffuse plot, *The Provoked Wife* remains Vanbrugh's solidest play. Its portrait of a bad marriage that somehow endures is memorable, while the discovery of the men in Sir John's closet, and his riotous encounters with the law, made it popular on-stage.[25]

Henceforth Vanbrugh abandoned original comedy for farcical adaptations and other pursuits. *The City Wives' Confederacy* (1705, from Dancourt), was usually (and better) called *The Confederacy*; not only wives but servants and children intrigue against rich old philandering husbands. Nothing is problematical, though: wit and clever plotting rule. *The Mistake* (1705) is Molière's *Le Dépit amoureux* teased out to five acts. Even then some questions remain, but the answers are not worth seeking: this is light entertainment, a vehicle for humorous servants with puzzled masters. *A Journey to London* had potential, but Vanbrugh left it unfinished (see below, p. 167). Surprisingly, his plays were performed more often than Congreve's.[26]

Richard Steele also participated in the dialogue, although his most important contributions came much later. Like Cibber, he spoke on both sides, having a good sense of humour as well as a moralizing bent. *The Funeral* (1701) has been called everything from farcical to sentimental, and most of the labels can be defended.[27] The character of Trusty and the reappearance of Lord Brumpton are emotive; Sable's instructions to his mourners and the mustering of the militia are comic; there are satiric and romantic vignettes; and the plot is farcically loose. (What Lady Brumpton really did to her husband, and Trusty's machinations, remain unclear; the climactic revelation of a prior marriage is a clumsy *deus ex machina*.) Occasionally entertaining, the play hardly coheres: it is a collage, a revue.

The Lying Lover (1703), from Corneille's *Le Menteur*, is more sentimental and strained. After treating Young Bookwit comically for three acts, Steele has him wound Lovemore in a drunken duel in order to manufacture emotional crises: Bookwit berating duels hysterically and accusing himself of parricide when his father faints; Lovemore contriving to announce his own demise to Penelope and exulting as she grieves affectionately – Steele's second straight attempt to create comedy from supposed death. Motives and feelings remain shadowy, but Steele asks us to 'pardon what he does, for what h'intends'.[28] That is to provide 'no improper Entertainment in a Christian Commonwealth', having 'just Regard to a reforming Age', and 'with Pity to chastise Delight/For laughter's a distorted passion'. The end result, though, is a flawed tragicomedy, which (Steele joked) was 'damn'd for its Piety'.

Yet Etherege might have envied the opening line of Steele's best play: 'Well Mr *Fainlove*, how do you go on in your Amour with my Wife?' In *The Tender Husband* (1705), Steele put his programme for moral betterment aside and produced a comedy.[29] The plot in which Clerimont, Sr reclaims his erring wife by arranging to catch her with Fainlove, a 'gallant' he has provided (really his ex-mistress Lucy), is at once an echo of Restoration mores and an anticipation of *The Lady's Last Stake*. Despite the title, Clerimont is tough in using his former paramour to humiliate his wife, triumphant in proclaiming, 'I've shewn you your Error' (v. 1). Her question, 'Is't possible you can forgive what you ensnar'd me into?' is a shrewd critique of his contrivance as well as a momentary softening of the mood. Lucy, since she cannot regain Clerimont, weds a 'Country Booby', Humphry Gubbin, while Clerimont's brother gets the hyper-romantic heiress Biddy Tipkin – characters raided by Goldsmith and Sheridan – in the livelier subplots. At this point, seemingly unsure of his mission and turning towards traditional comedy, Steele broke off from playwriting for some years.

George Farquhar's early plays gave little indication that he would make an important contribution to this dialogue. *Love and a Bottle* (1698) is in some respects such a bad play – ragged, conventional, hasty, and confusing – that it has been seen as a take-off on Restoration comedy.[30] Lyrick does ridicule Restoration drama, but Farquhar's ending is virtually what Lyrick mocks. Farquhar himself is usually read into Roebuck, 'an *Irish* Gentleman, of a wild roving temper, newly come to *London*', a penniless and charming libertine, 'Wild as Winds, and unconfin'd as Air'. Lovewell has his hands full guiding this mettlesome Hibernian through London's bogs to wedlock with his sister Leanthe, disguised as a page-boy. Others besides Roebuck are lively wits: Lucinda, Lyrick, and the drawing-master Rigadoon, who instructs Mockmode (a *bourgeois gentilhomme*) that '*Pythagoras* was a Dancing-Master; he shews the Creation to be a Country-Dance, where after some antick Changes, all the parts fell into their places' (II. 2). Often it sounds like early Shadwell, with less sense of direction. Farquhar could already locate good material, write comic dialogue, and do broad characterizations, but could not yet control or resolve what he could complicate.

The Constant Couple (1699) is more tightly constructed around a vamp and a rake. Several amusing suitors vie for the favours of Lady Lurewell, a professional tease who was herself jilted years ago.[31] Colonel Standard finally proves to be the youth who ruined her and (so help me) has been looking for her ever since. In the other plot Sir Harry Wildair besieges Angelica, informed that she is a prostitute; after blunders that foreshadow *She Stoops to Conquer*, he is disabused and marries her. The great popularity of Wildair, a new type of extravagant and humorous rake, led Farquhar to write a short sequel, *Sir Harry Wildair* (1701). As in his first comedy, Act v is a mess, and Farquhar seems unsure what to do with Sir Harry. Angelica has supposedly died of neglect in France, and Wildair is chasing Lurewell, who has also relapsed. Here he seems only a stylish villain: his attack on 'that old Thing call'd Love' as mean and unfashionable (III. 2), and his dismissal of honour as a schoolboy notion, are not palliated. At last he is 'reformed' by the 'ghost' of Angelica (whom he has not recognized impersonating his brother Banter!) and his behaviour is blamed on grief and French influence: one of several nationalistic touches. Finally, Wildair proffers a 'definition of a good Wife' untouched by feminism: 'uses all Arts to please her Husband', etc. (v. 6). Robert Wilks's charm pulled this off in 1701; Wildair's does not today.

The following year Farquhar produced a *Discourse Upon Comedy* and two unsuccessful examples. *The Inconstant* is an adaptation of Fletcher's *The Wild-Goose Chase*; about half the scenes are original and half the others recast.[32] *The Twin-Rivals*, an unusual and interesting play, pits the Wouldbe twins against each other: Ben fakes Hermes's death in his absence and seizes his estate. Ben and his accomplices, Mrs Mandrake the bawd and Subtleman the lawyer, make a strong team; unfortunately Farquhar, perhaps influenced by the reformers, crushes them under a ton of Virtue. Hermes returns spouting blank verse, and his reunion with Constance is handled sentimentally. So is Richmore's 'reform', which Farquhar tells us did not last![33] Ben, a likeable cad, finally ejects himself to 'Poverty and Contempt' (v. 4), possibly placating Collier, but leaving the play one more victim of the 'attractive rake problem'.

The Recruiting Officer (1706), though, written after Farquhar's own service as a recruiter, escapes from moral reform and drawing-room comedy into the countryside, as yet scarcely touched by Shadwell and Vanbrugh, nor mined by novelists. A warm, vigorous painting of Shrewsbury humours, it has both romantic and realistic strokes; Silvia disguised as a man follows Captain Plume, who tries to induct a pit man who 'has no visible means of a livelihood, for he works underground (v. 5).[34] Sergeant Kite's account of his gypsy background (III. 1) is a minor masterpiece of the picaresque. Farquhar presents his bumpkins with a gusto, and his women with a freedom, more Elizabethan

than eighteenth century, nor is the warmth ever sentimental, except where patriotism is concerned. Despite a loosely constructed plot, Farquhar had found his strength, and made a splendid theatrical vehicle for Wilks, Cibber, his own discovery Anne Oldfield, and their successors throughout the century.

Wilks and Oldfield scored again as Archer and Mrs Sullen in *The Beaux' Stratagem* (1707), still revived successfully. The setting is again the country (Lichfield), but seeming parallels with *The Recruiting Officer* are misleading; the principals remain indoors, and often have London in mind as a desideratum.[35] In place of the genial froth of the earlier play is a serious concern with money, marriage, class, and conscience. Wilks does not get Oldfield, who remains unhappily married; Farquhar's warmth is laced with colder currents. The Prologue invokes 'the Plain Dealer' and closes with an Etheregean remark about fools diverting men of sense. It is a play of paradoxes and contrasts, of hard and soft layers.

The two beaux, impecunious younger brothers who declare war on poverty, are a good example. Their project is sheer *Realpolitik*: pose as master and servant, marry a provincial fortune and go halves. Except for Aimwell's generous lapse in v. 4, which passes harmlessly, they do co-operate and keep faith, whereas earlier rakes were, like stags in rutting time, not so amicable. But only one of these is a rake: Archer exceeds his servant's brief to pursue Cherry and Mrs Sullen, and upbraids Aimwell's softness at the critical juncture. The captivated victim, Dorinda, urges Aimwell to reconsider their marriage, lest *he* be wedding concealed faults. 'Such goodness who could injure!' he exclaims, aside: 'I cannot, cannot hurt her' (v. 4).

His confession is a humane response, not sentimentality of Cibber's kind. Loveless 'reformed' with every inducement to do so, including entrapment; Aimwell confesses when he and Archer still have everything to lose. Shaftesbury would say that Dorinda's goodness has awakened his moral sense. It is an important passage – Cibber's false sentiment replaced with true – yet 100 lines later Aimwell greets news of his brother's death with 'Thanks to the pregnant stars that formed this accident'. Too bad for the late Viscount, but elder brothers sitting on title and fortune cannot expect fraternal affection too. Aimwell hands over Dorinda's fortune to Archer: now they need not split the bride's money. *Realpolitik* is re-established.

Another half-gesture towards humane feeling is the treatment of the Sullens' marriage. We are invited to pity the plight of young, attractive Mrs Sullen, married to 'a country blockhead, brutal to his wife', an amalgam of John Brute and Tunbelly Clumsey. Once, she breaks into rhetoric from Milton's divorce tracts: 'what evidence can prove the unaccountable disaffections of wedlock? . . . can radical hatreds be ever reconciled?' etc. (III. 3).[36] The powerful attraction between her and Archer makes her situation more poignant. Too honourable to cuckold Sullen, she resists Archer's advances, yet contemporary law granted separations only for adultery or extreme cruelty. What, then? Farquhar, unwilling to confirm her in a marriage as bad as the Brutes' and Fainalls', puts the Sullens through a catechism of divorce (borrowed with improvements from Shadwell's *Epsom-Wells*) that divides them symbolically, Miltonicly – but not legally. If this solution is fantastic, it is also effective theatre, and was perhaps the only way to end this plot comically. Besides, it is flexible: though most productions treat the conclusion as festive, it can be done ironically. Mrs Sullen will go to her brother, not to Archer. 'Consent' was certainly *not* 'law enough to set you free' in 1707: that is the point that may get lost in the age of the divorce kit.

Archer remains unattached at the end of the play, having refused the hand of Cherry, an innkeeper's daughter with two thousand pounds. 'Love's catechism' (II. 2) is humorous and spicy, stages well, and – unlike the Sullens' version – should unite the couple, both warm, attractive, and clever. But when Archer refuses Cherry's offer, she refuses his. We are well aware of his motives. The money is not enough, and moreover she is 'an innkeeper's daughter – ay, that's the devil. There my pride brings me off' (II. 2). Farquhar remains realistic here – the humanitarian revolution was only embryonic – and at the end, when Archer could afford her, Cherry has departed. It is tempting to believe that Goldsmith, more accustomed to levelling ideas, completed this interrupted relationship in *She Stoops to Conquer* (1773), whose earlier title was *The Belle's Stratagem*.

The Beaux' Stratagem is more humane and complex than earlier Farquhar; without abandoning his usual *vis comica* and liveliness, he closed the debate about *homo ludens* by affirming that some specimens, at least, have better instincts, consciences, to which one can appeal. At the same time he did not blink social problems – marriage, class pride – but noted them wittily, in profane catechisms. Farquhar's popularity was, and is, well deserved.

Lesser writers of this decade sought to please audiences by treating current topics in established ways. Mary Pix's comedies abound in problems arising from bad marriages.[37] *The Innocent Mistress* (1697) is a sprawling collection of manners and intrigues: Mrs Beauclair is clever and attractive as she bags her rake, but the Bellinda–Sir Charles relationship is pretentious, the other two plots are boring, and the ending is fortuitous. William Burnaby tried various angles without much success, treating reform ironically in *The Reformed Wife* (1700), satirizing fashionable foibles in *The Ladies' Visiting Day* (1701). *The*

Modish Husband (1702) blends sex, intrigue, farce, satire, and a touch of Southerne's seriousness: 'The Husband's Folly justifies the Wives' (v. 1). Thomas Baker almost defines manners comedy in his competent and entertaining *Tunbridge Walks* (1703), scrutinizing several urban and rural types: the yeoman, the fop, the transvestite, the witty parasite. Baker's dialogue is natural and the ending transcends convention; Woodcock accepts a London son-in-law only if *he* can raise a grandson on his estate: 'On those conditions, Heav'n bless you both' (v. 1).

Susannah Centlivre would become the most important of this group in due time; at first she was only trying to discover what the town wanted in their comic salad. 'Humour lightly tost up with Wit, and drest with Modesty and Air' is her conclusion in *Love's Contrivance* (1703), a medley from Molière.[38] Yet in 1705 she turned reformer of everyone's favourite problem, gambling; *The Gamester* (from Regnard's *Le Joueur*) adopts Steele's moralizing tone. Valere, a compulsive gambler even when faced with loss of love and inheritance ('I know I have no luck, yet can't forebear playing'), is finally reclaimed by Angelica's last shift: disguised as a gamester, she wins her own picture from him, then reveals herself. Like her namesake in *Love for Love*, she accepts the penitent as his father is disinheriting him. Less successful was *The Basset Table* (1705), which, keeping a lighter touch, reforms female gamblers. The most interesting character is Valeria, 'a philosophical Girl' – i.e. an amateur scientist – who enters pursuing 'a huge Flesh Fly' and dissects mammals. Her insistence (amid the usual society vapours) that women *are* fit to study science is refreshing, but she seems to be the object of satire.[39] In 1706 Centlivre, still searching for her style, switched to intrigue comedy, in which she would do her best work.

Stagnation: 1708–1727

The few notable comedies written between Farquhar's death and *The Beggar's Opera* were mostly deft applications of proven formulas; significant innovations were rare. It was a trying time for the theatre: the government viewed drama sternly, and occasionally intervened, but not firmly or consistently; audiences wanted decorous entertainment, not quality, satire, or experimentation.

Cibber's writing career fell victim to the cares of managing and acting. He did not write another important comedy until *The Non-Juror* (1717), an adaptation of Molière's *Tartuffe*; its timely anti-Jacobitism and Anne Oldfield as the lively Maria made it successful. When Maria is not ~persecuting Heartly, though, it is quite serious. In one scene Heartly recounts a tearful father–son reunion: Cibber's early style at a distance. *The Refusal* (1721) is equally topical. The South Sea Bubble backdrops some amusing intrigues, and the Wrangles' manoeuvres to match their daughters are also mercenary. Some of the courting games are fun; Cibber could still write effective scenes.

Mrs Centlivre's comedies were the most popular of the period, and two of them survived the *nineteenth* century. *The Busy Body* (1709), one of her longest-running triumphs, is a Spanish intrigue, by nature a brisk, unreflective form. Devoid of ideas, it abounds in good acting roles: Miranda, Sir George Airy, who acts both parts in a courtship scene (II. 1), and Marplot, who combines insatiable curiosity and good will with invincible stupidity. Mrs Centlivre had evidently decided that Restoration 'business', not reform, was the commodity in demand; Marplot resembles Dryden's Martin Mar-All, Sir Jealous Traffic parallels James Formal in Wycherley's *Gentleman Dancing-Master*, and Miranda goes masked to the park (despite Queen Anne's 1704 edict against vizards). It is light, conventional stuff – outwitting the *senex amans*, impersonating the expected suitor, etc. – but presented with clever twists such as the intercepted love-letter in code passed off as a toothache remedy. The faint serious undertone of forced marriage to a nasty old man recurs in *A Bickerstaff's Burying* and *Marplot in Lisbon* (both 1710), a sequel to *The Busy Body*. Marplot is several times called 'good-natured', clarifying the author's intention to make him amiably humorous, but his predictable meddling grows tiresome here.

Mrs Centlivre produced another successful Spanish intrigue, *The Wonder! A Woman Keeps a Secret*, in 1714. Set in Lisbon, it is as conventional as *The Busy Body* – tyrannical fathers, scheming servants, veiled trysts, mistaken identities – but the slick performance of old tricks elicited critical praise, and attracted good actors for two centuries.[40] The misunderstandings crucial to the genre, usually random events, are generated by Isabella's concealment at Violante's: the secret wondrously kept. Both are fine acting roles, as is Don Felix, one of Garrick's favourites. The low comedy is amusing, the language racy *ma non troppo*, and there are some patriotic bugles. Exaltation of English freedom over Spanish tyranny also occurs in *The Busy Body*, but Centlivre added something extra in the year of George I's accession, dedicating the play to him and awarding Isabella to Colonel Briton, a Scot, rather than to her local merchant admirer, as might have been expected. The anti-tyranny note is conspicuous at the end, where the two outwitted fathers stalk off-stage without softening. Far from senseless, the play makes its genre relevant, almost topical, at the end of the War of the Spanish Succession.

In her next comedy, *A Bold Stroke for a Wife* (1718), another colonel (Feignwell or Fainwell) wins the girl (Anne Lovely) against heavy odds. Fainwell and Anne have agreed to marry, but she wants her fortune, and her misanthropic father, who 'hated posterity' (I. 1), left her to the alternating care of four disparate guardians – Tradelove, a changebroker, the antiquary Periwinkle, the old beau Modelove, and the Quaker Obadiah Prim – all of whom must consent to Anne's marriage if she is to inherit. The action, then, has a classic simplicity: Fainwell must obtain the signatures of 'avarice, impertinence, hypocrisy and pride' (I. 1) on the marriage contract. Faced with the malicious irrationality of this situation, he resorts to trickery: *five* disguises, an actor's dream! Centlivre controls this material adroitly. The first and last impersonations, 'M. la Fainwell' (to Modelove) and 'Simon Pure' (versus Prim) succeed outright, whereas Tradelove's consent requires three scenes and Periwinkle's needs two disguises, these being interwoven.[41] Fainwell finally reveals himself to his dupes and closes on a patriotic and Anglican note, pitched at Prim and the Francophile Modelove. The improbabilities of *A Bold Stroke* struck some as farcical, but its acting qualities gradually established it in the repertoire, where it stayed into the nineteenth century.

The Artifice (1722), however, a disappointing finale to Centlivre's career, lacks both control and focus. She seems to lose touch with her strengths: it is too long, the multiple stories are poorly joined, the satire is gratuitous, and the reform scene (V. 3) sentimentalized. Whether Mrs Centlivre was only a symptom of 'the popular, clever, meaningless theatre of the time', possessing 'a sense of the theatre and little other sense at all', or rather 'an excellent craftsman for the stage, a precise observer of social trends', her three or four successful comedies of 1705–18 must determine.[42]

John Gay provided the most original comic artefacts of the period, satirizing critics, authors, and genres that seemed to the Scriblerians silly or pompous. The plays are not comedies: part of his game is obfuscating just what they are. *The Mohocks* (1712, not acted), an obscure satire, is called a 'tragi-comical farce'.[43] The roving bullies are first Miltonic demons or anarchist heroes who sing like the highwaymen of *The Beggar's Opera* ('Come, fill up the glass!') and terrorize the cowardly watch; later the roles reverse and firm justices arraign cowed Mohocks. *The What D'Ye Call It* (1715) is a 'tragi-comi-pastoral farce', whose 'Art . . . lies in interweaving the several Kinds of the Drama with each other, so that they cannot be distinguish'd'. This outflanks the genre critics who, when they criticize Gay as comedian or tragedian, will be reminded he is *farceur* or pastoralist, etc. Obviously the disintegrating genres still meant something. The play proves to be a rehearsal burlesquing pathetic tragedy and sentimental pastorals, whose absurdities are juxtaposed with rural realism.[44] Kitty's farewell to the 'happy fields' is accompanied by a 'Chorus of Sighs and Groans': 'Ah-O! – Sure never was the like before!' (II. 8). Later she goes mad, raving of 'Bagpipes in Butter, Flocks in fleecy Fountains' and 'Seas of Milk' like a bucolic Belvidera.

Three Hours After Marriage (1717), a collaboration with Pope and Arbuthnot, burlesques humans as well as genres. John Dennis, whose quarrelsome prefaces Gay had spoofed, now appears in person as the critic Sir Tremendous. Other traditional identifications – Phoebe Clinket as Mrs Centlivre, Plotwell as Cibber – are questioned by those who argue that the characters represent types.[45] Certainly they are humours, not people, as the dialogue is largely topical allusions and the plot a series of lazzi (farce 'turns'). Voilà, Gay smiles archly: such is modern drama. Three Hours is narrowly literary, like Book II of the 1744 Dunciad, and equally Scriblerian. Audiences did not like it.

Gay's satirical farces illustrate one tendency in Georgian comedy; Steele's last play exemplifies another, virtually the opposite. The Scriblerians prized wit and ridicule, techniques that Steele attacked in print long before The Conscious Lovers (1722) asked audiences 'To Chasten Wit, and Moralize the Stage'.[46] The seed was sown in 1704, when Steele sought to 'chastise Delight' in The Lying Lover (Epilogue). The sequence 'chastise' – 'chasten' is interesting: 'to punish', later 'to discipline', the old harsh comic responses ('For Laughter's a distorted passion'), to make them 'chaste'. Steele next attacked The Man of Mode, the reigning 'pattern of genteel comedy', as unnatural, rude, senseless, and dishonest (Spectator, no. 65, 1711). By 1713 he was writing a proper comedy, which his patent and reform mandate from George I (1715) certainly encouraged; in 1720, Steele introduced many of the play's characters in two periodical essays.[47] Five days before the première, John Dennis came to the 'Defence of Sir Fopling Flutter', arguing that Loveit and Sir Fopling are – quite properly – ridiculed, but evading Steele's complaints about Dorimant. It remains the classic confrontation between traditional and exemplary comic theory.

The play itself is less clear-cut than the critical positions. Steele said that he intended chiefly 'an innocent Performance' and 'scorn[ed] the Aids of Vice', yet Cimberton's appraisal of Lucinda 'as one that is to be pregnant' (III. 1) and some of the Tom and Phillis scenes are comical in the Restoration style and not overly delicate.[48] The Conscious Lovers's triumph and continued success are facts, but what attracted audiences: laughing scenes involving Cimberton, Tom and Phillis, and Myrtle disguised as Sir Geoffrey? Or the grave interviews between Bevil, Jr and Indiana, the moral lectures, the 'evasion of a duel' scene (IV. 1) for which Steele said the play was written, the tearful family reunion? Dennis argued that this solemn stuff (which Fielding called a sermon) was not comedy; Goldsmith would parody the sententious exchanges of the lovers; recent critics have questioned Bevil, Jr's conduct, especially in the duel scene.[49] Had he 'come clean' sooner, with his father, his friend, and his love, he would have seemed more exemplary and less priggish, but then Steele would have had no play. *The Conscious Lovers* is not *simply* moral or sentimental.

The play's sociology is more significant (and satisfactory) than its aesthetics. Romance motifs borrowed from Terence's *Andria* – piracy, long estrangement, providential reunion – are firmly grounded in the mercantile milieu of Steele's public, to whom the shape of the plot appealed: trader's daughter marries up into landed gentry. This type of social flexibility, also imaged in Richardson's *Pamela*, probably helped England release class tensions of the kind that were building in France. Mr Sealand, as 'conscious' (aware) as the young lovers, tells Sir John Bevil, 'we Merchants are a Species of Gentry, that have grown into the World this last Century, and are as honourable, and almost as useful, as you landed Folks, that have always thought yourselves so much above us' (IV. 2). Steele was not simply pandering to the merchants (though 'almost as useful' has a barb); he was, as usual, also trying to educate them. The other side of the upward-mobility coin was the quantification of human relationships, especially in the arranged marriage. Bevil, Jr twits his father on this point (I. 2), but Lucinda's feelings are understandably stronger: 'to be barter'd for, like the Beasts of the Fields . . . to be thus survey'd like a Steed at Sale', she rages (III. 1). *The Conscious Lovers* is most successful when Steele can make a serious point comically.

Of minor dramatists, Thomas Baker carried on the manners tradition; *The Fine Lady's Airs* (1709) might be subtitled 'Everyone in His Manner'. Baker could write lively dialogue, but plot and characters vacillate confusingly. Lady Rodomont, the finest lady, is a militant feminist whose sudden match-up with Colonel Blenheim is jarring. Mrs Lovejoy, an amorphous figure, tricks the merchant beau Nicknack into wedlock: initially ridiculous, he becomes a surprising spokesman for his class. The humours tradition survived in Charles Shadwell (son of Thomas), whose popular *The Fair Quaker of Deal; or, The Humours of the Navy* (1710), complete with villain, unlikely reform, and sentimental conclusion, anticipates the Victorian naval melodrama. A sequel, *The Humours of the Army*, followed inexorably in 1713.

For three decades, Charles Johnson essayed most of the current forms. *The Country Lasses* (1715) is the kind of idealized pastoral that Gay mocked: Flora and Aura prove too much for the London rakes, who, since 'The country bargain still is love for love' (Prologue), yield their freedom; a thief is so moved by good treatment that he confesses and is forgiven. *The Cobler of Preston* (1716), a simple-minded patriotic farce, sets the Induction of *The Taming of the Shrew* in the recent Jacobite Rebellion: Kit Sly becomes a pro-Stuart cobbler who is taught better politics through his metamorphosis. Johnson's threadbare invention labours, though, whenever he strays from Shakespeare.

The Drummer (1716) is a charming, unusual piece, supposedly Addison's, about an Odyssean husband who returns from the wars to find himself presumed dead and his house and grieving wife haunted by suitors.[50] The old steward Vellum would not disgrace Dickens, and Fantome's frightening of Tinsel ('Have compassion on my youth, and consider I am but a coxcomb') makes excellent theatre. The finale is *appropriately* sentimental: if a restored veteran and his loving wife cannot shed some tears, who can?

The New Wave: 1728–1737

The long comic drought ended in 1728 with the successful production of *The Provoked Husband*, 'compiled' by Cibber from Vanbrugh's unfinished *A Journey to London*.[51] In three and a half unruly acts, Vanbrugh sketched the rowdy misadventures of the Headpiece clan, freshly arrived in London, and the modish problems (chiefly gambling) of the Loverule marriage. Though both plots look promising, the exposition is so slow and full that neither has disclosed its final shape where Vanbrugh desisted. Presumably Sir Francis Headpiece's anger foreshadowed a return to the country, and Cibber says that the Loverules were intended to part ('To the Reader'). Judging this deficient in 'proper surprise' and 'too severe for comedy', however, Cibber inserted a tearful, eleventh-hour reclamation ('This may be called my wedding day!') at the end. His title (alluding to Vanbrugh's *The Provoked Wife*) shifts the emphasis from the rustics' bumbling to the urbanites' marital discord and reconciliation – the mode of *The Careless Husband* and *The Lady's Last Stake* – and his Dedication to the Queen promises 'to expose and reform the licentious irregularities' that disturb many marriages (p. 3).

Although the country plot also straightens out an erring wife, the Dedication can no more be trusted for the whole truth than the Prologue, which claims that Vanbrugh finally saw the error of his ways and adopted the exemplary view ('plays should let you see/Not only what you are, but want to be'), of which we have no evidence. Perhaps The *Relapse* did rankle after all. Cibber, as shrewd as ever, talks of moral improvement and provides one scene thereof, but sweetens the pill with the whole gamut of laughter, from fashionable diversions to country clowning. For Georgians, it was the perfect dosage.

Cibber said he was defending legitimate drama when he refused Gay's *Beggar's Opera* (1728).[52] If so, he paid the usual price. It had an unprecedented run at Lincoln's Inn Fields, making 'Gay rich and Rich gay'. Gay's 'ballad opera' – old tunes, new words – displaced Italian opera for a season, but its many imitators (including Cibber's *Love in a Riddle*) encroached on regular drama at Drury Lane thereafter. The idea sprang partly from Swift's suggestion for a 'Newgate pastoral' (*c.* 1716; Gay's 'Newgate Garland' (1725) foreshadows some ideas of *The Beggar's Opera*), partly from society's embrace of Italian-language opera: introduced to England *c.* 1705, boosted by Handel's arrival (1711) and very modish by 1715. For the Scriblerians, Italian opera was a toy of the rich – another example of false taste and cultural decay – and an assault upon Nature. The Beggar apologizes for not making his opera 'throughout unnatural, like those in vogue'; Pope later satirized the 'Harlot form' and 'Foreign . . . air' of opera.[53] The execution of the notorious highwayman Jonathan Wild (1725) provided the character of Macheath and the notion of 'a similitude of Manners in high and low Life' (III. 16). Wild's methods were often compared to Robert Walpole's, both being called 'great men'; Peachum, who buys and sells people, would suggest both. Gay's failure to obtain the 'place' he wanted (1726) added the final ingredient: disillusion with Court.

The finished text reflects long incubation, diverse influences, and Gay's characteristic persona: elusive, protean. Operatic absurdities are satirized (Polly versus Lucy as the rival divas Cuzzoni and Faustina), yet at times, as in Gilbert and Sullivan, the melodies are lovely and the mood is 'operatic'. Swift praised the work's morality; others condemned it for glorifying rogues; Johnson pronounced it likely 'to divert'.[54] When the highwaymen 'take the road' to the March from Handel's *Rinaldo*, are they ennobled or is opera tarred? Macheath, 'a great man', is, like Peachum, Walpole's surrogate, but does this exalt the rogue or abase the Prime Minister? Glancing up and down the social scale, Gay finds it a uniform cheat: 'each Neighbour abuses his Brother' (Air I). Satire is ubiquitous. Its major targets are, in *descending* order: women – Gay, like Congreve, never married – high society, courtiers and politicians, marriage, gentlemen, and lawyers. Six more subjects (including opera) are mentioned occasionally. But Gay's seriousness is questionable: everything is undercut so playfully and rapidly that the targets blend and the barbs fuse into a general, seemingly tongue-in-cheek cynicism.[55] Set alongside *Gulliver's Travels*, *The Dunciad*, or *The Threepenny Opera*, *The Beggar's Opera* appears bland.

Gay assembled the materials for a darker view of society than he actually took.

The music that delighted – and delights – audiences makes the same point about Gay's stance. Two-thirds of the tunes came from Durfey's popular collection *Pills to Purge Melancholy*, one-third from prominent composers such as Purcell and Handel, and most were twisted from their original qualities.[56] Bawdy originals got sweeter lyrics, while noble or romantic melodies received tough words. Air VI, for example, 'What shall I do to show how much I love her?' from Purcell's *Diocletian*, becomes 'Virgins are like the fair Flower in its Lustre' – in that both end up rotting and dying in Covent Garden – while 'Would you have a young virgin of fourteen years' (Air XXI) is exalted into Macheath's lyric 'If the Heart of a Man is deprest with Cares'. The result was a palimpsest whereon the effects of both texts could be felt pulling at each other, undercutting any single reaction. If Gay was serious about his satire, why dilute our responses with these contradictory associations? Again *The Threepenny Opera* is an instructive contrast: Weill's sinister settings of Brecht's words insist without qualification that 'Die Welt ist arm, der Mensch ist schlecht'. Gay is not so sure; wit and melody seem generous compensations.

In *Polly*, the suppressed sequel, Macheath has married Jenny Diver and is leading a West Indian pirate gang as 'Morano', a black; Polly comes looking for him and gets sold to a rich planter. Escaping in male attire, she falls in with pirates and natives, takes 'Morano' prisoner without recognizing him and delivers him to vigilante justice. *Polly* shows clearly how the ballad opera form works against serious social criticism; the familiar objects are repetitiously lambasted – 'great men', women, courtiers – until a jingle dissipates the gloom. So does Gay's pluralistic sensibility: the old theme ('In pimps and politicians/The genius is the same', Air V) has to compete with the new world, a noble savage, sympathy with distress. Stung by criticism of *The Beggar's Opera*'s morality, Gay simplified its complex ironies.[57] The Poet of the Introduction, 'unjustly accus'd of having given up my moral for a joke', sounds like Gay, preparing to give up his joke for a moral. A darker Macheath ('war's my pleasure') is executed, Polly becomes a figure of suffering virtue, and the finale idealizes Justice and Truth.

Henry Fielding succeeded Gay as satirist to the Opposition, styling himself 'H. Scriblerus Secundus' and continuing the Scriblerians' broad cultural concerns: art, society, and politics. Influenced by Gay and the 1728 *Dunciad*, he began to align himself with the anti-Walpole party in 1734, after which events moved swiftly towards the Licensing Act. But he and his theatre (the 'Little Hay') derived their anti-Ministry reputation from his last few plays: half his work was first produced at Drury Lane, and he wrote comedy and farce as as well as satire.

Between 1728 and 1737 he had some two dozen plays produced in London, making him its dominant dramatist and providing English drama with more excitement than anyone else for many a decade before or after.

Fielding began in regular comedy, but *Love in Several Masques* (1728), which paled beside *The Provoked Husband* and *The Beggar's Opera*, and *The Temple Beau* (1730), which is long, confusing, and careless, represent a false start, despite some good speeches. In the spring of 1730, however, Fielding found himself in *The Author's Farce*, his first play at the Little Hay and first essay in irregularity. Two acts of farce lead into a puppet show cum ballad opera conducted by the impoverished hero Luckless, a version of Fielding. Besieged in his garret by duns, rejected by booksellers and the managers of the patent theatres, he gives his play to the Haymarket, asking, 'What have been all the playhouses a long time but puppet shows?'[58] The performance is interrupted by the news that Luckless is actually the King of Bantam: he can marry his beloved and retire. *The Author's Farce* both satirizes and exploits the reigning theatrical follies, ridiculing Cibber (as the manager Marplay and the dramatist Sir Farcical Comic), Signior Opera, Monsieur Pantomime, etc., while using the absurd conclusion (and some of the tunes) of *The Beggar's Opera* – and of course *being* the form(s) it deplores.

Luckless's decision to take the freaks of his puppet show with him because they are 'All proper servants for the King of Bantam' (III, 860) is the germ of *Tom Thumb* (1730), Fielding's most famous play, which burlesques post-Restoration tragedy by cutting it down to size. It was so popular that Fielding expanded it from two to three acts, added a Scriblerian Preface mocking critics, and called it *The Tragedy of Tragedies* (1731). Ridicule by diminution is his Swiftian game; Tom is Gulliver (or Cibber) in Brobdingnag. Merlin, like Pope's Queen of Dulness, bids him

> See from afar a Theatre arise;
> There, Ages yet unborn, shall Tribute pay
> To the Heroick Actions of this Day:
> Then Buskin Tragedy at length shall choose
> Thy Name the best Supporter of her Muse.[59]

Giving Augustan tragedy a hero–muse commensurate with its stature, Fielding demolishes its epic similes, absurd exclamations, fatuous couplets, and endless comparisons through parody. Cleopatra and Octavia meet again, Sophonisba becomes Huncamunca, six murders and a suicide within eight lines brighten the finale: the targets were large and slow, and few escaped.

The first phase of Fielding's career ended with the banning of *The Grub Street Opera* (1731). An earlier version, *The Welsh Opera*, was popular, but when Fielding tried to enlarge it and sharpen his satire, the play was banned and the theatre closed.[60] In the Introduction, Scriblerus Secundus describes his piece as 'a sort of family opera', but it is the Royal Family: George II, Queen Caroline, and the Prince of Wales are impudently satirized as the Apshinkens, a troubled Welsh family whose servants are recognizably Walpole and other leading politicians. Without this key, however, the play is obscure and its characters are puzzling. The ideology seems populist rather than political: Mr Apshones preaches the rights of man against Owen, an arrogant aristocratic beau. Coupled with the democratic spirit is the patriotism enshrined in the play's best-known song, 'The Roast Beef of England'. The sixty-five airs would have carried it further than its slight text.

When Fielding returned to Drury Lane after this suppression, he also moved back towards comedy. The Prologue to *The Modern Husband* (1732) repents of youthful frolics and espouses Nature and Truth. A serious play in Southerne's vein, it exposes the corruption of a society where 'A willing Cuckold – sells his willing wife' (Prologue): 'a modern Trade', remarks Gaywit. Bellamant replies, 'ev'rything has its Price' (II. 1) – a theme that makes the Dedication to Walpole seem ironic. Moral criticism focuses on Lord Richly, the wife-purchaser. 'Where Grandeur can give Licence to Oppression', warns Bellamant, 'the People must be Slaves, let them boast what Liberty they please' (v. 2); Captain Merit can obtain a commission only by begging it from Richly. Though the satire on manners and class is keen, Fielding tries to do too much; several characters and plots could be dropped.

The translations from Molière (*The Miser*, *The Mock Doctor*) also represent an impulse towards comedy and farce, but *The Covent Garden Tragedy* (1732) is a burlesque along the lines of *Tom Thumb*, misapplying tragic diction and conventions to the bawds, bullies, and doxies of the red light district. Trivial as the play is, it shows how hostile to tragedy the prevailing temper had become – and contemporary tragedy was too frail to take much of this ridicule.

During his final phase Fielding still had plays produced at Drury Lane, but the more significant ones appeared at the Little Hay. *Don Quixote in England* (1734) identified him with the Opposition for the first time: the Dedication, praising Chesterfield's defence of a free stage, attacks corruption; the 'opera' drops the divinely mad knight and his squire into the midst of a venal country election. 'Money is the fruit of evil, as often as the root of it', observes Sancho. In *Pasquin, a Dramatick Satire on the Times* (1736), Trapwit's comedy shows how elections are rigged in a small town. The other play rehearsed, Fustian's tragedy, is a kind of *Dunciad* in which Queen Common-Sense is destroyed by Queen Ignorance, supported by the professions and the patent theatres. Obsessed by the parallels between theatrical and political corruption, Fielding was rapidly approaching the end of his tether. When *Eurydice*, a clever farce, failed at Drury Lane, he responded with *Eurydice Hissed* and *The Historical Register for 1736* (all 1737), sketchy rehearsal plays about evil managers in both spheres. In the last Walpole appears as Quidam, paying off 'patriots' and making them dance to his tune until his coins fall from their pockets. The playwright-manager Pillage in *Eurydice Hissed*, taken as 'an allegory on the loss of the Excise Bill', is another 'Great Man'.[61] A month after the première, Walpole's Licensing Act was law.

Whatever effect Fielding's satires had on Georgian society, their influence on his own subsequent work is unmistakable, and not only as the familiar 'theatricality' of his novels.[62] It is specifically the rehearsal format that carries over into the fiction: the author presenting a rehearsal to his friends becomes the novelist presenting his story to us. Fielding invented the 'normative' author, the type who acts as spokesman for the playwright's values. Before 1730, the typical rehearsal conductor was an anti-hero, like Bayes in *The Rehearsal* or Marsilia in *The Female Wits* (1697), but Luckless in *The Author's Farce* begins a series of sensible and sympathetic author-surrogates, notably Fustian in *Pasquin* and Medley in *The Historical Register*.[63] By an easy transition, the explicating persona of the rehearsal plays became the friendly author of *Tom Jones*, his armchair pulled up to the proscenium.

Reservations about Fielding's plays usually centre on *form*. Granting that he satirized legitimate targets – government corruption, social follies, theatrical nonsense – he did so in irregular forms that hastened the dissolution of comedy into the revue, the topical skit, etc. He himself used such labels as 'burlesque tragedy', 'operatic farce', and 'dramatic entertainment'; others have been harsher. Yet Fielding and some of his contemporaries and successors did their best work in just these *nouveaux* genres which, while they require readjustment, also open new possibilities.

The minor authors or this period produced a few odd plays that defy conventional categorization. Strange names had a vogue. Samuel Johnson of Cheshire's *Hurlothrumbo* (1729) is a mad, sometimes inspired play by an insane author (Johnson played Lord Flame, who admits, 'I rent my brain'). Several characters have metaphysical yearnings to transcend nature; the diction is extravagant, even apocalyptic. Everyone seems demented, or to have strayed from an allegorical masque. Addressed to 'Sons of Nonsense' and dedicated to Walpole (who took thirty copies), it had a good run. Henry Carey's *Chronon-hotonthologos* (1734) tries to burlesque tragedy in the manner of *Tom Thumb*. The parody of bombast and bathos is sporadically effective, but the action is vapid and many of the jokes operate on the level of the opening: 'Aldiborontiphoscophornio! Where left you Chrononho-tonthologos?' Carey also took off Italian opera in *The Dragon of Wantley* (1737), a good-humoured trifle with original music.

Farce throve in various guises. John Hippisley's *A Journey to Bristol* (1731) presents broad humours, beatings, and dousings until the last two scenes, which have a humane, affective tone. *The Devil to Pay* (1731), a short ballad opera by Theophilus Cibber from a play by Coffey and Mottley (from one by Thomas Jevon), was phenomenally successful, influencing European dramatists and remaining popular on Anglo-American stages for a century. Though flimsy and escapist – using magic to improve bad tempers – it has a pleasingly balanced structure and a sure sense of direction. James Miller's *The Coffee-House* (1737) combines comedy's usual conquest of the obstacles to young love with satirical 'Out-lines' of café types. Historians give it various labels; Miller himself classed it with the 'little additional Pieces' (i.e. afterpieces) whose rise, at the expense of regular comedy, was charac-teristic of Georgian theatre.

Of the more serious efforts, John Kelly's *The Married Philosopher* (1732, from Destouches) suffers from weak plotting, but the dialogue is pointed and several of the characters are both realistic and attractive. Though the good nature of old Bellefleur and the humanity of the ending have earned it the label 'sentimental', it never indulges emotion; the Prologue invokes Nature and common sense, not tears. Robert Dodsley's *The King and the Miller of Mansfield* (1737) also worships Nature, and humanity. The patriotic story of the incognito King impartially dispensing justice to courtiers and rustics skirts melodrama to reach comedy of a sober sort. The King's admonition to Lord Lurewell, 'he that Acts greatly, is the true Great Man', both echoes the venerable 'true nobility' theme (*The Wife of Bath's Tale*) and glances at Walpole. Thus the 'New Wave' ends as it began, criticizing immor-ality in high places: a subject henceforth liable to prior censorship under the Licensing Act.

Notes

1. Michael W. Alssid discusses the world as market in *Thomas Shadwell* (New York, 1967), p. 146; see also pp. 24 and 153–57. Other useful sources on the play include Kenneth Muir, *The Comedy of Manners* (London, 1970), p. 61; Louis Kronenberger, *The Thread of Laughter* (New York, 1952; 1970), pp. 101–03; and John H. Smith, 'Shadwell, the Ladies, and the Change in Comedy', *MP*, 46 (1948), 22–33 (p. 30).

2. Montague Summers's prefatory material in Volume IV of *The Works of Aphra Behn*, 6 vols (London, 1915) is helpful.

3. It is rated higher, as comedy, by Frank H. Moore, *The Nobler Pleasure* (Chapel Hill, 1963), p. 222; and by Arthur H. Scouten, 'Plays and Playwrights', in *The Revels History of Drama in English*, edited by T. W. Craik and C. Leech, 8 vols (London, 1975–83), V (1976), 177.

4. From the Dedication (London, 1697). See Leo Hughes, in *Restoration and Eighteenth-Century Drama*, edited by James Vinson (London, 1980), p. 121. Garrick's acting prolonged its life.

5. See Smith, 'Shadwell', p. 30; Scouten, *Revels History*, V, 207–08, and *Restoration and Eighteenth-Century Drama*, p. 65; and Peter Holland, *The Ornament of Action* (Cambridge, 1979), p. 158.

6. For example, J. H. Smith, *The Gay Couple in Restoration Comedy* (Cambridge, Massachusetts, 1948), p. 144; Muir, pp. 86–92; Scouten, *Revels History*, V, 212–13; and Robert D. Hume, *The Rakish Stage* (Carbondale, Illinois, 1983), pp. 191–93. My references are to Ralph Thornton's edition (Wynnewood, Pennsylvania, 1973). Professor Harold Love kindly sent me his copy, and the typescript introduction to his own forthcoming edition.

7. Dryden 'never saw such a first play in his life'. See Harold Love, 'Dryden, Durfey, and the Standard of Comedy', *SEL*, 13 (1973), 422–36 (pp. 433–34).

8. All references to Congreve's comedies are to Anthony G. Henderson's edition, *The Comedies of William Congreve* (Cambridge, 1977). On the wit, see Kronenberger, pp. 120–22.

9. Emmett L. Avery, *Congreve's Plays on the Eighteenth-Century Stage* (New York, 1951), pp. 155–56.

10. Avery, p. 155. On its popular farcing, see Kronenberger, pp. 128–30; on its humorists, especially Foresight, see Maximillian E. Novak, *William Congreve* (New York, 1971), p. 114. The successful première got the secessionist company at Lincoln's Inn Fields off to a good start.

11. Compare Novak, p. 123.

12. Norman Holland, *The First Modern Comedies* (Cambridge, Massachusetts, 1959), p. 164; but see Harriett Hawkins, *Likenesses of Truth in Elizabethan and Restoration Drama* (Oxford, 1972), pp. 98–112.

13. The 'letter', and Congreve's 'Amendments of Mr Collier's False and Imperfect Citations', are conveniently reprinted in *Restoration and Eighteenth-Century Comedy*, edited by Scott McMillin (New York, 1973).

14. The admirers include Paul and Miriam Mueschke, *A New View of Congreve's 'The Way of the World'* (Ann Arbor, 1958), p. 9; and Clifford Leech,

'Congreve and the Century's End', *PQ*, 41 (1962), 275–93 (p. 290). For the negative, see L. C. Knights, 'Restoration Comedy: The Reality and the Myth', *Scrutiny*, 6 (1937), 122–43 (pp. 128–29). On reception by audiences, see Avery, p. 155.

15. See John Traugott, 'The Rake's Progress from Court to Comedy', *SEL*, 6 (1966), 381–407 (p. 404).

16. See Gellert S. Alleman, *Matrimonial Law and the Materials of Restoration Drama* (Wallingford, Pennsylvania, 1942), pp. 123–24; and Novak, p. 153.

17. Thus Rose Zimbardo, *Wycherley's Drama* (New Haven, 1965), pp. 2, 8–10; compare *Comedies by William Congreve*, edited by Bonamy Dobree (1925; London, 1959), p. xv.

18. See Jean Gagen, 'Congreve's Mirabell and the Ideal Gentleman', *PMLA*, 79 (1964), 422–27 (p. 422); Novak, pp. 153–55; Knights, pp. 139–40; John Wain, 'Restoration Comedy and its Modern Critics', *EC*, 6, no. 4 (1956), 367–85 (p. 384); and John H. Wilson, *A Preface to Restoration Drama* (Cambridge, Massachusetts, 1965), pp. 180–82. On what follows, see Cleanth Brooks and Robert Heilman, *Understanding Drama* (New York, 1945), pp. 443–44.

19. See Cibber's *An Apology for the Life of Colley Cibber*, edited by B. R. S. Fone (1740; Ann Arbor, 1968), p. 118; and B. R. S. Fone, 'Colley Cibber's *Love's Last Shift* and Sentimental Comedy', *RECTR*, 7, no. 1 (1968), 33–43 (pp. 40–41).

20. For example, Paul Parnell, 'The Sentimental Mask', *PMLA*, 78 (1963), 529–35 (p. 532); Alan Roper, 'Language and Action in *The Way of the World*, *Love's Last Shift*, and *The Relapse*, *ELH*, 40 (1973), 44–69 (p. 69); and Arthur Sherbo, *English Sentimental Drama* (East Lansing, Michigan, 1957), pp. 103–6. R. D. Hume counts 23 rake-reforms before Loveless: *Rakish Stage*, p. 167.

21. References to *Love's Last Shift* and *The Careless Husband* follow Maureen Sullivan's edition of *Three Sentimental Comedies* (New Haven and London, 1973).

22. See Ernest Bernbaum, *The Drama of Sensibility* (Boston, 1915), p. 107; James J. Lynch, *Box, Pit and Gallery* (Berkeley and Los Angeles, 1953), p. 265; and Hume, *Rakish Stage*, p. 199.

23. See Hume, *Rakish Stage*, p. 190. Roper concludes that Vanbrugh sacrifices 'wholeness of action' (p. 69). L. C. Knights attacks the play, p. 122. Gerald M. Berkowitz labels it 'comedy of freedom' or 'expansion': Preface to *Sir John Vanbrugh and the End of Restoration Comedy* (Amsterdam, 1981).

24. See Berkowitz, pp. 16, 18–21, 23, 27; and P. Mueschke and J. Fleischer, 'A Re-Evaluation of Vanbrugh', *PMLA*, 49 (1934), 848–89 (pp. 886–89). The text is that of Anthony Coleman's edition of the play (Manchester, 1982), a good source of historical and critical material.

25. See Mueschke and Fleischer, 'Re-Evaluation', p. 889; Hume, *Rakish Stage*, p. 194; Berkowitz, pp. 61–65; and Lynch, *Box, Pit and Gallery*, p. 41. Originally Sir John donned a parson's garb; this had to be changed to a woman's dress.

26. Shirley S. Kenny, 'Perennial Favorites: Congreve, Vanbrugh, Cibber, Farquhar and Steele', *MP*, 73 (1976), S4–S11 (pp. S8–9).

27. There is a sharp attack in *A Comparison Between the Two Stages* (1702), edited by Arthur Freeman (New York and London, 1973), pp. 145–56. See also Bonamy Dobree, *English Literature in the Early Eighteenth Century* (Oxford, 1959), p. 235; and *The Plays of Richard Steele*, edited by Shirley S. Kenny (Oxford, 1971), p. 191. References to Steele's plays follow this edition.

28. Quotations from the Preface, Prologue and Epilogue in Kenny's edition; see also the Dedication. Kenny details the changes Steele made in Corneille's plot: pp. 103–4.

29. With help from Molière, Cibber, Burnaby, and Addison. See Kenny's edition, pp. 191–96; and Sherbo, p. 83.

30. Eugene N. James takes this dubious view in *The Development of George Farquhar as a Comic Dramatist* (The Hague, 1972), pp. 77, 85, 87, 97. Quotations come from *The Complete Works of George Farquhar*, edited by Charles Stonehill, 2 vols (London, 1930).

31. Modelled on Durfey's Madame Fickle and the real Mrs Manley, according to William Archer's note in his edition of *George Farquhar* (London, 1949), p. 32. Kronenberger has a good discussion of the play, pp. 167–71.

32. James considers Farquhar's version better organized than Fletcher's: pp. 160–62, 167, 183.

33. See the Preface. For discussion, see Muir, pp. 145–46; Kronenberger, pp. 174–75; and Eric Rothstein, 'Farquhar's *Twin-Rivals* and the Reform of Comedy', *PMLA*, 79 (1964), 33–41. William Archer compares the play to *The Double Dealer* as melodrama: *The Old Drama and the New* (London, 1923), p. 211.

34. References are to John Ross's New Mermaid edition (London and New York, 1977). On the two risqué passages excised from the second edition, see his note to v. 1, p. 96, and Appendix 1. See also Muir, pp. 146–49; and Kronenberger, pp. 175–79.

35. See Eric Rothstein's inn versus house reading in his *George Farquhar* (New York, 1967), pp. 151–58; and Judith Milhous and Robert D. Hume, '*The Beaux' Stratagem*: A Production Analysis', *Theatre Journal*, 34 (1982), 77–95 (pp. 81–82, 89–90). Textual references are to Charles N. Fifer's edition (Lincoln, Nebraska, 1977).

36. See M. A. Larson, 'The Influence of Milton's Divorce Tracts on Farquhar's *The Beaux' Stratagem*', *PMLA*, 39 (1924), 174–78. On separation and divorce at this time see Alleman, pp. 106–7, 112; and on Mrs Sullen's likely fate, Milhous and Hume, pp. 80–81, 88–89.

37. See Scouten, *Revels History*, v, 227.

38. The quotation is from John W. Bowyer, *The Celebrated Mrs Centlivre* (Durham, North Carolina, 1952), p. 54; see also pp. 55–56; and F. P. Lock, *Susanna Centlivre* (Boston, 1979), pp. 37, 39, 42–43.

39. See Lock, p. 53; and Bowyer, pp. 71–74, noting that Centlivre borrowed Anne Oldfield's copy of Fontenelle!

40. Percy Fitzgerald, *The Life of Catherine Clive* (London, 1888), p. 82; Lock, p. 94; and Bowyer, p. 183. On the significance of Colonel Briton, see Lock, pp. 96–98; Bowyer, pp. 152–53; and John Loftis, *Comedy and Society from Congreve to Fielding* (Stanford, 1959), p. 88.

41. The plotting is well summarized on p. xxiv of Thalia Stathas's edition (Lincoln, Nebraska, 1968), from which all quotations are taken; on the play's longevity, see pp. xv–xxi.

42. Quotations from Dobree, *English Literature*, p. 226; and Pat Rogers, *The Augustan Vision* (London, 1974), p. 161.

43. Patricia M. Spacks shows the difficulty of determining its object in *John Gay* (New York, 1965), pp. 129–31.

44. For discussion, see Dane F. Smith, *Plays About the Theatre in England, 1671–1737* (New York and London, 1936), pp. 94–100. Quotations follow *John Gay: Dramatic Works*, edited by John Fuller, 2 vols (Oxford, 1983).

45. Discussed by Richard Morton and William M. Peterson on pp. ii–v of their edition of the play (Painesville, Ohio, 1961).

46. Prologue; text from Shirley Kenny's edition. For another of Steele's attacks on wit, see *The Tatler*, no. 219 (1710).

47. *The Theatre*, nos 1 and 3 (1720). See John Loftis, *Steele at Drury Lane* (Berkeley and Los Angeles, 1952), pp. 184, 188, 194–96.

48. Theophilus Cibber said that his father contributed the Tom and Phillis sections. See Loftis, *Steele*, pp. 192–93. Steele's remarks are in the Preface and Prologue.

49. Notably Paul Parnell in 'The Sentimental Mask'; see also Malcolm Kelsall, 'Terence and Steele', in *Essays on the Eighteenth-Century English Stage*, edited by Kenneth Richards and Peter Thomson (London, 1972), pp. 23–25; and Michael M. Cohen, 'Reclamation, Revulsion, and Steele's *The Conscious Lovers*', *RECTR*, 14, no. 1 (1975), 23–30. Dennis's critique is in his 'Remarks on a Play Call'd, *The Conscious Lovers*' (1723); and Goldsmith's parody in *She Stoops to Conquer*, II. 1.

50. Steele claimed it for Addison. See Samuel Johnson's 'Life of Addison' in his *Lives of the English Poets*, 2 vols (London, 1952), I, 415; and Robert D. Hume, 'The Multifarious Forms of Eighteenth-Century Comedy', in *The Stage and the Page*, edited by George W. Stone, Jr (Berkeley and Los Angeles, 1981), pp. 15–16.

51. Published by Cibber in 1728, and printed in Volume III of *The Complete Works of Sir John Vanbrugh*, edited by Bonamy Dobree, 4 vols (London, 1927). In his edition of *The Provoked Husband* (Lincoln, Nebraska, 1974), Peter Dixon dates Vanbrugh's MS to the early 1720s (pp. xviii–xix); my references are to this edition. For Georgian reaction to Cibber's play, see Arthur Murphy, *The Life of David Garrick*, 2 vols (London, 1801), I, 118; and Hugh Blair, *Lectures on Rhetoric and Belles-Lettres*, 2 vols (Boston, 1802), II, 362; for a modern critique, Muir, p. 140.

52. In his *Apology*, pp. 135, 171.

53. From the Introduction to *The Beggar's Opera*; all quotations from Fuller's edition (Volume II). Pope's remark is in the 1744 *Dunciad*, IV, 45, 47.

54. 'Life of Gay', in *Lives of the English Poets*, II, 66. Spacks summarizes the reactions, pp. 122–25. For a Georgian stricture, see [Francis Gentleman,] *The Dramatic Censor*, 2 vols (London, 1770), I, 126.

55. Sven M. Armens argues otherwise in *John Gay, Social Critic* (New York, 1954); but compare Spacks, pp. 145–51; and Bertrand H. Bronson, 'The

Beggar's Opera', in *Studies in the Comic*, Univ. of California Publications in English, 8, no. 2 (1941), 197–231 (pp. 221, 223, 230).

56. See Bronson, pp. 202, 217.

57. *The Stage and the Licensing Act 1729–1739*, edited by Vincent J. Liesenfeld (New York, 1981), pp. x–xiii, cited by R. D. Hume, 'Henry Fielding and Politics at the Little Haymarket, 1728–1737', in *The Golden and the Brazen World*, edited by John M. Wallace (Berkeley, Los Angeles, and London, 1985), n. 34.

58. II. 7 in Charles B. Woods's edition (Lincoln, Nebraska, 1966).

59. III. 8 in L. J. Morrissey's edition (Berkeley and Los Angeles, 1970).

60. See Hume, 'Henry Fielding', pp. 98, 100–101, 112; and *The Grub-Street Opera*, edited by Edgar V. Roberts (Lincoln, Nebraska, 1968), pp. xii–xxii.

61. William W. Appleton quotes the Earl of Egmont's remark in his edition of *The Historical Register* and *Eurydice Hissed* (Lincoln, Nebraska, 1967), p. xiii; 'Great Man' appears on p. 56. There is not much of Fielding in Pillage (who could be Charles Fleetwood); Honestus is the author-surrogate.

62. On which see Frederick W. Bateson, *English Comic Drama 1700–1750* (Oxford, 1929), p. 142 (quoting Leslie Stephen); and Irvin Ehrenpreis, *Fielding: Tom Jones* (London, 1964), p. 8.

63. The sympathetic author appeared simultaneously in Gabriel Odingsell's *Bays's Opera* (1730); see Smith, *Plays About the Theatre*, pp. 150–51.

Chapter 10

Sister Arts: Operatic Drama
1689–1737

Music and Poetry have ever been acknowledg'd Sisters.
. . . As Poetry is the harmony of Words, so Musick is
that of Notes . . . sure they are most excellent when they
are joyn'd.

Henry Purcell (1691)

During the Restoration, masque and opera, sharing a reliance on music, spectacle, and (to a lesser extent) dance, had been practically indistinguishable, except perhaps by scale. We noted that Dryden's 1685 definition of opera ('a poetical Tale . . . represented by Vocal and Instrumental Musick, adorned with Scenes, Machines, and Dancing') suited most masques as well, and that John Blow's *Venus and Adonis* (*c.* 1683) has received both labels.[1] Similarly, few writers on post-Revolution opera, masque, or musical drama can differentiate them confidently. Roger Fiske describes Purcell 's *Fairy Queen* (1692) as a series of masques giving 'the effect of an opera'.[2]

The crucial distinction was still between English (or 'dramatic' or 'semi-') opera, which contained spoken dialogue, and Italian opera, which was all sung. Broadly speaking, semi-operas flourished from the Revolution until 1701, and survived until 1706. After a few seasons of *pasticcios* – Italian works sung in English or both languages – foreign opera took over with Handel's *Rinaldo* (1711). *The Beggar's Opera* (1728) initiated a third and final phase dominated by the ballad operas discussed above. All of these types, however classified or evaluated, were integral parts of the multifaceted 'whole show' for which Georgian theatre is famous.

The first period contains work of modest substance but great potential; musically it belonged to the Purcells. In Henry Purcell English opera discovered a major talent to which it was unable to do justice. For ten years he wrote incidental music to various plays before composing his first and finest opera, *Dido and Aeneas* (1689), and then it was for a girls' dancing school, not the public stage; when it did reach the latter (1700), it was as four masques interpolated in *Measure for Measure*. But *Dido* is a unified miniature opera, from the premonitory tensions of its overture to the catharsis of Dido's famous lament. Nahum Tate's much maligned libretto is mostly adequate for Purcell's purposes and was admirably suited to the venue: Aeneas is a cipher,

Dido and other women dominate, and there are seventeen dances.[3]
Tate's Dido is notably mellower than Virgil's as she sings her last:

> When I am laid in earth, may my wrongs create
> No trouble in thy breast.
> Remember me! but ah! forget my fate.[4]

What we remember is the chromatic beauty of Purcell's melody
soaring above an inexorable ground bass.

The music that Purcell wrote for Betterton's lavish *opéra-ballet The
Prophetess* (1690, from Fletcher and Massinger), especially the songs for
the spectacular masque in Act v, contributed to its enduring success
and set up Purcell's important collaboration with Dryden on *King
Arthur* (1691), not just another old play 'operatized' but a joint creation
of playwright and composer.[5] Dryden, who termed the result a
'dramatick Opera' (Preface), paid generous tribute to Purcell and
implied that he subordinated his libretto to the music, though the text
combines echoes of heroic drama with the lyrical jingoism of 'Alexander's Feast'. Oswald, who thinks 'ambition is a Godlike Fault',
engages in single combat with Arthur for England and Emmeline: the
old love/war recipe. There are also pacific pastorals such as 'How blest
are shepherds', and a proto-Wagnerian emphasis on quest and magical
transformations.[6] A grand finale tries to unite everything: the team's
loveliest song, 'Fairest Isle, all Isles Excelling', and a love-duet lead into
a 'Warlike Consort', a vision of the Order of the Garter, a procession
of heroes and a royalistic trumpet air evoking St George and the
English monarchy.

King Arthur was popular for a century, yet its promising lead was
not followed up; Purcell went back to incidental music, contributing
four masques to *The Fairy Queen*, Settle's (or someone's) adaptation
of *A Midsummer Night's Dream*. *The Fairy Queen* may be only a
'glorious revue hotchpotch', and it certainly cost the United Company
dear, but some of the music has worn well.[7] The familiar Rondeau has
a graceful beauty, and Winter's song in the masque of the seasons (IV)
is still impressive for its solemn sonorities; the ground bass from
Dido's lament here becomes a melody. Purcell also contributed music
for an alteration of Fletcher's *Bonduca* and a more extensive score to
a revival of *The Indian Queen* (both 1695) before his early death.

Other composers took up the slack. Henry's brother Daniel Purcell
teamed up with Jeremiah Clarke to 'musicalize' Settle's *The World in
the Moon* (1697): part comedy, part spectacle, part masque. 'So Great
an Undertaking . . . has never been on an English stage', crowed
Settle, and when the last scene discloses an eight-tiered platform,
sixteen classical statues, a twenty-four-foot-high marble staircase, floral

garlands extending fifty feet to the rear wall, etc., the reader understands his boast. The Italianate yet realistic comedy cum rehearsed
opera is unusual, and the 'unfashionable Spark' Palmerin Worthy interesting, but the production could not recover its expenses. John Dennis
had better luck with *Rinaldo and Armida* (1698), a spectacular farrago
brewed from Tasso, Shakespeare, Spenser, and heroic drama. Lincoln's
Inn Fields was too small for this epic, and audiences disliked the
conclusion, but John Eccles's music, well integrated with dramatic
mood, helped it to a fair run.[8] The great 'operatic' success of these
years was *The Island Princess* (1699), which the industrious Peter
Motteux extracted from Fletcher, with music by Daniel Purcell and
Clarke, and a *Masque of the Seasons* by the latter. Dramatic opera was
still viable.

The trickle of English operas had almost dried up when the aria-
and-recitative invasion began in 1705 with *Arsinoe, Queen of Cyprus*,
by Motteux, Thomas Clayton, and others. Audiences accustomed to
Italian songs and singers now had a chance to hear a full-length 'opera,
after the Italian manner: All sung' – but in English. An absurd pastiche
of Italian sources, *Arsinoe* was attached to comedies like a masque,
although it lacked the usual lavish scenery; its considerable success
made it important. Despite controversy, other Italiform operas
followed, notably *Camilla* (1706), *Rosamond* (1707), and *Almahide*
(1710).[10]

Daniel Purcell was also among those who submitted settings for
Congreve's masque *The Judgment of Paris*, four versions of which were
performed in 1701.[9] The text is short and straightforward, except that
a rather rakish Paris insists that he cannot possibly judge on faces alone:
the goddesses must disrobe. Apparently all-sung, the work is virtually
an operetta.

The champions of semi-opera rallied briefly in 1706. Lord Lansdowne's *The British Enchanters*, to William Corbett's music, resembles
heroic drama in its theme, extravagant emotions, stilted dialogue, fixed
postures – the stand-off between the magicians' and the lead couple
(IV. 1) recalls *The Indian Queen* – and happy ending for the principals.
The patriotic pageantry and extensive use of magic suggest *King Arthur*
as a model. Durfey's *Wonders in the Sun* (1706) provided both traditional and composed tunes in a comic framework – almost a ballad
opera – but failed to catch on. What finally destroyed semi-opera,
however, was the theatrical reorganizations of 1706–09 that prevented
first one house and then the other from performing its English operas:
spoken drama and Italian opera were protected, dramatic opera was
not.[11] Mixed or *pasticcio* opera dominated the years 1707–10, until
Handel's *Rinaldo* made all-Italian opera fashionable, and English opera
of any kind a rarity.

In effect, the foreign stranglehold on English musical drama was broken only when Scriblerian satire, trading on Italian opera's popularity, produced a native form that spoofed opera operatically. *The Beggar's Opera* was followed by five more ballad operas in 1728, eleven in 1729, eleven more in 1730: altogether sixty-four by 1737. Handel did not stop writing Italian operas; the balladeers' activity was *added* to the operatic scene. English opera rallied briefly: in 1732–33 six new operas with English libretti were staged, plus Arne's resetting of *Rosamond*.[12] Handel's exquisite 'English pastoral opera' *Acis and Galatea*, written about 1718 with lyrics later ascribed to Gay, was produced in London in 1731–32. All-sung, it lies between masque and operetta. Handel evidently did not respond to Aaron Hill's request (1732) to write an English opera – his English oratorios were a decade away – and, except for revivals such as *King Arthur* (1735–36), semi-opera sank again from view beneath the Italian and ballad alternatives.

A kindred form, the most potent of the novelties that appeared in the post-Revolution period, was the pantomime: a kind of operatic farce in which a mythical plot alternated with mimed escapades of Harlequin and Columbine emphasizing spectacular transformations.[13] The Restoration knew and used the Italian *commedia*, but an English version developed early in the eighteenth century when the afterpiece custom was established, rival playhouses were groping for weapons, and scenic resources were heftier.[14] Cibber recalled that pantomimes were at first narrative dances, 'a pleasing and rational Entertainment' used 'as Crutches to our weakest Plays'; only later did they become 'monstrous Medlies'. London's top producer of pantomimes – and as 'Lun', its best Harlequin – was John Rich, whose spectacles and tricks delighted crowds at Lincoln's Inn Fields in the 1720s, and, after 1732, at Covent Garden. Critics such as Pope and Fielding deplored the simple-minded visual wonders and surprises, and the desecration of old plays (e.g. *Harlequin Dr Faustus*, 1723). But the popular taste ran to special effects now, with serious consequences for regular drama, which was hard pressed to compete. Combining music, text, dance, scenes, and machines, pantomimes were not 'dramatic literature', but became in many ways the quintessential Georgian entertainment.

Notes

1. Dryden's definition appears in his Preface to *Albion and Albanius* (1685); on this and Blow's composition, see Chapter 6, p. 105 and n. 9. On the

uncertainties of definition, see Robert D. Hume, 'Opera in London, 1695–1706', in *British Theatre and the Other Arts, 1660–1800*, edited by Shirley S. Kenny (Washington, 1984), pp. 68–69; John Harley, *Music in Purcell's London* (London, 1968), p. 122; Eugene Haun, *But Hark! More Harmony* (Ypsilanti, Michigan, 1971), p. 118; and Robert E. Moore, *Henry Purcell and the Restoration Theatre* (Westport, Connecticut, 1961), p. 11.

2. Roger Fiske, *English Theatre Music in the Eighteenth Century* (London, 1973), p. 6.

3. See Eric W. White, *A History of English Opera* (London, 1983), p. 112. The master of the dancing school, Josias Priest, later choreographed some of Purcell's theatre operas.

4. *Dido and Aeneas*, edited by Margaret Laurie and Thurston Dart (London, 1966), pp. 70–71. For analysis see Curtis Price, *Henry Purcell and the London Stage* (Cambridge, 1984), pp. 225–62.

5. See Dennis Arundell, *Henry Purcell* (1927; Westport, Connecticut, 1971), pp. 71, 76–77; Edward J. Dent, *Foundations of English Opera* (1928; New York, 1965), Chapter 10; and Price, *Purcell*, p. 295.

6. Compare Dent, p. 209; and Haun, p. 140.

7. Arundell, p. 83. See also White, *History of English Opera*, pp. 122–25; Dent, p. 216; and Price, *Purcell*, pp. 336, 341.

8. See the Dedication to the 1698 edition; *A Comparison Between the Two Stages* (1702; New York and London, 1973), pp. 35–36; Hume, pp. 77, 80–81; and Curtis Price, *Music in the Restoration Theatre* (n.p., 1979), pp. 57–60. Hume also discusses *The World in the Moon* (p. 72) and *The Island Princess* (p. 81).

9. Eric W. White, *A Register of First Performances of English Operas . . .* (London, 1983), p. 17. See also Fiske, p. 14.

10. *Rosamond*, an English opera in Italian style by Addison and Thomas Clayton, failed. For early reaction to *pasticcios*, see *The Spectator*, nos 5, 13, 18, and 29; and *Roger North on Music*, edited by John Wilson (London, 1959), pp. 312–13. See also Curtis Price, 'The Critical Decade for English Music Drama', *Harvard Lib. Bull.*, 26 (1978), 38–76 (pp. 42–50); and Hume, pp. 84–88.

11. Price, 'Critical Decade', pp. 38–39, 59–61, 68, and 74.

12. See Fiske, pp. 132–44; pp. 62 and 133 on *Acis and Galatea*. Gay's involvement with the play is accepted by John Fuller, editor of *John Gay: Dramatic Works*, 2 vols (Oxford, 1983), I, 32–34.

13. See Mitchell Wells, 'Spectacular Scenic Effects of the Eighteenth-Century Pantomime', *PQ*, 17 (1938), 67–81; and A. B. Nicoll, *The World of Harlequin* (Cambridge, 1963), pp. 199–202.

14. Restoration usages include Aphra Behn's *Emperor of the Moon* (1687) and Nahum Tate's *A Duke and No Duke* (1685?). See the Introduction to Tate's play in *Ten English Farces*, edited by Leo Hughes and A. H. Scouten (Austin, Texas, 1948), and Hughes's *A Century of English Farce* (Princeton, 1956), Chapter 3. For Cibber's remarks, see Chapter 15 of *An Apology for the Life of Colley Cibber* (1740), edited by B. R. S. Fone (Ann Arbor, 1968), pp. 279–81.

Part Three

The High Georgian Era 1738–1779

Chapter 11
Britannia's Rules 1738–1779

The Age of Chatham

I know that I can save the country, and that I alone can.
                                    William Pitt, Earl of Chatham

Under Walpole's Stage Licensing Act, London theatre became almost apolitical, at least on the surface. Metaphorical renderings of current issues might sneak past the censor, allusions to 'liberty' could survive to be applauded by the Prince of Wales's adherents, and drama certainly reflected the ideas and feelings of the age, but any play treating contemporary political life directly – or offering a tendentious parallel – was simply banned, like John Kelly's *The Levee* (1741). Pitt's ringing words possess an urgency foreign to Garrick's theatre, which seldom took up (and then superficially) the great issues of imperial struggle, industrial revolution, and religious fervour that moved Georgians. From the historians of the period one discovers what the dramatists could only hint at, or had to ignore.

Even a quick survey shows what a violent time this was. Besides the 'official' conflicts – War of the Austrian Succession (1743–48), the Seven Years War (1756–63), the American Revolution (1775–83) – there was a maritime struggle with Spain (1739–43), ending Walpole's era of peace, clashes in India and America outside the war years, riots and another bloody Jacobite uprising (1745) at home. In more than half of the period's forty-two years, the Royal Navy or the army (or both) fired at someone in anger. The conflicts were increasingly global, possessing maritime, European, American, Indian, and African dimensions. In 1759 ('the Year of Victories'), for example, England won at Minden, and took Madras, Québec, Lagos, and Guadaloupe. During a 'peaceful' year, 1753, the English were forced out of the Ohio valley and there were anti-turnpike riots near Leeds. And all this time Black Africans were being torn from their homes and sold abroad to serve the Empire, though slavery was outlawed within England in 1772.

The domestic scene, on the whole relatively stable, was rarely sedate. The succession was finally settled *vi armis* in the Forty-Five, and Tories made peace with Hanover, especially after 'Farmer' George III, a genuine Englishman, acceded in 1760 and chose a Tory Prime Minister, Lord Bute.[1] Politics became a question of personalities and their policies rather than of such basic constitutional issues as had racked the nation in 1688 and 1714; often the significant division was not between Whig and Tory but between 'city' and 'country' or 'old' and 'new' Whig. The instabilities of the time were ministerial: gentlemen jockeying for position after a Walpole or a Pitt fell. Yet the clashes of kings, ministers, Parliament, and people could be sharp or protracted, and from the 1760s on the public grew testier. The reputation of Parliament sank dangerously low because of its class privileges, corruption, and resistance to reform; so did George III's, over *l'affaire* Wilkes and the American War.

Walpole finally resigned (1742) amid armed conflict, the first Prime Minister forced out by defeats in the House of Commons. Ironically, it was not the Opposition wolves who replaced Walpole but some of his own sheep; and perhaps, from the standpoint of stability, the nation was fortunate that the Pelhams managed – with some fumbling – to continue the 'Robinocracy' through the war years. By contrast, the revolving cabinets of the 1760s (six ministries in eight years) weakened government, divided the nation over the peace settlement with France, the treatment of Wilkes and colonial policy, and let it drift towards confrontation and a war of ignorance with America.[2] When George III finally did achieve stability (1770) it was with Lord North, who carried out his disastrous hard line on America against considerable popular and Parliamentary opposition spearheaded by Pitt.

William Pitt the Elder (later Earl of Chatham), the great statesman of the period, forms a sharp contrast with Walpole, the consummate politician of the previous era. A fiery orator with closer ties to City merchants than to party, he made a brilliant war leader, but could not create a lasting ministry by charming (and paying) 'the club', as Walpole had. The 'Age of Chatham' was therefore not a dynasty but a series of avatars. After making his mark in the 1730s as a 'Boy Patriot', championing Frederick, Prince of Wales, against George II and Walpole, Pitt was kept waiting until 1746 for a government post, and then it was a minor one. Dismissed in 1755, he returned as Prime Minister (1757–61) to lead England to victory in the Seven Years War. His second ministry (1766–68), however, was a period of division and paralysis; only in wartime were his best qualities realized.

It was an era of patriotism, even jingoism, about war, foreign trade, and imperial expansion, with the arts reflecting the national pride enshrined in Pitt's speeches. The stage glorified Shakespeare as a *British*

genius and contributed rousers such as 'Rule, Britannia' (in James
Thomson's masque *Alfred*, 1740). 'God Save the King' became the
national anthem after a concert audience sang it spontaneously during
the Forty-Five; William Hogarth signed himself 'Britophil'; successful
generals and admirals had their portraits painted by Sir Joshua
Reynolds; landscape gardeners represented the far corners of the
commercial empire in their plantings.[3] Such were the lighter aspects
of a lucrative imperialism that rested on enslavement and conquest.

From the top to the bottom of this multivalent society, higher
achievements more or less kept up with greater sins and sufferings.
Enclosure Acts – one exception to the general rule that important
developments rarely stemmed from the government – streamlined
farming, but made rural life untenable for the many peasants and
smallholders who had depended on access to commons.[4] Demographic
change proceeds ecologically: the poor became less landlocked, more
mobile, and were thus available for the factory jobs that began to open
around 1760, the traditional commencement of the Industrial Revolution. A new Royal Society was set up to 'Encourage' manufacturing,
etc. in 1754; Wedgwood's potteries, Hargreaves's spinning jenny,
Watt's steam engine, and Arkwright's spinner and water frame for his
factories all came into existence in the next fifteen years. Once Watt
teamed up with Matthew Boulton, a Birmingham entrepreneur, in
1773, eighteenth-century England's most radical revolution was fairly
under way.

Jobs were also available constructing the canals, roads, and iron
bridges that improved communications dramatically after 1750, and
further increased mobility. Much of this activity occurred in the
Midlands; by the time Parliament passed a General Turnpike Act
(1773), places like Leeds and Birmingham had been improving trans-
portation for years. Gradual advances in medicine, sanitation, and
agriculture reduced the death rate, and the population began to
increase, sharply after mid-century. This led to urban problems, partly
alleviated by private charities (such as foundling hospitals) that the
rising prosperity of middle-class philanthropists such as Captain
Thomas Coram made possible.[5] The first stirrings of the humanitarian
movement, led by Coram, Wilberforce, General Oglethorpe, and
others, began to agitate against the slave trade.

The Royal Navy exemplified many of the age's contradictions. It
scored brilliant victories over European fleets, such as Quiberon Bay
(1759), and protected the coast against French invasion, most notably
in 1745. Generally popular and prestigious, hymned as the ruler of the
waves, it was also engaged in backing the claims of English merchants
and settlers along the coasts of India and Africa, in seizing Spanish
treasure galleons, and in other acts of state piracy. Yet one of these

'pirates', Admiral Anson, circumnavigated the globe with his squadron, a significant feat in 1740–44. Of more scientific interest were Captain Cook's voyages (1768–79), the first disclosing Australia, the second reaching 71 ° S. in search of Antarctica, the third opening Oceania and the Pacific Northwest coast to Europeans. Even here there is ambiguity: although the voyages were co-sponsored by the Royal Society and produced a wealth of information for geographers, botanists, anthropologists, etc. – as well as art – they also allowed Europe to unleash the full panoply of her civilization upon the natives: traders, missionaries, soldiers, convicts.[6]

Sharp divisions between different economic groups, the beginnings of industrial fragmentation, characterized High Georgian society. Both paupers and consumers were conspicuous. On one hand, great peers increased their ownership of England's land by 5 per cent over the century (and land values almost doubled), while some industrialists made fortunes in iron, beer, or textiles; on the other, Poor Laws proliferated and by 1776 there were about two thousand parish workhouses.[7] Overall the standard of living was rising, creating surpluses and, for perhaps half the population, the leisure to enjoy travel, books, music, drama, gardening, horse-racing, hunting, etc.[8] The pursuit of happiness remained a handicap race for women in a frankly sexist society, but women made progress as wives and daughters, if not yet as citizens; the *mariage de convenance* decried by Steele grew less common. The urban poor could be seen – can still be seen, in Hogarth's famous print – making themselves 'dead drunk for a penny' in Gin Lane, though Parliament passed a Gin Act (1751). Government remained well behind social change, but kept on its trail, when Members' own interests and prejudices did not overpower the scent. The negativism of most Georgian legislation, from the Licensing Act to the Penal Acts against Massachusetts (1774), suggests an obsolete political structure dealing in an *ad hoc* manner with events it cannot comprehend.

The Age of Hume

'Tis not solely in poetry and music, we must follow our taste and sentiment, but likewise in philosophy.

David Hume

It has been called the Enlightenment, the Age of Reason, or of

Johnson, but the period resists labels. The cultural world continued to fragment as the ground common to writers, theologians, and philosophers diminished. The Enlightenment, primarily a European phenomenon, was opposed by strong forces in England; the reaction against reason was even more widespread. It could as well be termed the Age of Pulling Apart, of Unreason.

Nor can Dr Johnson's values (much as I revere them, and him) be called 'representative' of High Georgian culture as a whole. Virtually everything he wrote was grandly obsolescent: his poems moralize in heroic couplets, his tragedy *Irene* echoes heroic drama, his criticism is a valedictory for the neoclassical school, and *Rasselas* is a didactic fable, not a novel. His periodical essays continue Addison's form in a style reminiscent of Sir Thomas Browne's.[9] In politics an unreconstructed Tory, in bearing and outlook the last of the great literary arbiters, he dismissed Macpherson, the ballad revival, and Sterne; deplored Wesley and Wilkes; refuted Hume with a kick. The *Dictionary* (1755), a solid achievement, did help to spread literacy – which was increasingly employed on kinds of literature he detested.[10]

What Johnson does well represent is the right wing of Georgian letters, the hard edge that was least susceptible to the blandishments of innovation and sentiment. 'London' and 'The Vanity of Human Wishes' carry on the moral satire of Swift and Pope, as do the caricatures and paintings of William Hogarth, whose rakes, harlots, leering spectators, and distraught couples are grotesque exempla of excess and imprudence. Among novelists, Johnson preferred Richardson to Fielding, but Smollett, with his Grub Street toughness, is the most 'Johnsonian' of them. His and Johnson's travel narratives belong to the old moral/empirical tradition, not with the 'sentimental journeys'.[11] On-stage, while some plays luxuriated in emotionalism, the laughing comedies and farces shared Johnson's antipathy to 'cant' and 'humbug'.

Several great writers of non-fictional prose *could* be subsumed under an 'Age of Johnson', however much he reviled some of their premises: the massively studious historian of the Caesars, Edward Gibbon; Adam Smith, the prophet of acquiescence in the present economic order; and the early, anti-revolutionary Jeremy Bentham. Yet even here, pro-American Whigs such as Burke, men of the world like Chesterfield, garrulous self-advertisers like Cibber, and reformers such as Paine would need a different patron. Johnson's manners and morals were those of the cultural generation that passed away in the 1740s: Pope, Swift, Bentley, Bolingbroke, Lady Mary Wortley Montagu.

In that decade there emerged a new audience for the new blank verse, independent of Pope and Dryden: Reverend Young's *Night Thoughts* and Blair's *The Grave*, Mark Akenside's *The Pleasures of Imagination*, Joseph Warton's *The Enthusiast*, and his brother Thomas's

The Pleasures of Melancholy. The last initiated (or caught) a reflux of taste from Pope's 'Attic' art to the 'sweeter transport' of Spenser and a 'Gothic' aesthetic. James Thomson, known for tragedy and for *The Seasons*, brought out *The Castle of Indolence*, with Spenserian stanzas, diction, mood, and scenery, to acclaim in 1748. The Wartons' essays on Spenser and Pope (1754, 1756) confirmed a swing towards Spenser's more decorative and emblematic verse. The major poets of mid-century, Collins and Gray, differ markedly from Pope in their extensive use of the ode, their interest in archaic northern forms, and their love of minor keys and twilight hues. Gray's 'Elegy in a Country Churchyard' (1750) combines the mood of the graveyard school with a tribute to the common man; Johnson's generous praise of it in his 'Life of Gray' contrasts with his antipathy to most of Gray's canon. Johnson's own 'Vanity of Human Wishes' was, then, old-fashioned in 1749. His friend Oliver Goldsmith's poems, while they employ the versification of Pope (and Johnson), belong emotionally with the work of the younger generation.

The novel was the most significant literary innovation of the period. As Defoe had brought verisimilitude, Richardson imparted sensibility, and, in *Clarissa*, tragic grandeur, to the problems of more or less ordinary lives; Fielding gave epic sweep and seriousness to such characters and the form. The novel's usefulness as a vehicle for introspection and sensitivity is apparent in Sterne's *Tristram Shandy*, the publishing phenomenon of the 1760s, in Goldsmith's *The Vicar of Wakefield*, and in Fanny Burney's *Evelina*, though Smollett and Horace Walpole showed other ways to use it. Johnson played no part in this development: his penchant was towards the moral fable.

Whose age was it, then? In philosophy, David Hume's, though he lacked the reputation and influence of Hobbes or Locke. His weight made itself felt slowly – Adam Smith was his student and friend – and his views represent a ground swell in Georgian intellectual life that Johnson's do not. In Hume's central writings, *The Treatise of Human Nature* (1739) and *An Enquiry Concerning Human Understanding* (1748), Lockean concepts such as learning from sensory experience and the association of ideas are put to quite un-Lockean uses. The main thrust is against reason, or at least against rationalism. One casualty is Deism: 'Our most holy religion is founded on *faith*, not on reason', argued Hume, adding that the non-rational leap of faith is itself the one great Christian miracle.[12] 'The atheist Hume', as he became known, contended that our understanding of causation and nature comes about 'not by reason but by experience' (*ECHU*, IV. 1). The 'necessary connection' that we posit between causes and effects 'is nothing but an internal impression of the mind' (*THN*, III. 14).

Hume's universe is discontinuous, fragmentary; 'every effect is a distinct event from its cause'; 'objects have no discoverable connexion together' (*ECHU*, IV. 1; *THN*, III. 8). B follows A today, as it always has, but I can see no *reason* why it should do so tomorrow. Moreover, Humean man leads a hermetic existence, since 'we can never really advance a step beyond ourselves' in this world (*THN*, II. 6). *Pace* Locke, we have no sense of *self*, only a sense of perceptions. Our consciousness is 'a kind of theatre, where successive perceptions make their appearance', but we recognize neither the scene nor the story (*THN*, IV. 6). What enables us to operate at all is 'Custom, . . . the great guide of human life'; we do not *understand* existence, merely develop habits that give an illusion of regularity (*ECHU*, VI). 'Thus', concludes Hume, 'the observation of human blindness and weakness is the result of all philosophy' (*ECHU*, IV. 1).

The burden of Hume's argument is to place more importance on sentiment and intuition: an outlook that was beginning to permeate mid-eighteenth-century culture. It is feeling, not ratiocination, that causes us to believe one idea and not another; we have to feel about something before we can think about it. Hume insists that philosophy, like the arts, comes down to 'taste and sentiment' (*THN*, III. 8; *ECHU*, VI, VII). Such views encouraged – and coincided with – the growth of pre-Romantic and sentimental literature.

There was also a significant empirical tradition, extending rather than rejecting Locke. David Hartley was the most important exemplar: one of his followers was Joseph Priestley, from whom Jeremy Bentham derived his 'greatest happiness for the greatest number' doctrine.[13] Both Hartley and Priestley combined science with religion, moving from association of ideas to Optimism and meliorism. Hartley's *Observations on Man* (1749) is a remarkable synthesis of Hobbesian 'Sensory Vibrations' with a moral sense built up through association. Priestley, a product of one of the excellent dissenting academies, taught and ministered, wrote volumes on physics, metaphysics, ecclesiastical and secular history, politics, grammar, etc., and in his spare time discovered the law of inverse squares and isolated oxygen, among other scientific achievements. The empirical strain is also strong in Bentham, who, not yet Radical in the 1770s but a rather conservative utilitarian, appreciated Priestley's common sense about government and society, and in William Paley's theology.[14]

The great cultural phenomenon of the period, Methodism, offered an alternative to empiricism or rational dissent, and to much of Georgian life and thought. John Wesley came down on the eighteenth century like a new St Paul: proclaiming a mission to the poor, teaching the masses in the fields, denouncing slavery and corruption, organizing congregations and keeping them faithful through visits and letters.[15] One of the first great revivalists, he preached a religion of the heart in which salvation was through faith; like Hume, Wesley rated belief above reason, though man was also justified by good works such as tithing. Wesley concentrated on the lower classes, preaching education, cleanliness, and self-discipline as well as devotion. By 1760 Methodism was the most potent, coherent, and passionate ideology in England, averaging about a thousand converts a year; later it doubled that. High-Churchmen and aristocrats blamed Wesley for encouraging hysteria and insubordination in the mob ('I do not desire any discourse with any person of quality in England', he wrote), but David Hartley, who criticized national immorality in terms similar to Wesley's, praised the example of the Methodists. To their 'left', a host of evangelical sects turned a Calvinistic eye on society, reading the Bible literally and joining the widespread assault on reason.[16]

Not that the cultural picture was wholly bleak. The amount of time and money spent on books, music, and recreation increased dramatically.[17] The natural benevolence of man posited by the philosophers found expression in social and religious philanthropies. The writing of history reached new heights of sophistication and industry with Smollett, Hume, and Gibbon. Shakespeare received the most intelligent and imaginative treatment yet from actors (Garrick) and critics (Johnson). Novels proliferated, and poetry at least experimented with new modes. Research was conducted on everything from Norse ballads to physics. Yet there were, throughout the period and society, undercurrents of an instinctual resistance to all this enlightenment that forewarn of large upheavals in the offing.

The Age of Garrick

> Our [dramatic] poet's performance . . . must be tried in the manager's fire, strained through a licenser, suffer from repeated corrections . . . it may be a mere *caput mortuum* when it arrives before the public.
>
> Oliver Goldsmith, *Present State of Polite Learning* (1759)

The Licensing Act cast a long shadow over Garrick's theatre. By censoring regular drama and restricting it to Covent Garden and Drury Lane, it limited the market for dramatists and the menu for audiences. Together, the two theatres might stage nine premières a year, but fewer than half of these would be full-length plays. Dramatic talent was diverted elsewhere – Fielding is the best example – while an increase in the number of spectators encouraged the enlargement of London's playhouses and the spread of 'minor' theatres in the suburbs and provincial towns. Bristol, for example, acquired a Theatre Royal (1766) which is today our best example of an eighteenth-century English playhouse.[18]

Indeed the 'patent monopoly' was far from total. Even in London it was possible to operate without one: since John Rich at Covent Garden owned both patents, Drury Lane functioned under a series of licences. The century's greatest actor, David Garrick, made his debut at Goodman's Fields, outside of town and the patent system. The Haymarket Opera had a separate arrangement. Samuel Foote often ran the Little Theatre in the Haymarket under a licence before 1766. Out at Sadler's Wells, mostly a summer pantomime house, one visitor in 1774 found audiences better entertained than in the city theatres.[19]

Still, the twin foci of national drama were Drury Lane and Covent Garden, both remarkably stable in management, acting personnel, and premises. Garrick managed the Drury Lane company – still in Wren's 1674 building – from 1747 until his retirement in 1776, when R. B. Sheridan took over; many of the same actors returned year after year. John Rich operated Covent Garden from its construction (1732) until his death in 1761, when it passed to his son-in-law John Beard. Thereafter it was purchased (1767) by a diverse quartet, of whom Thomas Harris emerged as sole owner in 1774. Garrick staged an average of six new plays a year; Rich, with a less critical audience, ventured only three.[20]

As productions grew more elaborate, they became costlier to stage, so managers sought to accommodate more spectators. Drury Lane was altered in 1747 and 1762 to raise its seating capacity from an estimated seven hundred and fifty to around two thousand within the existing structure.[21] In 1775 Robert Adam lengthened the building by over 70 per cent – the auditorium by about 60 per cent, the stage by almost 100 per cent – and used slimmer pilasters and a higher ceiling to create an impression of spaciousness. At Covent Garden, John Rich found ways to boost his capacity from about fourteen hundred to two thousand or more by 1780, and built an antechamber that made his stage the longest in Europe. Foote even enlarged the Little Hay, adding seats in the upper gallery. Though the familiar form of the Restoration playhouse remained – a pit raked up to a 'U' of boxes, below two tiers of galleries – the characteristically English smallness was being lost.

The changes in physical layout naturally produced changes in acting: chiefly the retreat of the actors towards the proscenium arch.[22] Cibber calculated that the shortening of the forestage by four feet in 1696 had forced the actors at least ten feet back, and in 1775 Wren's original twenty-one-foot platform was further reduced to eleven feet in a much longer hall. The change in lighting that Garrick introduced after his return from the Continent in 1765 – immediately copied by Covent Garden – reinforced this pressure: the removal of the chandeliers over the platform and the increase of sidelighting in the wings were intended to reduce glare and improve visibility, but by enhancing the illumination of the deep-stage 'scene' at the expense of the forestage they too operated to draw the actors away from the audience, into a 'picture'.

The distancing of the actors in larger theatres accelerated the shift of emphasis 'from heads to ears . . . to eyes' that Pope had noted in 1737: at least the scene designers' spectacles were large enough to be appreciated from the upper gallery. So the simple side-wings, upper borders, and shuttered back flats inherited from the Restoration were steadily refined. All became machine-movable; back and side scenes painted on canvas were drawn off and on to rollers; and a front drop-scene began to be used as an act-curtain.[23] The standard of painting, both realistic and romantic, improved markedly after Garrick imported de Loutherbourg, a master of depth illusions and special effects such as the 'lighted transparency', in 1771. An actor's most dangerous competition no longer came from other actors. At the same time, costumes became more colourful and authentic.

The overall effect on acting and dramatic taste of this swing from verbal to visual and from cosy to grandiose was deleterious; the players were forced to yell, grimace, and broaden their gestures.[24] Most historians have blamed John Rich's spectacular pantomimes for debasing public taste, but both managers were heavily involved in the expensive competition. 'House charges' to authors doubled from Cibber's heyday to Garrick's, while total theatrical budgets increased four- or fivefold over the century. From the 1770s it was less an 'actors' age' than the scenists' and machinists'.

And yet if we had walked into a London theatre at any time before the 1790s, we would have thought it not cavernous but intimate; even after the remodellings of 1775 and 1782 hardly anyone was more than fifty feet from the stage in an auditorium only fifty feet wide. The spectators were intime as well, crowded on to the pit benches, talking to other regulars there or in the nearby boxes before (sometimes during) the play, often standing jampacked for major attractions. The theatrical public was growing, and broadening in social class, yet it retained coherent nuclei.[25] Aristocrats still attended (though many of them now preferred the opera), sitting mainly in the boxes; footmen considered the upper gallery their own; middle-class men (lawyers, clerks, merchants, intellectuals, students) dominated the pit; middle-class ladies preferred the lower gallery.

Whether this audience seems large or small, homogeneous or

heterogeneous, depends on one's perspective. A Restoration courtier would have thought Drury Lane in 1775 mobbed by *une foule*, whereas we would probably notice that the spectators were all middle class and above (except for the nobility's footmen). The need to procure seats well before the six p.m. curtain militated against the working man, who was also less able than his Elizabethan or modern counterpart to afford the cost.[26] While audiences were not courtly, they were still, then, in a sense, 'select'. A Georgian playwright distinguished between the noisy upper gallery, the yawning boxes, and 'the middle class and bulk of the assembly'; to a modern critic they were all *spiritually* middle class.[27] Garrick's public can be deemed heterogeneous by Restoration, but not by Jacobean, standards. The twelve thousand to fourteen thousand regular playgoers posited for the 1740s represent about 2 per cent of London's estimated population at the time; the comparable figure for 1605 is 13 per cent.[28]

The behaviour of Georgian audiences has defied rational analysis. Certainly they were capable of violence, rioting against French actors (1738, 1755), against price changes (1744, 1763), and on other occasions. At the Haymarket in 1738, an audience spokesman told the King's representatives 'That the Audience had a legal Right to shew their Dislike to any Play or Actor' and 'that the Judicature of the Pit had been acknowledged and acquiesced to, Time immemorial'.[29] Playgoers could also be quietly attentive to satisfactory productions, and downright adulatory towards their favourites, such as Garrick. But which type of conduct dominated, and were they getting better or worse? Assertions that spectators, for all their turbulence, gradually became more proper, or more indifferent, are balanced by declarations that they remained lively and did not mellow.[30] Evidently they were an exuberant medley who ran the gamut from general order to occasional riot, and increased in refinement as well as in boisterous whimsy as time passed; the last serious theatre riot of the period occurred in 1763. Playgoers were rowdiest before the opening curtain – throwing food and drink from the galleries, giving animal calls in the pit – but usually quieted when the play began unless angry at something, or unless a claque had been formed to 'clap' or damn a new play.[31]

To give a single truthful answer to the question of what these audiences wanted or expected is impossible: different groups had different wishes, and tastes change in forty years. 'Sentimental' comedies had a vogue in the 1760s, for example, whereas spectators of the 1770s were apt to ridicule them.[32] There were serious playgoers like Burke and Johnson, people concerned about a national drama (e.g. Whitehead), people willing to be instructed, even to weep over distress, benevolence, or patriotism, but most spectators probably went to the theatre to be entertained, not to be improved. If edification or sensibility was the pill, it had better be sugar-coated. *False Delicacy* and *The West Indian*, 'sentimental' successes of 1768 and 1771, market humour and satire as well as sensibility.

Georgian audiences had a keen sense of what was due them. If a scene was beneath their dignity, they might hiss it off as 'low': the fate of Goldsmith's bailiff scene in *The Good-Natured Man* (1768). If a performer was absent, or 'out' in a part, a handsome apology was exacted. Some still expected to be seated on-stage, and not until enough decided that their beloved theatrical illusion was thereby marred was Garrick able to banish them thence (1763). The high-spirited, carnival atmosphere of a Georgian playhouse has been vividly re-created by Allardyce Nicoll.[33] A time machine may be a scientific impossibility, but his description transports us, for a few minutes, into the veritable 'noise and tumult' of Garrick's theatre.

Notes

1. Useful sources on the political history of the period include: J. Carswell, *From Revolution to Revolution* (London, 1973), esp. pp. 96–114; R. W. Harris, *England in the Eighteenth Century* (London, 1963), esp. pp. 94, 114–15, 175–83; J. H. Plumb, *England in the Eighteenth Century* (Harmondsworth, 1950), esp. pp. 85, 105; Roy Porter, *English Society in the Eighteenth Century* (London, 1982); and W. A. Speck, *Society and Literature in England 1700–1760* (Dublin, 1983), esp. pp. 37–40.

2. Harris, p. 138.

3. Carswell, pp. 103, .108, 114; Porter, p. 22.

4. Asa Briggs, *A Social History of England* (London, 1983), pp. 172–77; see also p. 207, and Goldsmith's 'The Deserted Village' (1770). Other useful sources on the social history include Porter, esp. Chapter 1 and pp. 36–38, 42–43; Speck, esp. pp. 135–36; and Dorothy Marshall, *Eighteenth-Century England*, second edition (London, 1974), esp. p. 485.

5. See M. Dorothy George, *London Life in the Eighteenth Century* (1925; Harmondsworth, 1966), pp. 55–57; Carswell, p. 98; and Harris, p. 218.

6. An interesting account is Bernard Smith, *European Vision and the South Pacific* (Oxford, 1960).

7. Briggs, pp. 170–71, 176.

8. J. H. Plumb, *Georgian Delights* (London, 1980), p. 48 and passim; and Carswell, p. 96.

9. The observation of James Boswell, *Life of Johnson*, edited by R. W. Chapman, new edition (Oxford, 1952), p. 219 (1756).

10. Carswell, p. 109; see also p. 106.

11. See Thomas Curley, *Samuel Johnson and the Age of Travel* (Athens, Georgia, 1976), p. 49.

12. *An Enquiry Concerning Human Understanding*, Section x, part 2 (abbreviated as *ECHU*, x. 2). The texts of *ECHU* and *The Treatise of Human Nature* (*THN*) follow Charles W. Hendel, Jr's edition, *Hume: Selections* (New York, 1927; 1955). For brief discussions of Hume, see G. R. Cragg, *The Church and the Age of Reason* (Harmondsworth, 1960), pp. 168–69; and Basil Willey, *The Eighteenth-Century Background* (1940; Harmondsworth, 1965), pp. 109–24.

13. Willey, p. 164. I am generally indebted to Chapters 8 and 10.

14. See Cragg, pp. 170–71; and Leslie Stephen, *English Literature and Society in the Eighteenth Century* (1904; London, 1963), p. 111.

15. See Carswell, pp. 99–102, 165; Cragg, Chapter 10; Marshall, Chapter 18, Section 6; Plumb, *England*, Part II, Chapter 3; and Porter, pp. 192–93.

16. See Cragg, pp. 153–54.

17. Plumb, *Georgian Delights*, pp. 10, 26, 31.

18. On the suburban and provincial theatres, see Harry W. Pedicord, *The Theatrical Public in the Time of Garrick* (New York, 1954), pp. 23, 28, 30, 154; and 'The Changing Audience', in *The London Theatre World, 1660–1800*, edited by Robert D. Hume (Carbondale, Illinois, 1980), pp. 251–52; and Allardyce Nicoll, *Late Eighteenth-Century Drama*, second edition (Cambridge, 1952), p. 3. He describes the Bristol theatre in *The Garrick Stage* (Manchester, 1980), p. 41.

19. See Nicoll, *Garrick Stage*, p. 96; and Arthur H. Scouten, in *The London Stage 1660–1800*, 5 parts (Carbondale, Illinois, 1960–68), Part 3 (1961), p. xxxix. My debt to both of these sources is general. On patents and licences, see Judith Milhous, 'Company Management', in *The London Theatre World*, p. 9.

20. George W. Stone, Jr, *The London Stage*, Part 4 (1962), p. clxix, though my debt is wider. See also pp. xxx and xliii.

21. Estimates range from 500 to 1000 (1674) and 1800 to 2300 (1762). See Edward Langhans, 'The Theatres', in *The London Theatre World*, pp. 42, 47–48, 62; Pedicord, *Theatrical Public*, pp. 5–6; Stone, Part 4, p. xxxi; and Nicoll, *Garrick Stage*, p. 40. The Little Hay held around 1500 by 1790; see Stone, Part 4, p. xliii; and Langhans, p. 63. On compactness as an English speciality see Richard Southern, *The Georgian Playhouse* (London, 1948), p. 20; for a description of the typical playhouse, see Nicoll, *Garrick Stage*, pp. 23–24.

22. Colin Visser, 'Scenery and Technical Design', in *The London Theatre World*, p. 67. Cibber's remark is in *An Apology for the Life of Colley Cibber*, edited by B. R. S. Fone (Ann Arbor, 1968), p. 225. See also Langhans, p. 62; and Nicoll, *Late Eighteenth-Century Drama*, pp. 38–39; *Garrick Stage*, pp. 56, 116–18.

23. Nicoll, *Garrick Stage*, pp. 120–29, 137–41, 156–57; also *Late Eighteenth-Century Drama*, pp. 24–35; Stone, Part 4, pp. cxvii–cxx and *London Theatre World*, p. 184; and James J. Lynch, *Box, Pit and Gallery* (Berkeley and Los Angeles, 1953), p. 6.

24. Leo Hughes, *The Drama's Patrons* (Austin, Texas, 1971), pp. 181–84; and

Nicoll, *Late Eighteenth-Century Drama*, p. 23. Also helpful on the subject: Stone, *London Stage*, Part 4, pp. cxvii–cxx; and Milhous, p. 22.

25. See Nicoll, *Garrick Stage*, pp. 8, 84; and Pedicord, 'Changing Audience', p. 246.

26. Pedicord, *Theatrical Public*, p. 27; he argues (p. 154) that they were at the 'minor' theatres. See also Lynch, pp. 204–5; and Stone, *London Theatre World*, p. 192.

27. General John Burgoyne, Preface to *The Maid of the Oaks* (1774); Hughes, pp. 178–79.

28. Scouten, Part 3, pp. clxi–clxii; and Nicoll, *Garrick Stage*, p. 8 and n. 8.

29. Benjamin Victor, *History of the Theatres of London and Dublin*, 3 vols (London, 1771), I, 55–56.

30. Nicoll, *Late Eighteenth-Century Drama*, pp. 5–6, 9–11, 15–17, 22; Calhoun Winton, 'Dramatic Censorship', in *London Theatre World*, p. 308; Scouten, Part 3, pp. clxxi–clxxiii; and Pedicord, 'Changing Audience', p. 248. See also Hughes, pp. 32–33, 43, 53, 65, 74, 120–36, 155; Stone, *London Stage*, Part 4, p. clxxxiv; and Lynch, p. 206.

31. See Nicoll, *Garrick Stage*, pp. 86–91; and V. C. Clinton-Baddeley, *All Right on the Night* (London, 1954), esp. pp. 46–47, 55, 66–68, 76, 80, and 144.

32. Richard W. Bevis, *The Laughing Tradition* (Athens, Georgia, 1980), pp. 61–63. On audiences' desires (next sentence), see Nicoll, *Garrick Stage*, p. 95, quoting Thomas Davies.

33. In *The Garrick Stage*, pp. 78–100.

Chapter 12

The Luxury of Grief: Georgian Tragedy and Tragicomedy

From passions unrestrain'd what mischiefs grow.

David Mallet, *Elvira* (1763)

Tragic writing was inhibited for several decades by the Licensing Act. So was comic writing, but tragedy was the weaker, less popular genre, and the banning of both Brooke's *Gustavus Vasa* and Thomson's *Edward and Eleonora* in 1739 cannot have encouraged tragic dramatists. Whole seasons passed in the 1740s, 1750s, and 1760s without a new tragedy appearing. Not until the mid-1760s did the spurts become a flow; about half of the period's tragedies and tragicomedies were written and produced after 1765.

In these plays, the bourgeois trend of the 1730s was reversed; domestic tragedies were as scarce as if Lillo had not written. Instead there was a resurgence of Congrevian tragicomedy and heroic themes. It is almost a reversion to Stuart drama, without the poetry of Beaumont and Fletcher or the thunder of Dryden and Lee. Instead of eliciting tragedy from contemporary problems, as Charles Johnson had tried to do, the tragedians breathed doubtful life into such corpses as Mustapha and Essex, and developed the she-tragedy into the drama of exalted female nobility. Something in the age again lusted after heroics, though blank verse remained the norm. Many plays contain elements that can reasonably be called 'classical', but they are accompanied by appeals to pathos, and piteous touches are as likely to occur in a classical or heroic play as in a domestic one. In this confused picture it becomes more difficult to recognize 'schools' of tragedy: most writers seem to hold several degrees.

The Scottish contribution to British tragedy was notable in George II's reign, two veterans of the 1730s, Thomson and Mallet, dominating the first decade after the Act. Mallet's *Mustapha* (1739), a blank-verse adaptation of Boyle's 1665 heroic drama, changes it significantly, removing the Queen of Hungary plot to unify the action and shifting the emotional spectrum towards pathos. The shades of Solyman, Roxalana, Rustan, Mustapha, and Zanger dance to the quieter music invoked by Thomson's Prologue, where tragedy is the 'Queen of soft sorrows, and of useful fears'. Mustapha has a tearful reconciliation with Solyman and an effusive parting from his wife, who has a pathetic encounter with Roxalana; the Epilogue refuses to betray the 'fair virtue' and 'feeling pity' of the play with bawdy jokes. Mallet's characters also say they prefer 'Nature' to court life. *Mustapha* is competent mid-level writing: the diction is seldom strained, and Solyman is interesting (though frustrating) as a failed champion of civilization, too gullible to resist the knaves. The Emira plot, however, seems an afterthought, the attempts to heighten the mood are conventional, and Mallet demonstrates no great gift for language, character, or psychological analysis.

Thomson's *Edward and Eleonora* is also set in the Near Orient, but the characters are English Crusaders with a fondness for heroic rant. Here again feeling is indulged, especially in Daraxa's sorrowful narrative and the 'long farewell' of hero and heroine – possibly the longest pathetic passage in Georgian tragedy – yet the final scene exalts judgement and moderation above passion and the 'mistaken Zeal' of the Crusaders! The play's genre is as mixed as its value system: by saving both Edward and Eleonora from apparently fatal doses of poison and recasting the villain as hero, Thomson wrenches his tragedy to tragicomedy and cheapens the pathos of the royal couple's earlier parting. The first scene sufficed to get the play banned: Gloster's list of England's ills includes 'ministerial Rapine' and 'evil Counsellors . . . gather'd round the Throne' (later, Edward lashes 'corrupting Ministers and Favourites', those 'base servile Vermin of a Court'). 'One step to lawless Power . . . the least infringement of our Charters', warns Gloster, 'Would hurl the giddy Nation into Tempest'. And when he read that the 'Royal Heir' (the Prince of Wales) has a 'juster Claim' on his father than do 'Aliens' who make a 'Market of his Honour', the Examiner must have known what he had to do.[1] Altering the play in 1775, Thomas Hull excised the 'exceptionable Passages'.

When Henry Brooke published *Gustavus Vasa*, he included an apologia claiming that patriotism (then a code word among the Prince of Wales's adherents for opposition to the King and Walpole) was his 'great and single *Moral*'. His offences are less obvious than Thomson's, but in the charged atmosphere of 1739, the casting of Gustavus as 'Deliverer' of a country in 'Bondage' to 'a Tyrant's Sceptre' might have suggested to the Examiner the Prince of Wales; and his remark (to Sweden) 'thy brave Sons lie speechless,/And foreign Snakes engender' (I. 1) could have seemed pointed. *Honi soit qui mal y pense*. Despite Johnson's pamphlet ironically 'vindicating' the licenser, the play was not produced until 1744 – in Dublin, as *The Patriot*.

Tancred and Sigismunda (1745), Thomson's last original tragedy, subordinates heroic to domestic and emotive impulses. Tancred and Baron Osmond duel both for political power and for Sigismunda, daughter of Chancellor Siffredi, who attempts to manipulate them all.

This meshing of public and private considerations recalls Dryden and Otway, but Thomson's preoccupation is a father's power over his daughter's hand: a recurrent theme in Georgian drama. When she kneels to him and insists, 'Not to chuse/Without your wise direction, may be duty;/But still my choice is free' (III. 1), the play's emotions reach a first peak. Sigismunda chooses duty over love. At last Osmond, mortally wounded by Tancred, stabs her and dies, saying, ''Tis great!' (v. 4). Siffredi – who has a good deal to answer for – then points his moral at us: 'Ne'er with your children act a tyrant's part'. (The didacticism extends to the Epilogue, another that denounces irreverent epilogues.) An anonymous critical afterword in the 1774 Edinburgh edition pronounces the play monotonous, a 'closet' (reading) piece despite its stage success, and its language occasionally too 'sentimental' (sententious). Yet each of the sympathetic principals has a valid point, the plot is well joined, and the situation is genuinely tragic: the love of Tancred for Sigismunda is an insoluble problem, dooming all it touches.

Other tragedies of the 1740s gesture ineffectually in several directions: neoclassical, domestic, English history. Adaptations of Voltaire continued with James Miller's *Mahomet* and Aaron Hill's *Meropé* (1749), a new sort of heroic drama.[2] Eumenes, like Thomson's Tancred, is a true prince, but unknown to himself and to everyone save a foster-father, who gives him a bucolic upbringing to shield him from political danger: henceforth a popular type. The Prologue urges ladies to 'Nobly weep out', since '"Tis virtue's mark, to weep at others' woe'; the opening scene is a funereal pageant – 'Meropé, mournful on a couch; Ismene leaning melancholy below', bidding us 'See where the lone majestic mourner weeps' – and the foster-father, Narbas, meditates among the tombs. Yet the final axe falls only on the villains, sparing Eumenes, his mother Meropé, and Narbas. If any tragic feeling has survived the slow exposition, awkward diction, and formal *récits* of off-stage violence, it is dissipated when Hill settles for tragicomedy.

Irene (1749, written 1736) would be part of this ruck were it not by Dr Johnson. The good offices of Garrick sustained it for nine nights, but the difficulties posed by the diction and the essential 'untheatricality' of the material were (and are) insuperable.[3] The opening speeches, slowed by an attempt to give a large moral/historical view of Greece's fall, are choked with sentiment and aphorism; the second scene is equally ponderous; and Aspasia and Demetrius speak a combination of rant and 'Johnsonese' (see IV. 1). It is the language of a man who believed that theatrical audiences 'come to hear a certain number of lines recited with just gesture and elegant modulation' (*Preface to Shakespeare*). The formal exchanges of ideas (II. 1) and Mahomet's courting of Irene in couplets (II. 7) sound like heroic drama, but a religious solemnity suited to 'The Vanity of Human Wishes' undercuts the heroics; the last speech echoes the Prologue's 'mighty Moral for Mankind' and Aspasia's admonitions to Irene. Demetrius and Aspasia, with whom Johnson seems to identify, survive, so the play *feels* tragicomic despite Irene's horrible ending.[4] Since the escaped heroes are absent, however – their survival is only implied – our joy is muted at the final moral.

The 'star' of a modest tragic renaissance around 1749–50 was *The Roman Father*, the beginning of a long association between Garrick, who acted Horatius, and the academic poet William Whitehead. The play's formal symmetries and classical reserve approach parody of the Addisonian All-for-Rome tradition. Horatius out-Catoes Cato by donating *two* sons' lives to Rome, and scolds the third for surviving, until he learns his flight was strategic; untimely reminiscences of his own bygone martial exploits make him sound almost senile. His daughter Horatia is torn between her Roman family and her fiancé Curiatius, an enemy champion: 'To me death/Whoever conquers!' Similarly, her friend Valeria, whose brother Valerius covets Horatia, is caught 'betwixt this friend and this brother'. The tragedy – Horatia and Curiatius perish – is mitigated, though, by the closing pyrotechnics: Valerius's 'Friends, countrymen' elegy, and Horatius's salute to patriotism as the hero's 'first, best passion'. An adaptation of Corneille's *Horace*, *The Roman Father* was the most successful reworking of French neoclassicism since Philips's *The Distrest Mother*; its rhetorical excesses, which modern readers find difficult to take seriously, were 'receiv'd with Extravagant applause'.[5] The play entered the repertoire, and – perhaps the ultimate tribute – a ship was named for it.

Another classical tragedy by Whitehead, *Creusa, Queen of Athens*, appeared in 1754. Written in a flowery, ornate idiom, as if translated from a Greek ode, it neglected the prevailing tragic style and perished within a few seasons, but the final plight of Ilyssus, 'more an Orphan now,/Than when I knew no parents', is moving. Whitehead abandoned the genre with *Fatal Constancy* (1754), a 'sketch of a tragedy in the heroic taste' that gives only the hero's speeches. These include grotesqueries such as 'my starting eyeballs hang/Upon her parting steps', and end in scene directions like 'Exeunt severally, languishing at each other'. Point and match to the parodist.

A cluster of tragedies on British subjects appeared in 1753. Richard Glover's *Boadicia* is a heroic play depicting 'gen'rous valour' and 'faithful love' during the Roman–British Wars, but its language, full of predictable modifiers, lacks any distinction. The same failing mars Henry Jones's *The Earl of Essex*, though it was preferred to Banks's version and Henry Brooke's (1750), displacing them on-stage. The best and most important of this group was Edward Moore's *The Gamester*, not only English but contemporary in setting, and the only bourgeois tragedy of merit in the period.

Long a concern of moralists and satirists, gambling had been treated by comic dramatists as an excuse for fulsome eleventh-hour reclamations. Moore would have none of it. He was certainly not above sentimentalizing the action, as the tears over the loyalty of the old steward Jarvis (I. 3) and the generous sensibilities of Lewson and Charlotte (III. 4) show; and he includes two devices that might bring his gambler round: the dramatic reappearance of the supposedly murdered Lewson, and the death of a rich old uncle.[6] But Moore would not trivialize the action by letting Beverley suddenly outgrow his obsession; he was religious enough to take seriously his protagonist's words, 'I have warred against the power that blest me, and now am sentenced to the hell I merit' (IV. 5). In the Preface he defends Beverley's suicide (and the choice of prose) as suitable to the subject.

Moore writes with a stark intensity that can make his overstated characters seem surreal or mythic.[7] Beverley is a convincing portrait of a distraught man, and Lewson is rounder than most stage heroes' friends, though he is a moralizer. The villain is more problematical. Stukely, who wants Mrs Beverley, tells us his schemes in a bald soliloquy (I. 8), and seeks not only Beverley's ruin but his death. He and the saintly women belong to melodrama (though not of the most facile type: no sooner does Mrs Beverley proclaim 'Thus heaven turns evil into good' when Stukely is cornered (V. 11) than Beverley sickens and dies from poison). A villain so black blunts the anti-gambling point, the uncle's death and Lewson's 'rebirth' are too neat, and the reports of off-stage action are awkward: Moore actually observes neo-Classical decorum. The main weaknesses are in the plot, though; the prose, sometimes extravagant, is generally more natural than Lillo's. Initially unsuccessful, *The Gamester* became influential on the Continent and was revived well into the nineteenth century.

There was no general swing to English subjects; the next few seasons brought more classical tragedies. The Appius and Virginia story was dramatized three times, by Samuel Crisp, Frances Brooke, and John Moncrieff, in 1754–55. John Brown's *Barbarossa* (1754), a terse heroic tragicomedy about the overthrow of an Algerian tyrant, was occasionally revived for a century. But in 1756 Brown turned to Scottish lore for *Athelstan* and John Home to Scottish legend for *Douglas*, the *succès fou* of 1750s tragedy.

At the Edinburgh première, a proud member of the audience crowed, 'Whar's yer Willy Shackspeare nu?', but *Douglas*'s triumph at Covent Garden in 1757 raised it above any suspicion of mere chauvinism. It is tempting to call the play Romantic (or pseudo- or pre-

Romantic), Gothic or even Byronic, yet such terms, while they do capture one aspect of *Douglas*, convey a half-truth by making it seem forward-looking.[8] Actually Home's play trades in familiar eighteenth-century tragic staples, though it is a collage rather than a synthesis of them. Like *Jane Shore* and *The London Merchant* it drew on an old ballad, this one (published in Percy's influential *Reliques of Ancient English Poetry*) telling of Matilda's secret marriage to Douglas and its disastrous consequences. At one point Old Norval repeats a ballad refrain, ''Twas strange, they said, a wonderful discov'ry;/And ever and anon they vowed revenge'.[9] When young Douglas surfaces, he is in essence the 'true prince', rusticated and ignorant of himself, whom Thomson and Hill had popularized in the 1740s. With his medieval setting Home combined the pastoral melancholy of the 'graveyard poets', Young, Blair, Thomas Warton, and Gray, who wrote that Home had 'retrieved the true Language of the stage'.

It was Home's apparent artlessness and emphasis on nature, as well as his popularity, that invited the comparisons with Shakespeare (whom Johnson styled 'the poet of nature'). Some of the relationships seemed 'Shakespearean' – Douglas and Matilda as Romeo and Juliet, Lord Randolph and Glenalvon as Othello and Iago – and there are verbal echoes too, as when Lord Randolph denounces Glenalvon: 'Yon matchless villain did seduce my soul/To frantic jealousy' (v. 1). Like Dryden, Otway, and Rowe, Home can sometimes appear a rather pallid reflection of Shakespearean glories, a futile search for the lost Elizabethan chord.

Yet *Douglas* also contains the invocations of fate ('Fruit of fatal love'), the pitch for tears in Prologue and Epilogue, and the scenes of sentimental 'momism' (IV. 1, v. 1) that had become standard features of most Georgian tragic drama. It is a tragedy of sympathy rather than of fate, almost (through Lady Randolph) a 'she-tragedy'. Like Rowe, too, Home preserved the unities and kept violence off-stage, however awkward that might become; like Thomson and Whitehead, he was more poet than dramatist, preferring long speeches to action. The play's success, another tribute to Georgian acting, shows that audiences were ready for its blend of emotion, melancholy, ballad romanticism, and a yearning for the wild glens. But the flatness or failure of Home's later, mostly neoclassical tragedies (excepting the Ossianic *Fatal Discovery*) strengthens the suspicion that *Douglas* was a timely stroke by a writer with some feel for cultural undercurrents, not a calling for the stage.[10]

In the late 1750s tragic writers were scouting fresh fields. Robert Dodsley found in French legend the tale of Cleone, her husband, their friend, and a villain. But the story needs the delicacy of a Mme de La Fayette; *Cleone*'s approach to sexual intrigue is blunt, its blank verse woodenly formal. The play is interesting now chiefly for Dodsley's connections with the London literati, and George Anne Bellamy's triumph as Cleone.[11]

The shrewd and versatile Arthur Murphy had his first major success with *The Orphan of China* (1759), an adaptation of Voltaire's *L'Orphelin de la Chine*, anonymously translated in 1756 with a Dedication to Garrick recommending its production despite some weaknesses. Murphy's changes are instructive. The translation is a tragicomedy about a couple's efforts to preserve the true prince as Genghis Khan enters Peking: a formal heroic drama, full of static poses, emblematic characters, and ideology, designed to convince the conqueror that 'TO BE GOOD, IS TO BE GREAT'. Murphy's alteration – nearly half again as long – opens twenty years later under Timurkan, brings on the Prince and his changeling as young warriors, and enlarges the tragic element by letting the fostering old couple perish, though an uprising overthrows the barbarian tyranny. Claptraps for liberty and allusions to 'northern domination' – despite the Dedication to Bute – politicize the action, while references to Confucius enhance the veneer of *chinoiserie*, then in vogue. Displays of sentiment and sensibility increase. The verse becomes freer, with echoes of *Douglas*, of *Cato*, even of *Busiris*. Murphy was a kind of anthologist, collecting anything that had ever worked.

Few tragedies of the 1760s repay study; comedy was usurping the talent. Mallet's *Elvira* (1763), a heroically pathetic tale of the Renaissance Portuguese Court, suffers from an excess of self-descriptive speeches and a dangling conclusion. John Hoole's *Cyrus* (1768), an awful tragicomedy about royal manoeuvrings and mistaken identities in a grove, shares with *Merope*, *Douglas*, and *The Orphan of China* a prince brought back from provincial exile and revealed to himself and others. So does Murphy's popular *Zenobia*, where Rhadamistus is all this and the heroine's husband as well. His supposed death is the occasion for gratuitous pathos along the lines of *The Mourning Bride*: Zenobia first enters leaning on maidservants, moaning, 'A little onward, still a little onward/Support my steps'. Heroic descriptions, romantic encounters, and tearful effusions characterize Murphy's approach to the Hellenistic story. *Zenobia* is a pot-boiler, albeit with plainer, less ranting diction than the prevailing norm.

Murphy's *The Grecian Daughter* (1772) outshone his earlier successes and all other 'tragedies' of the 1770s, holding the boards for seven decades.[12] Moderns who – faced with Euphrasia's excruciating self-descriptions, the affected blank verse, the excesses of plot and character – find the appeal unfathomable, must remember the talents of Garrick, the Barrys, and (later) Sarah Siddons in acting and production. The text was greatly enhanced by spectacle, chiefly 'A wild romantic Scene amidst overhanging Rocks'. A master of the 'whole show' concept, Murphy provided a light-hearted Prologue, an uplifting Epilogue, patriotism, warfare, appeals to Nature and humane sentiment, and militant feminism. Euphrasia, the Grecian daughter, is both an inspirer ('War on, ye Heroes') who stabs the tyrant, and a devoted filialist (the epigraph is from Sophocles's *Electra*) who suckles her starving father in prison. A sympathetic guard describes the (off-stage) scene in a passage deeply expressive of Georgian sensibilities:

> And, ever and anon, amidst the smiles
> Of pure delight, of exquisite sensation,
> A silent tear steals down; the tear of virtue,
> That sweetens grief to rapture. All her laws
> Inverted quite, great Nature triumphs still.
>
> (II. 2)

From this welter of self-sacrifice and lachrymose pity Murphy pulls a tragicomedy: her father finally awards the government of Syracusa to Euphrasia ('A parent to her people').

The attempt to make ancient Sicilian issues relevant to England ('the freedom of this sea-girt isle') is far-fetched, but Murphy's attack on the Spanish treatment of nobly savage Peruvians in *Alzuma* (1773) was genuinely pertinent to a Christian imperial nation. Modelled on Voltaire's *Alzire*, it is Murphy's most substantial tragicomedy, treating real issues in relatively restrained language, yet it failed on-stage.[13] The heaviness of its anti-popery crusade, its strident maternalism ('And who shall dare oppose a mother's voice?'), and its emotional shrillness make revival unlikely.

In the 1750s William Mason had published two dramatic poems 'Written on the Model of the Ancient Greek Tragedy'; like Whitehead, another Cantabrigian, he hoped to turn drama back towards its classical sources. An extreme purist, Mason employed Choruses to chant odes, and argued the need to reject the great rule-breaking example of Shakespeare and recapture ancient simplicity.[14] He applied his ideas not to Greek but to British matter: Caractacus's war against the Romans, Elfrida's resistance to the advances of King Edgar and final withdrawal to a charnel vault. Whereas Whitehead actively sought theatrical success in London, Mason held aloof – till an unauthorized production of *Elfrida* at Covent Garden (1772) ran for over twenty nights. He then revised *Caractacus* for performance (1776), and brought out his own alteration of *Elfrida* (1779). These experiments enjoyed modest success, but Mason's radically reactionary Classicism led nowhere that the theatre was apt to follow.

Perhaps moved by wartime patriotism, a number of veteran and novice dramatists turned to English themes after 1775. Home's *Alfred* (1777) and Richard Cumberland's *The Battle of Hastings* (1778) are clear examples; Thomas Francklin's *Matilda* (1775) is less so, since it reworks a French source.[15] This persistent practice, which survived even the Napoleonic Wars, also produced Hannah More's *Percy* (1777), the finest tragedy of the 1770s.

Set in Durham in Crusading times, it recounts the mortal rivalry of Douglas and Percy for the heart of Elwina. The three strong principals have one intense interview after another, but it is More's gift for writing simple, direct, and flexible blank verse (with Shakespearean overtones) that makes *Percy* stand out. 'Why 'tis well!' exclaims Percy when Elwina confesses her forced marriage. 'Married to Douglas! By my wrongs I like it;/'Tis perfidy compleat, 'tis finished falsehood' (III. 1). Torn between the men representing love and duty, Elwina decides to take poison, which horrifies her maid. 'My gentle friend, what is there in a name?' Elwina asks her. 'The means are little where the end is kind' (v. 1). When Douglas tells her that he has killed Percy, she disdains conventional histrionics: 'No',

> The sorrow's weak that wastes itself in words.
> Mine is substantial anguish – deep, not loud;
> I do not rave. . . .
> Rage is for little wrongs – Despair is dumb.
>
> (v. 1)

Somehow, More escaped the infection of rant. The final scene invokes Desdemona and Ophelia too blatantly, but overall the action is admirably concentrated and the language at least adequate. After *Douglas*, no other English tragedy reaches this level for many a decade.[16]

The war years also brought the heroic strain back to the fore; noble love, patriotism, and military pageantry figure prominently in *The Battle of Hastings* and Robert Jephson's *Braganza* (1775), wherein high-minded native rebels overthrow a tyrannical foreign occupier. The scene is Portugal and the oppressors are Castilian, but it is an interesting production on the eve of the American War, and an accurate barometer forecasting foul tragic weather. The Duke and Duchess are impossibly virtuous, steadfast, disinterested leaders; Velasquez is a diabolical villain. Black or white characters, simplistic treatment of moral issues, and a language at once obvious and absurd are all symptoms of the drift into melodrama in the 1770s: little remains but to add the mood music.

Paul Hiffernan's *The Heroine of the Cave* (1774) is an egregious example of the tendency to overstate everything, which grew with the capacity of the theatres. Hiffernan expanded a three-act manuscript by

Henry Jones into a full-length portrait of Constantia's fidelity to her husband, unjustly imprisoned in Vienna's quicksilver mines. This 'finished Pattern of connubial Attachment, and heroic Exertions of true and becoming female Fortitude' is dedicated 'TO ALL VIRTUOUS WIVES'. Hiffernan's exposition is completely bald, his diction stagey, his grammar full of inversions and archaisms ('If that') for the metre's sake. (Jones's verse is marginally better, evoking the gloom of the cave; he has the prisoners sing a hymn and works in a tribute to British liberty.) At the end 'Vice is punished, Virtue reigns': the villain is executed while hero and heroine parade grandly.

Melodrama is one species of tragicomedy, which flourished generally in the 1770s. Hannah Cowley's *Albina* (1779) shows the lengths to which a determined tragicomedian would go: the villainous Gondibert steals to the wedding chamber to kill the heroine on her wedding night, but in the darkness accidentally stabs his accomplice Editha, then himself. In a spiteful Preface Cowley charged the 'coalition' of 'winter managers' (Sheridan and Harris) with sitting on her play for two years while Hannah More plagiarized *Percy* and *The Fatal Falsehood* (1779) from it. The resemblances she adduces, however, pertain wholly to stock situations of the time; and one has only to glance at *Fatal Falsehood*'s opening soliloquy, 'What fools are serious melancholy villains!/I play a surer game', to see that the differences in language are all in More's favour. Though unsubtle, the passage takes some original twists, and has an easy, natural movement foreign to Cowley and most contemporary stage speech. Nor is More's play shackled to the concept of poetic justice that vitiates *Albina* and many other Georgian 'tragedies': the villain falls, but so do Orlando and Emmelina.

For adherence to the tragic idea, compactness of plot and handling of blank verse, Hannah More transcends the 1770s and has few rivals in the whole period. But did her plays bear any significant relation to Georgian social concerns, or were they merely an elegant diversion from them, like the neo-medievalism of Chatterton's 'Rowley poems', or the glitter of Murphy's tragicomedies? In at least one respect, the former: *Percy*, like *Tancred and Sigismunda*, portrays the disastrous consequences of a father forcing his daughter into an unwanted marriage, a problem that also concerned social critics and writers of comedy.

Notes

1. On the Opposition political dimension of the play, see L. W. Conolly, *The Censorship of English Drama, 1737–1824* (San Marino, California, 1976), pp. 57–59. Quotations from the first edition, 1739.

2. For an account of *Mahomet*, see Bertrand H. Bronson, 'Johnson's *Irene*', in *Johnson Agonistes and Other Essays* (Berkeley and Los Angeles, 1965), pp. 116–17.

3. See Bronson, pp. 123–26, 131, 151–53. My account of *Irene* is generally indebted to this perceptive essay.

4. On Johnson's identification with Aspasia, and Demetrius, see Bronson, pp. 133, 136–38.

5. According to the Drury Lane prompter, Richard Cross, quoted in *The London Stage 1660–1800*, 5 parts (Carbondale, Illinois, 1960–68), Part 4, edited by George W. Stone, Jr (1962), p. 178.

6. References to the play follow Charles H. Peake's edition for the Augustan Reprint Society, series 5, no. 1 (1948). On its stage history, see his Introduction, p. 1.

7. Compare Robertson Davies's helpful discussion in *The Revels History of Drama in English*, edited by T. W. Craik and C. Leech, 8 vols (London, 1975–83), VI (1975), 153–54.

8. For such labels, see George H. Nettleton, *English Drama of the Restoration and Eighteenth Century* (New York, 1923), pp. 242–43; Allardyce Nicoll, *Late Eighteenth-Century Drama*, second edition (Cambridge, 1952), pp. 91–92; and Davies, p. 154.

9. References are to the text printed in *British Dramatists from Dryden to Sheridan*, edited by George H. Nettleton, Arthur E. Case, and George W. Stone, Jr, second edition (Boston, 1969).

10. See Nicoll, pp. 93–94; Davies, p. 164; and Conolly, p. 70.

11. At Covent Garden, Garrick having refused it at Drury Lane. See Ralph Strauss, *Robert Dodsley* (London, 1910), Chapter 10.

12. Robert D. Spector, *Arthur Murphy* (Boston, 1979), p. 149; and Davies, p. 167.

13. Spector gives the special circumstances of the failure and rates it his best play (pp. 153–54), as does Nicoll, pp. 76–77.

14. Letter II prefaced to *Elfrida*, second edition (London, 1752).

15. See Nicoll, pp. 60–61.

16. Nicoll compares *Percy* and *Douglas*, pp. 96–97.

Chapter 13
The Confused Muse: Georgian Comedy and Farce

> The theatre, in proper hands, might certainly be made the
> school of morality; but now, I am sorry to say it, people
> seem to go there principally for their entertainment!
>
> Sneer, in Sheridan's *The Critic*

Such was the vigour of the various comic forms that they multiplied
even under the Licensing Act. After some lean years in the 1740s and
early 1750s, comedies and farces burgeoned unstoppably from about
1756; close to two hundred comic pieces of all kinds – three or four
times the number of tragedies – were produced in London over these
forty seasons. Besides the classics of Goldsmith and Sheridan and other
regular comedies, they included dozens of afterpieces that still seem
fresh and lively.

But the numbers are deceptive here: despite its abundance, Georgian
comedy was sick, suffering from a theoretical blight and a surfeit of
reformers. On one side the Examiner of Plays forbad criticism of the
political and religious establishment; on another the moralists
demanded purity and edification. The Scots rhetorician Hugh Blair was
certainly not a *typical* Georgian playgoer, but he shows what a serious,
educated man of the time might ask of comedy. The general idea of
satirizing follies Blair thought 'moral and useful', though often perverted to immoral ends, as in the rake–plays. What Blair esteemed were
the *comédies larmoyantes*, which (he thought) were helping to cleanse the
British variety, and plays like *The Conscious Lovers* that mixed instruction with gaiety and ridicule.[1]

The Shaftesburian philosophers and aestheticians who promoted a
benign view of human foibles constituted a third front. Corbyn Morris
thought it the first task of comedy to 'exhibit the whimsical mis-
chievous oddities . . . of Persons in real life': those abundant English
eccentrics. 'And also', he added more traditionally, 'to expose and
ridicule their real Follies, Meanness, and Vices'.[2] *Humour* he
pronounced the English comic genius: it is benevolent where wit is
severe. Horace Walpole associated comedy with thinking, not feeling,
but generally his age admired sympathy, whereas comic theory has
tended to stress detachment (Henri Bergson's 'anaesthesia of the
heart').[3] In resisting the pressure towards sentimentality, comedy
became lighter, risking triviality; anticipating moral censure, it

censored itself, risking blandness. Now comedy, like tragedy before, was out of step with the culture.

A squadron of mostly short comedies sailed into the unknown waters beyond the Licensing Act, testing what might float. Robert Dodsley tried to cram the exemplary comedy into the compass of one act: *Sir John Cockle at Court* (1738) makes the 'Miller of Mansfield' (1737) a knight and brings him to London to satirize courtly fashions and be further sounded by the King, again disguised. Here Dodsley gets out of his depth; the flattery of the King is fulsome, the court scenes are puerile, and the manners overdrawn. He is more at home in the pastoral Never-never-land of *The Blind Beggar of Bethnal Green* (1741), a proto-melodrama that subordinates gaiety to sentiment and probability to exaggeration. All of a piece, it does possess a dated charm, if the critical faculties can be lulled, but few would repeat Dodsley's experiments with the sentimentalized afterpiece.

James Miller's full-length comedy *Art and Nature* (1738) juxtaposes a denizen of the colonized new world with well-established types of London comedy such as the dupe, the parasite, and the witty maid. The noble savage Julio roughens the stock situations, but his honesty and Violetta's wit expose a hypocrite and unite the lovers, whereupon Julio invites her to live a life of 'Nature and Common-Sense' with him in America. Miller assumes his savage's nobility too uncritically and his satire wavers, yet the perspective is fresh, and certainly the material had potential, partly realized in Cumberland's *The West Indian* (1771). Much less substantial is *The Picture* (1745), Miller's farce based on Molière's *Le Cocu imaginaire*; nineteen scenes are required to knit up and unravel the complications arising from a lost miniature of Heartly. And this, not the comedy of fresh perspectives, was the mode that Georgian writers usually followed: Miller's novel-mad Celia became Colman's Polly Honeycombe, who became Lydia Languish, and Murphy rewrote Molière's farce as *All in the Wrong* (1761).

David Garrick impressed London audiences as a playwright even before his acting debut. *Lethe; or, Esop in the Shades* (one act, 1740) is flyweight Fielding: a delightful satire on urban manners. Mortals are allowed to come to Hades once a year and drink of Lethe to forget their cares, after counselling with Aesop, who is alternately shocked and bemused. The episodic structure proved a theatrical strength: it was easy to drop some types and substitute others as the years and fashions passed. *The Lying Valet* (two acts, 1741), though less satisfying now, was equally popular. The plight and plan of Gayless and Sharp suggest *The Beaux' Stratagem* in a revision by Cibber. The 'reform' of Gayless *after* his public humiliation is meaningless and the closing moral reveals no understanding of the hero's errors, yet the tricks of witty servants and the 'roast' of Gayless, with a dash of 'generous Tempers', preserved the work for decades.

As Walpole fell, Henry Fielding resurfaced, though his licensed plays form a weak coda to the vigorous satires of the 1730s. *Miss Lucy in Town* (1742), a one-act farce, laughs at the follies of a country couple and exposes the London vices to which they are subjected. At times it uses the Restoration humours-and-manners style, yet rejects the city and affirms 'country' values: an oblique political statement.[4] The licenser insisted on revisions to clean up *The Wedding Day* (1743), an intrigue comedy from Cibber's mould; Millamour plays the field for four acts, then reforms. Blasted as ridiculous by a friend, he caves in: 'Too late I see . . . the fatal consequence of my ungoverned, lawless passion' (v. 1). Saddled with conventional virtue, Fielding proves as sad a nag as the Great Apologist he despised. His last play, *The Debauchees* (1745), is only a revision of *The Old Debauchees* (1732), used to attack the Jesuits: henceforth he was a novelist.

After the doldrums of the early war years, comedy began to revive with Charles Macklin's afterpiece *A Will and No Will* (1746), cut down from Regnard's five-act *Le Légataire universel* (1708), whose heroic couplets become terse colloquial prose. Thoroughly 'Englished' in tone and character, *A Will* offers brisk, racy entertainment along traditional lines: a virtuoso clever servant, Shark, helps young lovers obtain old Skinflint's legacy, and wed. Macklin's treatment of the miserly *senex amans* and the plots against him (including Harriet's threat that sex with her might be his death) is as tough as Juvenalian satire, and Shark's impersonations – an actor's delight – give convincing demonstrations of his wit. A novel Prologue has some actors, representing critics of the pit, anticipating the announced 'Prologue by the Pit'. But even good farces were destined for obscurity, and *A Will* sank with hardly a trace.[5]

Another French transplant provided the best short comedy of 1747: Garrick's *Miss in Her Teens*, from Dancourt's *La Parisienne*. Though the title-page calls it 'A Farce', Garrick's Prologue distinguishes between farcical drama and the *petite comédie*, where characters and 'Passions' imitate 'real Life', and 'Nature's Laws' are observed. It is, rather, *comedy*'s laws that seem applicable to this tale of young love routing its enemies. The types, situations, and structure are archetypal: the father rivalling his son for the hand of the *ingénue*, the braggart warrior exposed, the intriguing servants, the saturnalia. Garrick finds ample room inside this frame for farcing, satire, and topical allusions. Our hero is a deserving captain just back from the wars, full of praise for his 'royal general'; he kicks out a deserter and the effeminate Fribble (Garrick) after they have been amusingly exposed. Tension is resolved early so that we can enjoy these butts' discomfiture and the true hearts of the principals. Featherlight as it is, *Miss in Her Teens* may be the most perfectly crafted play Garrick ever wrote.

Regular (mainpiece) comedy was 'long given over, and even thought dead' – until Benjamin Hoadly's *The Suspicious Husband* (1747), widely hailed as the first genuine comedy since *The Provoked Husband*, which the title of course evoked, along with *The Careless Husband* and *The Tender Husband*.[6] The canny Hoadly provided something for every constituency. Belles who mask and walk in St James's Park, beaux who challenge them to trysts, and a rake named Ranger who stalks ladies' bedrooms at night, give the illusion of Restoration comedy, but they are only holograms: everyone is actually sincere and good-natured. The men, though quickly jealous, talk of valuing a woman's heart, not her wit or beauty; the ladies have a mutual admiration society. And Ranger, finding that his quarry is his friend's inamorata, derives a benevolist's pleasure from conveying her to him. Moralists appreciated this, and the final scene, wherein the suspicious husband 'reforms' and makes up with his virtuous wife. In the end nothing comes of all the licentious appearances: two young couples marry for love, and Ranger, though unattached, remains scoreless. The varied incidents, brisk pace, and especially the 'mistakes of a night' sequence in Act III gratified the lovers of stage business. *The Suspicious Husband* is very near the average of the popular comedies of the preceding century.

Immediately successful, it was the most frequently performed comedy of Garrick's tenure at Drury Lane and a reference point for Georgian dramatic taste. The anonymous pamphleteer of 1747 eulogized its moral decency, tender touches, and wealth of complicated incident 'more artfully contrived . . . than any *Spanish* novel I ever read', though Canker, an envious rival playwright in Macklin's *The New Play Criticiz'd* (1747), considered it 'mere incident . . . stuffed with escapes, pursuits, ladders of ropes . . . all a parcel of pantomimical finesses . . . Ranger is really the Harlequin'. By 1770 Francis Gentleman found the play 'indelicate', 'licentious', disrespectful towards women, 'flimzy and uninstructive'.[7] It should be in print anyway for its representativeness.

The only significant 'sentimental comedy' for a quarter century after the Licensing Act – and the most important between Steele and Hugh Kelly – was Edward Moore's *The Foundling* (1748), a rake-reform play that reworks *The Conscious Lovers*. Young Belmont is 'protecting' Fidelia, an apparent orphan who finally discovers her wealthy father, but Belmont's designs are *dis*honourable. Found out and challenged, he accepts the rebuke, repents, and proposes (successfully) to Fidelia. Henry Brooke's Prologue, promising drama that is exemplary ('a

Model of the virtuous Sort') and instructive ('more of Moral than of Sport'), applies the rhetoric of tragedy to Moore, who 'aims to draw the melting Sigh/Or steal the pitying Tear from Beauty's Eye'. Despite some funny scenes involving Faddle, the coquette Rosetta, and the Belmonts, most of the emphasis does fall on displays of virtue, the wonderful discovery of Fidelia's parentage, and the reformation of the rake. Belmont, after agreeing with Rosetta that they are the male and female versions of the libertine principle, becomes 'a Convert to Honour', producing a 'sentence' that Joseph Surface might envy: 'He who solicits Pleasure, at the Expence of Innocence, is the vilest of Betrayers'.

Although *The Foundling* had a fairly good run, Moore gave up sentimental comedy thereafter. *Gil Blas* (1751) concentrates on intrigue and laughter, adding a slightly moralized conclusion. There are lively scenes of low comedy – the Preface worries lest 'the town' think Gil 'too low for your acquaintance' – but also passages approaching high comedy between Gil and Aurora. For the quick humour of Gil, Moore was indebted to Le Sage's novel, but his skilful exposition and the nearly surreal confusion of Act v show some dramaturgical flair. Moore then turned to tragedy, where sentiment was uncontroversial.

The 1750s belonged mainly to afterpiece comedy, farce, and satire, the forms to which Samuel Foote devoted his career. Often dismissed as a mimic, a libeller or the skimpiest of *farceurs*, Foote worked from surprisingly serious views on comedy. Its aim, he held, was to correct minor vices and follies through satire; love was not to the purpose.[8] Rejecting Terence, Foote declared for Old Comedy: he liked to be called 'the English Aristophanes'. 'Dramatic satire' is the most accurate label for his plays, which have the sketchiness one would expect from a caricaturist whom the licensing system debarred from regular drama.

Foote's patron deity was Proteus. *Diversions of the Morning* (1747; sometimes billed as *Chocolate* or *Tea* to evade licensing restrictions) probably burlesqued tragedy, satirized critics, and mimicked 'Orator' Henley when it opened at the Little Hay. Later it metamorphosed into *The Auction of Pictures* (1748) and *Taste* (1752, also known as *The Virtuoso*), a Jonsonian exposé of both a shady art dealer with an 'old-master' factory in London, and his dupes. Further revisions (1758, 1761) set the plight of artists and some theatrical absurdities in a city versus country framework. Foote's earliest 'regular' play was *The Knights* (1749), which spoofs rural politicians and lubbers (based on actual people) in an amusing way that attracted Goldsmith and Sheridan.[9]

Productions of *Taste* and *The Knights* at Drury Lane gave Foote an entrée to the patent houses for a time: *The Englishman in Paris* (1753) and *The Englishman Returned from Paris* (1756) opened at Covent Garden, *The Author* (1757) at Drury Lane. All three mix hard and soft scenes as his Haymarket work rarely does. Though reasonably successful, the *Englishman* plays lack the wit and sure aim of Foote's best work. The first ridicules both 'men of mode' who affect French manners and Buck's boorish hostility to France, then unexpectedly turns romantic at the end; the sequel divides its attention between Buck's new Gallic foppery and a sentiment-tinged love plot.[10] *The Author*, a popular play whose central situation turns up in several major Georgian comedies, tells how a long-absent father returns to London, spies on his literary son, and, finding him poor but virtuous, reveals his paternity and wealth. Ever multifarious, Foote also satirizes Grub Street and a particular eccentric.

The afterpieces that proliferated in the 1750s are easy to denigrate as sketchy and ephemeral or to defend as theatrical. The full truth is more complex, involving numerous minute discriminations. Kitty Clive's *The Rehearsal* (1750) and Thomas Sheridan's popular *The Brave Irishman* (1754) offer little to a reader, nor does Tobias Smollett's patriotic farce *The Reprisal* (1757) reveal the novelist's hand. A kind of war casualty, it ridicules French pusillanimity and celebrates the true hearts of British tars, treating nautical material from *Roderick Random* (1748) at the level of a schoolboy revue.

But the farces can also surprise one. McNamara Morgan's *The Sheep Shearing* (1754), for example, a two-act prose version of the Florizel and Perdita plot in *The Winter's Tale*, ought to be a horror, yet Morgan's way of unifying the action at one locale is clever, his paraphrases of Shakespeare are sometimes pleasing, and his additions not inappropriate. It has the stylized charm of some Georgian pastoral painting – dim, vague, melancholy yet idealized – though the ecstatic finale is, as Florizel says, 'too much'. Quite different is *The Kept Mistress; or, The Mock Orators* (anonymous, 1756), an unusually frank portrayal of a fallen woman, her old keeper, her father, and her young lover who finally proposes. All this sounds above farce, and is, though the 'oratorical' subplot provides a rhetorical extravaganza and one of the maddest final scenes in eighteenth-century comedy.[11] The play shows the true *vis comica*, which had been scarce.

The war years, however, coincided with an upsurge in comic productions. Arthur Murphy's first play, *The Apprentice*, was produced in 1756 after a frustrating incubation and a quarrel with Foote.[12] Yet Foote's influence seems central to this satirical farce, some of whose characters were modelled on real people, and whose plot is just a ramshackle framework for portraits and scenes. Dick is a foppish apprentice to old Gangle and suitor to his daughter, but above all a devotee of 'spouting' (amateur theatrical declamation). The satire on the Spouters – amusing practitioners of Murphy's own trade – is unconvincing, and in places the writing is crude, but some witty dialogue and Dick's zany escapades made the play's popularity durable. Dick's father Wingate, a coarse, avaricious merchant, is a good character part.

With *The Upholsterer* (1758), Murphy found his comic self; he is our great anthologist in comedy as in tragedy. Borrowing liberally from Shakespeare, Molière and Augustan literature, Murphy retells the story of Quidnunc ('What news?'), whose 'vicious Excess of a Propensity to Politics' comes near to ruining him and his family.[13] Quidnunc is amusing in his weakness, nattering about the balance of power while his affairs unravel, so the satire has a good-natured ring, yet we can see that his foolish behaviour needs correction. Whereas Murphy struggled to make Dick a romantic hero, Quidnunc subsides into amiable harmlessness without changing his nature as the romance sidesteps him and his long-lost son reappears to take charge: a stroke that Murphy sentimentalized for the reading audience. *The Upholsterer* established Murphy as a skilful manipulator of inherited sources, and an entertaining moralizer.

For ten years after taking over at Drury Lane, Garrick was too busy managing and acting to compose original work, though he altered several of Shakespeare's plays. In the late 1750s, however, he re-emerged as an author of afterpieces. *Lilliput* (1756), like *Lethe*, ambushes English mores in an exotic setting, while assuring the public, 'To you these little folks have no relation' (Prologue). 'Lilliput' is an England infected with French manners, Lady Flimnap and friends become Restoration types, and Gulliver is a 'cit'. By focusing sharply on one episode, Garrick taps some of the strength of Swift's great farce. *The Male Coquette* (1757) also spotlights one action: ridiculing the effeminate slanderer Daffodil, whose counterpart, Fribble, was just one aspect of *Miss in Her Teens*. Here again the plot is resolved early, the whole second act being the exposure of the nasty capon. *The Guardian* (1759, from Fagan's *La Pupille*) is more serious, satirizing the reticence of Heartly and his ward Harriet about their feelings. The 'autumnal' Heartly is deemed not *too* old, since true love is involved. Garrick handles the material with bright superficiality, though the scene where Harriet dictates while Heartly writes is good *théâtre français*.

In these middle plays Garrick is more *engagé* than before; he has something to say to his audiences, with whose tastes, he believed, stage reform must begin.[14] In *Harlequin's Invasion* (1759), he dramatized the threat posed to legitimate drama by pantomimes, burlettas, scenic spectacles: all the bustling new forms. Ironically, he made the point in one of those irregular entertainments that he was deploring: a

'Christmas Gambol'. As Johnson said, those 'who live to please, must please to live'.

Even Dr Johnson confessed that James Townley's *High Life Below Stairs* (1759) 'is really very diverting when you see it acted', yet 'one may read it, and not know that one has been reading anything at all'.[15] It proved one of the most popular afterpieces of the next 100 years, though riotous footmen, resenting the exposé of servants who play while master's away, almost stopped it after one night. Their masters might also have objected, since the servants' aping of affected manners and modish vices cuts both ways, but they were too well entertained to complain. Even in print, the parody of the knocking at the gate in *Macbeth* and the reading of *The Servants' Guide to Wealth* (I. 3) are amusing. Townley passes along the uppity-servant joke from Steele to Goldsmith (whose 'fellows' also despise anything low), but seems serious about inversions of social order and servant misrule being dangerous: the faithful butler Robert and the closing speeches are heavily didactic.

Charles Macklin retired for a time after *Covent Garden Theatre* (1752), a plotless satire indebted to Fielding, was heavily censored and played only once. He resurfaced in 1759 with *Love à la Mode*, a farcical short comedy that supported him for the rest of his life. The plot is simplicity itself: Charlotte's four suitors – Jewish, Scottish, Irish, and equine – are exhibited and allowed to seek their own level. The Irishman, Sir Callaghan O'Brallaghan, emerges from the test 'true green' and wins the heiress. *Love à la Mode*'s pleasing symmetry, its comfortable predictability, and Macklin's accurate ear for regional and colloquial speech kept it on-stage for over half a century, but – like so many other plays of this era – it holds the mirror up to nothing except the stage's own conventions.

Comedy rebounded in the 1760s to such a degree that it becomes impossible to survey it all; every season brought five to seven new comic pieces. The war had turned headily in England's favour, and the trauma of the Licensing Act had been absorbed. The afterpiece proved a nursery of comic writers; success therein often fuelled the ambition to write full-length comedy. On 24 January 1760 Arthur Murphy presented two new three-act plays at Drury Lane. *The Desert Island*, a blank-verse rendering of Metastasio's *Isola Disabitata*, came first; called 'a dramatic poem', it offered pastoral romance amid exotic scenery. Its afterpiece was *The Way to Keep Him*, a genuine *petite comédie*. Garrick played Lovemore, a 'careless husband' who poses as 'Lord Etheridge' to stalk Widow Bellmour. When the saturnine Mrs Lovemore meets this 'other woman' she finds her amiable (which audiences found original) and they plot to expose and reclaim Lovemore.

The widow also educates the wife in the art of being an interesting woman: another fresh twist. Though not funny, the play *is* genteelly comic – a dramatization of Pope's society poems – and was so well received that Murphy added a loving couple, the Bashful Constants, some sentiment, and two acts to the 1761 version, which survived into the next century.

Murphy was just such a dramatist as Jeremy Collier had wanted – moral, didactic, etc. – but he was essentially a satirical *farceur*, and the afterpiece was his forte. Whenever he essayed large forms, he over-burdened himself. *All in the Wrong* (1761) is a five-act farce of misinterpreted circumstances that takes its source (Molière's *Le Cocu imaginaire*) far too seriously; a general assembly at any time would resolve the whole absurd tangle. Even more disorderly, *The School for Guardians* (1767) is overpopulated with incidents from three of Molière's plays.[16] Murphy's preference for situation over character and for episodic, 'comedy of errors' plots generally made three acts sufficient exposure, and at this length he usually succeeded. *The Old Maid* (1761), a farce that mocks its subject cruelly, was mined by Goldsmith and Sheridan and acted for a century.[17] *The Citizen* (1761) satirizes grasping 'cits' who barter their children in marriage, while the more even-handed and serious *What We Must All Come To* (1764) exposes both aristocratic and parvenu meannesses, making class tension palpable. *No One's Enemy But His Own* (1764) is a curious farce about a compulsive babbler. *The Choice* (1765), a popular short comedy, deals with family intrigue and reconciliation. More than anyone else, Murphy showed the *range* of afterpiece comedy. What he had to say fit very nicely into two or three acts.

Macklin followed him from afterpiece to mainpiece with *The Married Libertine* (1761), the most elaborate treatment yet of a careless husband. Lord Belville is also an irresponsible MP and a presumer upon privilege, so Lady Belville and friends arrange 'a private shame' to make him 'reflect, and see a folly that injures his fame and fortune' (I. 1).[18] Using the kind of 'life-theatre' visited upon Nicholas Urfe in John Fowles's *The Magus*, they go to barbarous lengths in terrifying and humiliating the old rake. Despite many weaknesses – it is long, prolix, at times sententious, and perfunctory (after all) in 'reforming' Lord Belville – the play retains interest as a pre-de Sade attempt at psychodrama. Personal opposition to Macklin soon stifled it, and killed his *True-Born Irishman* (1767), an anti-English farce, after one performance. Both plays, though, exhibit Macklin's gift for making conventional scenes vividly realistic.

Sam Foote's situation at the Little Hay did not encourage full-length comedy; he kept turning out satiric afterpieces, year after year. *The Minor* (1760), a notorious attack on Methodists and one more version of Terence's *Adelphi*, also includes the reformers' favourite: testing and reclaiming the prodigal, who 'experience[s] all the misery of real ruin, without running the least risk' (I. 1). Although the testing father is no benevolist, Foote risks sentimentality by introducing the pathetic Lucy in Act III. His real interest, as usual, is exposé: of Mother Cole, the bawd turned Methodist, of usurers through Shift. Foote played both. *The Minor*'s energy wants discipline, but shows Foote confidently expanding his empire. *The Lyar* (1762) gave him a good humours role as Young Wilding, who anticipates Sheridan's Beverley by courting in different guises.

Other plays of these years show Foote's weaknesses: personal satire and unwieldiness. *The Orators* (1762) takes off Thomas Sheridan and Methodist preachers; *The Patron* (1764) hits vain Maecenases and the poetasters who flatter them; *The Mayor of Garret* (1763) sends up country politics, soldiers, and (again) Methodists. It achieved popularity, but looks foolish in print. His best play in this period, *The Commissary* (1765), treats the war profiteer as a *bourgeois gentilhomme*. This happy stroke allows Foote to be both topical (the war had just ended) and universal, to hit both *nouveaux riches* and the parasites who swindle them. Foote's weapon was scattershot.

The success of George Colman's afterpiece *Polly Honeycombe* (1760) probably assisted his full-length comedy *The Jealous Wife* (1761), which opened two months later; in that interval Colman became the bright young hope of comedy. *Polly Honeycombe* is good entertainment that pretends to instruct. A 'Dramatick Novel of One Act', it ostensibly trumpets the dangers of the '*sentimental* . . . Stile' in fiction and, implicitly, in comedy: the first shot of the impending laughter versus sentiment war. But this is prologue propaganda; Polly, more sinned against than sinning, proves sympathetic as well as comical, and in the Epilogue upholds romantic novels still. The actual villain is her tyrannical father. This vagueness of purpose, and the satiric ending that declines to resolve confusion into marriage, do not, however, detract from the sparkle of the piece.

Colman, supposedly assisted by Garrick, altered his priorities significantly for a mainpiece. Instead of devising a single action and satirizing sentiment, he constructed a complex plot from Terence, Fielding, and *The Spectator*, muzzled satire and (briefly) indulged sentiment. Half of *The Jealous Wife* is the Allworthy – Squire Western – Tom and Sophia part of *Tom Jones* (Blifil is excluded), culminating in the fulsome reconciliation of the lovers; the rest is a gallery of humorists ranging from the title-character to the Congrevian Captain O'Cutter. Some of Fielding's characters are neatly dovetailed with their stage counterparts; Lady Freelove is Lady Bellaston reconceived as the conventional hateful Hobbesian. The best early dramatic use of the novel, it was the most competent comedy since the 1740s.

Colman next collaborated with Garrick on the most successful comedy of either's career: *The Clandestine Marriage* (1766). It has now been shown that Garrick's share was the larger of the two, though the pervasive class-consciousness smacks of Colman, whose 'great expectations' never materialized.[19] The tone is almost sociological. Mr Sterling, a wealthy merchant, will clearly be furious when he learns that his younger daughter Fanny has married his poor clerk Lovewell, just when her sister is preparing to wed Sir John Melvil. Before he finds out, both Sir John and his friend Lord Ogleby have fallen for Fanny, who, being four months pregnant, has her plate full. When the truth emerges, Lord Ogleby puts in a good-natured word for his kinsman Lovewell, and Sterling accepts the match. The play hedges its bets as shrewdly as *The Suspicious Husband*: playing the 'amiable delicacy' of Lovewell and Fanny for laughs, presenting traditional comedians like the malapropping Mrs Heidelberg, dramatizing class relations and cultivating 'cits' (as in *The Conscious Lovers*), lightly satirizing most topics that arise, even nudging us about Lovewell's visits to his wife's room. The romantic leads are vapid, but the two aristocrats are – against all odds – rounded characters, and Sterling is crassly strong.

The Clandestine Marriage owes more to afterpieces than its authors' apprenticeships, being indebted to two of James Townley's. *False Concord* (1764), which tells how a middle-class girl avoids an aristocratic marriage in order to wed her true love, provided a sketch of theme and plot; the servants who ape upper-class manners (Act II) plagiarize *High Life Below Stairs*. The *petites pièces* were both a mine of rough ideas, and a laboratory in which to experiment. Colman's best in these years, *The Deuce Is in Him* (1763), exposes morbid jealousy as a French refinement, while Garrick gave a *Peep Behind the Curtain* (1767) at spectators demanding and entrepreneurs providing spectacle and novelties. Garrick's rhetoric is typically opaque: the scenes and machines, the burletta, and the trendy producer Glib are half-sop, half-satire.

Part of the comic revival was a group of plays sometimes seen as a continuation of 'sentimental comedy', sometimes as a distinct phenomenon. Sententious, genteel, emotional, they resemble the novel of sensibility as much as they do anything by Steele or Moore. The first of them, Whitehead's *School for Lovers* (1762), is clearly nervous about its genre; Modely twits Caelia on talking 'like a sentimental lady in a comedy', and Garrick made significant revisions to Whitehead's original Prologue, which promised to 'play politely with your hopes and fears/And sometimes smiles provoke, and sometimes tears'. Garrick excised this couplet, and when Whitehead began to boast of his freedom from scene-shifting, Garrick cut in, acknowledging the English taste for 'change and show', and assuring the spectators, 'Write as *he* will, we'll act it as *you* please'. Whitehead's young sobersides Sir John Dorilant and delicate Caelia resemble Steel's Bevil, Jr and Indiana, a type of couple overdue for mockery. Ordinarily a 'school for lovers' would mean that they were being taught a lesson, but Whitehead, an indulgent schoolmaster, imparts no instruction. Dull in print, the play ran for thirteen nights and was later revived.

Frances Sheridan, whose family business was the theatre, produced a genteel comedy, *The Discovery* (1763), whose Prologue advertises decent, 'harmless satire'; she intended to 'touch the heart' and 'demand the melting tear'. Established sentimental motifs – gambling and reform, discovery of a lost child – coexist with the humours of the Flutters and the satiric portrait of the sententious lover Sir Anthony Branville. A writer for *Bell's British Theatre* (1791) called *The Discovery* 'rather a novel than a comedy' owing to its 'loose' and 'languid' dialogue and lack of surprising incident, but the dialogue ranges from tedious (the Medways) to revealing, and the action is resolved with pleasing ingenuity. Encouraged by her modest success, Mrs Sheridan presented *The Dupe* ten months later, again proclaiming allegiance to the grave and moral school. This time there is nothing to relieve the tedium of the lovers' sententiousness and the heaviness of reforming the dupe. Friendly, the benevolent intervener, is simply bland, but his wife, whose humour is loquacity, constitutes an active annoyance. Audiences soon consigned them all to oblivion.

Elizabeth Griffith's *The Platonic Wife* (1765), though taken from one of the sentimentalists' favourite sources, Marmontel's *Contes moraux*, is *anti*-sentimental in plot, ridiculing the 'foible' of Lady Frankland, who – intoxicated with 'vile romantic trash' and 'dying for sentimental passion' – is rejecting her husband. These 'Platonic' notions, nominally the villain, must be discredited, and 'the fallacy of sentimental love' disproved. The frightening ardour of her 'refined' suitor Belville accomplishes this, but the dialogue is so stilted and the Franklands' reunion so rapturous that the play's rhetoric turns against its plot; refinement is exploded *and* celebrated. *The Double Mistake* (1766) is more extreme. No critical perspective governs the sententiousness of Emily, Lord Belmont, and the Freeman brothers; what little incident the plot affords is mostly implausible. Griffith so idealizes the relations of the aristocrat with the business man and gives her lovers *such* delicate sensibilities that one looks for satire, but this is a desperate evasion. Reader, if you seek a standard for 'sentimental comedy', look no further.

The influence of this group may be gauged from Colman's *The Man of Business* (1767). Colman, who began by mocking sentimental affectations, now adapts Voltaire's *L'Écossaise*, adding some laughter, but focusing on types such as the gruff, good-hearted merchant Freeport, and tearful scenes of reunion and benevolence. All of the ridiculous people are finally ejected, leaving the stage to exemplars of domestic virtue. The theatrical climate encouraged displays of empathy and Doing the Right Thing. Garrick laundered Wycherley's *Country Wife* as *The Country Girl* (1766), which he vainly hoped would be 'innocent without being insipid'. Pinchwife becomes Moody, a rural humorist; Margery, not yet married, is awarded a proper young suitor; the Fidgets, Squeamishes, and Horner disappear; the dialogue is banal. Eunuchy, formerly a satiric device, becomes a quality of the writing.

Traditionally, the next six seasons have been seen as years of confrontation between the comic styles that Oliver Goldsmith later called 'laughing' and 'sentimental'. He and Sam Foote championed traditional comedy, while Hugh Kelly and Richard Cumberland purveyed a drama of sensibility. As usual, such generalizations obscure a more complicated reality: that comic mainpieces were all prudent mixtures of styles in various ratios.

Kelly's *False Delicacy* (1768), for example, supposedly the sentimental standard-bearer at Drury Lane, did provide an orphan, a good supply of moral *sententiae*, and three pairs of delicate lovers. Yet this delicacy – styled 'false' by the title – is the principal mischief-maker in the plot, estranging the right couples and assembling the wrong ones, until sensible people intervene: Mrs Harley and Cecil counterattack against reticence and stage-manage a final assembly that laughs the falsely delicate into proper 'life-force' behaviour. Still, a treacly benevolism drips over the lovers at last; Kelly cannot take a stand without yanking the rug from under his own feet. Refined Lady Betty exclaims, 'How has my folly undone me!' but Mrs Harley concedes that 'somehow, foolish as [delicacy] is, one can't help liking it'. The final speeches (and Garrick's humorous Prologue) are defensive about sentiments; then the Epilogue satirizes 'False Modesty'. *False Delicacy* is as self-critical as an unresolved antithesis.

Goldsmith's *The Good-Natured Man* premièred six days later at Covent Garden in an atmosphere of rivalry. According to the author's Preface, the qualities of 'the poets of the last age', 'nature and humour', were being set against Kelly's (and Garrick's) 'genteel comedy'. Again the actual dichotomy is less clear-cut than the theoretical. Lofty and Croaker did provide manners satire and situation comedy, though 'the public taste, grown of late, perhaps, too delicate' (Preface) judged the fine bailiff scene (III. 1) 'low', forcing its omission. But Goldsmith confused the issue by making a man of imprudent benevolence his protagonist and butt, then trying to embarrass and 'reform' him. The actor Powell warned Goldsmith that Young Honeywood was an intractable role.[20] The air of lovable eccentricity that surrounds Parson Primrose in *The Vicar of Wakefield* goes bad when the inept benevolist is bumbling around the stage in front of us, incommoding everyone with his unruly generosity. Those who read him ironically miss the point: it is difficult to be *comically* ironical about a man who is too disinterested for our world. To 'reform' this saintly fool is downright deep tragedy, not the traditional comedy Goldsmith wanted to write. 'Good nature' was not – especially in the eighteenth century – the easy target that jealousy, misers, and romantic maidens were.

Goldsmith's play, outperformed by Kelly's, failed to make comedy laugh. Mrs Griffith opened a *School for Rakes* (1769): for a rake and his accomplice who are already sententious penitents by the end of Act I. Richard Cumberland's *The Brothers* (1769), a popular *mélange* of romance and sentiment, may be our first melodrama.[21] Charlotte Lennox's *The Sister* (1769) is uniformly grave, except for the coquette, Miss Autumn. *A Word to the Wise* (1770), Kelly's dullest, most awkward comedy, ignores the proverbial wisdom of its title to moralize at inordinate lengths. These four plays contain less amusement than Shakespeare's major tragedies, but Cumberland's *The West Indian* (1771), often used as a sentimental touchstone, is now recognized as offering the most varied entertainment of any comedy from 1766 to 1773.[22]

Not that Cumberland's priorities are ever in doubt. The Prologue's repetition of 'hearts' signals the play's values: blessed are the benevolent, for they shall be rewarded at the final assembly. The title-character Belcour is a 'Good-Hearted Man', young, rash, and hot-blooded, observed secretly by the benign Stockwell, his unacknowledged father, who wants (of course) to test his heart. The distressed lovers Charlotte Rusport and Charles Dudley compete in kindness and sensibility; old Dudley loves Sterne for his benevolence; Louisa Dudley is self-consciously virtuous; and Major O'Flaherty has a heart of gold beneath his oddities. We wallow in goodness, and are not surprised when Louisa accepts Belcour, asking rhetorically, 'what must that heart be, which love, honour and beneficence like Mr Belcour's can make no impression on?' nor when Stockwell finds in him a 'heart beaming with benevolence'. (v. 6 & 8)[23] We knew it all along.

Yet Cumberland sought smiles, not tears; 'Rouse . . . Your good old humour', exhorts the Prologue. O'Flaherty and the villainous Lady Rusport are comical on-stage (though our laughter is amiable), and through the device of the 'noble savage', Belcour, Cumberland can satirize London's manners. Perhaps most important, he avoids the trap of gentility into which the legatees of Steele often fell. *The West Indian*, full-blooded, energetic, and sometimes risible, deserved its success.

His *Fashionable Lover*, a virtuous-orphan-in-distress melodrama, failed, however, as did Mrs Griffith's *Patience the Best Remedy* (both 1772). The latter starts promisingly and is well constructed, but lapses into sentimental clichés. When the anonymous 'Essay on the Theatre' appeared on 1 January 1773, no full-length 'laughing comedy' had succeeded since 1766, or, according to the essay, 1728.[24] The writer, believed to be Goldsmith, asks 'which deserves the preference, – the weeping sentimental comedy . . . or the laughing, and even low comedy?' but his own answer is unequivocal. Laughing comedy that ridicules vice and folly has the support of tradition; exemplary or 'sentimental' comedy is an upstart, a kind of 'bastard tragedy' that flatters our faults.

This 'puff preliminary' for *She Stoops to Conquer* was strongly seconded in February by Foote's funniest and deadliest satire: *The Handsome Housemaid; or, Piety in Pattens*. On one level it parodied Isaac Bickerstaffe's mawkish comic opera *The Maid of the Mill* (1765), but since that is a version of *Pamela*, sentimental literature is broadly indicted. Foote makes the lustful squire wonderfully asinine, his housemaid's '*vartue*' is staggering, and the butler turns no mean sentence: 'Beauty when join'd with Innocence, tho' naked will find out Admirers'.[25] At the last everyone is so determined to give that none can be found to receive; the apparent resolution goes catatonic with a spasm of 'oh! oh! oh!'s. (In the earliest version, Foote used puppets to suggest the mechanical qualities of dramatic benevolists.) *Piety*'s success was said to have prepared London to welcome Goldsmith's comedy.

She Stoops to Conquer, which opened in March, is not, of course, reducible to another attack on sentimental comedy, though the context of controversy, the Dedication, and Garrick's Prologue all encourage that view. It does needle those who preferred 'sentences' to 'anything that's low', and correct the prurient sentimentality of Cibber, but is broader and more complex than anti-sentimentalism. To a remarkable degree the play unified the High Georgian literary establishment in admiration: Garrick *and* Colman; Johnson, Burke, and 'The Club'; Cumberland and Fanny Burney. *She Stoops* was too popular, plays and reads too well, to have been merely polemical; of all eighteenth-century plays, it needs perhaps the least defence or explanation to-day.

In his last comedy Goldsmith transmutes the values he has inherited from the comic tradition we have been tracing. Not that he does so independently, without precedent, but he leads us from the foothills on to a summit from which we suddenly see how far we have come. What Thomson and Gray had effected in poetry, Fielding in the novel, Goldsmith does here for comedy. Liberated from the urban drawing-rooms, we are set in the country more firmly than in any comedy since *The Recruiting Officer*. Nor is this just a way to gain perspective on London (although it affords that); Antaeus-like, Goldsmith draws strength from the earth, finding in the country a source of values by which to guide his art. The domestic warmth of the Hardcastles and their servants corrects the anti-marriage, anti-family bias of much post-Restoration comedy. The rakes, the intrigues of the beau monde, the rule of wit, the knowledge and manipulation of manners: *ubi sunt? Où sont les neiges d'antan?* Natural goodness has become the sole test of character; it is all ye need to know, but nothing less will do. In 'The Deserted Village' and *The Vicar of Wakefield* Goldsmith had already shown himself a votary of the cult of benevolent feeling that Shaftesbury and Hutcheson and Sterne – building on Locke – had established in philosophy and the novel; here he joins the priesthood, a forerunner of Dickens.

Of the memorable characters that embody these values, the Hardcastles' *enfant terrible*, Tony Lumpkin, is perhaps the most significant. In essence a country bumpkin, he plays a remarkably large and honourable role: tricking Marlow, calling Hastings on his weathervane urban manners (v. 2), and assisting the lovers. His effect on the action rivals that of the Restoration Truewit, yet in personality he is the boorish anti-fop, like Sir Wilfull Witwoud. Tony's good nature is what allows Goldsmith (and us) to view him benignly; he is a natural man, an 'amiable humorist' whose freedom of manners expresses his British birthright, a domestic noble savage. [26]

Benevolence and manners also distinguish Marlow from his comic forebears. His inability to converse easily with a 'modest woman' (II. 1) makes him a virtual anti-rake; his inability to detect deceit would cast him as Witless, if wit were king. But his declaration of love to Kate (v. 3), whom he thinks a 'poor relation', parallels Aimwell's confession to Dorinda as a sign of decency, and contrasts favourably with Lovelace's treatment of Amanda, or Archer's of Cherry. Kate recalls the witty heroines of Restoration comedy (*The Belle's Stratagem* was one working title), but in her 'stooping' to save Marlow from his undemocratic version of the Englishman's malady there is something better than wit, or a good turn for an actress: something both beneficent and pragmatic. Not that many good catches will come her way out here; if she must play barmaid in order to unify an attractive suitor's split personality, the role is neither dishonourable nor, ultimately, undignified.

The play's achievement is to fuse diverse modes in harmonious synthesis while entertaining us. Some Georgians found it low and farcical, which it often is while Tony is on-stage, but the farcicality is an integral part of Goldsmith's mellow view of Tony, rural life, and human nature. Tony *earns* his pranks: his impish deceptions enable Kate to 'stoop' and Constance to elope. How would the couples have managed otherwise? The principal situations also teasingly evoke Restoration and sentimental comedies, only to reject or transcend them; London men are made to submit their fates to country folk, while Marlow's 'sober sentimental interview' with Kate takes off sententious comedy from Steele to Kelly. Romantic comedy is updated – Kate is not the first heroine to disguise herself for better access to a young man – and various contemporary foibles are gently satirized. What holds it all together is good nature: Tony's, Marlow's, Kate's, Hardcastle's. Even Hastings, safely eloped with Constance Neville, brings her back 'to appeal . . . to your humanity' (v. 3). Only superficially is *She Stoops to Conquer* a throwback to earlier comedy; many of the materials, and certainly the controlling idea of benevolence, are thoroughly Georgian.

In the interval between Goldsmith and Sheridan, Hugh Kelly provided manners satire and 'low' scenes in *The School for Wives* (1773), and Cumberland a bustling comedy of incident, *The Choleric Man* (1774). Though Colman's *The Man of Business* (1774) rivals *The London Merchant* in sobriety, overall the taste was running towards more laughter as Richard Brinsley Sheridan composed his first play. Often paired with Goldsmith, Sheridan was in fact quite different. Whereas Goldsmith wrote comedy in middle age, having suffered want, Sheridan began young, romantic, ambitious. The result was a modified comedy of wit, slightly brittle and more receptive to the artificialities of the manners tradition than was Goldsmith's comedy of humours and nature. With Sheridan we are back in the drawing-room.

In *The Rivals* (1775), however, it is *provincial* society, specifically Bath's, that entertains us. This was a shrewd choice of venue, for the newly developed spa was fashionable with the London gentry, and Sheridan's own romantic adventures there had been well publicized; in 1772 he had eloped with the famous *chanteuse* Elizabeth Linley (the heroine of Foote's *The Maid of Bath*, 1771) and had fought two duels over the escapade. Some of this turns up in the play – stolen visits, duelling rivals, etc. – but Sheridan's literary debts are also wide. Lydia Languish descends from Steele's Biddy Tipkin and Colman's Polly Honeycombe; Faulkland is the sentimental masochist, like Winworth in *False Delicacy*; Sir Lucius O'Trigger is the conventional stage Irishman; and Mrs Malaprop has an extensive gynaecology, including Mrs Tryfort in Frances Sheridan's *A Journey to Bath*, possibly her son's starting-point.[27] Sheridan formed these 'shreds and patches' into a coherent comedy that still resurfaces almost annually, as smart as ever, but the achievement did not come easily. Initially a failure at Covent Garden, *The Rivals* had to be rewritten (cut and toned down) before audiences approved, and Sheridan's further tinkerings left us with multiple versions.[28]

The famous second Prologue, which attacks 'the sentimental Muse' and espouses 'mirth' and 'love', disclaims any connection between 'our light scenes' and 'moral Truth'. Despite this unashamed retreat from the traditional moral claims of comedy, and the early release of tension reminiscent of Garrick, the play is not totally superficial. By bringing Lydia and Faulkland into line, it rules against their excesses.[29] The continuing debate over Faulkland – absurd or refined? – proves him a man of many hues and shadows, 'captious . . . without dissembling' and 'fretful without rudeness' (I. 2), proud yet humble, ardent yet reticent. Possibly Sheridan's self-portrait, he is a self-torturer who can be ridiculed or savoured, but not easily ignored. Too deep, perhaps, for light comedy, Faulkland and Julia, his critic and beloved, need more leisurely development and examination, along the lines of *The Clerk's Tale* or *Sense and Sensibility*. Then too, a rueful irony pervades Jack Absolute's relationship with his father, and even Acres is not quite a flat humours character. Of course Sheridan's theatrical genius is to make them all delightful, whatever else they are.

Sheridan was busy in the next two years with a farce, an operetta, alterations, and the purchase of Garrick's share of Drury Lane; there is nothing substantial until *The School for Scandal* (1777). Its penchant for reworking material from other comedies and its development around particular actors' strengths recall the genesis of *The Rivals*, but this is a larger and more serious statement than Sheridan's first comedy.[30] Inspired, perhaps, by the move to Drury Lane, *The School for Scandal* is a major revaluation of seventeenth- and eighteenth-century themes and characters, comparable to Goldsmith's last play. Wit, manners, feeling and the 'man of sentiment' are all nicely sifted through a Georgian sieve. Where the bubbling brightness of *The Rivals* is typically accused of superficiality, critics of Sheridan's second comedy suspect it of sentimentality.

If Sheridan actually joined two separate schemes, 'The Slanderers' and 'The Teasles', to make *The School*, it was a brilliant leap; they are united by a concern with benevolence that they share with the Surfaces plot and with Goldsmith.[31] Sir Peter Teasle's remark to Lady Sneerwell, 'true wit is more nearly allied to good nature than your ladyship is aware of' (II. 2), is both a gloss on her observation to Maria, 'there's no possibility of being witty without a little ill nature; the malice of a good thing is the barb that makes it stick' (I. 1), and the key to the play's values. Sheridan, like Addison and Pope, wants to analyse wit, to 'blame the false, and value still the true', but he links it to character or human nature (not to 'Nature'), which requires a distinction between true and false hearts. This paradigm works perfectly for the ill natures: Lady Sneerwell condemns herself, the scandalmongers are as malicious as clever, and Joseph Surface employs his silver tongue for hypocrisy and seduction. So malevolence produces false wit, but does benevolence produce true? Maria and Rowley, the most conspicuous incarnations of virtue, are figures from exemplary comedy, a bit dull and self-righteous. Sir Peter Teasle's goodness finally recovers his lady, but he is no wit. The generous natures of Charles and Sir Oliver Surface, however, are more spirited and humorous, especially in the auction scene.

Officially, then, Sheridan's true wit is good-natured, not cutting. Actually we eat our cake and have it too, laughing at false wit safely caged by condemnation; scandal is schooled, all right, but not until we have enjoyed its wickedness. The ostensible masks the real, for us and for the characters. The play's best-known screen falls in IV. 3, removing the barrier between truth and appearances for the four principals. Joseph's whole enterprise, of course, is screening his designs behind sentiments. Imprudence long obscures Charles's benevolence, as disguise does Sir Oliver's. Surfaces are what the play discusses: how they mislead, what they cover. Fashion and wit glitter, concealing malice and danger for a Lady Teasle. As in Goldsmith, manners are worthless, naturals win: 'amiable humorists' who sheathe a good heart in a rough case. The least noticed surface is the play's own rhetorical veneer: we can hardly say whether entertainment is superimposed on morality or vice versa.

The School for Scandal screens and assesses its comic inheritance. Like Goldsmith, Sheridan resurrects familiar types for revision: Lady Teasle is a 'country wife' who returns to her older husband when she recognizes his love and generosity; Sir Peter, a New Model *senex amans*, is miraculously constructed from the wreckage of many a Pinchwife and Fondlewife. Millamant's 'shoal of fools' and Olivia's flatterers are placed centre stage for our diversion and improvement. Contrasted brothers have clashed from Genesis and Terence to *Tom Jones* and Sheridan's *The Duenna* (1775), but Joseph is the grave young man of sentimental comedy as well as 'evil', and Charles 'the good' has the vigour of Cumberland's Belcour, with more humour. Uncle Oliver is the most genial (and comically vain) of the period's benign family spies. And so on. While amusing the weary business man, Sheridan manages to recycle, and implicitly evaluate, a century of comedy.

During this decade of major comedies, the afterpiece continued to flourish. Foote, one-legged after a riding accident (1766), bounced back with satirical sketches built around amputees. From 1770 he produced a play annually, of which *Piety in Pattens* was the most significant, *The Maid of Bath* the most lenient: even Foote thought Miss Linley above

satire. *The Nabobs* (1772), however, portrayed them so unfavourably
that some enraged Anglo-Indians had to be placated with a dinner. *The
Bankrupt* (1773) comes unusually close to sentimentality for Foote,
though the theme of 'a bankrupt age', in wit and credit, is provocative.
The Cozeners (1774), a well-constructed satire on smugglers, resembles
The Commissary and *The Alchemist*; Foote remained the 'dramatic
magistrate'. *The Trip to Calais* (1775), portraying the Duchess of
Kingston as Lady Kitty Crocodile, was forbidden at her request. Foote
revised (and tightened) it as *The Capuchin* (1776), but she harried him
out of the theatre and into an early grave.

Colman, who bought the Little Hay from Foote, was less prolific.
He too sensed a deficiency in the age, for which his metaphor was 'the
comic stubble' – an apt image for afterpieces, at least.[32] Burlettas and
spectacles aside, he produced *Man and Wife* (1769), a masquerade set
at Garrick's Shakespeare Jubilee, and *The Spleen* (1776), a farce satirizing the parvenus who frequented Islington Spa. Garrick's energy
went into the Jubilee, remodelling Drury Lane, producing spectacles,
managing, and acting. Besides minor work and alterations, he
burlesqued the theatrical scene in *The Meeting of the Company* (1774),
a one-act 'rehearsal', but the best play of his last decade was the
patriotic farce *Bon Ton; or, High Life Above Stairs* (1775). Trading on
the popularity of Townley's farce and the imminence of war, Garrick
exposes the decadent morals of the Frenchified rich, then uses the
Anglophile Sir John Trotley to denounce them. In print it seems
jingoistic; on-stage it became popular.

Murphy concentrated on comedy and tragedy. *Know Your Own
Mind* (1777), his final comedy, written in the 1760s but delayed by
quarrels and deaths, had the misfortune to be set against *The School
for Scandal*.[33] Some have thought it can stand the comparison. The
claim is not absurd: this is clearly a major comedy, possessing (in Lady
Bell, Dashwould, and Malvil) characters of some interest. It was at first
well received, and in the acting version – the Larpent MS, not the texts
Murphy prepared for readers – it could probably be revived.[34] A
retrial, however, would ultimately reach the same verdict. Like
Murphy's other comic mainpieces, *Know Your Own Mind* has more
people and situations than it needs: six eligible suitors – including a
sententious villain and a capricious man – mill around four women,
including a distressed orphan. Murphy's control had improved, and
on-stage the action might be comprehensible, but there is also the
problem of the play's cold, 'archaeological' feel. Murphy re-creates the
comedy of manners and wit (never humour) so perfectly you might
think his characters are alive, but he has nothing to say to or about
them; unearthed to no purpose, they are simply exhibited. In the long
run this neo-Classicism proved unsuitable: it did not hold audiences.

The play's Prologue is Murphy's valedictory, not only to his own career, but to a theatrical generation. Noting Garrick's retirement, he 'takes his leave' and 'hopes new poets will expand their wing'. They were needed. Goldsmith had died in 1774, Foote and Kelly in 1777; Garrick would die and Sheridan abandon the stage in 1779. An era was ending, though some mid-career writers continued, and some 'new poets' were stirring. What comedy most needed was a new style for or from them: the Restoration and Augustan Museum could be revisited only so many times, and was boring unless the guide was brilliant.

There are some glimmers of a new style in the serious and interesting plays that George Colman, now the doyen of comic writers, produced in his first summer seasons at the Little Hay. *The Suicide* (1778) deals forcibly with Tobine, a good-hearted rake who would rather die than renounce profligacy or continue hurting his friends; his beloved Nancy (disguised as 'Dick Rattle') gives him a fake poison. Tobine 'dies' repenting, so it is easy to reclaim him when he awakes, though his reform is assumed rather than emphasized. Combining humanitarian and problem drama, *The Suicide* presages the next decade's comedy.[35] Less avant-garde, but sporting some smooth and witty dialogue, *Separate Maintenance* (1779) satirizes decadent urban morals. The theme is old/country versus new/city: the rustic Oldcastles espouse traditional English values against the *bon ton* of their daughter and son-in-law, who are separated and skidding towards divorce. Part *Wives Excuse*, part Addison and Steele (who are specifically mentioned), *Separate Maintenance* indicts modern manners but ends comically. Both plays were unusually substantial summer fare, and experimented with a new length: four acts.

The 'new poets' for whom Murphy called were slow to soar. The one fresh talent that appeared was Hannah Cowley, and her initial efforts were uncertain. In *The Runaway* (1776), encouraged by Garrick, she tried to please everyone: Emily, fleeing from a forced marriage, hymns the beauty of the country amid her woes; George ridicules 'sentimental people', but delivers some 'sentences' of his own and rhapsodizes about Emily; an ageing belle and a coquette, Bella, work the Restoration vein; a foxhunt assembles musically; and sensible Drummond dispenses beneficence and patriotism. Here Cowley seems one of those Georgian writers embarrassed by a sense of responsibility to more styles than she can assimilate. Some scenes are humorous, and Bella is unexpectedly left at liberty, but overall the play tends to swing between the grave and the high-flown. *Who's the Dupe?* (1779) is a farce about a rich 'cit' and a college pedant, both duped by the young lovers. Cowley would do better work in the 1780s.

Of the also-rans who provide a standard for measuring achievement, Thomas Hull altered tragedies, comic operas, and comedies (including Tuke's *Adventures of Five Hours* as *The Perplexities*), and wrote farces of his own. Isaac Bickerstaffe, best known for comic opera, also adapted or composed comedies and farces. William Kenrick tried both intrigue and sentiment, achieving popularity only with *Falstaff's Wedding* (1766), a sequel to *II Henry IV* wherein the knight develops a Shaftesburian sense of humane amity. Generally, plays by these minor dramatists served to while away an hour without affecting the larger scheme.

   The Critic (1779) virtually closed Sheridan's theatrical career and ended a twenty-year boom in comedy. The wittiest of *The Rehearsal*'s offspring, it has no eighteenth-century rival as burlesque after *Tom Thumb*. The main target is post-Restoration tragedy, whose absurdities, from the leading question to the lingering stage death, are brilliantly parodied. Most of these foibles were antique (some of Buckingham's jokes are recycled); it is repertory, as much as current, tragedy that is sent up. Act I, though, is directed against comedy. Sneer's conversation with the Dangles pricks 'genteel comedy' (written in 'the true sentimental'), the 'school of morality', the social problem play, even the prudish, 'bungling reformation' of Vanbrugh and Congreve that Sheridan himself had performed.[36] Cumberland is portrayed as Sir Fretful Plagiary, a writer of tragedies; *The Battle of Hastings* had appeared the previous year, perhaps inspiring Sheridan's bitter-sweet final joke: a spectacle of the destruction of the Spanish Armada with patriotic music and a masque. In so far as it spoofs the 'musicalization' and 'spectacularism' of Georgian drama, it is well taken; but that Sheridan, like Garrick and Colman, judged it necessary to *give* the audience its 'show' even while mocking its mindlessness, boded ill for the theatre. *The Critic* half belongs with the plays of the next chapter.

Notes

1. Hugh Blair, 'Comedy', Lecture XLVII in *Lectures on Rhetoric and Belles-Lettres*, third American edition, 2 vols (Boston, 1802), II, 350, 351, 362–66.

2. Corbyn Morris, *An Essay Towards Fixing the True Standards of Wit, Humour, Raillery, Satire and Ridicule* (London, 1744), pp. 23, 32.

3. See Stuart M. Tave, *The Amiable Humorist* (Chicago and London, 1960), pp. 202–6. Bergson's phrase appears in Chapter 1, Section 1 of *Le Rire* (1900); see *Comedy*, edited by Wylie Sypher (New York, 1956), p. 64. Walpole's remark is printed by Moelwyn Merchant, *Comedy* (London, 1972), p. 2.

4. A sequel, perhaps only partly by Fielding, to his *Old Man Taught Wisdom*, it was suppressed for a while as supposedly caricaturing a 'man of quality'. See *The London Stage 1660–1800*, 5 parts (Carbondale, Illinois, 1960–68), Part 3, edited by Arthur H. Scouten (1961), p. 923; Leo Hughes, *A Century of English Farce* (Princeton, 1956), p. 260; James J. Lynch, *Box, Pit and Gallery* (Berkeley and Los Angeles, 1953), p. 222; and Charles B. Woods, 'The 'Miss Lucy' Plays of Fielding and Garrick', *PQ*, 41 (1962), 294–310. On *The Wedding Day* (below), see Scouten, p. 1035.

5. It was edited by Jean B. Kern in nos 127–28 (1967) of the Augustan Reprint Series; and appears in my *Eighteenth-Century Drama: Afterpieces* (London, 1970), which also contains *Miss in Her Teens* (below).

6. The quotation is from *An Examen of the New Comedy, call'd The Suspicious Husband* (London, 1747).

7. *The Dramatic Censor*, 2 vols (London, 1770), II, 335–36, 339, 346, 350. Macklin's play was edited for the Augustan Reprint Series by Jean Kern (see note 5), and proved prophetic: *Harlequin Ranger* appeared in 1751. See also *An Examen of the New Comedy . . . .*

8. See *The Roman and English Comedy Considered and Compared* (1747) and his Preface to *Taste* (1752).

9. Percy Fitzgerald, *Samuel Foote* (London, 1910), pp. 275–76, 283; and Mary M. Belden, *The Dramatic Works of Samuel Foote* (New Haven, 1929), p. 191. On this early period see Simon Trefman, *Sam. Foote, Comedian* (New York, 1971), Chapters 2 and 3; Elizabeth Chatten, *Samuel Foote* (Boston, 1980), Chapters 2 and 3; and Richard W. Bevis, *The Laughing Tradition* (Athens, Georgia, 1980), pp. 152–53.

10. *The Englishman Returned* is supposed (by some) to have been a steal of Murphy's idea: see Trefman, pp. 73–74; and Chatten, p. 45. For *The Author*'s influence on Cumberland, Goldsmith, and Sheridan, see Trefman, p. 84; and Bevis, *Tradition*, p. 155.

11. It is included in my *Afterpieces* volume, and discussed in my *Tradition*, pp. 116–20.

12. *The Apprentice* was written in 1753 or 1754 but revised: see Robert D. Spector, *Arthur Murphy* (Boston, 1979), p. 58. On the quarrel (over a sequel to Foote's *Englishman in Paris*), which still divides scholars, compare Trefman, pp. 73–74, with Spector, p. 65. *The Spouter* (1756) was part of Murphy's revenge.

13. See particularly *The Tatler*, nos 155, 160, *The Spectator*, no. 403, and Fielding's *Rape Upon Rape* (1730), sometimes called *The Coffee-House Politician*. For discussion, especially of Murphy's changes to the printed text, see my *Afterpieces*, p. 195, n. 24; and *Tradition*, pp. 38–39.

14. Garrick's interesting comments are reprinted by George W. Stone, Jr, in *The London Theatre World, 1660–1800*, edited by Robert D. Hume (Carbondale, Illinois, 1980), p. 204; and in *The London Stage*, Part 4 (1962), p. cxcii.

15. In James Boswell, *The Life of Samuel Johnson*, edited by R. W. Chapman (London, 1952), p. 1070. Also see Robertson Davies's account in *The Revels History of Drama in English*, edited by T. W. Craik and C. Leech, 8 vols (London, 1975–83), VI (1975), 157.

16. *L'École des femmes*, *L'École des maris*, and *L'Étourdi*.

17. There are echoes in both *She Stoops to Conquer* and *The Rivals*. See *The Way to Keep Him and Five Other Plays by Arthur Murphy*, edited by John P. Emery (New York, 1956), p. 245.

18. Reference is to J. O. Bartley's edition, *Four Comedies by Charles Macklin* (London, 1968). On opposition to this play and *The True-Born Irishman*, see *The London Stage*, Part 4, p. 841; *Thespian Magazine*, 8 (1792), p. 64; and *Four Comedies*, pp. 125 and 81.

19. On the shared authorship, see Eugene R. Page, *George Colman the Elder* (New York, 1935), pp. 111–23; Frederick L. Bergmann, 'David Garrick and *The Clandestine Marriage*', *PMLA*, 67 (1952), 148–62; George W. Stone, Jr and George M. Kahrl, *David Garrick* (Carbondale, Illinois, 1979), pp. 242–43; and *The Plays of David Garrick*, edited by Frederick L. Bergmann and Harry W. Pedicord, 7 vols (Carbondale, Illinois, 1980–82), I, 413–17.

20. According to John Forster, *The Life and Times of Oliver Goldsmith*, third edition (London, 1890), p. 294. For a reading of the play as ironic, see Ricardo Quintana, *Oliver Goldsmith* (London, 1969), pp. 143–51.

21. See William Archer, *The Old Drama and the New* (London, 1923), p. 233.

22. By Cecil J. L. Price, *Theatre in the Age of Garrick* (Oxford, 1973), p. 164; and Arthur Friedman, 'Aspects of Sentimentalism in Eighteenth-Century Literature', in *The Augustan Milieu*, edited by Harry K. Miller, Eric Rothstein, and G. S. Rousseau (Oxford, 1970), p. 249.

23. Quotations follow the text in *British Dramatists from Dryden to Sheridan*, edited by George H. Nettleton, Arthur E. Case, and George W. Stone, Jr, second edition (Boston, 1969).

24. That is, *The Provoked Husband* ('the laughing, and even low comedy . . . last exhibited by Vanbrugh and Cibber'). See *Westminster Magazine* for December 1772; the textual note in *British Dramatists*, p. 937; and Bevis, *Tradition*, pp. 81–83.

25. As edited by Samuel N. Bogorad and Robert G. Noyes, *Theatre Survey*, 14, no. 1a (1973), 30. My debt to this well-executed edition is general. On *Piety's* influence, see *The Morning Chronicle* for 19 March 1773; Thomas Davies, *Memoirs of the Life of David Garrick*, 2 vols (London, 1780), II, 140–41; and Arthur Murphy, *The Life of David Garrick*, 2 vols (London, 1801), II, 52.

26. Tony fits the argument of Tave, esp. Chapter 5. Quotations and scene references follow *The Collected Works of Oliver Goldsmith*, edited by Arthur Friedman, 5 vols (Oxford, 1966), v.

27. An unfinished play, printed in *Sheridan's Plays . . .*, edited by W. Fraser Rae (London, 1902). See *The Rivals*, edited by Richard L. Purdy (Oxford, 1935), pp. xxxix–xli; *The Dramatic Works of Richard Brinsley Sheridan*, edited by Cecil J. L. Price, 2 vols (Oxford, 1973), I, 37–39; and John Loftis, *Sheridan and the Drama of Georgian England* (Oxford, 1976), p. 45, n. 6. Allardyce Nicoll considers *The Rivals* overrated, 'a thing of shreds and patches': *Late Eighteenth-Century Drama*, second edition (Cambridge, 1952), p. 160.

28. We have the Larpent MS and various editions. The two versions opened on 17 and 28 January 1775. For accounts see Purdy's Introduction to his edition; Cecil Price, *Sheridan's Plays* (Oxford, 1975; the source of my quotations), pp. x–xi; and Bevis, *Tradition*, pp. 217–19.

29. See Price, *Sheridan's Plays*, pp. xi and xiii on these points.

30. Compare Nicoll, p. 160; Price, *Sheridan's Plays*, pp. xiii, xix–xx; and Arthur C. Sprague, 'In Defence of a Masterpiece: *The School for Scandal* Re-examined', in *English Studies Today*, 3rd series, edited by G. I. Duthie (Edinburgh, 1964), pp. 128–30.

31. On the joining see *Works of Sheridan*, I, 293; and Andrew Schiller, '*The School for Scandal*: The Restoration Unrestored', *PMLA*, 71 (1956), 694–704 (p. 699).

32. Prologue to Charlotte Lennox's *Old City Manners* (1775).

33. Spector clarifies the situation and discusses the possible influence of Murphy's play on Sheridan's, pp. 121–22; Emery compares the two plays in his *Five Plays*, p. 334.

34. Murphy altered the play for a reading audience in the first edition (1778) and his 1786 *Works*. For comparisons of the versions, see Emery's edition, and Bevis, *Tradition*, p. 200.

35. Charles Dibdin considered it his best play after *The Clandestine Marriage*: *A Complete History of the Stage*, 5 vols (London, 1795), v, 276. The play was edited (along with *Separate Maintenance*) by Ross Grossman in his Ph.D. dissertation at the Claremont Graduate School, 1976.

36. See Price, *Sheridan's Plays*, pp. xviii–xix.

Chapter 14

Lay All Aristotle's Rules Aside: Musicals and Irregular Forms 1738–1779

The plain unornamented drama is too flat, Sir. Common dialogue is a dry imitation of nature, as insipid as real conversation; . . . Dramatick pieces, unadorned by dance and scenery, will never be able to make a stand against opera and pantomime.

Crochet in George Colman's *New Brooms!* (1776)

Non-traditional forms of drama continued to flourish and proliferate: in the long run, perhaps, the most significant theatrical development of the period. The Licensing Act restricted drama to the two patent houses, so new minor theatres such as Sadler's Wells did a roaring trade with irregular entertainment.[1] Here was, in Colman's phrase, 'the comic stubble'. A variety of labels was attached – with cheerful irresponsibility – to the pieces submitted to the Examiner and/or published, and today it is difficult to sort out the inherited generic confusion. What distinguishes a 'musical farce' from a 'comic opera'? General John Burgoyne's popular *The Maid of the Oaks* (1774) can stand for many another original blend; a sentimental love plot loosely binds together songs, scenic effects, magical characters, dancing, and 'vaudevill'. It calls itself a 'Past'rol Fete' ('Where young and old take fancy for their guide,/And lay all Aristotle's rules aside'), while modern scholars term it comedy or 'musical entertainment', but such a work defies *any* traditional classification; it is musical–pastoral–spectacle–comedy. Gay's *The What D'Ye Call It* proved prophetic.

Of the innovations, pantomime remained popular, especially (until 1761) under John Rich at Covent Garden. Though never again quite as lordly as in the 1720s, it was potent and influential.[2] Garrick took over Drury Lane hoping 'to banish pantomime, rope-dancing, and the Smithfield muses', said Murphy.[3] If so, he failed. During the 'playhouse war' of 1750 Garrick accepted the inevitable:

Unwilling we must change the nobler scene
And, in our turn, present you Harlequin.

He accordingly unleashed his own Rich, Henry Woodward, who produced *Queen Mab* (1750), *Harlequin Ranger* (1751, from *The Sus-*

picious Husband), and other pantomimes for both managers. Garrick's Prologue to *The School for Lovers* (1762) acknowledges the 'eager transport' that 'crowded Pantomimes' aroused. After all, the three plays most frequently performed at the two patent theatres during his career were pantomimes. The form itself, a blend of mythic operetta with Italian farce, scenic wonders, and tumbling, hardly changed, having no need to. Rich is said to have believed in pantomime as an art form.[4] The form, largely his own creation, was unique.

Burlesques, though less numerous and successful than in the 1730s, were still alive.[5] Henry Carey followed *The Dragon of Wantley* with *Margery; or, A Worse Plague Than the Dragon* (1738); Catherine Clive made awkward obeisance to Buckingham in *The Rehearsal; or, Bays in Petticoats* (1750); and Macklin tried (unsuccessfully) to unite Fielding with Buckingham in *Covent Garden Theatre; or, Pasquin Turned Drawcansir* (1752). The best burlesques were by managers: Garrick's *A Peep Behind the Curtain* (1767), an interesting exposé of the pressures pushing managers toward vulgarity, his *Meeting of the Company* (1774), another of Bayes's rehearsals, and Sheridan's *The Critic*, easily the class of the field (see also Ch. 13). Act I satirizes comedy, opera, and theatre-goers; Acts II and III use a rehearsal to burlesque tragedy and 'spectacularism'. It may be the only eighteenth-century imitation of a Restoration play that is fully as good as the original. Both *A Peep* and *The Critic* are double agents, though, indulging false taste while mocking it.

Ballad opera, associated with opposition politics, generally gave way to *comic* opera, wherein the best light composers of the day – usually Thomas Arne or Charles Dibdin – composed original scores for stories of romantic love.[6] Whereas ballad opera belongs to the history of folk music, burlesque, and political satire, comic opera is part of the development of musical comedy. It became the native answer to Italian opera – which remained fashionable, and dominant over serious English opera such as Arne's *Artaxerxes* (1762) – but comic opera developed as much from comedies with songs and 'musical farces' like Arne's *Don Saverio* (1750) as from opera.

By far the most important author of Georgian comic operas was Isaac Bickerstaffe, who virtually invented the form, though Sheridan's *The Duenna* (1775) was its greatest single success. Bickerstaffe's close association with John Beard, manager at Covent Garden from 1762, was the main reason why that theatre, a pantomime house under Rich, became an operetta house.[7] Bickerstaffe staked out his territory in *Thomas and Sally* (1760), a 'musical entertainment', but *Love in a Village* (1762, based on Johnson's *Village Opera*, 1729) was more successful, defining the style and preparing inherited clichés for transmission to us. The situations and types were already standard (three of the four romantic leads are fleeing forced marriages, and the fourth emulates

Wycherley's 'gentleman dancing master'), the exposition is juvenile and much of the dialogue 'stagy' and affected. Yet it suffices to introduce Arne's next song, and the surface is always bright, warm, and cheerful. Melodious escapism of a kind still popular, it was revived in the 1920s.[8]

A sequel, *Love in the City* (1767), missed the mark, and the fatuous absurdities of *The Maid of the Mill* (1765), a version of *Pamela*, deserved the ridicule of Foote's *Piety in Pattens*, but in 1768 Bickerstaffe produced his best opera, *Lionel and Clarissa*. Harman and Diana are clever and spirited, most other characters are humorous, and much of the dialogue is fairly intelligent. There are genuine moral dilemmas, and the sentimental title couple have to work theirs through. With music by Dibdin, it too was popular for a century and revived in the 1920s. Bickerstaffe's other comic operas – and his imitators – do not reach this level.

They included Sheridan, who gave the period its most popular comedy, burlesque, and comic opera; *The Duenna*, scored by his father-in-law Thomas Linley and others, had an astonishing first run of over ten weeks. Its 'Spanish intrigue' plot and characters, less interesting than *Lionel and Clarissa*'s, seem superficial and well-worn in print, but cannot really be judged without the staging and songs. Lopez is Figaro with a dash of Sancho Panza, and Sheridan's wit occasionally flashes in the dialogue. The play's phenomenal success was part of a pattern of popularity for the form: *The Beggar's Opera, Love in a Village*, and *The Duenna* ran two, three, and four in performances of mainpieces from 1775 to 1800.[9]

'Legitimate' or not, operettas were established, and spawning prodigiously. One by-blow was the burletta, a sort of musical farce burlesquing a Classical myth. Italian burlettas were followed on the London stage by translated and then English ones.[10] Kane O'Hara was the Bickerstaffe of the form, his *Midas* (1764) being the first English burletta, and *The Golden Pippin* (1772) also influential. Conceptually a mere sophomoric debasement of myth, burlettas depended for their charm on music and a jangling wit. Criticism dies laughing at the outrageous doggerel of *Midas* – at one point O'Hara rhymes fifteen lines in a row – but the final chorus warns, 'Now critics lie snug. . . . Remember the fate of Midas'. More pernicious and worth less than sentimental comedy, the burletta played an important role in English theatrical history. Because it was not considered a play and hence fell outside the Licensing Act, it *could* be performed at the non-patent theatres. As a result, the term 'burletta' was steadily broadened until it might mean almost any drama fitted up with some music in order to sidestep the theatrical monopoly.[11] Finally, patrons at the patent theatres, where O'Hara had begun, demanded their burlettas back.

'Preludes' emerged as an agreeable way of airing current theatrical issues. Generally penned by actor-managers whose careers depended on understanding and appeasing the various factions in the audience, they descended from dramatized prologues (Macklin's for *A Will and No Will*) and topical 'gambols' (Garrick's *Harlequin's Invasion*).[12] Foote and Colman wrote 'occasional preludes' for the Haymarket and Covent Garden before Garrick took up the idea. *The Meeting of the Company*, rhetorically a burlesque but *called* a 'prelude', displays obnoxious dramatists, actors, and spectators. To mark the opening of his last season and the splendid alterations to Drury Lane Garrick produced a 'musical prelude', *The Theatrical Candidates* (1775), in which Tragedy, Comedy, and Pantomime argue their claims. *New Brooms!*, the prelude Colman donated to introduce the new managers of Drury Lane in 1776, is a sprightlier presentation of these and other topics. An actor, a spectator, and writers of comedy, pantomime, and opera debate what the theatre is and ought to be. Each persona has a distinct viewpoint, behind which Colman hides; but it is clear that comic opera and spectacle were now real threats to regular comedy (and that Colman accepted the need to compromise: in *The Spanish Barber*, his 1777 adaptation of Beaumarchais's *Le Barbier de Seville*, Figaro becomes Lazarillo, the archetypal picaresque rogue, and the Harlequin of this pantomime, while songs 'garnish' and vary the action). Murphy's lively *News from Parnassus* (1776) is weightier and even broader.

Still other forms led shadowy existences. 'Pieces', 'sketches', and 'dramatic (or 'musical') entertainments' often claimed the right to operate outside the restrictions of traditional generic criticism. Pastoral usually occurred as part of another genre, such as comic opera, but occasionally set up independently, as in Garrick's *Florizel and Perdita* (1756), a 'dramatic pastoral'. Garrick eventually tried almost everything: masques, interludes, 'dramatic opera', and 'dramatic romance', besides the forms already mentioned. 'Spectacles' were important, but usually attached to something else, such as Garrick's interlude *The Jubilee* (1769). Anyone who glances at a list of the types of plays put forward in the period can see that the traditional genres, while still important, were crumbling, and that their stones were being used to erect a variety of quite different buildings.

Notes

1. Vincent J. Liesenfeld, *The Licensing Act of 1737* (Madison, Wisconsin, 1984), prints the Act, pp. 191–93. See also Allardyce Nicoll, *Late Eighteenth-Century Drama*, second edition (Cambridge, 1952), p. 208.

2. See Leo Hughes, *A Century of English Farce* (Princeton, 1956), Chapter 3, esp. p. 93; and Nicoll, *Late Eighteenth-Century Drama*, p. 209.

3. Arthur Murphy, *The Life of David Garrick*, 2 vols (London, 1801), I, 136.

4. See Paul Sawyer, 'John Rich's Contributions to the Eighteenth-Century London Stage', in *The Eighteenth-Century English Stage*, edited by Kenneth Richards and Peter Thomson (London, 1972), p. 91; but contrast Leo Hughes, *The Drama's Patrons* (Austin, Texas, 1971), pp. 97–108, esp. 101–2. See also Allardyce Nicoll, *The World of Harlequin* (Cambridge, 1963), pp. 202, 217; and Mitchell Wells, 'Spectacular Scenic Effects of the Eighteenth-Century Pantomime', *PQ*, 17 (1938), 67–81.

5. See Hughes, *Century*, Chapter 4.

6. Carey's *Margery* and Dibdin's *The Waterman* and *The Cobler* (1774) are called ballad operas, but here again the terminology was and is slippery. See Eric W. White, *A Register of First Performances of English Operas . . .* (London, 1983), esp. p. v; Part Three of his *A History of English Opera* (London, 1983); and Roger Fiske, *English Theatre Music in the Eighteenth Century* (London, 1973), Chapters 4–10: all splendid sources.

7. See Murphy, II, 172; and Nicoll, *Late Eighteenth-Century Drama*, p. 198.

8. See Robertson Davies, *The Revels History of Drama in English*, edited by T. W. Craik and C. Leech, 8 vols (London, 1975–83), VI (1975), 162, n. 1.

9. Cecil J. L. Price, *Theatre in the Age of Garrick* (Oxford, 1973), p. 112.

10. See P. T. Dircks, 'The Eighteenth-Century Burletta', *RECTR*, 10, no. 2 (1971), 44–52.

11. See, besides the above sources, George Rowell, *Victorian Theatre* (Oxford, 1956), pp. 9–13; V. C. Clinton-Baddeley, *All Right on the Night* (London, 1954), pp. 161–62; Watson Nicholson, *The Struggle for a Free Stage in London* (1906; New York, 1966), pp. 281–85.

12. Robert D. Spector suggests the French *pièce à tisoir* as the source in *Arthur Murphy* (Boston, 1979), p. 92.

Chapter 15
Epilogue: The 1780s

Matrices: politics, society, culture

> After 1782, almost every available statistical series of
> industrial output reveals a sharp upward turn.
>
> T. S. Ashton, *The Industrial Revolution*

> On Tuesday I gave notice of my design to preach upon
> (what is now the general topic) Slavery.
>
> John Wesley's *Journal*, 1788

The 1780s form a coda to the story of Restoration and eighteenth-
century drama. Clearly one play is ended, though not forgotten; most
of its cast has bowed out; winds are blowing from new quarters.
Virtually every aspect of English life is in transition. Janus seems the
patron of the decade.

It began darkly, at home and abroad. The American War widened
to include Holland, and the 'Armed Neutrality of the North' further
taxed the resources of the Royal Navy. Cornwallis's defeat at York-
town (1781) meant the loss of America, confirmed by the Versailles
peace treaty in 1783. The Gordon Riots over increased civil rights for
Catholics (1780) – a *déjà vu* unpleasantly reminiscent of 1680 – aroused
conservative fears of popular revolt and stiffened resistance to needed
reforms.[1] Dunning's Resolution 'that the power of the Crown has
increased . . . and ought to be diminished' (1780) signalled renewed
struggle between the Royal and Parliamentary spheres. Ministries rose
and tumbled: North's was replaced by Rockingham's Whigs, who
soon gave way to the unholy Fox–North coalition (1782), which
yielded to the younger Pitt (1783). Confirmed by the general election
of 1784, however, he embarked on the longest period of rule since the
'Robinocracy': nearly two decades.

Pitt was a Tory, though the labels 'Whig' and 'Tory' no longer
meant much. The Whigs began dividing into reformers and Radicals;

Tories – and most Englishmen – were 'Pittites'. His stewardship, beginning as the war ended, was generally constructive (or reconstructive) and peaceful, until events in France overwhelmed Europe. Pitt's genius was to learn from others and to sail blithely over the wreckage of his own defeats. Fox's India Bill failed in 1783; a year later Pitt steered a sounder India Act through successfully. Behind his Parliamentary Reform Bill (1785) lay years of official and unofficial agitation – the Committee on Parliamentary Reform, the Societies for Constitutional Information, etc. – but when it was defeated he simply moved on to the next task. Burke had spoken and written on economic reform for years; Pitt – a disciple of Adam Smith – reorganized the national finances, carried retrenching budgets, and negotiated a lucrative commercial treaty with France (1786). He spoke against slavery, but would not force the issue in Parliament.[2] Overall Pitt gave England an interval of stability after decades of strife, and it prospered.

The prevailing climate of reform also gave Pitt's prime ministry one of its least creditable episodes. The East Indian Company – and nabobs generally – were widely suspected of exploiting the natives; when Warren Hastings returned from India he was charged with misgovernment and impeached.[3] His sensational trial (1788–95) was dominated by impassioned Whig orators – Burke, Sheridan, Fox – but Pitt, probably from a genuine concern for colonial justice, allowed the harassment to continue. Though Hastings, a decent man and a capable administrator, was a poor choice of scapegoat, the episode demonstrates the momentum the humanitarian movement had acquired.

The government lacked the means to control or direct the unfamiliar forces sweeping through society. Reformers existed within Parliament, but organizations for dealing with social problems usually arose outside it, and had a high mortality rate. The Yorkshire Movement for redistributing Parliamentary seats, formed in 1779, splintered in 1780; the General Chamber of Manufacturers of Great Britain (1785) also had a swift demise. Yet reform committees, including one for abolishing the slave trade (1787), and provincial cultural groups like the Manchester Literary and Philosophical Society (1781), kept appearing. The government did try to improve the workhouse system and regulate chimney sweeping, and there were MPs in Wilberforce's Clapham Sect, which established Freetown, Sierra Leone, for freed slaves (1787).[4] But popular power usually operated outside the establishment, not through it. Wesley finally and reluctantly broke with the Anglican Church in 1784 because it would not ordain his American ministers. The Gordon Riots showed how little Parliament understood its proletarian constituency, which, faced with automation, smashed factories and equipment in the Midlands.

But England's revolution was, finally, industrial; the system absorbed the social forces.[5] Entrepreneurs devoted great energies to commercial development and expansion, which lay outside Parliament's ken, and the economy quickened its pace, especially after the war. Though England had fought to protect her colonial revenues, post-war exports to the United States increased sharply in value. Cotton imports had to octuple in the century's last two decades to satisfy the mills; to carry this trade, shipbuilding increased. Land was enclosed at a faster rate, and its value and productivity mushroomed. The mechanization of agriculture helped boost food production, assisting the population to grow by 50 per cent between 1750 and 1800. Coal output doubled and pig iron quadrupled in that period, and Henry Cort's 'puddling process' brought them into profitable alliance. Other capitalists turned to transport, building canals and turnpikes; by the 1780s one could travel between Manchester and London in half the time required in the 1750s.

All this progress – the quantum leaps in many economic and demographic indices, the giant strides towards industrialization – had its price. The enclosures and factories caused social dislocations, of which riots and Poor Laws give hard if scattered evidence. Prices as well as production went up, and there were shortages amid the abundance. If Wigan Pier was still over the horizon, Marx's class conflict was already on it, but prosperity was more visible and yields readier data. As Brecht wrote,

> Denn die einem sind im Dunkeln
> Und die andern sind im Licht.
> Und man siehet die im Lichte
> Die im Dunkeln sieht man nicht.[6]

Wesley excepted, serious thinkers of the 1780s treated this new world distantly or obliquely. Joseph Priestley, though living in Birmingham and clubbing with James Watt, concentrated on church history until he read Adam Smith. Then he revised his *Lectures on History* (1788), written in the 1760s, to include a rosy picture of economic individualism. He thought 'Men of wealth and influence' could be 'the greatest blessing to human societies' if they 'conscientiously make their power subservient to the good of their country', which they would do, if properly educated. Moreover, 'the only proper object of government' is '*the happiness of the people*'.[7] This side of Priestley – the social responsibility of the powerful – was developed by Jeremy Bentham during the 1780s into the 'principle of utility', whereby an action is judged good if 'the tendency it has to augment the happiness of the community is greater than any it has to diminish it'.[8] This attempt to found happiness on 'reason' and 'law' was, however, abused and discredited by those 'utilitarians' who ignored the moral stipulations of Bentham's theory.

The other major serial publications of the decade, Gibbon's *Decline and Fall of the Roman Empire* and Sir Joshua Reynolds's *Discourses*, did not examine society's fractures, although social corollaries could be deduced from Gibbon's critique of clerics and Christianity. Reynolds's concern was aesthetics, specifically the reconciliation of neo-Classical formalism with the growing conviction that art must possess spontaneity and intuition if it is to live. His respect for the rules, for decorum and training, his sense of art as artefact, all operate within the assumption that the arts arise from, imitate, and address themselves to imagination, feeling, and sensibility. (The decade's principal work of European philosophy was likewise synthetic, or dialectic: Immanuel Kant's *Critique of Pure Reason* (1781) attempts to balance the world of natural law against man's duties to the moral law, knowledge against faith, which he finally prefers.[9])

Imaginative literature passed from Augustan concerns and Georgian style to the first heady draughts of 'the blushful Hippocrene'. The dominant English poets of 1780–85, William Cowper and George Crabbe, retain Pope's sense of social norms. Crabbe's *The Village* (1783) debunks poetic fictions about rural life (in heroic couplets) and discusses its actual problems. The troubled Cowper, who retired to 'sing the SOFA', sketched a realistic picture of the countryside he loved, where the cotter dips water from a weedy ditch, 'Angry and sad, and his last crust consumed./So farewell envy of the *peasant's nest*!'[10] But the second half of the decade belonged to younger poets more attuned to the new mood being established in Europe by Goethe's *Werther* (1774) and *Egmont* (1789). Burns's whole-hearted embrace of bohemianism and democracy separates his 1786 poems from most eighteenth-century verse, though he still quotes Pope. Blake's verse in the 1780s is visionary and prophetic; it was the French Revolution that politicized him. The novel, which might have engaged the great social issues, stood in a Gothic recess, waiting for Austen and Scott. The decade's most notable English novel, Beckford's *Vathek* (1786), an intriguing but esoteric piece of orientalia written and first published in French, is closer to stage melodrama than to contemporary life.

Theatre and drama

Nothing goes down now but mirth and fun.

European Magazine (1783)

London theatre continued to expand, one way or another. The patent companies remained stable, Covent Garden under Harris and Thomas Hull, Drury Lane under the Sheridan group until J. P. Kemble took over (1788).[11] In 1782 Covent Garden was lengthened by about sixty feet (c. 50 per cent) and its seating increased proportionately to about two thousand, both figures in line with the 1775 Drury Lane; the auditorium of Vanbrugh's opera-house in the Haymarket was also deepened. John Palmer opened a new London theatre, the Royalty (1787), but could not get regular drama established there.[12] Scenic spectacles kept increasing in importance, expense, and ingenuity, even after de Loutherbourg abandoned Drury Lane (1781). Attendance remained high. Histrionically, Sarah Siddons's success at Drury Lane (1782) redeemed an earlier failure and began to make amends for the loss of Garrick; J. P. Kemble, her brother, made his debut the next year. A popular team, idols of 'the Kemble religion', they seem to have moved away from the relative naturalism of Garrick towards a more formal style, both statuesque and exaggerated, that was the starting-point of nineteenth-century actors.

An average of about two new tragedies or tragicomedies appeared annually in the 1780s. Few can claim any distinction, but some claim notice as signs of the times. The increasingly melodramatic temper of the theatre (and a critical eulogy in 1781) produced a renewal of interest in Lillo's *Fatal Curiosity*, which was altered by Colman (1782) and by the novelist Henry Mackenzie (1784).[13] Colman (still managing the Little Hay) cut the play down to about three-fifths the usual length of Georgian tragedies, and toned down some of Lillo's excesses. Mackenzie took the opposite tack, expanding it to five acts and painting moral qualities in starker terms; Old Wilmot becomes another of the period's saintly profligates, and Mackenzie sends a villain to foreclose on him. Colman's version fared slightly better.

Richard Cumberland, the decade's only significant tragic writer, led the drift into melodrama, meaning here not a type of musical drama but a style exaggerated in predictable ways: type characters running to extremes of good and evil; conventionally improbable romance-plots, featuring *coups de théâtre*; unnatural, ranting dialogue; lurid scenes – in effect, a stage version of the Gothic novel.[14] . Indeed, Horace Walpole's *The Castle of Otranto* furnished hints for Robert Jephson's tragedy *The Count of Narbonne* (1781); and Walpole's unacted but influential *The Mysterious Mother* (1768) prompted Cumberland's *The Mysterious Husband* (1783).[15] Cumberland softened Walpole's double incest to bigamy, and a son who marries one of his father's wives, but reinforced this plot with some extravagant prose. Lord Davenant, who married Dormer's beloved from mercenary motives, then married his sister as well, soliloquizes: 'Curs'd be the hour in which I wrong'd this man! . . . 'Sdeath! how I loath myself! Damnation! what a wretch I am!' etc. (II. 1). Dormer and Lady Davenant speak the language of romantic fiction, full of periods and stilted formalities (III. 1); under duress, she rants like Murphy's heroines: 'Inexplicable distress! . . . Fate labours as with mother's pangs!' (IV. 1). Finally Lord Davenant takes poison, apologizes to his wife as to a 'saving angel', *and* stabs himself.

When Cumberland essayed tragedy, he often fell short. *The Mysterious Husband*'s villain doubles as tragic protagonist; Lord Davenant is strong, never good or admirable. That the effect of evil perishing while good survives is tragicomic, not tragic, is shown again in *The Carmelite* (1784), whose only casualty is Lord Hildebrand. He perishes of guilt at having killed St Valori twenty years ago and usurped his lands; only in his last moments does he learn that his 'victim', disguised as a Carmelite, has been at his side for years, prodding his conscience. St Valori is finally reunited with his widow Matilda and son Montgomeri (Siddons and Kemble), whose play it largely is. Cumberland indulges Siddons with the kind of hysterical scenes that Murphy had given Mrs Barry (*The Grecian Daughter* was one of Siddons's great triumphs), turning his play into *The Norman Widow*, a tangle of misplaced grief and verbal raptures that deflect the plot. St Valori long suspects that Montgomeri is Matilda's lover because she was seen to embrace the young man and murmur, 'My husband!' (II. 1). But that is just the way she talks when revealing herself to her son and appointing him her champion against her husband's 'murderer'. Most of the play is a froth of ecstatic language, withheld information, and Gothic paraphernalia: a shipwreck on a wild coast, a funeral chapel with despairing somnambulist.

Cumberland's most genuine tragedy was *The Arab* (1785; later called *Alcanor*), which treats Judaean dynastic quarrels after Herod's death. Rome's choice is Herod's supposed bastard, the noble savage Alcanor, raised in desert exile. The Sanhedrin would prefer the legitimate son 'in David's line', Herodian. Both sons are noble, but Alcanor has more scope; 'in the desert', he explains, 'We think and act at large', whereas in 'the guilty world' the feelings contract (IV. 1). Even Herodian apostrophizes the 'blessed solitudes' where 'the soul,/Expanding with the space it contemplates,/Grows like the scene, magnificent and vast'. Thus Cumberland transmits the embryonic 'aesthetics of the infinite' from Addison and Burke to the nineteenth century.[16] Alcanor's plight becomes tragic when, already enthroned, he learns that he is actually a commoner. Unable to face the loss of his mission and of the beautiful Glaphyra to Herodian, he abdicates and stabs himself. Glaphyra predicts that 'Nature's child/Will, with the God of Nature, meet forgiveness' (v. 3). Cumberland plays Alcanor's nobility and naturalness fortissimo, and his use of the 'gloomy Western Tower' and the 'Magnificent Hall' of the Sanhedrin relates the play to Gothic spectacle, but plot and hero *are* tragic, and the blank verse, while unpointed, is at least smooth and competent.

Hannah More, whose *Percy* was the best tragedy of the previous decade, wrote four *Sacred Dramas* (1782) that were not performed. Nor were they intended to be: 'It would not be easy', she thought, 'to introduce Sacred Tragedies on the English Stage'.[17] That a serious writer of proven talent and some stature should turn from the stage to closet drama was a significant and ominous development.

That *Werther*, Frederick Reynolds's first play, did reach Covent Garden in 1786 despite obvious weaknesses is also significant. More an evocation of Goethe's mood than a rendering of his novel, *Werther* offers three short acts of *Sturm und Drang*. With no preparation, Reynolds winds up Werther and Charlotte to the highest pitch and leaves them there: they rave, read *Ossian*, weep, embrace, fall, and are 'supported off'. Amid the welter of feeling, bathos passes almost unnoticed. Werther: ''Tis not for ever that we now divide.' Charlotte: 'No, for tomorrow we will meet again' (I. 2). Buckingham and Fielding stir in their graves. A new *Zeitgeist* announces itself, between sobs, and settles down for a long stay.

Comedy, a larger, stronger field (three to four new comedies and farces annually in London), was not dominated by anyone. Of established dramatists, Hannah Cowley excelled with three plays in the decade's first four years. *The Belle's Stratagem* (1780) is an ambitious attempt to twist worn strands into workable rope. Letitia Hardy, the scheming belle, first appals Doricourt as a country booby, then, having jogged his indifference, converts hate to love as a masked wit. Counterpointing this Farquhar–Goldsmith plot is a Wycherley–Sheridan motif wherein Courtall pursues a country wife. Endowed with a lively masquerade where Doricourt is captivated, a 'screen scene' where Courtall is deceived, exposed, and ridiculed, a fringe of social satire, and some provocative remarks about the world being more masked than the stage (Epilogue), the play is rich. But it squanders its wealth in an irrelevant conclusion where the characters, forgetting what the belle's stratagem was, try to make the issue English reserve versus Continental assurance. The patriotic ending reminds us it was wartime,

and throws into relief the thinness of Cowley's plot compared to Goldsmith's. Letitia's roles and Doricourt's response prove nothing
important about them or us.

Which Is the Man? (1782) is another lively social comedy with a
'screen scene', but *its* patriotic theme is integral. A merry young
widow, Lady Bell Bloomer, chooses a gallant officer, Beauchamp,
over Lord Sparkle, a rake in whom are satirized various Georgian
corruptions: he bought his borough, won the gift of an ecclesiastical
living at dice, raises his tenants' rent to finance his dissipations, etc.
Though Fitzherbert's treatment of his ward in the subplot is unsatis-
factory, Lady Bell and the dialogue are lively. *A Bold Stroke for a
Husband* (1783), a Restoration-style Spanish intrigue, is just witty fluff
making deep bows to Virtue, 'our first, most awful duty'.

After a decade of rejections, eighty-year-old Charles Macklin finally
obtained a licence for *The Man of the World* (1781).[18] It is nearer to the
'problem play' than to any type of Georgian comic drama. The
problem is how to handle the ambitious, energetic Sir Pertinax
Macsycophant (Macklin), who, having disinherited one son, Sandy,
for liberal leanings, wants to marry the other, Egerton, to Lord
Lumbercourt's daughter Rodolpha and propel him into the Ministry.
Egerton, however, likes Constantia better, and Rodolpha prefers
Sandy. By the end a political match seems likely after all, but Macsycophant has broken with his whole family, and stalks out cursing like
a Scottish Malvolio. Macklin shares with greater writers the inability
to make passive virtue as interesting as evil activity – if indeed he
wanted to. An actor first, he wrote himself the best role; the upright
Egerton, the sententious clergyman Sidney, and the limp Constantia
pale beside him. Only the Lumbercourts – as crudely, broadly Scottish
as he, though less gifted – can hold the stage with Macsycophant,
whose dark power recalls Sir Giles Overreach.

Cumberland continued to produce, mirroring the times yet
remaining himself. *The Walloons* (1782), a wartime comedy, pits Royal
Tar Davy Dangle against a treacherous lot: bigamous Lady Dangle,
a papist termagant; Father Sullivan, a 'huge lazy' Franciscan; and his
accomplice Daggerly, who are spying at Plymouth. The Prologue,
however, embraces everyone 'Whose kindred virtues speak their
British race'. *The Natural Son* (1784) resembles *The West Indian* in its
wish to redeem one of society's pariahs, in Major O'Flaherty's role as
amiable humorist, and in the benevolism of its conclusion. The illegitimate, seemingly orphaned Blusherly, at first too quiet and delicate
to please anyone, gains interest and confidence as he learns his
parentage and receives inheritances, first from his dead mother, then
(had you guessed?) from his living father. With all its warmth, the play
can be tough; Blusherly, Lady Paragon, and Phoebe Latimer (a learned

Lady Wishfort) are all teased cruelly when most vulnerable. It is saved by eccentrics: O'Flaherty, the compleat angler Jack Hustings, Dumps and Ruefull, whose 'rough shells' of misanthropy cover (of course) 'virtue at the heart' (III. 1).

Cumberland's *The Imposters* (1789) deserves to be better known: the Contrasted Brothers meet the Rogues' Stratagem with entertaining results. 'Lord Janus' ('his ingenuity almost excuses his iniquity') and 'Polycarp' are clever, Oliver is funny, Captain Sapient manly, Sir Charles noble, and Eleanor, a new type of active heroine who goes riding, attractively spirited.[19] Warm and witty, *The Imposters* shows Cumberland still observant and responsive, ready for the new decade.

In 1801, Arthur Murphy pronounced John Burgoyne's *The Heiress* (1786) 'the best comedy that has appeared since *The School for Scandal*'.[20] Murphy *would* like this complex weave of drawing-room intrigues, disclosures, reunions, marriages, and social satire. The Alscrips are memorable *nouveaux riches*: the rakish father a pushy, usuring lawyer, the purse-proud heiress a crass climber who rages like a fishwife when crossed; her 'Uncle's Pig-Iron' fortune seems symbolic. Sir Clement Flint is more believable and striking while judging others by his own selfishness than when he finally turns philanthropist because 'to reward the deserving . . . is self-interest in the extreme' (v. 3), though his name presages the change. The virtuous characters, except for vivacious Lady Emily, are inevitably less colourful, yet Burgoyne has to be taken seriously here; II. 1, where Flint watches Clifford play chess with Emily (who likens them all to literary genres), has multiple levels, the satirical passages are finely detailed, and the precise stage directions suggest a heightened concern with gesture and blocking. But loose ends and implausibilities mar the play: Blandish's schemes fade out unmentioned, the brother-finds-sister plot is strained, and the non-duel in Hyde Park is as contrived as anything in Steele. *The Heiress* is finally not in Sheridan's class.

The first significant new dramatist to appear was Thomas Holcroft, whose unslumbering social conscience typically created comedies of concern. *Duplicity* (1781) is, despite Holcroft's demurrer, a version of Moore's *The Gamester* wherein the duplicitous friend is only a *seeming* villain: Osborne finally reveals it was all a scheme to cure Harry of his infatuation with gambling, and returns the money he's won! (This surprising turn makes Osborne's aside in I. 2 – 'This old fool is become suspicious, I must be sudden' – look, well, duplicitous.) Holcroft's intensity about reforming gamblers produces some didactic moments, yet his rural humorists, the Turnbulls, are delightful, especially in IV. 2, where Clara translates polite London English into the Zomerzetzhire proverbs they understand. In his Preface Holcroft worries that such characters have become 'hazardous' through disuse, for which he blames sentimental comedy, introduced 'about fourteen years ago' (1767–68), and 'A sense of propriety [that] spreads in proportion as people read'.

Holcroft remained *engagé*, translating Beaumarchais's mildly revolutionary success *The Marriage of Figaro* (Paris, 1784) for Covent Garden (1785). (On his own, he did not write saucy speeches for the lower classes, though Figaro's observations on the pride of rank and fortune could provide mottoes for some of Holcroft's aristocratic villains.) *Seduction* (1787) interminably exposes the real or affected levities and dissipations of 'the town'; it has witty passages, but, as in *Duplicity*, there are unfair surprises at the end. This feature, and stage directions that pose the actors in 'pictures' at crucial moments, foreshadow Holcroft's later melodramas.

The rise of women writers that, beginning in the 1760s, had already gone beyond any previous period, continued with the advent of Elizabeth Inchbald, an actress who wrote comic drama and later published collections of plays. Her competence and penchant for moralization and pathos are manifest from her earliest work. In *I'll Tell You What* (1785), the marital question comes full circle from Farquhar: divorce is too easy. 'Divorces happen every day now', observes Major Cyprus, whose wife's brother 'compelled' her to leave her suspicious first husband (I. 2, 3). Finally the Cypruses separate, for they met in intrigue, and 'No lasting friendship is formed on vice' (v. 3). Harriet Cyprus and women are then lectured on virtue. The subplot wherein an angry father disinherits his son, driving his family nearly to ruin, contains more emotional energy; the scenes of reconciliation are tearfully effusive, triumphs of charity over obduracy. With its slick *coups de théâtre*, contrived assemblies, and too neat use of the title, the play has the 'well made' feel of some Victorian comedies.

Such Things Are (1787), less regular but more interesting, exhibits the same sure touch on dialogue. Set in Sumatra, it might be Aphra Behn's except for the pathos centring on Haswell, a concerned liberal who virtually empties Sumatra's prison after discovering that the Sultan's beloved wife has languished there unknown for fourteen years. On his first visit Haswell meets Zedan, who picks his pocket. Later Haswell gives him money; Zedan, 'holding his heart' and feeling something he 'never felt before – it makes me like not only you, but all the world besides', returns the pocket-book. Haswell: 'Oh, nature!' (II. 4). This gives a good idea of Inchbald's desideratum, though there is much – perhaps too much – else going on, including manners satire. Haswell's benevolences finally yield fantastic returns: granted 'power to redress the wrongs of all who suffer', he releases prisoners with suitable rebukes or absolution, makes a match, receives thanks, and is praised fulsomely by all. Mrs Inchbald's farces, such as *Appearance Is Against Them* (1785), are less sentimental.

Leonard MacNally, who tried most of the lighter forms, wrote one play worth a second look: *Fashionable Levities* (1785), set at Bath. The early acts, long-winded and disorderly, are oddly anachronistic; the primitives sharking around the spa seem to have stepped from a wit comedy by Davenant or Killigrew. Then, against all odds, the play becomes solemn and substantial, facing the issues directly. In an exemplary scene (IV. 3), the old guardian Ordeal shows a good heart – without losing his quirky wit - as he releases his ward to her honourable young lover. Next, Lady Flippant Savage, the focus of the title's concern, rejects her 'dissipated life' (blamed on a vicious education in 'foibles and levities') and proclaims her sensibility (v. 2). Even her husband Sir Buzzard Savage, steamrollered by Georgian benevolence, at last agrees to return home, reform, and be happy. MacNally saves whom he can, and wittily.

The Dramatist (1789), also set in Bath, shows that Frederick Reynolds's *métier* was farcical comedy; once warmed up the play is quite delightful. Its comic centre is the playwright Vapid, a wonderful confuser of life and art, perpetually making a fool of himself and getting caught, but embracing every reverse with a cry of 'Here's incident!' Tucked behind sofas or in closets, he is sure to pop out at the worst moment, offering or finishing an epilogue. Perceiving everything as a comic episode, he stage-manages Act v as if he were writing or directing Reynolds's play; 'go to her', he begs Neville, 'preserve the unity of action'. Eventually he wins a play-loving heiress who will build him a theatre. *The Dramatist* ends self-reflexively, saluting the 'Joys domestic . . . cherished on the throne', an application of Vapid's formula: 'say it's a translation from the French and interweave a few compliments on the English' (v. 1). Could that be Dickens's Vincent Crummles in the wings, awaiting his cue?

A comedy as charming as Reynolds's was by then a rarity. John Pinkerton was not alone in lamenting

> how much our stage hath declined . . . since the retreat of
> Garrick. It is overwhelmed with floods of Irish nonsense,
> and stuff more stupid than stupidity, where not one
> glimmer of sense or wit appears.[21]

'Indeed', he remarked, 'pantomime is now the best entertainment we find in our theatres'. Sarcasm or hyperbole aside, more 'irregular' plays – mostly musicals – were being written and performed than ever before. Miscellaneous comic pieces now constituted a plurality of new plays and also of performances, for more of the 'hits' were musicals too.[22] A smaller proportion of acted drama reached print, though: these plays were designed to be seen, not read, and have seldom gratified readers. It was in this decade that the proto-vaudevillian forms first took over from what remained of regular comedy and tragedy. Critics might rage against 'floods of nonsense', but the physical theatres – well advanced towards cavernous music-halls – encouraged a loud, cheerful, unreflective drama, and the theatres were full.

Spectacular pantomimes, after about 1785 more often revivals than premières,[23] became a Boxing Day treat, burlettas and masques appeared sporadically, but comic operas, which increasingly alternated original tunes with melodies from European opera and British folk music, were more numerous and popular. The greater rewards brought forward new composers. Arne had died (1778); Dibdin, persisting despite difficulties with managers, wrote and succeeded less often.[24] Samuel Arnold, whose first credit was *The Maid of the Mill*, and William Shield emerged as the principal composers of the 1780s. Though Colman popularized musicals at the Little Hay, Covent Garden generally led in this area until 1788, when Drury Lane acquired the talented composer Stephen Storace. John O'Keeffe, the author of *Wild Oats*, was the leading librettist of a large group that included most practising dramatists: Cumberland, Holcroft, MacNally, Frances Brooke, Colman the Younger, Burgoyne, etc.

As texts, even the successful 'irregulars' have little but historical interest: they depended on music, scenery, and sometimes topicality for their appeal. Shield's and Frederick Pilon's *Siege of Gibraltar* (1780) appeared while the real siege was continuing, after Rodney's temporary relief; Shield's and O'Keeffe's *Omai* (1785) exploited the visit of the famous Tahitian carried by Captain Cook. Productions such as Shield's and Miles Andrews's *The Enchanted Castle* (1786) and Storace's and James Cobb's *The Haunted Tower* (1789) *required* the scenic effects that both used and intensified the Gothic horror vogue.[25] Popular operas like *The Lord of the Manor* (1780) and *Rosina* (1782) are nothing without their songs, some of which became Victorian staples. Yet Colman the Younger's *Inkle and Yarico* (1787) can hold a reader's interest even without Arnold's music. Set in 'an American forest' and at Barbados, it tells how a mercenary young English trader, Thomas Inkle, falls in love with a helpful native girl, Yarico, then tries to sell her into slavery: a version of a story recounted by Steele.[26] Using a noble savage to satirize Europe and trading on the slavery debate, *Inkle and Yarico* succeeded, and retains an appeal that most of the Gothic, pastoral, and exotic operettas have lost.

The late 1780s, like the late 1770s, ended an era, this time of European history as well as English drama. George III went mad and recovered (1787–88), presaging the Regency; the Bastille fell, foreshadowing Napoleon's wars. Vanbrugh's Haymarket Opera burned down (1789), and the remaining theatres were being radically altered. Tragedy had largely dissolved into melodrama, comedy was moving into new regions, and light novelties were more vigorous than either. The Old Guard – except Cumberland – stepped aside. Colman the Elder relinquished the Little Hay to his son in 1787, Thomas Linley handed over Drury Lane's music to Storace in 1788, and Charles Macklin, who was a year older than *The Way of the World* and had worked with Cibber and Fielding and Garrick and Foote and everyone since, retired in 1789. It is time to stop. Like him, we can still haunt the theatres, admonishing the startled actors, 'Speak up, sir! We can't hear you!'

Notes

1. See Roy Porter, *English Society in the Eighteenth Century* (London, 1982), pp. 135–36; and Gerald R. Cragg, *The Church and the Age of Reason* (Harmondsworth, 1960), pp. 219–23.

2. J. H. Plumb, *England in the Eighteenth Century* (Harmondsworth, 1950), p. 191.

3. For a defence of Hastings see R. W. Harris, *England in the Eighteenth Century* (London, 1963), p. 173.

4. See Plumb, *England*, pp. 158–59; and Porter, p. 148.

5. Asa Briggs, *A Social History of England* (London, 1983), p. 180. For the data in the balance of the paragraph, see Briggs, pp. 170–74, 186, and 206–7; Porter, pp. 329–34 and 350; and Dorothy Marshall, *Eighteenth-Century England*, second edition (London, 1974), pp. 476–78.

6. The concluding lines of *Die Dreigroschenoper* by Kurt Weill and Bertolt Brecht: 'For some live in darkness, and others in light. And we see the ones in brightness: Those in shadow go unseen'.

7. Basil Willey quotes and discusses this and other passages from Priestley in *The Eighteenth-Century Background* (1940; Harmondsworth, 1965), pp. 180, 190–93.

8. From Chapter 1 of *An Introduction to the Principles of Morals and Legislation* (1780–89).

9. See Cragg, pp. 250–54.

10. *The Task* (1785), Book i, ll. 246–47.

11. See Judith Milhous, in *The London Theatre World, 1660–1800*, edited by Robert D. Hume (Carbondale, Illinois, 1980), pp. 24–25. The figures in the next sentence come from Edward Langhans, in *London Theatre World*, pp. 63–65.

12. Allardyce Nicoll, *Late Eighteenth-Century Drama*, second edition (Cambridge, 1952), p. 230, cites the patentees' opposition as the cause of failure.

13. For an account of both alterations, and James Harris's critique, see the Introduction to William H. McBurney's edition of *Fatal Curiosity* (Lincoln, Nebraska, 1966), pp. xiv–xvii, a useful source. Mackenzie's version was called *The Shipwreck*.

14. See Bertrand Evans, *Gothic Drama from Walpole to Shelley* (Berkeley and Los Angeles, 1947).

15. See Robertson Davies, 'Plays and Playwrights', in *The Revels History of Drama in English*, edited by T. W. Craik and C. Leech, 8 vols (London, 1975–83), VI (1975), 164–65, 177–78.

16. The phrase is from the subtitle of Majorie H. Nicolson's *Mountain Gloom and Mountain Glory* (1959; New York, 1963).

17. Quoted by Davies, p. 178.

18. Earlier versions were refused by the Examiner in 1770 and 1779. A three-act prototype, *The True-Born Scotsman*, played Dublin in 1764. See *Four Comedies by Charles Macklin*, edited by J. O. Bartley (London, 1968), pp. 28–32; Dougald MacMillan, 'The Censorship . . . of Macklin's *Man of the World*', *Huntington Lib. Bull.*, 10 (1936), 79–101; and William W. Appleton, *Charles Macklin* (Cambridge, Massachusetts, 1960), pp. 136, 207–16.

19. See J. H. Plumb, *Georgian Delights* (London, 1980), pp. 17–19 on the growing enjoyment of landscape and mountain-climbing. Of course equestriennes were not new, except as comic heroines.

20. Arthur Murphy, *The Life of David Garrick*, 2 vols (London, 1801), II, 105.

21. 'Robert Heron' [John Pinkerton], 'On Comedy', in *Letters of Literature* (London, 1785), pp. 202–3.

22. See my *Laughing Tradition* (Athens, Georgia, 1980), pp. 65–66 on the new plays being submitted; and Harry W. Pedicord's analysis of the repertoire in *The Theatrical Public in the Time of Garrick* (New York, 1954), Appendix C.

23. Roger Fiske, *English Theatre Music in the Eighteenth Century* (London, 1973), p. 446. Fiske is a major source of what follows.

24. Eric W. White, *A History of English Opera* (London, 1983), pp. 203–6.

25. On which see Fiske, pp. 473, 501.

26. In *Spectator*, no. 11: see Fiske, p. 477.

Chronology

Note: A selection of notable plays, writings and events in the period. Dates of plays refer to first production. Here and in the Author Bibliographies (pp. 293–325), the London theatres are abbreviated as follows:
CG = Covent Garden; DG = Dorset Garden; DL = Drury Lane;
GF = Goodmans Fields; H² or Little Hay = Little Theatre in the Haymarket; Hay = the Haymarket Opera; LIF = Lincoln's Inn Fields.
In addition, the following abbreviations are used:

b. = born	Polit. = Political
Brit. = Britannica	Prins = Principles
co(s) = company/–nies	pub. = published
d. = died	Reg. = Register
ed. = edition	ret. = retired
Engl. Dram. = English Drama	rev. = revised
govt = government	Sec. = Secretary
Hist. = History	St = Street
Lit. and Phil. = Literary and	tr. = translation/–ting/–ted
Philosophical	trans. = translator
mo(s) = month(s)	vs = against

DATE	PLAYS	OTHER WORKS	HISTORY AND CULTURE
1660	Tatham *The Rump*	Corneille *Discours*	Restoration of King Royal patents create King's and Duke's Cos Royal Society begins Pepys starts diary
1661	Davenant *Siege of Rhodes*, I and II Cowley *Cutter of Coleman Street*		Rescissory and Corporation Acts

DATE	PLAYS	OTHER WORKS	HISTORY AND CULTURE
1662	R. Howard *The Committee* *The Surprisal* Boyle *The General* (Dublin)	Molière *L'École des femmes* Kirkman *The Wits*	Uniformity Act Charles II marries Smock Alley Theatre opens (Dublin)
1663	Tuke *Adventures of Five* *Hours* Dryden *Wild Gallant* J. Howard *English Monsieur* Wilson *Cheats*		Theatre Royal, Bridges St, opens Women start to wear masks
1664	R. Howard/Dryden *The Indian Queen* Etherege *The Comical Revenge* Dryden *Rival Ladies* Boyle *The General* (London) *Henry V*	Killigrew *Thomaso*	Conventicle Act Five Mile Act Nell Gwyn joins King's Co.
1665	Dryden *Indian Emperor* Boyle *Mustapha* J. Howard *All Mistaken* R. Howard *Vestal Virgin*		Second Dutch War Princess Anne b. Plague closes theatres
1666		Molière *Le Misanthrope*	Great Fire Pentland uprising Theatres reopen

DATE	PLAYS	OTHER WORKS	HISTORY AND CULTURE
1667	Dryden *Secret Love* *Wild Gallant* (rev.) (/Newcastle) *Martin Mar-All* (/Davenant) *Tempest* Boyle *Black Prince* E. Howard *Change of Crownes*	Milton *Paradise Lost* Molière *Tartuffe* Racine *Andromaque*	Dutch Navy in Thames; theatres close for July Clarendon dismissed
1668	Etherege *She Wou'd If She Cou'd* Shadwell *Sullen Lovers* Sedley *Mulberry Garden* Dryden *Evening's Love* R. Howard *Great Favourite*	Dryden *Essay of Dramatic Poesy*	Triple Alliance Dryden, Poet Laureate Davenant d. Betterton, Harris manage Duke's Co.
1669	Dryden *Tyrannick Love* R. Howard/ Buckingham *Country Gentleman*		Theatres close for Queen's death Pepys ends diary
1670	Shadwell *The Humorists* Betterton *Amorous Widow* Dryden *Conquest of Granada* (I)	Racine *Bérénice*	Second Conventicle Act Congreve b.

DATE	PLAYS	OTHER WORKS	HISTORY AND CULTURE
1671	Dryden *Conquest of Granada* (II) Wycherley *Love in a Wood* Buckingham *et al* *Rehearsal*	Milton *Paradise Regained* *Samson Agonistes*	DG theatre opens C. Cibber b. N. Gwyn retires
1672	Dryden *Marriage à la Mode* *The Assignation* Shadwell *Miser* *Epsom-Wells* Wycherley *Gentleman Dancing Master* Ravenscroft *Citizen Turned Gentleman*		Third Dutch War Declaration of Indulgence Bridges St theatre burns Addison, Steele b.
1673	Settle *Empress of Morocco* Behn *Dutch Lover*	Molière *Le Malade imaginaire*	Test Act Eliz. Barry acting Molière d.
1674	Lee *Nero* Shadwell *et al.* *The Tempest* Newcastle *Triumphant Widow* Duffett *Mock Tempest*	Rymer, trans. *Reflections on Aristotle* (Rapin)	Third Dutch War ends Wren's DL opens Milton,Clarendon, Tuke d. Rowe b.

DATE	PLAYS	OTHER WORKS	HISTORY AND CULTURE
1675	Wycherley *Country Wife* Dryden *Aureng-Zebe* Lee *Sophonisba* Shadwell *Psyche* *The Libertine* Crowne *Calisto* Otway *Alicibiades*		
1676	Etherege *Man of Mode* Wycherley *Plain Dealer* Shadwell *Virtuoso* Lee *Gloriana* Behn *Town Fop* Durfey *Madame Fickle* Otway *Don Carlos* *Titus and Berenice* *Cheats of Scapin*		
1677	Dryden *All for Love* *State of Innocence* Lee *Rival Queens* Behn *The Rover* Sedley *Antony and Cleopatra* Durfey *Fond Husband*	Racine *Phèdre*	Charles Killigrew replaces father as manager of King's Co.

DATE	PLAYS	OTHER WORKS	HISTORY AND CULTURE
1678	Dryden *Limberham* (/Lee) *Oedipus* Lee *Mithridates* Shadwell *Timon* *True Widow* Otway *Friendship in Fashion* Durfey *Trick for Trick*	Bunyan *Pilgrim's Progress* Rymer *Tragedies of Last Age*	Popish Plot First Society for Reformation of Manners Farquhar b. Marvell, Flecknoe d.
1679	Lee *Caesar Borgia* Shadwell *Woman-Captain* Tate *Loyal General*	Burnet *History of the* *Reformation*	Exclusion Bill Duke of York expatriated Bothwell Brig rising Ann Bracegirdle joins Duke's Co. Hobbes, Boyle d.
1680	Otway *Orphan* *Caius Marius* *Soldier's Fortune* Dryden *Spanish Friar* Lee *Lucius Junius Brutus* *Theodosius*	Burnet *Rochester*	Duke of York returns from Scotland Butler, Rochester d.
1681	Lee *Princess of Cleve* Ravenscroft *London Cuckolds* Banks *Unhappy Favourite* Tate *Lear* Shadwell *Lancashire Witches*	Dryden *Absalom and Achitophel*	Charles II dissolves Oxford Parliament Mrs Verbruggen joins King's Co.

DATE	PLAYS	OTHER WORKS	HISTORY AND CULTURE
1682	Otway *Venice Preserved* Lee/Dryden *Duke of Guise* Banks *Virtue Betrayed* Southerne *Loyal Brother*	Dryden *Macflecknoe* *Religio Laici* Durfey *Pills to Purge* *Melancholy*	King's Co. collapses; union of two companies
1683	Crowne *City Politiques* Lee *Constantine* Otway *The Atheist*		Rye House Plot Killigrew d.
1684	Banks *Island Queens* Tate *Duke and No Duke* Lacy *Hercules Buffoon*		Lee enters Bethlehem Hospital
1685	Crowne *Sir Courtly Nice* Dryden *Albion and Albanius*		Charles II d.; theatres close 3 months James II accedes Monmouth's Rebellion Edict of Nantes revoked Gay, Handel b. Otway d.
1686	Behn *Lucky Chance* Jevon *Devil of a Wife*		
1687	Sedley *Bellamira* Behn *Emperor of the Moon*	Dryden *Hind and Panther* Newton *Principia*	Buckingham and Nell Gwyn d.

DATE	PLAYS	OTHER WORKS	HISTORY AND CULTURE
1688	Shadwell *Squire of Alsatia*		Glorious Revolution Flight of James II Lee recovers Pope b. Bunyan d.
1689	Dryden *Don Sebastian* Shadwell *Bury Fair* Tate/Purcell *Dido and Aeneas* Lee *Massacre of Paris* Behn *Widow Ranter*	Gould *The Playhouse: a Satire*	William and Mary accede Constitution adopted War of League of Augsburg begins Toleration Act James II invades Ireland Shadwell Poet Laureate Behn d.
1690	Southerne *Sir Anthony Love* Dryden *Amphitryon* Shadwell *Amorous Bigotte* *Scowrers* Betterton/Purcell *Prophetess*	Locke *Essay on Human* *Understanding* *Discourses on* *Government* *Letter on Toleration*	Battle of the Boyne Cibber, Doggett begin to act
1691	Southerne *Wives Excuse* Durfey *Love for Money* Dryden/Purcell *King Arthur*	Rochester *Poems* Racine *Athalie* Langbaine *Account of Engl. Dram.* *Poets*	Societies for Reformation of Manners flourish Etherege d.
1692	Dryden/Southerne *Cleomenes* Shadwell *Volunteers* Settle ?/Purcell *Fairy Queen*		Royal proclamation against vice DL altered Killigrew mentions 'after-money' Lee, Shadwell d. Tate Poet Laureate

DATE	PLAYS	OTHER WORKS	HISTORY AND CULTURE
1693	Congreve *Old Batchelor* *Double Dealer* Durfey *Richmond Heiress*	Rymer *Short View of Tragedy*	Lillo b.
1694	Southerne *Fatal Marriage* Dryden *Love Triumphant* Durfey *Don Quixote* I–II	Bossuet *Réflexions sur la comédie* J. Wright *Country Conversations*	Queen Mary d.; theatres closed Religious societies propose 'National Reformation of Manners'
1695	Congreve *Love for Love* Southerne *Oroonoko* Purcell (operas) *Indian Queen* *Bonduca* Durfey *Don Quixote* III	Locke *Reasonableness of Christianity*	Actors' revolt: Betterton *et al.* to LIF Press censorship lapses Purcell, Killigrew, Halifax d.
1696	Cibber *Love's Last Shift* Vanbrugh *Relapse* Ravenscroft *Anatomist* Manley *Royal Mischief*	Toland *Christianity Not Mysterious*	Demise of the Crown Act Lord Chamberlain requires that all plays be licensed C. Rich shortens Drury Lane forestage
1697	Congreve *Mourning Bride* Vanbrugh *Provoked Wife* Settle *World in the Moon* Granville *Heroic Love*		Treaty of Ryswick ends war with France Ravenscroft d.

DATE	PLAYS	OTHER WORKS	HISTORY AND CULTURE
1698	Farquhar *Love and a Bottle* Dennis *Rinaldo and Armida* Trotter *Fatal Friendship*	J. Collier *Short View of . . . Stage* Dennis *Usefulness of Stage*	First Partition Treaty Parliament passes Act against debauchery Royal proclamation vs stage profanity Wilks joins DL R. Howard d.
1699	Farquhar *Constant Couple* Durfey *History of Massaniello* Dennis *Iphigenia* Motteux *et al.* *Island Princess*	Wright *Historia Histrionica*	Second Partition Treaty Tate proposes stage reform and censorship William III proclaims against vice
1700	Congreve *Way of the World* Rowe *Ambitious Stepmother* Burnaby *Reformed Wife* Cibber *Love Makes a Man*	T. Brown *Amusements* Blackmore *Satyr Vs Wit*	Whigs form Kit-cat Club Anne Oldfield begins acting Barton Booth joins LIF Co. Thomson b. Dryden d.
1701	Rowe *Tamerlane* Steele *Funeral* Farquhar *Sir Harry Wildair* Congreve *Judgment of Paris*	Steele *Christian Hero*	James II d.; France recognizes Pretender as 'James III' War of Spanish Succession begins Act of Settlement Two general elections Sedley d.
1702	Farquhar *Twin-Rivals* *Inconstant* Cibber *She Would and She Would Not* Burnaby *Modish Husband*	Dennis *Large Account . . .* Clarendon *History of the Great Rebellion* Anon. *Comparison Between 2 Stages*	William III d. Anne becomes Queen 'Encouragement of Piety and Virtue' proclaimed *Daily Courant* begins publishing

DATE	PLAYS	OTHER WORKS	HISTORY AND CULTURE

1703	Rowe
	Fair Penitent
	
	Steele
	Lying Lover
	
	Baker
	Tunbridge Walks
			Great storm wrecks
			  DG
			J. Wesley, Dodsley, T.
			  Cibber b.
			Pepys d.

1704	Cibber
	Careless Husband
	
	Banks
	Albion Queens (rev.)
	
	Dennis
	Liberty Asserted
	
	Congreve/Vanbrugh/
	  Walsh
	Squire Trelooby
		Swift
		Tale of a Tub
		Battle of Books
		
		Newton
		Opticks (English tr.)
		
		Defoe's
		Review begins
			Battle of Blenheim
			Gibraltar captured
			Anne suppresses
			  wearing of vizards
			Locke d.

1705	Steele
	Tender Husband
	
	Centlivre
	Basset Table
	Gamester
	
	Vanbrugh
	Mistake
	Confederacy
	
	Clayton
	Arsinoe
	
	Rowe
	Ulysses
		Bedford
		Serious Reflections
			General election
			Queen's Theatre,
			  Haymarket, opens
			Anne appoints
			  Congreve and
			  Vanbrugh to inspect
			  plays
			Daily Courant begins
			  printing playbills
			Halley calculates
			  cometary orbit

1706	Farquhar
	Recruiting Officer
	
	Granville
	British Enchanters
	
	Durfey
	Wonders in the Sun
		Dennis
		Essay on Operas
		
		Bedford
		Danger of Stage Plays
			Battle of Ramillies
			Vanbrugh leases Hay
			  to Swiney
			Hay to do plays, DL
			  operas
			Banks d.

DATE	PLAYS	OTHER WORKS	HISTORY AND CULTURE
1707	Farquhar *Beaux' Stratagem* Cibber *Double Gallant* *Lady's Last Stake* Addison *Rosamond*	Le Sage *Crispin rival de son* *maitre* Watts *Hymns*	Union with Scotland C. Rich silenced by Lord Chamberlain A. Bracegirdle ret. Fielding b. Farquhar d.
1708		Swift *Argument Vs Abolishing* *Christianity* Downes *Roscius Anglicanus*	Union of companies at DL Hay to do operas, DL plays
1709	Centlivre *Busy Body* Dennis *Appius and Virginia* Baker *Fine Lady's Airs*	Rowe's edition of Shakespeare Steele begins *Tatler* Pope's and Philips's *Pastorals*	Battle of Malplaquet Betterton's troupe returns to Hay Rich expelled from DL DG demolished Sacheverell sermon Johnson b.
1710	Centlivre *Marplot in Lisbon* C. Shadwell *Fair Quaker of Deal* Hill *Elfrid*	Berkeley *Principles of Human* *Knowledge* Essays on tragedy in *Tatler*	Tories replace Whigs Copyright Act Wren finishes St Paul Sacheverell trial Companies united at DL under Cibber *et* *al.* E. Barry retires Betterton d.
1711	Settle *City Ramble . . .* Cibber *Hob*	Pope *Essay on Criticism* Addison, Steele begin *Spectator* Shaftesbury *Characteristiks*	Occasional Conformity Act Marlborough dismissed Hay again restricted to operas Handel reaches London
1712	Philips *Distrest Mother* C. Johnson *Wife's Relief*	Pope *Rape of the Lock* *Spectator* attacks modern comedy	Barrier Treaty Moore b.

DATE	PLAYS	OTHER WORKS	HISTORY AND CULTURE
1713	Addison *Cato* Gay *Wife of Bath*	Tate *et al.* *Monitor*	Treaty of Utrecht Scriblerus Club forms Sterne b. Rymer d.
1714	Rowe *Jane Shore* Centlivre *The Wonder!* Theobald *Electra*		Queen Anne d. George I accedes Whigs replace Tories Schism Act J. Rich's co. at LIF Steele governor of DL C. Rich d.
1715	Gay *The What D'Ye Call It* Rowe *Lady Jane Grey* C. Johnson *Country Lasses*	Pope *Temple of Fame* *The Iliad* I Le Sage *Gil Blas*	Jacobite Rebellion Battle of Preston Steele receives patent for DL Rowe Poet Laureate Loius XIV, Tate d.
1716	Addison *Drummer* C. Johnson *Cobler of Preston*	Gay *Trivia*	Septennial Bill Gray b. Wycherley d.
1717	Gay *et al.* *Three Hours After Marriage* Cibber *Non-Juror*		Triple Alliance Bangorian controversy Addison Sec. of State Garrick b.
1718	Centlivre *Bold Stroke for a Wife*	Prior *Poems*	Quadruple Alliance War with Spain Occasional Conformity Act repealed DL managers rebel Rowe d.

DATE	PLAYS	OTHER WORKS	HISTORY AND CULTURE
1719	Young *Busiris* Dennis *Invader of His Country*	Defoe *Robinson Crusoe* Bedford *Serious Remonstrance*	Jacobite landing in Scotland Peace with Spain Peerage Bill Schism Act repealed Steele patent revoked Addison d.

1720	Hughes
	Siege of Damascus
		Gay
		Poems
		
		Steele
		The Theatre
		
		Anon.
		Stage Plays . . . .
		  Condemned
		
		Pope finishes tr. *Iliad*
			South Sea Bubble
			War with Spain
			Steele removed from
			  DL
			Little Theatre in
			  Haymarket opens
			Foote b.

1721	Young *Revenge* Cibber *Refusal* Hill *Fatal Extravagance*	Montesquieu *Lettres persanes*	'Bubble Act' Walpole First Minister Steele restored to DL Smollett b.
1722	Steele *Conscious Lovers* Centlivre *The Artifice*	Defoe *Moll Flanders* *Journal of Plague Year*	Atterbury Plot Young Pretender b.
1723	Fenton *Mariamne*		General Workhouse Act Durfey, Centlivre d.
1724	Gay *Captives*	Defoe *Roxana* Swift *Drapier's Letters*	Wood's Halfpence Settle d.
1725	Ramsay *Gentle Shepherd*	Pope edits Shakespeare; begins tr. *Odyssey* Hutcheson *Beauty and Virtue*	Treaty of Hanover First Treaty of Vienna

DATE	PLAYS	OTHER WORKS	HISTORY AND CULTURE
1726	Welsted *The Dissembled Wanton*	Swift *Gulliver's Travels* Thomson *Winter* Law *Unlawfulness of Stage* . . . Dennis *Stage Defended*	Voltaire in England Vanbrugh, Collier d.
1727	Theobald *Double Falsehood*	Newton *Principia* tr. Gay *Fables* Destouches *Le Philosophe marié*	George I d. George II accedes Annual Indemnity Acts begin Murphy b. Newton d.
1728	Gay *Beggar's Opera* Cibber/Vanbrugh *Provoked Husband* Fielding *Love in Several Masques*	Pope *Dunciad 1–3* Law *Serious Call . . .*	Booth ret.
1729	Gay *Polly* Cibber *Love in a Riddle* C. Johnson *Village Opera* S. Johnson *Hurlothrumbo*	Swift *Modest Proposal*	Treaty of Seville Oglethorpe's exposé of Newgate GF Theatre opens Kitty Clive's début Congreve, Steele d.
1730	Thomson *Sophonisba* Fielding *Temple Beau* *Tom Thumb* *Author's Farce*	Thomson *The Seasons* Tindal *Christianity Old as* *Creation*	Cibber Poet Laureate Goldsmith b. A. Oldfield d.

DATE	PLAYS	OTHER WORKS	HISTORY AND CULTURE
1731	Lillo *London Merchant* Mallet *Eurydice* Coffey *et al.* *Devil to Pay* Fielding *Grub St Opera*	*Gentleman's Magazine* begins Law *The Case of Reason* Marivaux *Mariamne*	Second Treaty of Vienna Sugar Bill Giffard operates GF Cowper b. Defoe d.
1732	C. Johnson *Caelia* Fielding *Mock Doctor* *Modern Husband* *Covent Garden Tragedy* Kelly *Married Philosopher*	Berkeley *Alciphion* Franklin *Poor Richard's Almanac* Voltaire *Zaïre*	'Patriots' oppose Walpole government J. Rich opens new CG Theatre Giffard opens new theatre in Ayliffe St Cumberland, Colman b. Gay, Wilks d.
1733	Fielding *Miser* Gay *Achilles*	Pope *Essay on Man* 1–3	Family Compact Excise Bill T. Cibber leads DL actors' revolt
1734	Fielding *Don Quixote in England* Gay *Distrest Wife* Carey *Chrononhotonthologos*	Pope *Essay on Man* 4 Theobald edits Shakespeare Hill *Prompter* Voltaire *Lettres anglaises* Goldoni *Belisaire*	Fleetwood proprietor of DL Dennis d.
1735	Hill *Zara* Fielding *Old Man Taught* *Wisdom*	Pope *Arbuthnot* Abbé Prévost *Manon Lescaut*	Wesley to Georgia Giffard buys DL patent

DATE	PLAYS	OTHER WORKS	HISTORY AND CULTURE

1736	Lillo
	Fatal Curiosity
	
	Fielding
	Pasquin
	
	Hill
	Alzira
		S. Duck
		Poems
		
		Butler
		Analogy of Religion
			Prince of Wales
			  quarrels with King
			Gin Act
			Witchcraft Acts
			  repealed
			Fielding's company at
			  H²

1737	Fielding
	*Historical Register for
	  1736*
	Eurydice
	
	Dodsley
	Miller of Mansfield
	
	Carey
	Dragon of Wantley
		Wesley
		Psalms and Hymns
		
		Shenstone
		Poems
		
		Manchester Magazine
		  begins
			Queen Caroline d.
			Porteous Riots
			Civil List crisis
			Footmen's Riot
			Prince of Wales leads
			  opposition to Walpole
			Stage Licensing Act

1738	Thomson *Agamemnon* Miller *Art and Nature* Dodsley *Sir John Cockle at Court*	Bolingbroke *Idea of a Patriot King* *Scots Magazine* begins	Third Treaty of Vienna Wesley begins missionary work Anti-French riots at H²

1739	Thomson
	Edward and Eleonora
	
	Mallet
	Mustapha
	
	H. Brooke
	Gustavus Vasa
		Hume
		*Treatise of Human
		  Nature*
			Naval war with Spain
			Famine in Ireland
			Wesley begins open-air
			  preaching
			T. Coram's Foundling
			  Hospital

1740	Garrick
	Lethe
	
	Dodsley
	Blind Beggar . . .
	
	Thomson/Mallet and
	  Arne
	Alfred
		Richardson
		Pamela
		
		Cibber
		Apology . . .
		
		Thomson and Arne
		Rule Britannia
			Giffard's company at
			  GF
			Peg Woffington's
			  début
			CG stage deepened

DATE	PLAYS	OTHER WORKS	HISTORY AND CULTURE
1741	Garrick *Lying Valet* Kelly *The Levee*		General election Walpole's govt often defeated Garrick's début
1742		Pope, *Dunciad* in 4 books Fielding *Joseph Andrews* Young *Night Thoughts* I	Walpole resigns England enters European hostilities GF closed; Giffard's company at LIF Nash's code for Bath
1743	Cooke *Love the Cause and Cure of Grief*	Blair *The Grave* Fielding *Jonathan Wild*	Battle of Dettingen Wesley's code for Methodists Garrick, Macklin lead actors' strike at DL
1744	Havard *Regulus* Miller *Mahomet*	Dodsley's edition of *Old Plays* Akenside *Pleasures of Imagination* J. Warton *The Enthusiast* *God Save the King*	War with France Carteret resigns 'Broad Bottom' govt Anson's voyage Methodist conference Price riots at DL LIF Theatre abandoned Pope d.
1745	Thomson *Tancred and Sigismunda* Fielding *The Debauchees*		Battle of Fontenoy Jacobite invasion Lacy manages DL Swift d.
1746	Macklin *A Will and No Will*		Battle of Culloden Pitt enters govt
1747	Hoadly *Suspicious Husband* Garrick *Miss in Her Teens* Foote *Diversions of a Morning* Macklin *New Play Criticized*	Collins *Odes* T. Warton, Jr *Pleasures of Melancholy* Warburton's ed. of Shakespeare Goldoni *Arlequin Serviteur*	General election: Pelhams restore majority Garrick buys into DL Foote acts at H^2

DATE	PLAYS	OTHER WORKS	HISTORY AND CULTURE
1748	Moore *The Foundling*	Richardson *Clarissa* Thomson *Castle of Indolence* Hume *Human Understanding*	Peace of Aix-la- Chapelle ends War of Austrian Succession Discovery of Pompeii Thomson d.
1749	Johnson *Irene* Hill *Meropé* Foote *Knights*	Fielding *Tom Jones* Johnson *Vanity of Human Wishes* Hartley *Observations on Man*	Nova Scotia founded Westminster Bridge built Riot at H²
1750	Whitehead *Roman Father* Brooke *Earl of Essex*	Gray's *Elegy* Johnson begins *Rambler*	H. Walpole begins Strawberry Hill S. Barry joins CG
1751	Moore *Gil Blas*	Fielding *Amelia* Hume *Enquiry Concerning the* *Principles of Morals*	Clive's defence of Arcot Diderot proposes encyclopaedia Quin retires Prince of Wales d.
1752	Foote *Taste* S. Cibber *The Oracle* Macklin *Covent Garden Tragedy*	Whitefield's *Letter to* *Wesley*	Crown acquires Georgia London Hospital Local Licensing Act New Style dates begin
1753	Moore *Gamester* Glover *Boadicea* Jones *Earl of Essex* Foote *Englishman in Paris*	Richardson *Grandison* Smollett *Ferdinand, Count* *Fathom*	English driven from Ohio valley Marriage Act 'Jew Bill' Anti-turnpike riots near Leeds

DATE	PLAYS	OTHER WORKS	HISTORY AND CULTURE
1754	Whitehead *Creusa* Brown *Barbarossa* Crisp *Virginia* T. Sheridan *Brave Irishman* Morgan *Sheep Shearing*	T. Warton *Observations on The Fairy Queen* Bolingbroke's *Works* begin	General election Newcastle PM Albany Congress Royal Society to encourage manufacturing Fielding, Pelham d.
1755	Moncrieff *Appius*	Johnson *Dictionary* Lessing *Miss Sara Sampson*	Hostilities with France Lisbon earthquake Corsican rebellion Riots vs French at DL
1756	Home *Douglas* Garrick *Lilliput* Murphy *Apprentice* Brown *Athelstan* Foote *Englishman Returned* Anon. *Kept Mistress*	Gray *The Bard* Burke *Sublime and Beautiful* J. Warton *Essay on . . . Pope*	Seven Years War begins Pitt Sec. of State Calcutta, Minorca, etc. lost Black Hole of Calcutta
1757	Foote *Author* Garrick *Male Coquette* Smollett *Reprisal*	Hume *Natural History of Religion* Smollett *Hist. of England* Jenyns *Enquiry into . . . Evil*	Clive victorious in Bengal Devonshire govt collapses; Pitt PM Cumberland defeated C. Cibber, Moore d.
1758	Dodsley *Cleone* Murphy *The Upholsterer*	Johnson begins *Idler* Diderot *Le Père de famille*	Wolfe takes Louisburg French lose Senegal Bridgwater Canal

DATE	PLAYS	OTHER WORKS	HISTORY AND CULTURE
1759	Murphy *Orphan of China* Macklin *Love à la Mode* Townley *High Life Below Stairs* Garrick *Guardian* *Harlequin's Invasion*	Johnson *Rasselas* Voltaire *Candide* Goldsmith *Present State of Polite* *Learning* *Annual Reg.* founded Sterne *Tristram Shandy* begins	'Year of Victories': Minden, Niagara, Québec City, etc. Wedgwood Pottery founded Sankey Cut in Liverpool Canal Theatre riots
1760	Colman *Polly Honeycombe* Foote *The Minor* Murphy *Way to Keep Him* Bickerstaffe *Thomas and Sally*		George II d. George III accedes English capture Montréal, Guadaloupe Traditional beginning of Industrial Revolution P. Woffington d.
1761	Colman *Jealous Wife* Murphy *All in the Wrong* *Old Maid* *Citizen* Macklin *School for Husbands*	Hume *History of England* Goldsmith *Citizen of the World* Churchill *Rosciad*	General election: Pitt falls; Bute PM J. Rich d. Beard takes over CG
1762	Bickerstaffe *Love in a Village* Whitehead *School for Lovers* Foote *The Lyar* *The Orators*	Macpherson *Ossian* Hurd *Chivalry and Romance* Rousseau *Social Contract*	English capture Pondicherry Newcastle resigns DL enlarged Theatre riot

DATE	PLAYS	OTHER WORKS	HISTORY AND CULTURE
1763	F. Sheridan *Dupe* *Discovery* Mallet *Elvira* Colman *Deuce Is in Him* Foote *Mayor of Garrett*	Smart *Song to David*	Treaty of Paris ends Seven Years War Grenville PM Wilkes Riots Pontiac's Rebellion Half-Price Riots Garrick clears patrons from stage; leaves for Europe
1764	Murphy *No One's Enemy But . . .* *What We Must All . . .* Foote *Patron* Townley *False Concord* O'Hara *Midas*	Goldsmith *Traveller* Walpole *Castle of Otranto*	Wilkes expelled from Parliament Sugar Act Literary and Brooks's clubs form Hogarth d.
1765	Foote *Commissary* Bickerstaffe *Maid of the Mill* Griffith *Platonic Wife*	Percy *Reliques* Blackstone *Commentaries*	Stamp Act (America) Rockingham PM Garrick introduces sidelights Young d.
1766	Garrick/Colman *Clandestine Marriage* Griffith *Double Mistake* Kenrick *Falstaff's Wedding* Carey *Cottagers*	Goldsmith *Vicar of Wakefield* H. Brooke *Fool of Quality* Lessing *Laokoön*	Chatham (Pitt) PM Stamp duty repealed Cavendish discovers hydrogen Foote receives patent for H^2 Garrick hires Barry F. Sheridan, Quin d.

DATE	PLAYS	OTHER WORKS	HISTORY AND CULTURE
1767	Murphy *School for Guardians* Colman *English Merchant* *Oxonian* Macklin *True-Born Irishman* Garrick *Peep Behind the Curtain*	Dickinson *Letters from a Farmer* . . . Beaumarchais *Eugénie*	Chatham collapses; govt drift Townshend's import duties on America Manchester, Liverpool linked by canal Beard sells CG to Colman, Harris, etc.
1768	Kelly *False Delicacy* Goldsmith *Good-Natured Man* Bickerstaffe *Lionel and Clarissa* Murphy *Zenobia* Hoole *Cyrus*	Sterne *Sentimental Journey* Priestley *Principles of Government* Encyclopaedia Brit. begins	Pitt resigns Grafton PM General election Wilkes re-elected Arkwright's spinner Royal Academy founded Captain Cook sets sail Sterne d.
1769	Cumberland *Brothers* Home *Fatal Discovery* Bickerstaffe *Captive* Colman *Man and Wife*	Letters of Junius begin	Wilkes excluded Society for Defence of Bill of Rights Watt's steam engine Severn iron bridge Garrick's Stratford Shakespeare Jubilee
1770	Kelly *Word to the Wise* Colman *Portrait* Bickerstaffe *'Tis Well It's No Worse* Foote *Lame Lover*	Goldsmith *Deserted Village* Burke *Thoughts on the Present Discontents*	North PM 'Boston Massacre' Cook finds Australia Bruce finds source of Blue Nile Hargeaves's jenny Chatterton d.

DATE	PLAYS	OTHER WORKS	HISTORY AND CULTURE
1771	Cumberland *West Indian* Foote *Maid of Bath* Bickerstaffe *He Would If He Could*	Smollett *Humphry Clinker* Mackenzie *Man of Feeling*	First coloured fashionplate De Loutherbourg at DL Gray, Smollett, Smart d.
1772	Murphy *Grecian Daughter* Foote *Nabob* Mason *Elfrida*	Burgh *Political Disquisitions*	Slavery declared illegal in England Cook sails again Stourport Canal
1773	Goldsmith *She Stoops to Conquer* Foote *Piety in Pattens* Kelly *School for Wives* Waldron *Maid of Kent* Murphy *Alzuma*	Wesley *Thoughts on . . .* *Scarcity of Provisions*	Boston Tea Party Hastings Gov.-Gen. of India Regulating Act for East India Co. General Turnpike Act Watt and Boulton team up Chesterfield d.
1774	Cumberland *Choleric Man* Colman *Man of Business* Burgoyne *Maid of the Oaks* Garrick *Meeting of the Company* Hiffernan *Heroine of the Cave*	Chesterfield's *Letters* pub. Goethe *Werther* Burke *Speech on American* *Taxation*	Québec Act; Penal Acts vs Massachusetts Continental Congress in Philadelphia Wilkes resumes seat Priestley isolates oxygen Goldsmith d.

DATE	PLAYS	OTHER WORKS	HISTORY AND CULTURE
1775	Sheridan *The Rivals* *The Duenna* Garrick *Bon Ton* Jephson *Braganza*	Beaumarchais *Le Barbier de Seville* Johnson *Journey to the Western Islands*	Battles of Concord, Lexington, Bunker Hill Sunday Observance Society founded Adam redecorates DL
1776	Foote *Trip to Calais* *Capuchin* Cowley *Runaway* Colman *New Brooms* Mason *Caractacus* ?Kelly *Man of Reason*	Smith *Wealth of Nations* Gibbon *Decline and Fall*, vol. I Paine *Common Sense* Bentham *Theory of Legislation*	American colonies declare independence Parliament considers reform; rejects universal male suffrage Garrick retires Sheridan manages DL Hume d.
1777	Sheridan *School for Scandal* More *Percy* Murphy *Know Your Own Mind* Colman *Spanish Barber*	Priestley *Matter and Spirit* Burke *Letter To Sheriffs of Bristol*	Burgoyne surrenders at Saratoga Colman sells CG to Harris, moves to H² Foote, Kelly, and Barry d.
1778	Cumberland *Battle of Hastings* Sheridan *Camp* Colman *Suicide*	Burney *Evelina*	Franco–American alliance Relief Act Voltaire, Rousseau d.

DATE	PLAYS	OTHER WORKS	HISTORY AND CULTURE

1779	Sheridan
	Critic
	
	Colman
	Separate Maintenance
	
	More
	Fatal Falsehood
	
	Cowley
	Albina
	Who's the Dupe?
		Johnson
		Lives of the Poets I
		
		Hume
		Dialogues Concerning
		  Natural Religion
			Spain enters war vs
			  England; Siege of
			  Gibraltar; Dutch join
			  Armed Neutrality
			'Crompton's Mule'
			De Loutherbourg's
			  Wonders of Derbyshire
			Garrick d.

1780	Cowley
	Belle's Stratagem
	
	Burgoyne
	Lord of the Manor
	
	Lee
	Chapter of Accidents
	
	Pilon
	Siege of Gibraltar
		Lessing
		Education of Mankind
		
		Burke
		Speech on Economical
		  Reform
		
		Bentham
		Morals and Legislation I
			War with Holland
			Gordon Riots
			Dunning Resolution
			Committee on
			  Parliamentary Reform
			Society for
			  Constitutional
			  Information

1781	Macklin *Man of the World* Holcroft *Duplicity* Jephson *Count of Narbonne*	Crabbe *Library* Kant *Critique of Pure Reason* Schiller *Die Räuber*	Cornwallis surrenders General election Manchester Lit. and Phil. Society founded

1782	Cumberland
	Walloons
	
	Cowley
	Which Is the Man?
	
	More
	Sacred Dramas
	
	Colman
	Fatal Curiosity (rev.)
	
	MacNally
	Retaliation
		Cowper
		Poems
		Table Talk
		
		Priestley
		Corruptions of
		  Christianity
			North's govt falls
			Rockingham Whig
			  govt
			Fox–North coalition
			Burke's Economic
			  Reform Bill
			Gilbert's Poor Law
			S. Siddons succeeds at
			  DL
			CG, H² enlarged

DATE	PLAYS	OTHER WORKS	HISTORY AND CULTURE

1783	Cowley
	Bold Stroke for a
	Husband
	More Ways Than One
	
	Cumberland
	Mysterious Husband
		Crabbe
		Village
		
		Blake
		Poetical Sketches
		
		Blair
		Lectures on Rhetoric
			Treaty of Versailles
			  ends American War
			Fox–North govt falls
			Younger Pitt PM
			Act of Renunciation
			Fox's India Bill thrown
			  out
			J. P. Kemble's début

1784	Cumberland *Carmelite* *Natural Son* Holcroft *Noble Peasant*	Beaumarchais *Les Noces de Figaro*	Pitt's India Act Wesley breaks with Anglican Church Johnson d.

1785	Inchbald
	I'll Tell You What
	
	Cumberland
	Arab
	
	Macnally
	Fashionable Levities
	
	Reynolds
	Werther
		Cowper
		Task
		
		Boswell
		Tour to the Hebrides
		
		Paley
		Prins of Moral and Polit.
		  Philosophy
		
		Daily Universal Register
		  begins
			Pitt's Parliamentary
			  Reform Bill
			Gen. Chamber of
			  Manufacturers of
			  Great Britain
			Whitehead d.

1786	Burgoyne *Heiress* Cowley *School for Greybeards* Inchbald *Widow's Vow*	Burns *Poems* Beckford *Vathek* Mozart *Les Noces de Figaro*	Pitt's Sinking Fund Trade agreement with France Hastings charged

1787	Inchbald
	Such Things Are
	
	Holcroft
	Seduction
	
	Colman the Younger
	Inkle and Yarico
	
	Dibdin
	Harvest Home
	
	Powell
	Narcotic
		Mozart
		Don Giovanni
			King's first madness
			Hastings impeached
			Sierra Leone founded
			  for freed slaves
			Committee for
			  Abolishing Slave
			  Trade
			Palmer's Royalty
			  Theatre opens

DATE	PLAYS	OTHER WORKS	HISTORY AND CULTURE
1788	Cowley *Fate of Sparta* O'Keeffe *Prisoner at Large*	Blake *No Natural Religion* Gibbon *Decline and Fall* completed	Triple Alliance Hastings trial begins New S. Wales established Regulating Act for chimney sweeps Kemble manages DL
1789	Reynolds *The Dramatist* Cumberland *The Imposters*	Blake *Songs of Innocence* Goethe *Egmont* E. Darwin *Botanical Garden* begins	Bastille falls Estates General meet George III recovers Haymarket Theatre burns Macklin retires

General Bibliographies

Note: *Titles have been selected for their interest or historical importance; for supplements, see (iv) A. Each section is arranged alphabetically. Place of publication is London, unless otherwise stated. Boston is Boston, Massachusetts.*

(i) English drama: history and criticism

Archer, W.	*The Old Drama and the New* (1923). (Readable, interesting, opinionated, sometimes unfair.)
Bentley, E.	*The Life of the Drama* (New York, 1965). (Provocative observations on dramatic genres, etc.)
Brooks, C., and R. B. Heilman (eds)	*Understanding Drama* (New York, 1945). (Elucidates the principles of dramatic criticism; includes stimulating discussions of several eighteenth-century plays.)
Nicoll, A. B.	*British Drama*, 4th edn (1947). (A *tour de force*, setting eighteenth-century developments in a broader perspective.)
Palmer, J.	*Comedy* [1914]. (A notable effort to define the 'English genius' in comedy.)
Sypher, W. (ed.)	*Comedy* (New York, 1965). (Contains Bergson's *Laughter*, Meredith's *Essay on Comedy*, and Sypher's *The Meanings of Comedy*. Wider than drama.)
Thorndike, A. H.	*English Comedy* (New York, 1929); *Tragedy* (Boston, 1908). (Necessarily quick surveys of large territories.)

(ii) Restoration and eighteenth-century background

Briggs, A.   *A Social History of England* (1983). (Rapid coverage
                  of vast field, yet rich in detail; Chs 5–7 relevant.)

Carswell, J.   *From Revolution to Revolution: England 1688–1776*
                  (1973). (A chronological and thematic treatment of
                  political, social, economic, and cultural history.)

Cragg, G. R.   *The Church and the Age of Reason* (Harmondsworth,
                  1960). (Broad perspective; particularly useful on
                  seventeenth-century strife and the appeal of
                  Wesley.)

George, M. D.   *London Life in the Eighteenth Century* (1925;
                  Harmondsworth, 1964). (A voluminous social
                  history of the metropolis, especially its poor,
                  showing that 'London was becoming less, not
                  more, industrial as the century went on'.)

Harris, R. W.   *England in the Eighteenth Century* (1963). (Mostly
                  political history; rather plodding but informative.)

Kenyon, J. P.   *Stuart England* (Harmondsworth, 1978).
                  (Formidably revisionist, with enough Tory bias to
                  offset what the author sees as a century of 'Whig
                  hagiography'.)

Laslett, P.   *The World We Have Lost* (1965). (Throws unusual
                  lights on seventeenth- and eighteenth-century
                  society.)

Marshall, D.   *Eighteenth-Century England*, 2nd edn (1974). (Fine
                  large canvas; thorough treatment of social issues.)

Plumb, J. H.   *England in the Eighteenth Century (1714–1815)*
                  (Harmondsworth, 1950). (The standard short
                  history by the leading authority; mostly politics,
                  economics.)
                  Georgian Delights (1980). (Fills in the brighter
                  aspects of the social picture.)

Porter, R.   *English Society in the Eighteenth Century* (1982).
                  (Panorama of Georgian culture; full of interesting
                  details.)

Willey, B.   *The Eighteenth-Century Background* (1940). (The
                  intellectual context, especially 'the Idea of Nature'.)
                  The Seventeenth-Century Background (1934). (History
                  of ideas; valuable on Hobbes, Locke, Deism, heroic
                  poetry, etc.)

(iii) Restoration and eighteenth-century literature

Baugh, A. C. (ed.) *A Literary History of England*, 2nd edn (New York, 1967). (Part III has chapters on drama by George Sherburne.)

Burton, K. M. P. *Restoration Literature* (1958). (Contains a generally hostile discussion of Restoration drama.)

Dobree, B. *English Literature in the Early Eighteenth Century* (Oxford, 1959). (Masterful; some sharp opinions on drama.)

Speck, W. A. *Society and Literature in England 1700–1760* (Dublin, 1983). (Argues that literature was more ideological than realistic; dramatists 'created their own fictional worlds'.)

Stephen, L. *English Literature and Society in the Eighteenth Century* (1904). (The classic early study of this relation.)

Sutherland, J. L. *English Literature of the Late Seventeenth Century* (Oxford, 1969). (Volume VI of the *Oxford History*; informative and acute chapter on drama.)

Tave, S. *The Amiable Humorist* (Chicago, 1960). (Includes dramatic exemplars of the benevolization of humour.)

(iv) Restoration and eighteenth-century drama

A. Bibliographies

Armistead, J. M. *Four Restoration Playwrights* (Boston, 1984). (Exhaustive bibliographies for Shadwell, Behn, Lee, and Otway.)

Arnott, J. F., and J. W. Robinson *English Theatrical Literature, 1559–1900* . . . (1970). (An updating of Lowe's *Bibliographical Account of English Theatrical Literature*, 1888.)

Link, F. *English Drama, 1660–1800. A Guide to Information Sources* (Detroit, 1976). (Histories, collections, dramatic criticism, etc. and bio-bibliographies of 156 dramatists.)

MacMillan, D. *Catalogue of the Larpent Plays in the Huntington Library* (San Marino, California, 1939). (A useful introduction to the Larpent Collection.)

Stratman, C. J. *et al.*   *Restoration and Eighteenth-Century Theatre Research: A Bibliographical Guide, 1900–1968* (Carbondale, Illinois, 1971).

Vinson, J. (ed.)   *Restoration and Eighteenth-Century Drama* (1980). (Includes primary and selected secondary bibliographies.)

B. Audiences

Clinton-Baddeley, V. C.   *All Right on the Night* (1954). (Readable introduction to the atmosphere of Georgian theatre.)

Hughes, L.   *The Drama's Patrons* (Austin, Texas, 1971). (A thorough examination of the eighteenth-century audience.)

Lynch, J. J.   *Box, Pit and Gallery* (Berkeley and Los Angeles, 1953). (A detailed study of Georgian 'stage and society'.)

Pedicord, H. W.   *The Theatrical Public in the Time of Garrick* (New York, 1954). (A pioneering and still useful enquiry; see his update, 'The Changing Audience', in *The London Theatre World, 1660–1800*, ed. by Robert D. Hume [1980].)

Smith, D. F.   *The Critics in the Audience of the London Theatres from Buckingham to Sheridan* (Albuquerque, New Mexico, 1953). (Uses plays and other primary sources to obtain glimpses of playgoers.)

C. Aspects of the theatre

Boswell, E.   *The Restoration Court Stage* (Cambridge, Massachusetts, 1932). (Sets the scene in the royal theatres.)

Conolly, L. W.   *The Censorship of English Drama, 1737–1824* (San Marino, California, 1976). (Based on the Larpent Collection.)

Fowell, F., and F. Palmer   *Censorship in England* (1913). (Includes drama; useful on period before 1737, where Conolly takes over.)

Highfill, P. H., Jr, K. Burnim, and E. A. Langhans   *A Biographical Dictionary of Actors, Actresses, Musicians, Dancers, Managers and Other Stage Personnel in London, 1660–1800*, 16 vols (Carbondale, Illinois, 1973–). (Excludes dramatists. Publication reached vol. x, up to Nash, in 1984.)

Hotson, L.   *The Commonwealth and Restoration Stage* (Cambridge, Massachusetts, 1928). (Standard; valuable on Commonwealth theatricals.)

Hume, R. D. (ed.)   *The London Theatre World, 1660–1800* (Carbondale, Illinois, 1980). (Useful update on trends in theatrical scholarship.)

Lawrence, W. J.   *Old Theatre Days and Ways* (1935). (Delightful recollections and research.)

Leacroft, R.   *The Development of the English Playhouse* (Ithaca, New York, 1973).

Liesenfeld, V. J.   *The Licensing Act of 1737* (Madison, Wisconsin, 1984). (Covers events leading up to the Act, 1729–37.)

Nicholson, W.   *The Struggle for a Free Stage in London* (Boston and New York, 1906). (Sets eighteenth-century events in a larger context.)

Nicoll, A. B.   *The Garrick Stage* (Manchester, 1980). (The master's last book, a vivid re-creation of Georgian theatre.)

Price, C. J. L.   *Theatre in the Age of Garrick* (Oxford, 1973). (Reliable account of audiences, repertoire, and the stage.)

Richards, K., and P. Thomson (eds)   *Essays on the Eighteenth-Century English Stage* (1972). (Includes Steele, Rich, and Harris.)

Southern, R.   *Changeable Scenery* (1952); *The Georgian Playhouse* (1948). (The leading expert on Restoration and eighteenth-century theatres explains how they looked and worked.)

Sprague, A. C.   *Beaumont and Fletcher on the Restoration Stage* (Cambridge, Massachusetts, 1926). (Demonstrates their popularity.)

Stone, G. W., Jr (ed.)   *The Stage and the Page. London's 'Whole Show' in the Eighteenth-Century Theatre* (Berkeley and Los Angeles, 1981). (Essays on diverse subjects by expert hands.)

Troubridge, St V.   *The Benefit System in the British Theatre* (1967). (Erudite, thorough; traces practice to the Restoration.)

Van Lennep, W. *et al.* (eds)   *The London Stage 1660–1800*, 5 parts, 11 vols (Carbondale, Illinois, 1960–68.) (The major research tool for the period, listing all known performances with a wealth of associated information.)

Wilson, J. H.   *All the King's Ladies* (Chicago, 1958). (Informative and entertaining account of Restoration actresses.)

D. Selected primary sources

Baker, D. E., S. Jones, and I. Reed   *Biographica Dramatica*, 3 vols (3rd edn, 1812). (Biographies and play-lists.)

Cibber, C.	*An Apology for the Life of Colley Cibber, Comedian* (1740). (A wealth of material on London theatre 1690s–1730s.)
Downes, J.	*Roscius Anglicanus* (1708). (An important account of Betterton's theatre by its prompter; two modern editions.)
Genest, J.	*Some Account of the English Stage, 1660–1830*, 10 vols (Bath, 1832). (Annotated play-lists and theatrical commentary.)
[Gentleman, F.]	*The Dramatic Censor*, 2 vols (1770; repr. 1969). (Detailed critiques of particular plays and actors.)
Wright, J.	*Historia Histrionica* (1699). (A dialogue on drama.)

E. General history and criticism

Birdsall, V. O.	*Wild Civility* (Bloomington, Indiana, 1970). (Argues the seriousness and Englishness of major Restoration comedies.)
Boas, F. S.	*An Introduction to Eighteenth-Century Drama 1700–1780* (Oxford, 1953). (Monographs on the principal dramatists.)
Craik, T. W., and C. Leech (gen. eds)	*The Revels History of Drama in English*, 8 vols (1975–83). (Vols v (*1660–1750*) and vi (*1750–1880*) are an indispensable gathering of first-rate scholarship on society, theatre, and drama in the period.)
Cunningham, J. E.	*Restoration Drama* (1966). (A plain introduction to the period and its major playwrights for the general reader.)
Dobree, B.	*Restoration Comedy* (Oxford, 1924); *Restoration Tragedy* (Oxford, 1929). (Provocative; still good starting-points.)
Donohue, J. W.	*Dramatic Character in the English Romantic Age* (Princeton, 1970). (Keen analyses of major plays late in period.)
Hume, R. D.	*The Development of English Drama in the Late Seventeenth Century* (Oxford, 1976). (Studies changes in dramatic types, 1660–1710, proposing new phases and labels.) *The Rakish Stage* (Carbondale, Illinois, 1983). (Essays new and collected on diverse topics.)
Kronenberger, L.	*The Thread of Laughter* (New York, 1952). (Literate discussions of several major comedies in the period.)
Krutch, J. W.	*Comedy and Conscience After the Restoration* (New York, 1924). (Classic study of how social changes affected comedy; but see Loftis.)

Loftis, J.   *Comedy and Society from Congreve to Fielding* (Stanford, 1959). (Updates and corrects Krutch's work).
The Politics of Drama in Augustan England (Oxford, 1963). (Theatre and government, 1702–1737.)

Nicoll, A. B.   *A History of English Drama 1660–1900*, 6 vols (Cambridge, 1952–59). (Vols I–III remain the most thorough critical survey of English drama 1660–1800.)

Schneider, Ben R., Jr   *The Ethos of Restoration Comedy* (Urbana, Illinois, 1971). (Shows what moral values were praised or condemned.)

Wilson, J. H.   *A Preface to Restoration Drama* (Cambridge, Massachusetts, 1965). (Readable introduction to the whole theatrical spectrum.)

F. Forms and subgenres

Bernbaum, E.   *The Drama of Sensibility* (Boston and London, 1915). (Pioneering but outdated study of sentimental drama; see Sherbo.)

Brown, L.   *English Dramatic Form, 1660–1760* (New Haven and London, 1981). (An attempt to explain genre in cultural terms.)

Clinton-Baddeley, V. C.   *The Burlesque Tradition in the English Theatre After 1660* (1952). (Traces the development of the form from its English origins through Sheridan and beyond.)

Deane, Cecil V.   *Dramatic Theory and the Rhymed Heroic Play* (Oxford, 1931). (Long the standard treatment, but see the Kirsch listing under Dryden in the author bibliographies.)

Evans, B.   *Gothic Drama from Walpole to Shelley* (1947).

Fujimura, T. H.   *The Restoration Comedy of Wit* (Princeton, 1952). (Proposes an alternative to the 'comedy of manners' cliché.)

Holland, N.   *The First Modern Comedies: The Significance of Etherege, Wycherley and Congreve* (Cambridge, Massachusetts, 1959). (A landmark in the critical acceptance of Restoration comedy.)

Hughes, L.   *A Century of English Farce* (Princeton, 1956). (Defines and traces the form, especially 1650–1750.)

Kern, J. B.   *Dramatic Satire in the Age of Walpole 1720–1750* (Iowa, 1976). (Elucidates types of satiric drama.)

Knights, L. C.   'Restoration Comedy: the Reality and the Myth', *Scrutiny*, 6 (1937), 122–43. (Famous harangue against Carolean drama – not only comedy – as 'trivial, gross and dull'.)

Loftis, J.   *The Spanish Plays of Neoclassical England* (New Haven, 1973). (Studies the influence and the form.)

Marshall, G.   *Restoration Serious Drama* (Norman, Oklahoma, 1975). (Interesting chapters on seriousness, diction, genres, etc.)

Muir, K.   *The Comedy of Manners* (1970). (Uneven treatment of the major critical issues; useful discussions of plays.)

Palmer, J.   *The Comedy of Manners* (1913). (Readable pioneer work.)

Perry, H. T. E.   *The Comic Spirit in Restoration Drama* (1925). (Valiant effort to fit the period into the history of comedy.)

Rothstein, E.   *Restoration Tragedy* (Madison, Wisconsin, 1967). (The leading modern study; has a useful chapter on tragic theory.)

Sherbo, A.   *English Sentimental Drama* (East Lansing, Michigan, 1957). (Important reassessment, demolishing inherited clichés.)

Smith, D. F.   *Plays About the Theatre in England . . . 1671–1737* (New York and London, 1936); with M. L. Lawhorn, *Plays About the Theatre in England, 1737–1800* (Lewisburg, Pennsylvania, 1979). (Studies of rehearsal-plays and other drama that mirrors its own milieu.)

G. Sources, themes, conventions

Alleman, G. S.   *Matrimonial Law and the Materials of Restoration Drama* (Wallingford, Pennsylvania, 1942). (Full of detailed information on law and comedy; well indexed; esp. useful on 1690–1707 period.)

Bevis, R. W.   *The Laughing Tradition* (Athens, Georgia, 1980). (The civil war of dramatic comedy, 1737–1779.)

Donaldson, I.   *The World Upside-Down: Comedy from Jonson to Fielding* (Oxford, 1973). (Insightful study of comic inversions.)

Goldgar, B. A.   *Walpole and the Wits* (Lincoln, Nebraska, 1976). (The political influence on Gay, Fielding, etc., and their responses.)

Harbage, A.   *Cavalier Drama* (New York, 1936). (Traces the aristocratic strain in drama 1629–69, showing Court influence.)

Hawkins, H.   *Likenesses of Truth in Elizabethan and Restoration Drama* (Oxford, 1972). (A rebuttal to theological criticism.)

Holland, P.   *The Ornament of Action. Text and Performance in Restoration Comedy* (Cambridge, 1979). (The influence of theatrical context on dramatic meaning.)

Lynch, K. M.   *The Social Mode of Restoration Comedy* (New York, 1926). (A study of Caroline-Restoration continuity.)

Smith, J. H.   *The Gay Couple in Restoration Comedy* (Cambridge, Massachusetts, 1948). (Seminal analysis of a characteristic convention.)

Waith, E. M.   *The Herculean Hero* (New York, 1962). (From Marlowe onwards; Dryden gets a chapter.)
Ideas of Greatness: Heroic Drama in England (1971). (The 'Ideals of Chivalry' are traced through the heroic plays and on to Rowe and Addison.)

Wilkinson, D. R. M.   *The Comedy of Habit* (Leiden, 1964). (How the idea of 'gallantry' influenced Restoration comic writers.)

H. Opera and musical drama

Fiske, R.   *English Theatre Music in the Eighteenth Century* (1973). (Massive, authoritative, readable treatment of all aspects of subject; some coverage of Restoration developments.)

Harley, J.   *Music in Purcell's London* (1968). (Emphasizes social background, musical types and venues: homes, fairs, Court, etc.)

Haun, E.   *But Hark! More Harmony* (Ypsilanti, Michigan, 1971). (Focuses on 'The Libretti of Restoration Opera in English'.)

Moore, R. E.   *Henry Purcell and the Restoration Theatre* (Westport, Connecticut, 1961). (A chapter on each of Purcell's major operas.)

Price, C. A.   'The Critical Decade for English Musical Drama, 1700–1710', *Harvard Lib. Bull.*, 26 (1978), 38–76. ('Three major revolutions' that subverted Purcell and English opera.)
Henry Purcell and the London Stage (Cambridge, 1984). (Learned and literate treatment of his theatre music.)

White, E. W.   *A History of English Opera* (1983). (Places Augustan and Georgian developments in a five-century European context.)
A Register of First Performances of English Operas and Semi-Operas from the Sixteenth Century to 1980 (1983).

Wilson, J. (ed.)   *Roger North on Music* (1959). (Selections from the essays (1695–1728) of a qualified observer.)

Individual Authors

Notes on biography, editions, and criticism

Each entry is divided into three sections:
(a) *Outline of author's life and literary career.* Dates of plays refer to first
    performance.
(b) *Selected works, letters, and biographies.* Here and in (c), place of publication is
    London unless otherwise stated. Boston = Boston, Massachusetts.
(c) *Selected critical studies, etc.* of author's *plays* (not other genres), listed
    chronologically. Works of history and criticism in the General Bibliography,
    and Link and Vinson under (iv) A., should also be consulted.
Modern editions of plays, *modern critical essays* and *general histories* are not
systematically cited here. In addition to abbreviations for learned journals and for
theatres given earlier, the following abbreviations are used:
anon. = anonymous(ly); asst = assistant; b. = born in; *c.* = about;
ch(s). = chapter(s); co-ed. = co-editor; C = comedy; ed(s) = editor(s), edited
(by); educ. = education/-ted (at); F = farce; fl. = flourished; Hosp. = Hospital;
m. = married; poss. = possibly; prob. = probably; prod. = produced/ction;
pub. = published; repr. = reprinted (in); rev. = revised/sing/sion; T = tragedy;
TC = tragicomedy; trans = translated/tions.

ADDISON, Joseph (1672–1719), b. Milston (Wilts.), son of a clergyman; educ.
Charterhouse (where he met Richard Steele) and Oxford (Queen's, 1687);
Classical learning gained him appointment at Magdalen College (MA,
1693, Fellowship 1698–1711). Took pupils; gained reputation for Latin
verse. Pub. poetic compliment to Dryden, trans from Latin, English prose
and verse (1693–97); poems extolling King (1695, 1697). Considered taking
orders, but Congreve introduced him to Charles Montagu, who procured
him a pension; travelled on Continent (1699–1703); pension ended with
death of William (1702). Joined Whig Kit-cat Club on return to England;
held minor political appointments from 1704. Pub. *A Letter from Italy*
(1701) and *Remarks on Several Parts of Italy* (1705), latter well received.
Pub. poem on Battle of Blenheim; made Under-secretary of State (1706).
Helped Steele with *Tender Husband*. Opera *Rosamond* (1707), intended to
popularize English music, failed. Devoted friends included Swift, Steele,
and Philips; Lady Mary Wortley Montagu, Young, for a time Pope, found
him charming; may have drunk to overcome shyness. Occasional political
pamphleteer; elected MP 1708, but never spoke. Contributed to Steele's

The Tatler (1709–10). Lost office when Whigs fell (1710); bought a country estate; kept Chelsea lodgings (once Nell Gwyn's). With Steele, prod. *The Spectator*, landmark in journalism, popularizing the familiar essay (1711–12). Finished writing *Cato*, based on a play seen in Italy; prod. successfully and profitably (1713). Contributed to *The Guardian* (1713) and the new *Spectator* (1714). Regained government offices at Queen Anne's death; wrote for *The Freeholder* (1715–16). Gave Steele *The Drummer*, which failed (1716). In same year m. the Countess of Warwick, an old friend. Served as Secretary of State (1717) until ill health forced resignation (1718). Fell out with Steele in print. Died a few months after daughter's birth.

> Tickell, T., ed., *The Collected Works of Joseph Addison*, 4 vols (1721). (Preface contains important biographical material.)
> Hurd, R., ed., *The Works of Joseph Addison*, 6 vols (1811; reissued 1856). (Contains minor material difficult to come by.)
> Guthkelch, A. C., ed., *The Miscellaneous Works of Joseph Addison*, 2 vols (1914). (Includes plays.)
> Graham, W., ed., *The Letters of Joseph Addison* (Oxford, 1964).
> Smithers, P., *The Life of Joseph Addison*, 2nd edn (Oxford, 1968). (The standard biography.)

> See: Donaldson, I., 'Cato in Tears: Stoical Guises of the Man of Feeling', in *Studies in the Eighteenth Century II*, ed. R. F. Brissenden (Toronto, 1973), pp. 377–95.
> Otten, R. M., *Joseph Addison* (Boston, 1982). (Twayne Series; good general introduction; has a ch. on the plays.)

BANKS, John (*fl.* 1677–96); little is known of his life. Apparently studied law; associated with New Inn. *The Rival Kings*, an imitation of Lee's *Rival Queens*, prod. in 1677 and *The Destruction of Troy* in 1678, but first success was *The Unhappy Favourite* (1681), a tragedy about the Earl of Essex. *Virtue Betrayed* (1682), the story of Anne Boleyn, was his most popular play. Then his luck changed. *Cyrus the Great*, a heroic drama, had been prohibited in 1681; his tragedies about Lady Jane Grey (*The Innocent Usurper*, 1683) and Elizabeth and Mary, Queen of Scots (*The Island Queens*, 1684) were banned as politically incendiary, though the latter was pub.. Of the three banned plays, the first was performed for a few nights in 1695–96; the second pub. in 1694; and the last, rev. as *The Albion Queens*, prod. in 1704. Nothing is heard of Banks after 1696.

> Blair, T. M. H., ed., *The Unhappy Favourite* (New York, 1939). (Includes a sketch of Banks's life and works, etc.)

> See: Hochuli, Hans, *John Banks* . . . (Berne, Switzerland, 1952). (A study; in German.)

BEHN, Aphra (1640?–89); of her birth, parentage, and early life little is known. As a youth resided briefly in Surinam, Dutch Guiana, where (she said) she knew the original 'Oroonoko'. Returned to England in early 1660s; m. Mr Behn, a wealthy merchant of Dutch descent; may have attended Court. Widowed by 1666; sent to Antwerp as a spy, but little heeded or paid. Returning to England without inheritance or income, was imprisoned for debt; became first female professional writer in London, prod. verse, prose fiction, and drama of all kinds after initial rejection. Formed close tie with Edward Ravenscroft, friendships with Killigrew, Dryden, Otway, Southerne. Prod. *The Forced Marriage* (TC) 1670, *The Amorous Prince* (C)

1671, and *The Dutch Lover* (C) 1673; complained that its poor reception was due partly to male prejudice. Made comeback in 1676 with *Abdelazar* (T) and *The Town Fop* (C). *The Rover* (1677), a comedy about banished Cavaliers (from Killigrew's novel *Thomaso*), was her most successful play; two other comedies of that year may be hers. *Sir Patient Fancy* (C, 1678) was criticized for raciness and plagiarism. Two or three more plays appeared in 1679–80 before her outspokenly Tory sequel to *The Rover* (1681); also prod. *The False Count* (C) in that year. *The Roundheads* (1681) and *The City Heiress* (1682) were Tory plays based on earlier comedies. *Like Father, Like Son* (1682) prod. but not printed. Arrest (1682) for attacking Monmouth in an epilogue caused four-year vacation from stage, during which she pub. poems and fiction. Returned to comedy with *The Lucky Chance* (1686) and *The Emperor of the Moon* (1687), but last pubs mostly non-dramatic verse and prose; most important was novel *Oroonoko* (1688), later dramatized by Southerne. Buried in Westminster Abbey (1689). *The Widow Ranter* (C, 1690) and *The Younger Brother* (C, 1696) appeared posthumously, as did several pieces of fiction.

> Summers, M., ed., *The Works of Aphra Behn*, 6 vols (1915). (The standard modern edition, though the texts are unreliable.)
> Armistead, J. M., *Four Restoration Playwrights . . . a Reference Guide* (Boston, 1984). (Lists writings about Behn 1675–1980.)
> Woodcock, G., *The Incomparable Aphra* (1948). (Still the most readable biography, though superseded by Link.)

See: Link, F. M., *Aphra Behn* (New York, 1968). (Twayne series; most reliable modern biography and sound criticism.)
Goreau, A., *Reconstructing Aphra* (New York, 1980). (A feminist interpretation.)

BICKERSTAFFE, Issac (1733–*c*. 1808), served as page to Lord Chesterfield (1745) and in army (1745–55) before beginning to write for stage (1756); later served in the Marines. About twenty of his plays, mostly musicals, were prod. between 1760 and 1775. *Thomas and Sally* (1760) and the oratorio *Judith* (1761) were less popular than his comic opera *Love in a Village* (1762), which defined the form, and *The Maid of the Mill* (1765), which continued it. Two adaptations, *Daphne and Amintor* and *The Plain Dealer*, also appeared in 1765. Charles Dibdin wrote the music for *Love in the City* (1767) and *Lionel and Clarissa* (1768). Two musicals, a cantata, a farce, and an adaptation also appeared in 1768; at height of fame, enjoyed society of Boswell, Johnson, and their circle. Followed in 1769 with a farce and two musicals, *The Captive* and *The Ephesian Matron*. In 1770 prod. *'Tis Well It's No Worse* (from Calderón), and two more Dibdin musicals, *The Recruiting Sergeant* and *He Would If He Could*. Accused of homosexuality (a capital crime), fled England, living abroad for the rest of his life. William Kenrick insinuated a connection between Bickerstaffe and Garrick in 'Love in the Suds' (1772). A musical, *The Sultan*, appeared in 1775. Last heard of in France (1808), living on a Marine pension.

See: Tasch, P. A., *The Dramatic Cobbler* (Lewisburg, Pennsylvania, 1971). (The only full study, superseding earlier work.)

BOYLE, Roger, first Earl of Orrery (1621–79), eleventh child of Earl of Cork; educ. Trinity (Dublin) and privately; resided on Continent in 1630s; m. Lady Margaret Howard (1641); helped suppress Irish rebellion in same year. A Royalist, served the English Protestant interest in Ireland against

natives, Catholics, and French as soldier and general under Charles I,
Cromwell, and Charles II. MP from 1654, Lord President of Munster and
Earl from 1660. Personal friendship with Charles II; acceptance of his
suggestion to write heroic dramas led to *The General* (Dublin, 1662;
London, 1664; also called *Altemera*), *Henry V* (1664), *Mustapha* (1665), *The
Black Prince* (1667), and other heroic plays. Pub. a multi-volume romance,
Parthenissa (complete 1665). Survived a Parliamentary effort at
impeachment (1669) with able defence and King's help. *Guzman* (C) and
Mr Anthony (C) performed 1669 and 1672. Fell from power (1672) for
outspoken anti-Catholicism; lived retired in Ireland, ill with gout.

> Clark, W. S., ed., *The Dramatic Works of Roger Boyle*, 2 vols
> (Cambridge, Massachusetts, 1937). (Exhaustive; scholarly.)
> *A Collection of the State Letters of the Right Honourable Roger Boyle,
> the First Earl of Orrery* (1742).
> Lynch, K. M., *Roger Boyle, First Earl of Orrery* (Knoxville,
> Tennessee, 1965). (Standard biography; devotes two chs to plays.)

> See: Lynch, K. M., 'Conventions of Platonic Drama in the Heroic Plays
> of Orrery and Dryden', *PMLA*, 44 (1929), 456–71.

BUCKINGHAM, George Villiers, second Duke of (1628–87), son of the first
Duke, Charles I's favourite, assassinated 1628. Raised by Charles I; educ.
Trinity, Cambridge (MA, 1642). Served in royal cavalry; travelled on the
Continent; joined Charles II in exile. Retained royal favour after
Restoration; recovered sequestered estates, but twice imprisoned in Tower
for intrigues. Friend of Cowley, Etherege, Wycherley. Main author of *The
Rehearsal* (1671), burlesque of heroic drama; adapted *The Chances* (1667?)
from Fletcher, and *The Restoration* (1683) from *Philaster*. Another play was
printed posthumously. Died of a chill.

> *Miscellaneous Works Written by His Grace, George, late Duke of
> Buckingham*, 1 vol. (1704); 2 vols (1715). (The only collected
> editions; contain letters.)
> Wilson, J. H., *A Rake and His Times* . . . (New York, 1954). (The
> most satisfactory scholarly biography.)

> See: O'Neill, J. H., *George Villiers, Second Duke of Buckingham* (Boston,
> 1984). (Twayne format: life, criticism, bibliography.)

CENTLIVRE, Susannah (1669–1723), née Freeman, of a dissenting family, in
Lincolnshire; parents prob. died when she was young; poss. m. and
widowed twice in mid-1680s, but accounts of her youth are anecdotal until
1700, when first play, *The Perjured Husband* (TC) prod. at DL. Also pub.
in collections of letters (1700–01). Very productive thereafter, mainly in
comedy; *The Beau's Duel* and *The Stolen Heiress* (TC) appeared 1702, and
Love's Contrivance, from Molière, 1703. The latter two appeared anon. for
fear of anti-female prejudice. None made much impression on the public,
but *The Gamester* (1705), a serious moral comedy, did; followed with a
similar play, *The Basset Table* (1705). In 1706 prod. *Love at a Venture* and
The Platonick Lady; while acting in former met Joseph Centlivre, Yeoman
of the Mouth (royal cook), at Windsor; m. him (1707); friendships with
Rowe, Farquhar, Steele. *The Busy Body* (1709), first pub. in her own
name, a big success, leading to a sequel, *Marplot in Lisbon* (1710). Only
minor plays for several years: *The Man's Bewitched* (1709), *A Bickerstaff's
Burial* (1710), *The Perplexed Lovers* (1712). Pub. *The Masquerade*, a poem,

and moved to Buckingham Court (1713). *The Wonder!* (C, 1714) was a triumph. A dedicated Whig, greeted George I with two poems. Pub. two unacted farces (1715) and prod. *The Cruel Gift* (T, 1716); satirized by Pope (1716–17). Last hit was *A Bold Stroke for a Wife* (C, 1718); taken ill 1719; final play, *The Artifice* (1722), unsuccessful.

> *Dramatic Works of the Celebrated Mrs Centlivre*, 3 vols (1872).
> Bowyer, J. W., *The Celebrated Mrs Centlivre* (Durham, North Carolina, 1952). (The standard biography; reprints much primary material.)

See: Lock, F. P., *Susanna Centlivre* (Boston, 1979). (Twayne series; life, useful criticism, and annotated bibliography.)

CIBBER, Colley (1671–1757), son of a Danish sculptor; educ. Grantham Free School (Lincs.); unable to gain election to Winchester, went to London (1687); joined levy for William of Orange but soon left to serve Earl of Devonshire (1688). Joined Theatre Royal, Drury Lane (1690); acted numerous roles, some with success. In 1693 m. Katherine Shore; ten children. Discontent with reputation led him to write comedies with good parts for self: e.g. Sir Novelty Fashion in *Love's Last Shift* (1696). Followed with *Woman's Wit* (C, 1697), *Xerxes* (T, 1699), and *King Richard III* (T, 1700), but generally accepted that comedy was his forte. Became adviser to the manager, 1700, as well as actor and dramatist. Followed with comedies *Love Makes a Man* (1700), *She Wou'd and She Wou'd Not* (1702), and *The Careless Husband* (1704), one of his best, before moving to Haymarket Theatre (1706) amid lawsuits and turbulence. *The Comical Lovers, The Double Gallant*, and *The Lady's Last Stake* all appeared there in 1707. When the two theatres consolidated (1708), became co-owner and manager of DL, but company acted at Hay until 1712. Wrote little substantial for some years: *The Rival Fools* (1709), *The Rival Queens* (1710, burlesquing Lee), *Hob*, an adaptation (1710), *Ximena* (1712), musicals, etc. Survived suits and countersuits over theatrical management (1714–15). *The Non-Juror* (1717), adapted from *Tartuffe*, was successful. More managerial troubles 1719–21. Prod. *The Refusal* (1721) and *Caesar in Egypt* (1724) before his last big success, *The Provoked Husband* (1728), from an unfinished MS by Vanbrugh. Ballad opera *Love in a Riddle* (1729) was damned; named Poet Laureate (1730). Retired from DL 1733 but made occasional appearances until 1745. Wrote libretto for *Polypheme* (1734); pub. *Dramatic Works* (1736); literary feuds with Pope, Fielding; pub. his autobiographical *Apology* (1740). Last play, *Papal Tyranny in the Reign of King John* (1745), ridiculed.

> *The Dramatic Works of Colley Cibber*, 5 vols (1777).
> Barker, R. H., *Mr Cibber of Drury Lane* (New York, 1939). (The standard biography, well written and thoroughly documented.)

See: Ashley, L. R. N., *Colley Cibber* (New York, 1965). (Standard Twayne layout; termed 'somewhat uneven' by Link.)

COLMAN, George, the Elder (1732–94), b. Florence, Italy, son of the English envoy; brought up after father's death by uncle, William Pulteney, Earl of Bath; educ. Westminster and Oxford (BA, 1755). Co-ed. *The Connoisseur* (1754–56); studied law at Lincoln's Inn, 1755–57; barrister 1757; MA 1758; m. an actress, Miss Ford; son George became a dramatist. Met Garrick.

Went on Oxford circuit, 1759–64, but drawn to stage. First play, one-act *Polly Honeycombe*, prod. successfully 1760; turned out some three dozen more, including preludes, adaptations, and musicals. *The Jealous Wife* (1761, with Garrick) first full-length play; *The Musical Lady* (1762) and *The Deuce Is in Him* (1763) are lively afterpieces. At Bath's death (1764), received enough money to give up law, though less than hoped. *The Clandestine Marriage* (1766, with Garrick) was his major success in regular comedy. Purchased one-quarter share of CG (1767) and managed it until 1774. Wrote short comedies such as *Oxonian in Town* (1767) and *Man and Wife* (1769); adapted longer plays from Shakespeare, Beaumont and Fletcher, and Voltaire (*The English Merchant*, 1767). Began to write libretti for burlettas with *The Portrait* (1770), working with composers such as Arnold and Arne. Prod. a serious comedy, *The Man of Business* (1774), and retired to Bath; wrote for *The London Packet* and stage. Afterpiece *The Spleen*, an adaptation of Jonson's *Epicoene*, and a prelude, *New Brooms*, all prod. 1776. Bought H^2 from Foote (1777) and managed it until 1789. Among adaptations from Gay and Shakespeare and Beaumarchais (*The Spanish Barber*, 1777), pub. his *Dramatic Works* (1777) and wrote substantial comedies: *The Suicide* (1778) and *The Separate Maintenance* (1779). Prod. only pantomimes, preludes, and an adaptation of Lillo's *Fatal Curiosity* (1782) before a stroke (1785) left him enfeebled. Pub. his *Prose on Several Occasions* (3 vols, 1787). After one more adaptation and a musical, relinquished the H^2 to son George (1789) and retired.

> Peake, R. B., *Memoirs of the Colman Family, Including Their Correspondence*, 2 vols (1841).
> Page, E. R., *George Colman the Elder* (New York, 1935). (Solid biography; considerable dramatic criticism.)

CONGREVE, William (1670–1729), b. Bardsey, Yorkshire, son of an army officer; family moved to Ireland (1674), settling at Youghal; educ. at Kilkenny school and Trinity College, Dublin (1686), contemporary with Swift; in England after the Revolution, entered Middle Temple (1691), but gave up law for literature. Pub. a romance or proto-novel, *Incognita* (1692), and minor verse. First play, *The Old Batchelor* (C, 1693), highly praised by Dryden and others, a great success; *The Double Dealer* (C, 1693) less so. Assisted Dryden in translating Juvenal; other minor verse 1693–94. Friendship with Anne Bracegirdle. Established Betterton's new company at LIF with highly successful *Love for Love* (1695); made shareholder, promised a new play a year; became licenser of hackney coaches and wrote *Concerning Humour in Comedy* (1695). Saved Betterton's company with tragicomedy *The Mourning Bride* (1697) and became manager of LIF (until 1705). Attacked by Jeremy Collier for immorality, replied in *Amendments to Mr Collier's False and Imperfect Citations* (1698). After lukewarm reception of masterpiece, *The Way of the World* (1700), withdrew from stage and went to Europe, though his masque *The Judgment of Paris* prod. in 1701, and *Squire Trelooby*, a collaboration with Vanbrugh and William Walsh, in 1704. Pub. minor verse and met Duchess of Marlborough (1703). Left LIF to help Vanbrugh manage new Queen's Theatre, Haymarket, but soon retired (1704–05). Made commissioner of wine licences (1705), and held other minor government posts. Pub. *Works*, including opera *Semele* (1710). Made Secretary for Jamaica (1714); lived comfortably, a friend of Scriblerians, respected as major literary figure. Ed. Dryden's plays (1717). Involved with Duchess of Marlborough, who bore him a daughter (1723).

Declining health; visited by Voltaire, severe gout (1726); moved to Bath 1728, where injured in fall. Buried in Westminster Abbey.

> Davis, H., ed., *The Complete Plays of William Congreve*, 2 vols (Chicago, 1967).
> Henderson, A. G., ed., *The Comedies of William Congreve* (Cambridge, 1977).
> Hodges, J. C., *William Congreve the Man* (New York, 1941). (The standard modern biography 'from new sources'.)
> Hodges, J. C., ed., *William Congreve: Letters and Documents* (New York, 1964).
> Bartlett, L., *William Congreve: A Reference Guide* (Boston, 1979). (Exhaustive and annotated list, 1729–1977.)

See: Dobree, B., *William Congreve* (1963).
> Van Voris, W. H., *The Cultivated Stance* (1965). (Time and design in the plays; and Congreve's values.)
> Novak, M. E., *William Congreve* (New York, 1971). (Superior biocritical work in the Twayne format.)
> Morris, B., ed., *William Congreve* (1972). (Various modern critical approaches; with an introduction on his relevance.)
> Love, H., *Congreve* (Oxford, 1974). (Focuses on the comedies in the theatre; deals with the case against Congreve's importance.)
> Williams, A. L., *An Approach to Congreve* (New Haven and London, 1979). (Argues the 'essential compatibility' of Congreve's works and Christian interpretations of life.)
> Lyons, P., ed., *Congreve: Comedies* (1982). (An anthology of shorter critical reactions from Collier to Love.)

COWLEY, Hannah (1743–1809), née Parkhouse, b. Tiverton, Devon, daughter of a bookseller; privately educ.; m. a captain in the East India Co., bearing him two children. Thinking she could equal what was on-stage, sent Garrick a comedy, *The Runaway*, which he prod. (1776). In 1779 contributed a scene to a pantomime, extracted a farce, *Who's the Dupe?* from Centlivre's *Stolen Heiress*, and prod. a tragedy, *Albina, Countess Raimond. The School of Eloquence* and *The Belle's Stratagem*, possibly her best comedy, appeared in 1780, and *The World as It Goes* in 1781. Her most productive year was 1783: *A Bold Stroke for a Husband* (C), *Which Is the Man?* (F), and *More Ways Than One* all appeared then. *A School for Greybeards* (1786) was an adaptation from Aphra Behn, and *The Fate of Sparta* (1788) a moderately successful tragedy. Pub. three volumes of verse in the 1780s, and prod. two more plays in the 1790s before retiring in disgust at the 'vitiated taste of the town'.

> *The Works of Mrs Cowley: Poems and Dramas*, 3 vols (1813). (Contains a brief biography.)

See: Rhodes, R. L., '*The Belle's Stratagem*', *RES*, 5 (1929), 129–42. (Plot summary and some discussion.)

CROWNE, John (*c.* 1640–1712), b. Shropshire; lived in Nova Scotia with family on land granted by Cromwell, 1656–*c.* 1660; poss. attended Harvard; in London, served as usher to a gentlewoman. Pub. a romance, *Pandion and Amphigenia* (1665); then turned to stage, beginning with serious plays. *Juliana* and *Charles the Eighth* prod. in 1671, and *Andromache*, a translation from Racine, in 1674. *Calisto* (1675), a successful court masque, and *The*

Country Wit (1676) are lighter, but *The Destruction of Jerusalem by Vespasian* (1677) is massively heroic. In 1679–81 Crowne prod. *The Ambitious Statesman, The Misery of Civil War, Thyestes,* and *Henry the Sixth* without conspicuous success. That came when he turned to comedy, with *City Politiques* (1683) and especially *Sir Courtly Nice* (1685), requested by Charles II, whose death Crowne saluted in verse. Alternated serious and comic work, producing *Darius* (1688), *The English Friar* (1690), *Regulus* (1692), *The Married Beau* (1694), an interesting comedy, and *Caligula* (1698). A few other minor plays are sometimes attributed to him. Co-authored with Dryden and Shadwell an attack on Settle's *Empress of Morocco* (1674), and pub. two heroic poems (1692). Little else is known of his life, except that he was patronized by Queen Mary.

> Maidment, J., and W. H. Logan, eds, *The Dramatic Works of John Crowne,* 4 vols (Edinburgh, 1872–74). (Omits several plays.)
> McMullin, B. J., ed., *The Comedies of John Crowne: A Critical Edition* (New York, 1984). (Useful issue of the important plays.)
> Winship, George P., *The First Harvard Playwright: A Bibliography of Crowne* (1922).

See: White, A. F., *John Crowne: His Life and Dramatic Works* (Cleveland, 1922).
> Ward, A. W., 'Crowne's Place in Restoration Comedy', in *Dryden and His Contemporaries,* ed. C. M. Gayley and A. Thaler (New York, 1936).

CUMBERLAND, Richard (1732–1811), b. Cambridge, a descendant of Bishop Cumberland and of Bentley, the Classical scholar; educ. at Westminster and Trinity, Cambridge (1744–51); private secretary to Lord Halifax (1751–). Pub. first poem 1754; m. Elizabeth Ridge (1759; seven children). Appointed Ulster Secretary; given offices pertaining to American colonies; and pub. first play, *The Banishment of Cicero,* not prod. (1761). Clerk of Reports to Board of Trade (1762). First prod. play, *The Summer's Tale* (1765), only moderately successful, but *The Brothers* (1769), a melodrama, more so, and *The West Indian* (1771) a major triumph. Friendships with Garrick, Johnson, Goldsmith. Next few comedies anti-climactic: *The Fashionable Lover* (1772), *The Note of Hand* (1774), and *The Choleric Man* (1774). Secretary to Board of Trade (1775). Prod. a tragedy, *The Battle of Hastings* (1778), then several minor plays, musicals, and adaptations (1778–1780). Sent on peace mission to Spain, which failed; abolition of Board of Trade reduced income; retired to Tunbridge Wells (1780). Pub. *Anecdotes of Eminent Painters in Spain* and prod. *The Walloons* (C, 1782). *The Mysterious Husband* (1783) and *The Carmelite* (1784) are melodramas, but *The Natural Son* (1784) is a comedy and *The Arab* (1785) a tragedy. In 1789 prod. *The Imposters,* rev. *The Country Attorney* (1787) as *A School for Widows,* and pub. a novel, *Arundel.* Subsequently wrote two more novels, pub. three religious poems, and prod. some twenty more plays, of which the most important were *The Jew* (1794) and *The Wheel of Fortune* (1795). His *Memoirs* (1806–07) are a mine of material on Georgian theatre. Buried in Westminster Abbey.

> *The Posthumous Dramatic Works of the Late Richard Cumberland,* 2 vols (1813). (Incomplete; not the modern edition needed.)
> Williams, S. T., *Richard Cumberland: His Life and Dramatic Works* (New Haven, 1917). (The best life; includes some criticism.)

See: Dircks, R. J., *Richard Cumberland* (Boston, 1976). (A Twayne
       volume, the only modern book-length study; two chs on plays.)

DAVENANT, William (1606–68), b. Oxford, son of the mayor, a vintner and
publican; godson of Shakespeare; educ. at Lincoln College; early service as
page to nobility (1620–23) introduced him to Court; began writing poetry
and tragedies, some performed at the Blackfriars. Began military career
c. 1626, seeing foreign action and gaining lieutenancy and royal favour by
1629. Married (1632), though ill with syphilis that disfigured his nose.
Established self as playwright (1634) with *The Wits*, a comedy, and *Love
and Honour*, a heroic tragicomedy whose success encouraged him to
continue in that vein. Between 1634 and 1638, ten more of his plays were
licensed. In 1638, pub. *Madagascar* and other poems; succeeded Jonson as
Poet Laureate; obtained a patent to build a theatre (1639) but did not carry
through; served in the 'Bishops' Wars' (1639–40); master of the Cockpit
Theatre company (1640). Arrested for involvement in First Army Plot
(1641), was released on bail; fled to Queen in France; served in Royalist
army (1642–); knighted (1644). After defeat, returned to writing,
beginning epic *Gondibert* with Hobbes's encouragement in France (1648).
Captured during mission to America (1651), was imprisoned by Parliament
in Tower (1651–52); continued to work on epic; remarried soon after
release; rearrested for debt but pardoned 1654. His wife dying, travelled to
France and remarried (1655); returned to London and began to prod.
operatic drama with help of Bulstrode Whitelock; presented an
'Entertainment at Rutland House', his London residence, then *The Siege of
Rhodes* (1656), later expanded to two parts. *The Cruelty of the Spaniards in
Peru* (1658) and *The History of Sir Francis Drake* (1658–59) followed.
Arrested for involvement in Royalist uprising (1659) but released; granted
patent to operate London theatre (1660); after brief tenure at Salisbury
Court, moved to LIF, which he equipped with elaborate scenes and
machines. Successfully mixed Shakespearean revivals and adaptations,
notably *The Tempest* (1667), with his own plays: the two-part *Siege of
Rhodes* (1661), *Law Against Lovers* (1662), *A Playhouse to Be Let* (1663), *The
Rivals* (1664) and *The Man's the Master* (1668). Buried in Westminster
Abbey.

> Maidment, J., and W. H. Logan, eds, *The Dramatic Works of Sir
> William Davenant*, 5 vols (Edinburgh, 1872–74; repr. New York,
> 1964). (Includes all but two Shakespearean adaptations.)
> Blaydes, S. B., and P. Bordinat, *Sir William Davenant: An Annotated
> Bibliography, 1629–1985* (New York, 1986). (Brief biography;
> 'comprehensive' primary and secondary bibliography.)
> Harbage, A., *Sir William Davenant* (Philadelphia, 1935). (Biography
> and criticism.)
> Netherot, A. H., *Sir William Davenant* (Chicago, 1938). (Focuses on
> Davenant's theatrical career.)

See: Collins, H. S., *The Comedy of Sir William Davenant* (The Hague,
       1967). (With some biography, comic history, and theory.)
       Bordinat, P., and S. B. Blaydes, *Sir William Davenant* (Boston,
       1981). (Standard Twayne format; analyses the plays.)

DENNIS, John (1658–1734), b. London, son of a saddler; educ. at Harrow and
Caius, Cambridge (1670–79; MA 1683); settled in London (1680); toured
France and Italy (1688). Returning, became acquainted with Dryden,

Wycherley, Congreve, and other writers. Began to pub. poetry (1692), eventually issuing ten books of increasingly patriotic verse, none of them important. Launched distinguished career as essayist with *The Impartial Critic* (1693). First play was *A Plot and No Plot* (C, 1697). Prod. *Rinaldo and Armida*, a heroic tragicomedy with music, and *The Usefulness of the Stage*, an answer to Collier, in 1698. *Iphigenia* (1699), a spectacular tragedy, had few performances; his alteration of *The Merry Wives of Windsor*, *The Comical Gallant* (1702), also failed. In 1704 turned back to heroic tragicomedy with *Liberty Asserted*, and pub. the interesting essay 'The Grounds of Criticism in Poetry'. After living on paternal inheritance for some time, gained patronage of Duke of Marlborough and post in Customs House, and prod. *Gibraltar* (F, 1705). Pamphleteered on behalf of Whigs; prod. *Orpheus and Eurydice* (1707) and *Appius and Virginia* (T, 1709), condemned for rant; avoided the stage for a decade. Attacked Pope's *Essay on Criticism* (1711) and underwent bankruptcy proceedings; career declined into poverty and literary feuds. Pub. *An Essay Upon the Genius and Writings of Shakespeare* (1712). Issued his *Select Works* (1718) and altered *Coriolanus* as *The Invader of His Country* (1719), a final stage failure. Debated theory of comedy with Steele in *A Defence of Sir Fopling Flutter* (1722) and *Remarks upon . . . 'The Conscious Lovers'* (1723). After more attacks on Pope and another defence of the stage (1726–29), died in poverty.

> Johnson, J. W., ed., *The Plays of John Dennis* (New York, 1980). (Facsimiles; omits the Shakespearean adaptations.)
> Hooker, E. N., ed., *The Critical Works of John Dennis*, 2 vols (Baltimore, 1939–43). (Superb edition; includes letters).
> Paul, H. G., *John Dennis: His Life and Criticism* (New York, 1911). (Standard but outdated.)

See: Murphy, A. J., *John Dennis* (Boston, 1984). (Twayne format; includes biography and about twenty-five pages on Dennis's plays.)

DRYDEN, John (1631–1700), b. Aldwinckle All Saints, Northants.; educ. Westminster and Trinity College, Cambridge (1646–54); received small paternal inheritance (1654); moved to London (1657). May have held minor employment with Cromwell government and worked for a bookseller. Began writing verse in school; early poems mainly eulogized great men, including Cromwell ('Heroick Stanzas', 1659) and Charles II ('Astraea Redux', 1660). In 1663 m. his friend Sir Robert Howard's sister Lady Elizabeth, joined the Royal Society, and saw his first play, *The Wild Gallant*, prod. unsuccessfully; the following year collaborated with Howard on *The Indian Queen*, first heroic drama prod. in London. Also in 1664 prod. *The Rival Ladies*, mixing heroic and low comedy. Wrote sequel to his and Howard's effort, *The Indian Emperor* (1665), on his own, launching successful career as playwright. After plague-enforced vacation, came back in 1667 with *Secret Love*, a heroic comedy, *Sir Martin Mar-All*, a popular farce, *The Tempest*, an adaptation of Shakespeare, and *Annus Mirabilis*, a poem about 1666. Named Poet Laureate; signed contract to write for Theatre Royal, becoming England's first professional playwright; pub. *Of Dramatic Poesy*, important work of dramatic criticism; and prod. *An Evening's Love*, a popular farcical comedy (all 1668). Named Historiographer Royal (1669); dominated heroic drama with *Tyrannick Love* (1669) and *The Conquest of Granada* (2 parts, 1670, 1671). Adverse reaction turned him to comedies: *Marriage à la Mode*, one of his best, and *The*

Assignation (both 1672). Returned to heroic style with *Aureng-Zebe* (1675) and *The State of Innocence and Fall of Man* (unacted, 1677), an 'operatic' version of *Paradise Lost*. Joined swing to blank-verse tragedy with *All for Love* (1677), most admired play, then wrote a low sex farce, *The Kind Keeper* (1678), at King's instigation. In years disturbed by Popish Plot prod. *Oedipus* (1678) and *The Duke of Guise* (1682) with Nathaniel Lee, both political; *Troilus and Cressida* (1679) from Shakespeare; and *The Spanish Friar* (TC, 1680); but concentrated on political satires: *Absalom and Achitophel* (1681–82), *The Medal*, and *Macflecknoe* (both 1682). Increasingly preoccupied with religion, wrote *Religio Laici* (1682) to defend his Anglicanism; but conversion to Catholicism *c.* 1685 led to *The Hind and the Panther* (1687). Wrote an opera, *Albion and Albanius* (1685). Loss of offices at Revolution forced return to stage for livelihood; *Don Sebastian* (1689), a major tragedy, was followed by *Amphitryon* (1690), an elegant farce, and *King Arthur* (1691), a dramatic opera. *Cleomenes* (T, 1692) and *Love Triumphant* (TC, 1694) closed his playwriting career, but continued to pub. verse and trans. Juvenal, Virgil, Ovid, etc. and *Fables Ancient and Modern* (1700). In latter years, held place among coffee-house wits at Will's.

Hooker, E. N., H. T. Swedenberg, Jr, *et al.*, eds, *The Works of John Dryden*, 19 vols (Berkeley, Los Angeles, and London, 1956–). (20 vols projected; definitive texts; uneven criticism.)

Ward, C. E., ed., *The Letters of John Dryden with Letters Addressed to Him* (Durham, North Carolina, 1942).

Ward, C. E., *The Life of John Dryden* (Chapel Hill, 1961). (The standard biography.)

Macdonald, H., *John Dryden: A Bibliography of Early Editions and of Drydenia* (Oxford, 1939). (Superb scholarship.)

Hall, J. M., *John Dryden: A Reference Guide* (Boston, 1984). (An annotated list of writings about Dryden, 1668–1981.)

See: Moore, F. M., *The Nobler Pleasure: Dryden's Comedy in Theory and Practice* (Chapel Hill, 1963). (Determines phases of his career; finds increasing interest in moral questions.)

Wasserman, G. R., *John Dryden* (New York, 1964). (Standard Twayne format; two chs on drama; brief analyses of the plays.)

Kirsch, A. C., *Dryden's Heroic Drama* (Princeton, 1965). (Authoritative treatment of theory and dramatic context.)

Eliot, T. S., *John Dryden* (New York, 1966). (Posthumous collection of three essays, one on Dryden as dramatist.)

King, B., *Dryden's Major Plays* (1966). (Notable for seeing the heroic plays as satires; discusses all dramatic genres.)

Barbeau, A. T., *The Intellectual Design of John Dryden's Heroic Plays* (New Haven, 1970). (Sees them as plays of ideas.)

Myers, W., *Dryden* (1973). (Useful overview of whole career.)

Hughes, D., *Dryden's Heroic Plays* (1981). (Largely a reply to King, emphasizing Dryden's 'Idealization of Man'.)

DURFEY (or D'URFEY), Thomas (1653–1723), b. Exeter of Huguenot descent; moved to London by the 1670s; abandoned study of law for literature; made himself welcome at Court, pleasing monarchs from Charles II to Anne with his wit and songs. Little known of life except his works; beginning 1676 prod. some 27 plays (only 5 adaptations), 28 vols of verse and 2 collections of tales. Three of his plays prod. in 1676, of which the sex farce *Madame Fickle* became popular; Durfey wrote another such, *A*

Fond Husband, in 1677. *The Virtuous Wife* (1679) has its admirers. During the Plot years, wrote political plays: *Sir Barnaby Whigg* (1681) and *The Royalist* (1682). Of his four other plays in the 1680s, three are adaptations of Jacobean works. In the 1690s wrote comedies of more substance: *Love for Money* (1691), *The Richmond Heiress* (1693) and *The Comical History of Don Quixote* in three parts (1694–95). *The Rise and Fall of Massaniello* (two parts, 1699) was a rare (and unsuccessful) foray into tragedy. Late in career wrote an interesting musical, *Wonders in the Sun* (1706); later pub. *New Operas* (1721). Poems ran gamut from Pindaric odes to burlesques. Pub. six collections of own songs, 1683–99; but most important edition was *Wit and Mirth; or, Pills to Purge Melancholy* (1719–20), source of numerous songs in *Beggar's Opera*. Lived on patronage, benefits, sales of songs and plays, but popularity and finances declined from *c*. 1713 to death.

> Vaughn, J. A., ed., *Two Comedies by Thomas D'Urfey* (Rutherford, New Jersey, and London, 1976). (*Madam Fickle* and *A Fond Husband*.)

See: Forsythe, R. S., *A Study of the Plays of Thomas D'Urfey*, 2 vols (Cleveland, 1916–17). (Repr. *A Fool's Preferment*, 1688.)
   Lynch, K. M., 'Thomas D'Urfey's Contribution to Sentimental Comedy', *PQ*, 9 (1930), 249–59. (Anticipates the new mode.)
   Graham, C. B., 'The Jonsonian Tradition in the Comedies of Thomas D'Urfey', *MLQ*, 8 (1947), 47–52. (Allusions and influence.)

ETHEREGE, George (1636–1692), prob. b. Berkshire, eldest son of a Royalist who died in France; little known of early life; poss. educ. at Cambridge; apprenticed to lawyer (1658); entered Clement's Inn (1659); may have travelled abroad. Resurfaced in London 1663; first play, *The Comical Revenge*, prod. 1664; success led to literary friendships and royal favour; supposedly had a child by Mrs Barry, the actress. Triumph of second comedy, *She Would If She Could*, appointment as Gentleman of the Privy Chamber, and departure on embassy to Istanbul as secretary to English ambassador, all 1668; embassy to Holland (1671). Over next few years, involved in brawling and duelling incidents. Responded to Rochester's summons (1675) with last comedy, *The Man of Mode* (1676), another triumph. Knighted in late 1670s (or 1680s); m. Mary Arnold, a wealthy widow (*c*. 1680). Troubled by gambling debts, accepted embassy to Bavaria (1685), living in Ratisbon until 1689, when change of government ended appointment. Last years obscure; may have lived in Paris, poss. a Catholic.

> Cordner, M., ed., *The Plays of Sir George Etherege* (Cambridge, 1982). (Fine modern edition, superseding Brett-Smith.)
> Bracher, F., ed., *The Letters of Sir George Etherege* (Berkeley and Los Angeles, 1974). (Includes a short biography.)
> Mann, D. D., *Sir George Etherege: A Reference Guide* (Boston, 1981). (The best guide to other sources.)

See: Underwood, D., *Etherege and the Seventeenth-Century Comedy of Manners* (New Haven, 1957). (Relates him to pre-Restoration drama and to seventeenth-century thought and society.)
   Holland, N. N., *The First Modern Comedies* (Cambridge, Massachusetts, 1959). (Close analyses of Etherege, Wycherley, and Congreve.)

Birdsall, V. O., *Wild Civility* (Bloomington, 1970). (Includes two
chs on the 'comic spirit' in Etherege's plays.)

FARQUHAR, George (1677?–1707), b. Londonderry, son of a poor clergyman;
educ. Trinity, Dublin (1694–96), not without problems; acted briefly at
Smock Alley, Dublin, meeting Robert Wilks; accidental stabbing of fellow
actor caused him to leave for London *c.* 1697. Pub. a novella, *Adventures of
Covent Garden*; first comedy, *Love and a Bottle*, prod. at DL same month
(Dec. 1698). Supposed to have discovered Anne Oldfield and introduced
her to stage. Second play, *The Constant Couple* (1699), a big success, but
next three – *Sir Harry Wildair*, a sequel (1701), *The Inconstant*, and *The
Twin Rivals* (both 1702) – failed; financial difficulties. Also pub. *A
Discourse upon Comedy* and a miscellany of verse and letters (1702). Poss.
tricked by false story about her dowry, m. Margaret Pemell (1703); despite
success of *The Stage-Coach* (1703), joined army (1704–06); experiences as
recruiter led to *The Recruiting Officer* (1706). Visited Ireland (1706); sold
lieutenancy; became ill. Died in same month that *The Beaux' Stratagem* was
prod. (March 1707).

> Stonehill, C. A., ed., *The Complete Works of George Farquhar*, 2 vols
> (1930). (Currently the standard edition; should be superseded by
> S. S. Kenny's.)
> Connely, W., *Young George Farquhar: The Restoration Drama at
> Twilight* (1949). (Needs to be checked against Rothstein).

See: Rothstein, E., *George Farquhar* (New York, 1967). (Superior
> Twayne volume; several substantial chs on the plays.)
> James, E. N., *The Development of George Farquhar as a Comic
> Dramatist* (The Hague, 1972). (Long introduction on history of
> critical reactions to Farquhar.)
> Anselment, R. A., ed., *Farquhar: The Recruiting Officer and The
> Beaux' Stratagem: A Casebook* (1977). (Early vs modern reactions.)

FIELDING, Henry (1707–54), b. Sharpham Park, Somerset, son of an army
officer; educ. Eton (1719–24) and University of Leyden, Holland
(1728–29); lived in London, 1724–28. Pub. *The Masquerade, a Poem* under
pseudonym Lemuel Gulliver, and had first comedy, *Love in Several
Masques*, prod. at DL (1728). Returning from Leyden, threw self into
career as writer of comedy, farce, and burlesque; *The Temple Beau*, *The
Author's Farce*, *Tom Thumb*, and *Rape Upon Rape* all prod. 1730. In 1731
rev. *Tom Thumb* as *The Tragedy of Tragedies*, prod. *The Letter-Writers* and
The Welsh Opera, soon rev. as *The Grub Street Opera*. In 1732 dominated
DL: *The Lottery*, *The Modern Husband*, *The Old Debauchees*, *The Covent
Garden Tragedy*, and *The Mock Doctor* all prod. there. *The Miser* (from
Molière) and *Deborah* appeared 1733. In 1734 m. Charlotte Craddock; prod.
The Intriguing Chamber Maid and *Don Quixote in England* same year. After
An Old Man Taught Wisdom (1735), *The Universal Gallant* failed at DL;
moved to H^2, where *Pasquin*, a political satire, and *Tumble Down Dick*
were successful (1736). Similarly, after *Eurydice* failed at DL (1737),
succeeded at H^2 with *The Historical Register for 1736*, a satire on Walpole,
and *Eurydice Hiss'd*. After Licensing Act closed H^2, began studying law at
Middle Temple (1737). Ed. *The Champion* (1739–41); called to bar (1740).
Under pseudonym of Connie Keyber, pub. *Shamela*, satirizing
Richardson's *Pamela* (1741); own novel, *Joseph Andrews* (1742), followed.
Prod. conventional comedies, *Miss Lucy in Town* (1742) and *The Wedding*

Day (1743). Pub. *Miscellanies*, including *Jonathan Wild* (1743). Wife d.,
leaving him with children (1744); edited anti-Jacobite *The True Patriot*
(1745–46) and *Jacobite's Journal* (1747–48); m. Mary Daniel, first wife's
maid (1747). Justice of the Peace for Westminster (1748). Pub. *Tom Jones*
(1749); made magistrate for Middlesex. Pub. *Amelia* and *An Enquiry into
the Causes of the Late Increase in Robbers* (1751). Ed. *Covent Garden Journal*
(1752). Worked on reducing crime and providing for poor (1753); became
ill, voyaged to Lisbon and died nearby (1754).

> Henley, W. E., ed., *The Complete Works of Henry Fielding, Esq.*,
> 16 vols (1903). (Will be superseded by *The Wesleyan Edition*
> (Middletown, Connecticut, 1967–) when the plays are available.)
> Dudden, F. H., *Henry Fielding: His Life, Works, and Times*, 2 vols
> (Oxford, 1952). (Now standard; vol. II has a large bibliography.)
> Stoler, J. A., and R. D. Fulton, *Henry Fielding: An Annotated
> Bibliography of Twentieth-Century Criticism, 1900–1977* (New York,
> 1980). (Has a section on criticism of plays.)

> See: Irwin, M., *Henry Fielding: The Tentative Realist* (Oxford, 1967).
> (One ch. on plays; concludes he failed as dramatist.)
> Paulson, R., and T. Lockwood, eds, *Henry Fielding: The Critical
> Heritage* (1969). (A little, mostly early, criticism on plays.)
> McCrea, B., *Henry Fielding and the Politics of Mid-Eighteenth-Century
> England* (Athens, Georgia, 1981). (Argues that he was politically
> and artistically uncertain while a playwright.)
> Dircks, R. J., *Henry Fielding* (Boston, 1983). (Twayne vol.; treats
> the plays mostly as a prelude to novels.)
> Hume, Robert D., 'Henry Fielding and Politics at the Little
> Haymarket, 1728–1737', in *The Golden and the Brazen World*, ed.
> by J. M. Wallace (Berkeley, Los Angeles, and London, 1985),
> pp. 79–124. (Develops a theory of the theatrical years.)

FOOTE, Samuel (1720–77), b. Truro, Cornwall, son of mayor, an MP; educ.
Worcester College, Oxford (1737–40), but left without degree; may have
studied law in London. In 1741 m. Mary Hickes; squandered inheritance,
leading to debtors' prison (1742–43); turned to acting for livelihood
(1744–). After failure in tragedy, succeeded in comic roles; spent 1745–46
in Dublin, but usually acted in London. Turned author (1747) with two
treatises, on comedy and 'the Passions', and an eclectic entertainment,
Diversions of the Morning, in which he acted at H². Operating without a
patent and staying one step ahead of the Examiner of Plays, called same
material *Tea* and *Chocolate*, and used some of it in *The Auction of Pictures*
(1748) and *Taste* (1752). *The Knights* (1749) was his first 'regular' short
comedy. Broke into patent theatres with satiric *Englishman in Paris* (1753)
and its sequel, *Englishman Returned from Paris* (1756), both prod. at CG; hit
stride with *The Author* (1757) at DL. *The Minor* (1760), attacking
Methodists, prod. successfully in Dublin, then London. *Tragedy à la Mode*
(1761) and *The Lyar* (1762) played at patent theatres; moved back to H²
with *The Orators* (1762), *The Mayor of Garratt* (1763), *The Patron* (1764),
and *The Commissary* (1765), some of his best and most popular plays.
Riding accident led to loss of leg (1766); in compensation, granted summer
patent; opened redecorated H² 1767. Next plays, *The Devil Upon Two
Sticks* (1768) and *The Lame Lover* (1770), built around his disability;
returned to topical satire with *The Maid of Bath* (1771) and *The Nabob*

(1772). Charmed angry nabobs (as well as Dr Johnson) with wit. *Piety in Pattens* (1773) spoofed sentimental clichés, but *The Bankrupt* (1773) came close to sentimentality. Prod. *The Cozeners* (1774); refused licence for *A Trip to Calais* (1775), caricaturing Duchess of Kingston; rev. it as *The Capuchin* (prod. 1776); her agent prosecuted him on sodomy charge. Acquitted; sold H² to Colman (1777); died at Dover; buried in Westminster Abbey.

> *The Dramatic Works of Samuel Foote*, 2 vols (1809; New York, 1968). (Badcock's 1830 edition has not been reprinted.)
> Trefman, S., *Sam. Foote, Comedian* (New York, 1971). (The only modern or scholarly biography; includes critiques of plays.)

See: Belden, M. M., *The Dramatic Work of Samuel Foote*, Yale Studies in English, no. 80 (New Haven, 1929; New York, 1970). (Still useful for research into caricatures and analyses of plays.)
> Chatten, E. N., *Samuel Foote* (Boston, 1980). (Twayne volume; best work on Foote as afterpiece dramatist in humours tradition.)

GARRICK, David (1717–79), b. Angel Inn, Hereford, son of an army recruiter; educ. Lichfield Grammar School and Samuel Johnson's school nearby; walked to London with Johnson (1737); entered Lincoln's Inn; engaged in wine trade with brother (1738–41). Success of first play, *Lethe* (1740), a satiric afterpiece, turned him towards stage; acted at Ipswich and Goodman's Fields, London, at first under assumed name, and prod. a short comedy, *The Lying Valet* (1741). Immediately popular, he acted at Smock Alley, Dublin (1742) and at DL (1742–45); co-managed Smock Alley (1745–46); played for a season at CG (1746–47), where short comedy *Miss in Her Teens* was successful (1747), before taking over as manager and joint patentee at DL (1747–76). Acting and managing left little time for composition, but rev. old plays almost annually; about half of forty-odd plays are adaptations; generally his versions of Shakespeare moved back towards original texts. In 1749 m. Eva Maria Veigel or Violetti, a dancer. Prod. two satires, *Lilliput* (1756) and *The Male Coquette* (1757); adapted a French play as *The Guardian* and commented on theatrical taste in *Harlequin's Invasion* (1759). Prod. only minor plays, *The Enchanter* (1760) and *The Farmer's Return* (1762), before taking leave to make Grand Tour (1763–65); well received on Continent; returned with new ideas on staging. With George Colman the Elder, prod. *The Clandestine Marriage* (1766), most important comedy. Adapted *Neck or Nothing* from Le Sage (1766); wrote two musicals with Michael Arne and prod. satire on audience taste, *A Peep Behind the Curtain* (all 1767). Organized lavish and controversial 'Shakespeare Jubilee' at Stratford; wrote a musical about it, *The Jubilee* (1769). Besides adaptations and musicals, prod. *The Irish Widow* (1772), a farce, and two satires, *The Meeting of the Company* (1774) and *Bon Ton* (1775), in last years. Retired to great acclaim, selling share of DL to Sheridan and founding Theatrical Fund (1776); buried in Poets' Corner.

> Pedicord, H. W., and F. L. Bergmann, eds, *The Plays of David Garrick*, 7 vols (Carbondale, Illinois, 1980–82). (Definitive critical edition; first two vols are Garrick's own plays.)
> Little, D. M., and G. M. Kahrl, eds, *The Letters of David Garrick*, 3 vols (Cambridge, Massachusetts, 1963). (Over 1300 letters, 1733–76.)

Stone, G. W., Jr, and G. M. Kahrl, *David Garrick: A Critical Biography* (Carbondale, Illinois, 1979). (Massive and definitive; includes a ch. on his plays and one on his adaptations.)

Berkowitz, G. M., *David Garrick: A Reference Guide* (Boston, 1980).

See: Stein, E. P., *David Garrick, Dramatist* (1938; New York, 1967). (Still useful for detailed analyses of plays.)

Burnim, K. A., *David Garrick, Director* (Pittsburgh, 1961). (Studies his managerial role and adaptations, not his own plays.)

Dircks, P. T., *David Garrick* (Boston, 1985). (Usual Twayne format; two chs on his plays and two on adaptations.)

GAY, John (1685–1732), b. Barnstaple, Devon; educ. at local grammar school; apprentice to silk mercer (1702?–1706); secretary to Aaron Hill in London (1707). Pub. first poetry, *Wine* (1708); met Pope; pub. *The Present State of Wit* (1711) and *The Mohocks* (unacted C, 1712). Became steward in household of Duchess of Monmouth (1712). Made literary mark by pub. *Rural Sports, The Fan*, and poems in Steele's *Poetical Miscellanies*, becoming secretary of Scriblerus Club, and having first comedy prod., *The Wife of Bath* (all 1713). Pub. *The Shepherd's Week* and undertook diplomatic mission to Hanover as Clarendon's secretary (1714). *The What D'ye Call It*, a multigeneric spoof, prod. 1715; pub. *Trivia* (1716). Collaborated with Pope and Arbuthnot on satire *Three Hours After Marriage* (1717); visited Continent (1717, 1719). Pub. *Poems on Several Occasions* (1720), but lost money in South Sea Bubble. Made Commissioner of State Lottery (1723); *The Captives* (TC) prod. 1724. *The Beggar's Opera* accepted by Rich at LIF; huge success made 'Gay rich and Rich gay', popularized ballad operas (1728). Pub. *Polly*, the forbidden sequel; lost apartments in Whitehall; moved in with Queensberrys, his patrons (1729). *Acis and Galatea*, with music by Handel, prod. 1732. Buried in Westminster Abbey. *Achilles* (1733), *The Distress'd Wife* (1743), *The Rehearsal at Goatham* (1754), and *Polly* (1777) were prod. posthumously.

Fuller, J., ed., *John Gay: Dramatic Works*, 2 vols (Oxford, 1983). (The definitive edition; useful criticism, good annotations.)

Burgess, C. F., ed., *The Letters of John Gay* (Oxford, 1966).

Irving, W. H., *John Gay: Favorite of the Wits* (Durham, North Carolina, 1940). (Best biography; superabundant background information.)

Klein, J. T., *John Gay: An Annotated Checklist of Criticism* (Troy, New York, 1973). (An adequate guide to secondary sources.)

See: Schultz, W. E., *Gay's 'Beggar's Opera': Its Content, History and Influence* (New Haven, Connecticut, 1923). (Comprehensive.)

Bronson, B. H., 'The Beggar's Opera' (1941), in his *Facets of the Enlightenment* (Berkeley and Los Angeles, 1968). (The best critique of the music; see also the essay on *Acis and Galatea*.)

Spacks, P. M., *John Gay* (New York, 1965). (Twayne format; fine, insightful criticism of Gay's work and masks.)

Lewis, P. E., *John Gay: The Beggar's Opera* (London, 1976). (The fullest recent study; emphasizes underlying seriousness.)

Erskine-Hill, H., 'The Significance of Gay's Drama', in *English Drama: Forms and Development*, ed. by M. Axton and R. Williams (Cambridge, 1977). (Examines the plays in larger contexts.)

GOLDSMITH, Oliver (1728 or 1730–74), b. Pallas, County Longford, Ireland, son of a poor clergyman; educ. at small-town schools and Trinity College, Dublin (1745–49); left Ireland (1752) after being rejected for ordination, missing boat for America and losing money at cards. Studied law or medicine in Edinburgh (1752–53), leaving without a degree to travel in Europe and study medicine at Leyden and Padua (1754–56). In London, calling self 'Doctor', worked as assistant apothecary and school usher (1756); began literary career with editorial work on *Monthly Review* and trans (1757–58); pub. *An Enquiry into the Present State of Polite Learning in Europe*, ed. *The Bee*, and wrote for other periodicals (1759). His 'Chinese Letters', *Memoirs* of Voltaire, and other writings led to meeting with Johnson (1761) and other London literati. Pub. *The Citizen of the World* (1762), trans. Plutarch's *Lives* (1763); founded The Club with Johnson, Reynolds, Garrick, etc.; pub. his *History of England* and *The Traveller* (1764). Always writing but perenially short of money, pub. novel *The Vicar of Wakefield*, poems and trans (1766). First play, *The Good-Natured Man*, coolly received (1768); after pub. of *Roman History* (1769), made Professor of Ancient History at Royal Academy (1770); pub. *The Deserted Village* and biographies (1770). *She Stoops to Conquer* successfully prod. 1773; afterpiece *The Grumbler* followed, his last play. Ten-day illness led to sudden death (1774); two histories, in all ten vols, pub. posthumously.

Friedman, A., ed., *The Collected Works of Oliver Goldsmith*, 5 vols (Oxford, 1966). (Standard; plays in vol. v; contains all but *The Grumbler*, ed. by A. I. P. Wood in 1931.)

Balderston, K. C., ed., *The Collected Letters of Oliver Goldsmith* (Cambridge, 1928).

Wardle, R., *Oliver Goldsmith* (Lawrence, Kansas, 1957). (Reliable; a great improvement on J. Forster's nineteenth-century account.)

Ginger, J., *The Notable Man: The Life and Times of Oliver Goldsmith* (1977). (Non-academic but well documented; tries to re-create context and understand workings of period.)

Woods, S. H., Jr, *Oliver Goldsmith: A Reference Guide* (Boston, 1982). (Lists secondary sources; for primary material see T. Scott, *Oliver Goldsmith: Bibliographically and Biographically Considered*, New York, 1928.)

See: Jeffares, N. A., *A Critical Commentary on Goldsmith's 'She Stoops to Conquer'* (London, 1966). (Solid work from an able hand; includes a short biography.)

Kirk, C. M., *Oliver Goldsmith* (New York, 1967). (Twayne format; ch. on plays emphasizes issue of sentimental comedy.)

Quintana, R., *Oliver Goldsmith* (New York, 1967). (Biography cum criticism; one ch. on plays; stresses use of irony.)

Rousseau, G. S., ed., *Goldsmith: The Critical Heritage* (1974). (Reprints some contemporary reactions to the plays.)

Danziger, M. K., *Oliver Goldsmith and Richard Brinsley Sheridan* (New York, 1978). (Includes two introductory-level chs on Goldsmith's plays and biocritical introduction.)

HILL, Aaron (1685–1750), b. London, son of a dissipated attorney who died young; educ. at Devon grammar school and Westminster to age 14; travelled to Istanbul to visit a relative, Lord Paget, the English

Ambassador, who provided a tutor and a tour of the Middle East (1700–03). After return to England, employed as tutor, travelling abroad until 1706 or 1707; secretary to Earl of Peterborough and Monmouth (1707–10). Began literary efforts with *Camillus* (1707), first of fourteen pub. poems; followed with *A Full Account of the Present State of the Ottoman Empire* (1709); managed DL (1709–10); first plays performed there: *Elfrid* (T), *The Walking Statue*, and *Squire Brainless* (all 1710). In same year m. Miss Morris of Exeter; nine children. Managed Hay (1710–13); adapted two plays by G. Rossi as operas with music by Handel: *Rinaldo* (1711) and *Il Pastor Fido* (1712). Literary friends included Pope. Involved in various projects, many unsuccessful. *The Fatal Vision* (T, 1716) and *Fatal Extravagance* (T, 1721) were last original works performed; managed H² (1720–33); adapted Shakespeare's *Henry V* (1723). Co-ed. *The Plain Dealer* (1724–25) and ed. *The Prompter* (1734–36). Rev. *Elfrid* as *Athelwold* (1731). Four of his adaptations of Voltaire prod.: *Zara* (1735), *Alzira* (1736), *Merope* (1749), and *The Roman Revenge* (1753). Retired to Essex 1738; buried in Westminster Abbey. *The Insolvent* prod. posthumously (1758).

> *The Dramatic Works of Aaron Hill, Esq.*, 2 vols (1760). (The only collected edition; includes five unacted plays.)
> Brewster, D., *Aaron Hill; Poet, Dramatist, Projector* (New York, 1913). (Good bibliography; supersedes Ludwig's *Life and Works*.)

See: Dobson, A., *Rosalba's Journal and Other Papers* (1915). (Includes biographical and some critical discussion of Hill.)
Bruce, H. L., 'Voltaire on the English Stage', in *Univ. of California Publications in Modern Philology*, 8, no. 1 (1918), 1–152. (Includes about thirty pages on Hill's adaptations.)

HOLCROFT, Thomas (1745–1809), b. London, son of a poor cobbler; no formal educ.; worked as stableboy in Newmarket and as apprentice shoemaker in London; taught reading in Liverpool (1764). First of four marriages *c.* 1765. After work as cobbler, secretary, and tutor, met Macklin (1770); theatrical prompter in Dublin (1771); strolling player in England for *c.* six years thereafter; minor actor at DL (1778–early 1780s). Began literary career 1777 with *Elegies*, first of three vols of pub. verse; first play, *The Crisis*, prod. unsuccessfully 1778; *Manthoon*, anon. novel of same year, may be his. Contributed to various magazines and reviews. *Alwyn*, first of a half-dozen acknowledged works of fiction, appeared 1780, as well as his *Plain and Succinct Narrative* of the Gordon Riots; henceforth showed growing interest in politics. Quit acting for writing soon after success of *Duplicity* (C, 1781). Worked in Paris as secretary and journalist (1782–83); back in London for prods of musical *The Noble Peasant* and *The Follies of a Day*, his version of Beaumarchais's *Marriage of Figaro*, both with democratic bias (1784). *The Choleric Fathers*, another musical, prod. 1785; pub. *Sacred Dramas* (1785), not prod. In Paris, met Paine, Godwin, Mary Wollstonecraft (1785–86). Serious comedy *Seduction* (1787) last play of period. Of some eighteen later plays, most notable are melodramas: *The Road to Ruin* (1792) and *A Tale of Mystery* (1802); continued to pub. verse, fiction, political essays; indicted for high treason (1794), briefly imprisoned and released. Fourth marriage 1799; lived in Hamburg and Paris (1799–1802); problems with debt, ill health, public hostility. *Memoirs*, left incomplete at death, finished by Hazlitt.

> Colby, E., ed., *The Life of Thomas Holcroft*, 2 vols (New York, 1925). (Holcroft's memoir, completed by Hazlitt in 3 vols, 1816.)

Colby, E., ed., *A Bibliography of Thomas Holcroft* (New York, 1922). (Primary materials only.)

See: Colby, E., 'Thomas Holcroft: Man of Letters', in *South Atlantic Quarterly*, 22 (1923), 53–70. (Six pages on the plays.)
Stallbaumer, V. R., 'Thomas Holcroft: A Satirist in the Stream of Sentimentalism', *ELH*, 3 (1936), 31–62. (Sees him as a satirist forced to compromise with prevailing taste.)

HOWARD, Robert (1626–98), b. London, son of first Earl of Berkshire; brothers Edward and James were also dramatists. May have attended Magdalen College, Oxford (1641) but did not graduate; knighted for bravery in battle (1644); m. Ann Kingsmill (1645); six or more children. Arrested and imprisoned *c*. 1657; released 1660. Pub. his *Poems*, including an unacted comedy, *The Blind Lady* (1660). Appointment as Clerk of the Patents of Chancery (1660) first of several minor government posts; commissioned infantry colonel (1660); elected MP for Stockbridge but also briefly imprisoned (1661). Signed agreement with Killigrew and others to build theatre in Bridges St (1661). His comedies *The Surprisal* and *The Committee* acted at Vere St theatre (1662). Collaborated with Dryden, who had m. his sister Elizabeth (1663), on *The Indian Queen* (1664), first heroic drama. *The Vestal Virgin* (1665) has both tragic and tragicomic endings. Quarrelled in print with Dryden over use of rhyme in drama, 1665–68; lent money to King; remarried (1665) after first wife d.; played important role in Parliamentary issues (including impeachments of Penn and Clarendon) from 1666. *The Great Favourite* (TC, 1668) very successful; but controversial comedy *The Country Gentleman* (1669, with Buckingham) not prod. Secretary of the Treasury (1671); again lent money to King (1672); other offices (1673); ill health and involvement in Exchequer scandal 1676–77; third marriage, to Mary Uphill; agent for Nell Gwyn in matter of property given her by King; Auditor of the Exchequer (1677–); MP for Castle Rising, Norfolk, 1678–98; Privy Council, 1688–89; fourth marriage (1692 or 1693); further offices and commissions (1690–). Buried in Westminster Abbey.

The Dramatic Works of Sir Robert Howard (1722). (Identical with *Five Plays*, 1692. There are modern editions of several plays.)
Arundell, D. D., ed., *Dryden and Howard: 1664–1668* (Cambridge, 1929). (Includes text of *The Great Favourite.*)
Oliver, H. J., *Sir Robert Howard* (Durham, North Carolina, 1963). (The standard critical biography.)

See: Scott, F., *The Life and Works of Sir Robert Howard* (New York, 1946).

INCHBALD, Elizabeth (1753–1821), née Simpson, b. Stanningfield, near Bury St Edmunds, daughter of a Catholic farmer; rejected for acting position at Norfolk (1770). Left for London (1772); soon m. actor/painter Joseph Inchbald, went to Bristol and began to act. Acted in Scotland 1772–76; travelled to Paris; acted in the English provinces 1776–80. Began writing fiction. After husband's death (1779), acted at CG and H^2 in London, as well as in Shrewsbury, Dublin, and elsewhere (1780). Her first play, *A Mogul Tale*, acted at H^2 1784; followed with comedies and farces such as *I'll Tell You What* and *Appearance Is Against Them* (both 1785). *The Widow's Vow*, first of a number of adaptations from Continental dramatists, prod. 1786. *Such Things Are*, set in Sumatra, *The Midnight*

Hour, and *All On a Summer's Day* appeared 1787, *Animal Magnetism* 1788. *The Child of Nature* (1788) and *The Married Man* (1789) were both adapted from the French. After retirement from acting (1789), wrote about ten more plays, half adapted from French and German sources; most were performed 1791–1805; only *Every One Has His Fault* (1793) has been ed. Pub. two novels in the 1790s, and ed. three collections of plays, totalling 42 vols, 1808–09.

> Boaden, J., *Memoirs of Mrs Inchbald*, 2 vols (1833). (Makes extensive use of letters; prints two unacted plays.)
> Joughlin, G. L., 'An Inchbald Bibliography', *Studies in English, Univ. of Texas*, 14 (1934), 59–74. (Primary; with prod. tables.)

See: Littlewood, S. R., *Elizabeth Inchbald and Her Circle* (1921). (Primarily biographical; two chs on the plays.)

JOHNSON, Charles (1679–1748), intended for the law, lodged at Middle Temple (1701); turned to stage after meeting Robert Wilks; wrote prolifically, usually following current fashions. Long interval after first play, *The Gentleman Cully* (1701), was followed by sustained productivity: *The Force of Friendship* and *Love in a Chest* appeared in 1710, *The Generous Husband* and *The Wife's Relief*, a popular tragicomedy adapted from Shirley, in 1711, and *The Successful Pyrate* in 1712. Little known of his life outside theatre. After *The Victim* (1714), prod. two of his best plays, *The Country Lasses* (1715) and *The Cobler of Preston* (1716), followed by *The Sultaness* (1717) and *The Masquerade* (1719). *Love in a Forest* (1723) is a clever adaptation of *As You Like It*. Unproductive in 1720s, except for *The Female Fortune* (1726); Gay's popularization of ballad opera suggested *The Village Opera* (1729), later adapted by Bickerstaffe. More serious are *The Tragedy of Medea* (1730), *The Ephesian Matron* (1732), and *Caelia* (1732), a prose domestic tragedy prompted by success of *The London Merchant*. Thought to have married a young widow (1733) and set up a tavern, retiring upon her death and living comfortably.

See: Shudovsky, M. M., 'Charles Johnson and Eighteenth-Century Drama', *ELH*, 10 (1943), 131–58. (Sees him as representative of period; analyses several plays, including *Caelia* and *Country Lasses*.)

KELLY, Hugh (1739–77), b. Killarney, Ireland, son of a Dublin publican; little educ.; apprenticed to a staymaker. Went to London (1760); pub. a play, *L'Amour A la Mode* (not acted); worked as a staymaker and copying clerk; m. (1761, five children); wrote newspaper articles and political pamphlets; ed. magazines and daily papers. Lived at the Middle Temple. Pub. a verse elegy for the Earl of Bath (1765), *Thespis*, a poetic critique of London actors (1766), a novel, *Memoirs of a Magdalen* (1767), and *The Babler* (1767), a collection of his newspaper essays. Achieved fame and some fortune with *False Delicacy* (1768), a comedy shrewdly mixing satire with sentiment. Received government employment (1770); *A Word to the Wise* (1770) was shouted down; received a pension from Lord North. After *Clementina* (1771), adapted *The School for Wives* from Molière and *The Romance of an Hour*, an afterpiece, from Marmontel. Having studied law, was called to the bar (1774). His final (anon.) play, *The Man of Reason* (1776), lasted one performance.

> Carrer, L., ed., *The Plays of Hugh Kelly* (New York and London, 1980). (Facsimile of 1778 *Works*; introduction questionable.)

See: Schorer, M., 'Hugh Kelly: His Place in the Sentimental School',
       PQ, 12 (1933), 389–401 (Demonstrates his critical objections to
       sentimentalism, and contradictions in plays.)
       Rawson, C. J., 'Some Remarks on Eighteenth-Century "Delicacy",
       with a Note on Hugh Kelly's *False Delicacy*', *JEGP*, 61 (1962),
       1–13. (*Formally* sentimental, the play is a satire.)

KILLIGREW, Thomas (1612–83), b. London, son of a courtier; little or no
formal educ., but a voracious reader; early introduction to theatres and
Court; became court page (*c*. 1625). Travelled on Continent; began to
write plays: *Claricilla*, *The Prisoners*, and *The Princess* (1635–36) may have
been prod. about this time, but performance data uncertain. In 1636
m. Cecilia Crofts (d. 1638); pub. *Claricilla* and *The Prisoners*, and wrote
The Parson's Wedding, best known comedy (1641). Arrested for supporting
Royalists (1642), whom he joined in Oxford (1644) and Paris (1647).
Wrote *The Pilgrim*, *c*. 1646, *Bellamira her Dream*, *c*. 1651. Appointed
Resident at Venice by Charles II (1651), but resigned after complaints;
travelled throughout Europe, writing closet drama *Thomaso; or, The
Wanderer*, *c*. 1654; m. Charlotte de Hesse (1655). Granted patent by Charles
II to operate theatre in London (1660), headed King's Men, first at Vere
Street (1660–63), then at Bridges St, the first Theatre Royal, Drury Lane
(1663–72). Prod. at least three of his own comedies in first seasons; pub.
eight *Comedies and Tragedies* (1664). After first DL burned, commissioned
Christopher Wren to build second (1674). Succeeded Henry Herbert as
Master of the Revels (1673); yielded control of King's Men to son Charles
(1677). Remained an intimate of King, who paid part of his burial costs in
Westminster Abbey.

       Killigrew, T., *Comedies and Tragedies* (1664; New York, 1967).

See: Harbage, A., *Thomas Killigrew, Cavalier Dramatist* (1937; New York,
       1967). (Includes some criticism of plays; bibliography.)
       Reich, W. T., ed., *Claricilla by Thomas Killigrew* (New York, 1980).
       (Critical edition; introduction discusses Cavalier milieu.)

LEE, Nathaniel (*c*. 1645/52–92), b. Hatfield, Herts. or Walthamstow, Essex, son
of a rector, later chaplain to the King; educ. Charterhouse (1658–65) and
Trinity, Cambridge (BA 1668/9), where pub. an elegy (1670). To London,
poss. as Buckingham's protégé (1671); short acting career, abbreviated by
stage fright (1672–73); turned to writing. First play, *The Tragedy of Nero*
(1674), unsuccessful; dedicated popular tragedy *Sophonisba* (1675) to
Rochester, either acknowledging a previous connection or appealing for
support; instead Rochester attacked play. Dedications to *Gloriana* (1676)
and *The Rival Queens* (1677), a great success, show him abandoning
Rochester's circle for the Earl of Mulgrave's, which included Dryden, with
whom he exchanged commendatory verses (1677) and collaborated on
Oedipus (1678), another success. By *Mithridates* (1678), enjoyed patronage
of Earl of Dorset. In contract controversy, moved from DL to DG
(1678–79). *The Massacre of Paris* (T) banned for militant anti-Catholicism,
but prod. *Caesar Borgia* (1679); Dedication acknowledges critical disfavour.
Success of *Theodosius* revived reputation, but *Lucius Junius Brutus* was
banned after a few performances (1680). *The Princess of Cleve*, from Mme
de La Fayette's novel, prod. between 1680 and 1683; pub. occasional
poetry, shifted from Whig to Tory (1681–82); collaborated with Dryden
again on *The Duke of Guise* (DL, 1682). Last play, *Constantine the Great*,

prod. 1683. Confined in Bethlehem Hospital for insanity 1684–88; after discharge, received pension from Theatre Royal; pub. poems, *Princess of Cleve*; *The Massacre of Paris* performed (1689). Sank into obscurity (1690–92).

> Stroup, T. B., and A. L. Cooke, eds, *The Works of Nathaniel Lee*, 2 vols (New Brunswick, New Jersey, 1954–55). (General biocritical introduction; brief historical prefaces to all the plays.)
>
> Ham, R. G., *Otway and Lee* (New Haven, 1931). (As much drama criticism as biography; sees Lee as a 'heroic' playwright.)
>
> Armistead, J. M., *Four Restoration Playwrights: A Reference Guide . . .* (Boston, 1984). (Includes secondary material on Lee.)
>
> McLeod, A. L., 'A Nathaniel Lee Bibliography, 1670–1960', *RECTR*, 1, no. 2 (1962), 27–39. (Supplements above with primary sources.)

See: Dobree, B., 'Nat. Lee and the Tragedy of Humours', in *Restoration Tragedy* (Oxford, 1929). (Lee typifies heroic rant.)

> Knight, G. W., 'The Plays of Lee', *Venture*, 1 (1960), 186–96.
>
> Armistead, J. M., *Nathaniel Lee* (Boston, 1979). (Twayne volume; short biography; ch. on every play but the collaborations.)

LILLO, George (1693–1739), b. London, son of a Dutch jeweller; family were Dissenters. Worked in the City as partner in father's jewellery business; little else is known of life. First play, *Silvia; or, The Country Burial*, a ballad opera, failed in 1730; but *The London Merchant* (1730), a domestic tragedy in prose, was very popular. Prod. a patriotic masque, *Britannia and Batavia*, for royal wedding (1734); *The Christian Hero* (1735), a heroic and spectacular verse drama, had moderate success, as did *Fatal Curiosity* (1736), a verse domestic tragedy more popular with writers than with public. Adapted *Pericles* as *Marina* (1738); last play, the pastiche *Elmerick* (1740), was performed posthumously.

> Drucker, T., ed., *The Plays of George Lillo*, 2 vols (New York and London, 1979). (Facsimile edn of 1775 *Works*, with introduction and selected bibliography.)
>
> Palette, D. B., 'Notes for a Biography of George Lillo', *PQ*, 19 (1940), 261–67.
>
> Burgess, C. F., 'Further Notes for a Biography of George Lillo', *PQ*, 46 (1967), 424–28. (Presents new documentary evidence.)

See: Hudson, W. H., 'George Lillo and *The London Merchant*', in his *A Quiet Corner in a Library* (Chicago, 1915; New York, 1968). (Accords play historical importance; prefers *Fatal Curiosity*.)

> Burgess, C. F., 'Lillo Sans Barnwell, or the Playwright Revisited', *MP*, 66 (1968), 5–29. (Finds Lillo's other work more interesting than the 'too popular' *London Merchant*.)

MACKLIN, Charles (*c.* 1699–1797), b. Culdaff, Inishowen, County Donegal, Ireland; details of early life sketchy. Father d. 1704; mother then m. a publican; educ. at Island Bridge near Dublin, where stage career prob. began; poss. attended Trinity College, Dublin; may have worked at London tavern *c.* 1713. Prob. acted around Bristol and Bath with strolling companies by 1717; London acting début, poss. by 1720, certainly by 1725, apparently unsuccessful; appeared briefly again in 1730, but not hired as regular by DL until 1733. Fathered an illegitimate child by Ann Grace, an actress; involved in actors' dispute (1733); acted at H² (1734), but soon returned to DL (1734–48). Accidentally killed a fellow actor, was tried for murder but acquitted with light punishment (1735); returned to acting; m. Ann Grace (1739); friendship with Garrick strained by 1743 strike; began to teach acting; brief tenure at H² (1744) followed by return to DL. After failure of first play, *King Henry VII* (1746), turned to afterpieces: *A Will and No Will* (1746), from Regnard, and *The New Play Criticized* (1747), parasitic on Hoadly's *Suspicious Husband*. In 1748 prod. *The Club of Fortune-Hunters* (lost) and *The Lover's Melancholy*, from Ford. Went to Dublin with wife, acting for Thomas Sheridan there 1748–50; acted at CG (1750–52), producing *Covent Garden Theatre* (1752), a Fieldingesque satire. 'Retired' from stage (1753) to open a coffee-house and lecture; declared bankruptcy (1755). Plans for theatre in Dublin shelved at wife's death (1758); m. Elizabeth Jones and returned to acting (1759); prod. successful afterpiece, *Love à la Mode* (1759), his most popular play; shifted to CG, where *The School for Husbands*, a reform comedy, prod. (1761). Death of Rich sent him to Dublin (1761–64), where comedies *The True-Born Irishman* (1762) and *The True-Born Scotsman* (1764, first version of *The Man of the World*) appeared. After commuting between Dublin and London for three years, rejoined CG, producing *The Irish Fine Lady*, the London version of *The True-Born Irishman* (1767). Involved in legal proceedings against six playgoers for 'riotous conspiracy to deprive Mr Macklin of his livelihood', ending in landmark victory (1773–75). Most important comedy, *The Man of the World* (rev. of *The True-Born Scotsman*), finally prod. after repeated rejections, with author starring (1781). Retired 1789: lived in poverty but continued theatre-going in 1790s.

> Bartley, J. O., ed., *Four Comedies by Charles Macklin* (London, 1968). (A biocritical sketch and the last four comedies.)
> The Augustan Reprint Series has reproduced *The Man of the World* (no. 26, 1951), *Covent Garden Theatre* (no. 116, 1965), *A Will and No Will* (no. 127, 1967), and *The New Play Criticized* (no. 128, 1967).
> Appleton, W. W., *Charles Macklin: An Actor's Life* (Cambridge, Massachusetts, 1960). (The standard biography.)

See: Findlay, R. R., 'The Comic Plays of Charles Macklin', *Educ. Theat. Jour.*, 20 (1968), 398–407. (Emphasizes his 'dark satire' and contributions to laughing comedy.)
Bevis, R. W., 'Charles Macklin', in *The Laughing Tradition* (Athens, Georgia, 1980), pp. 129–38. (Discusses all the comedies.)

MOORE, Edward (1712–57), b. Abingdon, Berks, son of a dissenting minister; educ. privately and at a school in East Orchard, Dorset; apprenticed to a linendraper in London. Worked as a factor in Ireland; in London, entered linen trade, but turned to writing when it failed. *Solomon: A Serenata* with music by Boyce prod. 1743; his verse *Fables for the Female Sex* pub. 1744. Met a number of the literati through Henry Brooke, who contributed Prologue to *The Foundling* (1748), a successful sentimental comedy. Pub. minor verse; m. Jenny Hamilton (1749) despite poverty; one son. The lively *Gil Blas* (C, 1751) was unsuccessful, but *The Gamester* (1753), a domestic tragedy in prose, had a good run. Friendships with Fielding and Lord Lyttleton, who secured him work writing for *The World*, which he ed. 1753–56, and 6 vols of which pub. (1755–57). Pub. his own works by subscription (1756).

Poems, Fables, and Plays by Edward Moore (1756).
The Dramatic Works of Edward Moore (1788).
Caskey, J. H., The Life and Works of Edward Moore (New Haven, 1927). (The standard biography; treats plays historically.)

See: Van Bellen, E. C., 'Trois joueurs', Neophilologus, 9 (1924), 161–72. (Relates The Gamester to Saurin's Beverley, 1768).
Collins, R. L., 'Moore's The Foundling – an Intermediary', PQ, 17 (1938), 139–43. (Between Clarissa and Tom Jones.)
Peake, C. H., ed., The Gamester, ARS no. 14 (1948). (Introduction discusses domestic tragedy and moral reform movement.)

MURPHY, Arthur (1727–1805), b. Clomquin, Roscommon, Ireland, son of a merchant (d. 1729); straitened family moved to London (1735); lived with aunt in Boulogne 1736–38; educ. at English College, St Omer, France (1738–44), using uncle's family name, French; studied accounting and bookkeeping at Webster's Academy, London (1744), but also read literature and met actors, including Foote; sent to Cork as clerk to merchant (1747–49), but refusal to sail for plantations led to French disowning him; bookkeeper in London banking house (1750); friendship with Fielding. Began literary career by editing Gray's Inn Journal (1752–54); failing to inherit anything from French, took up acting (1754–56), appearing at both theatres with modest success. First play, The Apprentice, refused by Garrick (1754), finally staged 1756; pub. The Spouter (1756), satirizing Garrick, Foote, and others; Englishman from Paris had only one performance (1756), as Foote had already prod. sequel to own Englishman in Paris. Admitted to Lincoln's Inn (1757); afterpiece The Upholsterer staged 1758; wrote theatrical commentary for The London Chronicle; The Orphan of China, adapted from Voltaire, first big success (TC, 1759). Presented The Desert Island and The Way to Keep Him (as afterpiece) on same programme (1760); popularity of latter led to five-act version (1761). Pub. three satirical poems (1760–61); affair with Ann Elliot. Co-managed DL with Foote (summer) and prod. three more comedies, The Old Maid, The Citizen, and All in the Wrong (1761). Occupied with edition of Fielding, polemical writing; called to the bar (1762); had two short comedies staged, No One's Enemy But His Own and What We Must All Come To (1764). Prod. The Choice; appointed commissioner for bankruptcy in London (1765). Returning to full-length plays, presented School for Guardians (C, 1767) and Zenobia (T, 1768); quarrelled with Garrick; death of Ann Elliot and involvement in copyright case (1769); prod. The Grecian Daughter (1772), a triumph, and the unsuccessful Alzuma (1773), both tragicomedies. Meditating retirement, rev. earlier plays, presented News from Parnassus, a prelude (1776) and Know Your Own Mind, a five-act comedy long in the making (1777), his last play in this period. Made up with Garrick, served as recorder of Sudbury (1779–89), opposed the Gordon Riots (1780), ed. his plays (1786); did miscellaneous writing. Retired from the bar (1788); pub. a biocritical essay on Johnson (1792); prod. The Rival Sisters, ed. Macklin and trans. Tacitus (1793); became ill (1797); pub. a tragedy, Arminius, attacking French Revolution (1798); pub. Life of Garrick (1801); received pension from George III (1803) and sketched a Life of Foote (1805).

The Works of Arthur Murphy, Esq., 7 vols (1786).
Schwartz, R. B., ed., The Plays of Arthur Murphy, 4 vols (New

York and London, 1979). (Garland facsimile edn; short
introduction.)

Emery, J. P., ed., *The Way to Keep Him and Five Other Plays* . . .
(New York, 1956). (*Apprentice, Upholsterer, Old Maid, What We
Must*, and *Know Your Own Mind*.)

Emery, J. P., *Arthur Murphy* (Philadelphia, 1946). (Fairly even
coverage of Murphy's long and active life.)

See: Carkey, J. H., 'Arthur Murphy and the War on Sentimental
Comedy', *JEGP*, 30 (1931), 563–77. (Shows his attachment to
traditional theories of comedy.)

Dunbar, H. H., *The Dramatic Career of Arthur Murphy* (New York,
1946). (Biocritical treatment of the years 1754–77.)

Spector, R. D., *Arthur Murphy* (Boston, 1979). (Usual Twayne
format; thorough coverage; useful discussions of plays.)

OTWAY, Thomas (1652–85), b. Trotten or Woolbeding, Sussex, son of a rector;
educ. at Winchester College, Hants. (1668) and Christ Church, Oxford
(1669–71); stage fright marred acting début (1670); at father's death, left
Oxford without degree, settling in London (1671). Tried acting again but
soon turned to writing tragedies; *Alcibiades* (1675) a reasonable success, but
Don Carlos (1676) much more popular and lucrative. Ensuing personal and
critical attacks embittered him. Prod. *Titus and Berenice* (from Racine) and
The Cheats of Scapin (from Molière, poss. first English afterpiece) together
in 1676; and a dark comedy, *Friendship in Fashion* (1678). Joined
Monmouth's regiment as ensign, receiving lieutenancy in Flanders (1678);
returned to London after disbanding. Another tragedy, *Caius Marius*,
staged 1679; literary quarrel with Settle; prod. both *The Orphan*, a
domestic tragedy, and *The Soldier's Fortune*, a problem comedy, in 1680.
Pressed by financial (and other) worries, tutored Charles Beauclerk, son of
Charles II and Nell Gwyn; and pub. verse satire, *The Poet's Complaint of
His Muse* (1680). After *Venice Preserved* (1682), his most esteemed tragedy,
prod. a dark comedy, *The Atheist* (1683), a sequel to *The Soldier's Fortune*.
Pursued by creditors, did translations; death surrounded by mystery.

Ghosh, J. C., ed., *The Works of Thomas Otway*, 2 vols (Oxford,
1932). (Standard; includes poems and letters as well as plays.)

Ham, R. G., *Otway and Lee* (New Haven, 1931). (Necessarily
succinct, but the best extended account of his life.)

Armistead, J. W., *Four Restoration Playwrights: A Reference Guide* . . .
(Boston, 1984). (Includes an annotated secondary bibliography on
Otway to 1980.)

See: Taylor, A. M., *Next To Shakespeare* (Durham, North Carolina, 1950).
(Stage history and criticism of *The Orphan* and *Venice Preserved*.)

Waith, E. M., 'Tears of Magnanimity in Otway and Racine', in
French and English Drama of the Seventeenth Century (Los Angeles,
1972). (Comparatist approach to *Venice Preserved* and *The Orphan*.)

Warner, K. P., *Thomas Otway* (Boston, 1982). (Twayne format;
good biographical ch. distinguishes fact and legend.)

RAVENSCROFT, Edward (*c.* 1650–*c.* 1700); virtually nothing is known until his
enrolment at Middle Temple (1671); prob. of an old Flintshire family.
Began playwriting with *The Citizen Turned Gentleman* (1672; sometimes
prod. as *Mamamouchi*), like most of his plays cribbed from Molière and ·

other European comedy; ran for nine nights, pleasing public but not
critics; Prologue attacked Dryden, initiating a literary quarrel. Followed
with *The Careless Lovers* (1673) and *The Wrangling Lovers* (1676); turned
more directly to *commedia dell'arte* with *Scaramouche a Philosopher* (1677).
Took a new path with *The English Lawyer* (1677), from a Latin play, and
King Edgar and Alfreda (1677), a serious history play; poss. his alteration of
Titus Andronicus was acted 1678. Returned to Molière and Italian comedy
for *The London Cuckolds* (1681), a great and lasting success. The Epilogue
to *Dame Dobson* (1683), from T. Corneille, attacked the Whigs. After a
long lapse, reappeared with *The Canterbury Guests* (1694) and *The Anatomist*
(1696), which was popular for two centuries after being reduced to an
afterpiece. Closed career with *The Italian Husband* (1697), more serious but
unsuccessful. Nothing further is known.

> There is no collected edition; *London Cuckolds* has been ed. by both
> M. Summers and N. Jeffares.

See: Parshall, R. E., 'The Source of Ravenscroft's *The Anatomist*', *RES*,
       12 (1936), 328–33. (A Hauteroche farce.)

REYNOLDS, Frederick (1764–1841), b. London, son of a prominent attorney;
educ. at boarding school and Westminster; entered Middle Temple (1782)
but soon turned to playwriting. Began with tragedies – *Werther* (Bath,
1785; London, 1786) and *Eloisa* (1786) – but switched to comedy with *The
Dramatist* (1789), a great success. Thereafter prod. comedies almost
annually. Of post-1789 efforts, *How to Grow Rich* (1793) was very popular,
but *The Rage* (1794), *Fortune's Fool* (1796), *Cheap Living* (1797), and *Folly
as It Flies* (1801) read better now and give a fair idea of his style. Also
collaborated with Miles Peter Andrews on several melodramas, such as
The Mysteries of the Castle (1795).

> There is no collected edition; *The Dramatist* appears in Nicoll's
> *Lesser English Comedies of the Eighteenth Century* (Oxford, 1927).
> *The Life and Times of Frederick Reynolds, Written by Himself*, 2 vols
> (1826; New York, 1969).

ROWE, Nicholas (1674–1718), b. Little Burford, Bedfordshire, son of a lawyer;
King's Scholar at Westminster School, London (1688); entered Middle
Temple (1690 or 1691). Inherited five hundred pounds p.a. at father's
death (1692); called to the bar (1696), but slighted law for literature. In
1698, m. Antonia Parsons (died 1706); one son. Began theatrical career as
writer of heroic dramas: *The Ambitious Step-Mother* (1700) and *Tamerlane*
(1701), performed on 4 or 5 November for many years in honour of King
William; but tried domestic tragedy in *The Fair Penitent* (1703). Despite
success, essayed comedy in *The Biter* (1704), a failure, and heroic themes
again in *Ulysses* (1705) and *The Royal Convert* (1707). Pub. first of state
poems complimenting royalty (1707); turned to trans. and ed., notably
Shakespeare (1709); received official appointments as ducal secretary,
Secretary of State for Scotland (1709). Returned to literature 1714 with *The
Tragedy of Jane Shore*, a popular blend of domestic pathos with the
Shakespearean history play, and *Poems on Several Occasions*. Given a
Customs post (1714); prod. *The Tragedy of Lady Jane Gray*, complimenting
Hanover; made Poet Laureate and given clerkship (1715). In same year m.
Anne Devenish; maintained numerous literary friendships with Steele,
Addison, Cibber, etc.; trans. Ovid and Lucan. Buried in Westminster
Abbey.

Devenish, A., ed., *The Works of Nicholas Rowe* . . ., 2 vols (1747). (First collected edn; contains a biography.)

Sutherland, J. R., ed., *Three Plays by Nicholas Rowe* (1929). (Contains the best modern biography and a bibliography, besides editions of *Tamerlane*, *Fair Penitent*, and *Jane Shore*.)

See: Burns, L. C., *Pity and Tears* (1974). (Rowe's tragedies.)

Canfield, J. D., *Nicholas Rowe and Christian Tragedy* (Gainesville, Florida, 1977). (Emphasizes Rowe's primarily theological approach to problem of evil.)

Jenkins, A., *Nicholas Rowe* (Boston, 1977). (Twayne format; sees him as didactic, topical, and melodramatic.)

SEDLEY, Charles (1639?–1701), b. London, some months after father's death; Royalist connections caused difficulties for mother, who took family to France, 1646–48; educ. Wadham College (Oxford), 1656–57 (no degree). Acceded to brother's baronetcy (1656); m. Katherine Savage (1657, one daughter); collaborated with Edmund Waller and others in trans. *Pompey the Great* from French (prod. *c.* 1663); fined and briefly imprisoned for notorious show of public nakedness and profanity at Cock Tavern (1663); in France *c.* 1665–67; MP for New Romney (1668, re-elected 1679, 1681, 1690). *The Mulberry Garden* (C, 1668) was first unaided play. Accompanied King on a progress through East Anglia (1668); hired a ruffian to beat up actor Edward Kynaston, who had imitated him on-stage; diplomatic mission to France with Buckingham and others (1670); committed insane wife to convent and m. Ann Ayscough (1672, one son). Prod. a tragedy, *Antony and Cleopatra* (1677). Fell ill; apparent conversion to Christianity. Comedy *Bellamira* prod. 1687. Defeated at New Romney but opponent vacated seat (1695). Three unacted plays (one an alteration of his *Antony and Cleopatra*) were pub. posthumously.

Sola Pinto, V. de, ed., *The Poetical and Dramatic Works of Sir Charles Sedley*, 2 vols (1928). (Standard; good bibliography.)

Sola Pinto, V. de, ed., *Sir Charles Sedley* (1927). (The standard life and works; contains most of the existing criticism on the plays.)

SETTLE, Elkanah (1648–1724), b. Dunstable, Bedfordshire, son of a taverner; educ. Westminster School and Trinity College, Oxford (1666), taking no degree but writing a heroic drama, *Cambyses*, prod. in London *c.* 1667–71. Pub. an anti-Dutch poem (1666). Settled in London; gained patronage of Rochester but enmity of Dryden, esp. after success of spectacular heroic play *The Empress of Morocco* (1671 or 1673); m. Mary Warner (1673 or 1674); prod. *Love and Revenge* (1674), an adaptation that led to a quarrel with Shadwell. Turned out heroic dramas for DG: the gory *Conquest of China by the Tartars* (1675), *Ibrahim the Illustrious Bassa* (1676), and *Pastor Fido* (1676) from Guarini's influential play. After a three-year hiatus, reappeared in 1679, managing a pope-burning ceremony for the Whigs; prod. *The Female Prelate* and *Fatal Love* for DL (1680), his outlet for the next decade; pamphleteered for Whigs and wrote verse reply to *Absalom and Achitophel* (1682); prod. *The Heir of Morocco* (1682); quarrel, poss. duel, with Otway; became Tory and inherited estate (1683). After another gap, prod. *Distressed Innocence* (1690); appointed Poet to the City of London (1691), writing the annual Lord Mayor's pageant until 1708. Pub. two works of fiction (1692). Henceforth wrote for both theatres, prod. *The Fairy Queen* (1692, with Purcell's music) for DG, *The Ambitious Slave*

(1694) and an adaptation of *Philaster* (1695) for DL, and *The World in the Moon* (1697), an opera-like Italianate farce, for DG. Defended dramatic poetry against Collier (1698). *The Virgin Prophetess* (1701) and *The City-Ramble* (1711) appeared at DL, but his fortunes were declining; wrote drolls for the fairs; admitted to the Charterhouse as a poor brother in the year his last play, *The Lady's Triumph*, prod. (1718).

> Brown, F. C., *Elkanah Settle: His Life and Works* (Chicago, 1910).
> (The standard biography; good bibliography; some criticism.)

SHADWELL, Thomas (1641 or 1642–92), b. Santon Hall or Broomhill, Norfolk, son of a wealthy Royalist; educ. privately, at grammar school in Bury St Edmunds and at Gonville and Caius, Cambridge (1656), but left without degree; entered Middle Temple (1658). Clerk to Auditor of the Exchequer; travelled in Ireland and poss. in Europe *c.* 1664–65; m. Anne Gibbs, an actress, *c.* 1663–67; four children. Encouraged by Duke of Newcastle, began career as dramatist with *The Sullen Lovers* (1668), a successful comedy, followed by *The Royal Shepherdess* (TC, 1669) and *The Humorists* (C, 1670), all at LIF. Argued with Dryden in print over nature of comedy, championing Jonson and humours. *The Hypocrite* prob. prod. *c.* 1671 at LIF; *The Miser* was prod. anon. at Bridges St (1672), and *Epsom-Wells* appeared at DG (1672), his venue until 1688. Then turned to 'opera', rev. the Davenant–Dryden *Tempest* (1674) and working on *Psyche* (1675). Joined Dryden and Crowne in attacking Settle (1674). *The Triumphant Widow* (1674) was apparently finished by William Cavendish from Shadwell's original. *The Libertine* (1675), his Don Juan play, defies generic labels. Returned to comedy with *The Virtuoso* (1676) and *A True Widow* (1678), but also rev. *Timon of Athens* (1678). Played to the farce-lovers in *The Woman-Captain* (1679) and to anti-Catholic sentiment in *The Lancashire Witches* (1681). Drawn into Plot polemic, attacked Dryden in prose and verse (1682–83). After financial difficulties, returned to stage (henceforth DL) with *The Squire of Alsatia* (C, 1688); welcomed William and Mary in verse (set to music by Purcell), was appointed Poet Laureate, succeeding Dryden, and prod. *Bury-Fair* (C, 1689). *The Amorous Bigotte* and *The Scowrers* both prod. in 1690; *The Volunteers* (1692) prod. posthumously.

> Summers, M., ed., *The Complete Works of Thomas Shadwell*, 5 vols (1927). (Long introduction and biography; textually unreliable.)
> Armistead, J. M., *Four Restoration Playwrights* (Boston, 1984). (Bibliography of secondary sources on Shadwell, among others.)
> Borgman, A. S., *Thomas Shadwell: His Life and Comedies* (New York, 1928). (Both biographical and critical.)

> See: Alssid, M., *Thomas Shadwell* (Boston, 1967). (Superior Twayne volume, the best critique of the plays; emphasizes satire.)
> Kunz, D., *The Drama of Shadwell* (Salzburg, 1972). (Useful.)

SHERIDAN, Richard Brinsley (1751–1816), b. Dublin, son of Thomas, actor, manager, and playwright, and Frances, novelist and playwright; educ. Harrow (1762–68) and Waltham Abbey School (1772–73). Family left Dublin 1754, lived in London and France, where Frances died; settled with father in Bath (1770). Pub. some minor verse. Eloped to France with Elizabeth Linley, the singer, and twice duelled with Captain Mathews over the affair, being wounded the second time (1772); m. her (1773); one son.

Entered Middle Temple (1773) but turned to writing for stage. First comedy, *The Rivals*, succeeded after initial failure and revision (1775); *St Patrick's Day* (F, 1775) was written for the benefit of a helpful actor. Collaborated with father-in-law Thomas Linley on *The Duenna* (1775), a popular comic opera. From profits, bought part-ownership of DL on Garrick's retirement and became manager (1776): altered several earlier plays for prod., most importantly *The Trip to Scarborough* (1777), from Vanbrugh's *The Relapse*. Elected to the Literary Club on Johnson's nomination; soon after scored greatest success with *The School for Scandal* (1777). Poss. wrote *The Camp* (1778), with music by Linley, and *The Wonders of Derbyshire* (1779). *The Critic*, a burlesque, was last important original play (1779). Elected MP 1780, serving for three different constituencies until 1812; retained business connection with DL but did little dramatic work thereafter. Wrote an interlude for a pantomime (1780), and *Robinson Crusoe* (1781), his own and Linley's pantomime. Held Cabinet posts in the Rockingham and coalition ministries (1782–83); spoke against Hastings at impeachment proceedings and managed his trial by Parliament (1787–94); advised Prince of Wales during Regency crisis (1788). Had DL enlarged (1794); remarried (1795) after Elizabeth's death; contributed to collaborative musicals and did alterations from Kotzebue, notably *Pizarro* (1799). Again member of Cabinet (1806) and Privy Council. Lost heavily when DL burned (1809). Buried in Westminster Abbey.

Price, C. J. L., ed., *The Dramatic Works of Richard Brinsley Sheridan*, 2 vols (Oxford, 1973). (Definitive; a condensed version pub. in paperback by OUP in 1975.)

Price, C. J. L., ed., *The Letters of Richard Brinsley Sheridan*, 3 vols (Oxford, 1966).

Sichel, W., *Sheridan: From New and Original Material . . .*, 2 vols (1909). (An important supplement and corrective to Thomas Moore's 1825 *Memoirs of . . . Sheridan*, the starting point.)

Rhodes, R. C., *Harlequin Sheridan: The Man and the Legends* (Oxford, 1933). (Another important update; most readable.)

Gibbs, L., *Sheridan* (1947). (General and informal.)

Durant, J. D., *Richard Brinsley Sheridan: A Reference Guide* (Boston, 1981). (Chiefly secondary; some attention to texts.)

See: Durant, J. D., *Richard Brinsley Sheridan* (Boston, 1975). (Twayne format; short life, criticism; annotated bibliography.)

Auburn, M. S., *Sheridan's Comedies* (Lincoln, Nebraska, 1977). (A full critical and historical examination; some debatable judgements.)

Loftis, J., *Sheridan and the Drama of Georgian England* (Cambridge, Massachusetts, 1977). (Informative study of plays' contexts.)

Danziger, M. K., *Oliver Goldsmith and Richard Brinsley Sheridan* (New York, 1978). (Chronologies; milieux; critical discussions.)

SOUTHERNE, Thomas (1659–1746), b. Dublin; educ. in grammar school there and at Trinity College, Dublin (1675–78); entered Middle Temple, London, 1678 or 1680. Having met Dryden, made a false start in drama with *The Loyal Brother* (T, 1682), which complimented the Duke of York, and *The Disappointment* (1684), an awkward comedy. Commissioned an ensign in Princess Anne's Regiment (1685), rose to company command by 1688, but Revolution forced him back to the theatre, under Dryden's tutelage. *Sir Anthony Love* (C, 1690) was very successful, but *The Wives Excuse* (1691), a serious comedy, was much less so. After another try at comedy, *The Maid's Last Prayer* (1693), turned two of Aphra Behn's stories into popular tragedies: *The Fatal Marriage* (1694) and *Oroonoko* (1695); m. Agnes Athyns, who may have had money, *c.* 1696–1700. Failure of *The Fate of Capua* (T, 1700) virtually ended playwriting career, though *The Spartan Dame*, a rev. of a play banned in 1687, prod. 1719 and *Money the Mistress* in 1726. Served as a regimental agent; advised Pope on his pastorals at the poet's request.

> *Plays Written by Thomas Southerne, Esq.*, 3 vols (1774). (A modern edition, ed. by R. J. Jordan and H. Love, is forthcoming.)
> Dodds, J. W., *Thomas Southerne, Dramatist* (New Haven, 1933). (Short standard biography and some criticism; reissued 1970.)

See: Waith, E., 'Admiration in the Comedies of Thomas Southerne', in *Evidence in Literary Scholarship*, ed. by R. Wellek and A. Ribeiro (Oxford, 1979). (A trope derived from heroic drama.)
> Root, R. L., Jr, *Thomas Southerne* (Boston, 1981). (Usual Twayne format; a fair introduction; each important play gets a ch.)

STEELE, Richard (1672–1729), b. Dublin, son of a poor gentleman; educ. at Charterhouse, London (1684–89), where he knew Addison, and Christ Church, Oxford (1690); postmaster at Merton College, 1691–94. Joined Troop of Life Guards (1692); left Oxford without degree (1694); pub. verse elegy for Queen Mary (1695); regimental ensign (1695) and secretary to Lord Cutts (1696–97). Captain in Tower Guards; fathered an illegitimate child; pub. poem defending Addison (1700) and *The Christian Hero*, a moral tract (1701). First comedy, *The Funeral*, prod. at DL 1701. Made regimental captain (1702). *The Lying Lover* (DL, 1703) was unsuccessful; *The Tender Husband* (C, 1705) did better, but turned to periodical writing, government posts. In 1705 m. Margaret Stretch, who d. the following year; m. Mary Scurlock (1707; four children). An ardent Whig, ed. government's *London Gazette* (1707–10); with Addison, wrote *The Tatler* (1709–11) and *The Spectator* (1711–12); ed. *The Guardian* (1713) and *The Englishman* (1713–14). Elected MP 1713; expelled from Parliament by Tories (1714), but given offices, including governorship of DL, on accession of George I (1714); knighted, re-elected MP and given life patent for DL (1715). Ed. *The Englishman*, second series (1715), three other periodicals (1715–16), *The Plebian* (1719), and *The Theatre* (1720). Wrote pamphlets on theatre and South Sea Bubble (1720). Re-elected MP and prod. *The Conscious Lovers*, most popular comedy (1722); in ill health, arranged to pay debts and retired to Wales (1724).

> Kenny, S. S., ed., *The Plays of Richard Steele* (Oxford, 1971). (Definitive edition; textual notes and critical commentary.)
> Blanchard, R., ed., *The Correspondence of Richard Steele* (Oxford, 1941; rev. 1968).
> Winton, C., *Captain Steele: The Early Career of Richard Steele* (Baltimore, 1964); *Sir Richard Steele, M.P.: The Later Career* (Baltimore, 1970). (Together, the standard biography; a useful supplement is John Loftis, *Steele at Drury Lane*, Berkeley and Los Angeles, 1952.)

See: Kenny, S. S., 'Richard Steele and the "Patterns of Genteel Comedy"', *MP*, 70 (1972), 22–37. (Shows how he gradually built up his dramatic formula over four plays.)

Novak, M. E., 'The Sentimentality of *The Conscious Lovers* Revisited and Reasserted', *MLS*, 9, no. 3 (1979), 48–59.
Dammers, R. H., *Richard Steele* (Boston, 1982). (Twayne format; two chs on plays; sees Christian dogma informing whole *opus*.)

TATE, Nahum (1652–1715), b. Dublin, son of a dissenting clergyman; educ. Trinity College, Dublin (1668–72). Moved to London (1672); began writing; pub. his *Poems* in 1677. Entered theatre as tragic dramatist, prod. *Brutus of Alba* (1678, from *The Aeneid*), *The Loyal General* (1679), and his notorious alterations of Shakespeare's *Richard II*, *Lear*, and *Coriolanus* (1680–81). First of many trans was *Ovid's Epistles* (1680); others included Juvenal and Lucian. Collaborated with Dryden on Part II of *Absalom and Achitophel* (1682). Returned to stage with farcical comedies, the popular *A Duke and No Duke* (F, 1684) and *Cuckold's Haven* (1685, from *Eastward Ho*). This failed, as did *The Island Princess* (1687, from Fletcher). Wrote libretto for Purcell's opera *Dido and Aeneas* (1689), but thenceforth concentrated on poems, trans and editions, notably of Boyle's *Guzman* and Davies's *Nosce Teipsum*. Versified Hall's *Characters* (1691); Poet Laureate (1692); Historiographer Royal (1702). *Injured Love* (T) pub. 1707 but not acted. Last poem was elegy for Queen Anne (1714).

See: Scott-Thomas, H. F., 'Nahum Tate and the Seventeenth Century', *ELH*, 1 (1934), 250–75.
        Spencer, C., *Nahum Tate* (New York, 1972). (Twayne format; includes three chs on the plays; the only substantial modern work.)

THOMSON, James (1700–48), b. Ednam, Roxburghshire, son of a Presbyterian minister; educ. at church grammar school (1712–14), at the College of Edinburgh (1715), and its Divinity Hall (1718), where he stayed four years. Moved with family to Edinburgh, 1716. Pub. poems in *The Edinburgh Miscellany* (1720) and *The Plain Dealer* (London, 1724). Moved to London (1725), where he pub. *The Seasons* one by one (1726–1730), besides other verse. Established in Aaron Hill's circle. First tragedy, *Sophonisba*, prod. at DL 1730. Resided in Europe, 1730–33; returning, pub. *Liberty* and travel poems (1735–36). Had *Agamemnon* prod. at DL (1738), but *Edward and Eleonora* (TC, 1739) was forbidden under the Licensing Act. His and Mallet's masque *Alfred*, containing 'Rule, Britannia', prod. privately (1740). Rev. and expanded *The Seasons* (1744). *Tancred and Sigismunda* (T, 1745) was acted at DL. Pub. Spenserian *Castle of Indolence* shortly before death; his alteration of *Coriolanus* was acted posthumously (1749).

Adams, P. G., ed., *The Plays of James Thomson*, 2 vols (London and New York, 1979). (A Garland facsimile.)
McKillop, A. D., ed., *James Thomson . . . Letters and Documents* (Lawrence, Kansas, 1958). (Standard.)
Grant, D., *James Thomson* (1951). (The standard biography; but little mention of the plays.)

See: Campbell, H. H., *James Thomson* (Boston, 1979). (The only twentieth-century critical study; gives one ch. to plays.)

VANBRUGH, John (1664–1726), b. London, fourth of nineteen children of an ardent Protestant; prob. educ. at King's School, Chester, to 1683; poss.

studied architecture in France (1683–85). Brief service as ensign in regiment of foot (1686); imprisoned in France for spying on behalf of William III (1688–92); arrested in England but released (1692); auditor for Duchy of Lancaster; captain of regiment of Marines (1695–96). First play, *The Relapse* (1696), a riposte to Cibber, was followed by the two-part *Aesop* (1696–97), first of many adaptations of French plays. *The Provoked Wife* (1697), his best comedy, was original. *The Country House* (1698), however, was adapted from Dancourt, *The Pilgrim* (1700) from Fletcher, *The False Friend* (1702) from Le Sage, and *Squire Trelooby* (1704, with Congreve and Walsh) from Molière; *The Confederacy* (1705), *The Mistake* (1705), and *The Cuckold in Conceit* (1707) also have French sources. Wrote a *Short Vindication* of his plays against Jeremy Collier (1698); worked with Wren (1698) and Hawksmoor (1699) on architectural projects before launching own career with Castle Howard (1701), the Haymarket Opera (1703), Blenheim Palace (1705, incomplete), etc.; became a regimental captain and Comptroller of the Board of Works (1702). Member of Kit-cat Club; Board of Directors of Greenwich Hospital (1703); officer of College of Heralds (1703–). Managed Hay with Congreve (1705–06); knighted (1714); made Surveyor of Greenwich Hospital (1715); m. Henrietta M. Yarborough (1719; one son); last years marred by squabbles over Blenheim; left MS of *Journey to London*, completed by Cibber, unfinished at death.

> Dobree, B., and G. Webb, eds, *The Complete Works of Sir John Vanbrugh*, 4 vols (1921–28). (Standard edition; vol. IV contains a good many letters.)
>
> Whistler, L., *Sir John Vanbrugh* (New York, 1939). (Still the standard biography.)
>
> Bingham, M., *Masks and Facades: Sir John Vanbrugh . . .* (1974).

See: Husebo, A. R., *Sir John Vanbrugh* (Boston, 1976). (Twayne format; gives four chs to plays, some biography.)

> Berkowitz, G. M., *Sir John Vanbrugh and the End of Restoration Comedy* (Amsterdam, 1981). (Best recent treatment; argues that he helped comedy break free of Restoration stereotypes.)

WHITEHEAD, William (1715–85), b. Cambridge, son of a baker, educ. Winchester College (1729–35) and Clare Hall, Cambridge (1735–39, Fellow, 1742, MA 1743). Began pub. verse with *The Danger of Writing Verse* (1741). Tutor to nobility; gave up fellowship and moved to London *c.* 1745. Poem 'To Mr Garrick' began long association. First play, *The Roman Father* (T, 1750), adapted from Corneille, was successful; second, *Creusa, Queen of Athens* (1754), was less so. *Poems on Several Occasions* (1754) includes *Fatal Constancy*, burlesquing heroic tragedy. Accompanied noblemen on Grand Tour (1754–56); Secretary of Order of Bath (1756); Poet Laureate (1757). Reader of plays for DL and prod. a fairly popular comedy, *The School for Lovers*, 1762; *A Trip to Scotland* (F, 1770) also well received. Pub. little thereafter.

> *Plays and Poems by William Whitehead . . .*, 2 vols (1774); 3 vols, with W. Mason's Memoir (1788).
>
> Dobson, A., 'Laureate Whitehead', in *Old Kensington Palace and Other Papers* (1910).
>
> Broadus, E. K., *The Laureateship* (Oxford, 1921).

WYCHERLEY, William (1641–1715), b. Clive, Shropshire, son of a nobleman's steward; educ. privately; resided in France, 1655–59, joining Mme de Montanoier's circle and converting to Catholicism. Returning to England, entered Inner Temple and briefly attended Queen's College, Oxford, where he reconverted to Protestantism (1660). Served in Ireland with Earl of Arran's Guards (1662); poss. accompanied English ambassador to Madrid (1664) and served in Second Dutch War (1665). Pub. *Hero and Leander*, a burlesque, anon. (1669). May have acted and managed before success of first play, *Love in a Wood* (1671), brought affair with Duchess of Cleveland and friendship with Buckingham, in whose regiment he was commissioned (1672–74). Adopted Spanish intrigue style in *The Gentleman Dancing-Master* (1672). Enjoyed friendship and patronage of King. *The Country Wife* (1675) was controversial as well as popular, and *The Plain Dealer* (1676), his last play, is a retort to the town's hypocrites. Supported Buckingham (gaoled in the Tower) in a verse letter and fell ill (1677); King's help enabled him to recover in France. On return to England (1679), was offered post as tutor to King's bastard son, but marriage to Countess of Drogheda forfeited royal favour and imbroiled him in debt and litigation. When she d. (1685) he was gaoled for her debts; released and pensioned by James II (1686); lost pension in 1688. Father's death (1697) brought an encumbered estate, not an income, for his retirement. Pub. *Miscellany Poems*; friends with Pope (1704). Eleven days before own death, m. Elizabeth Jackson.

> Friedman, A., ed., *The Plays of William Wycherley* (Oxford, 1979). (Standard, superseding G. Weales's quite good 1966 edition.)
>
> McCarthy, B. E., *William Wycherley* (Athens, Ohio, 1979). (Somewhat dry but scholarly, and much more reliable than the lurid imaginings of earlier biographers.)
>
> McCarthy, B. E., *William Wycherley: A Reference Guide* (Boston, 1985). (Annotated; traces critical responses over the years.)

See: Zimbardo, R. A., *Wycherley's Drama* (New Haven and London, 1965). (Argues that it links Elizabethan to Augustan satire; a landmark in the acceptance of Wycherley as an artist.)

Rogers, K. M., *William Wycherley* (New York, 1972). (Twayne volume; good short biography; analyses of plays.)

Chadwick, W. R., *The Four Plays of William Wycherley* (The Hague, 1975). (Estimable discussions of the plays, tracing their descent into pessimism; thorough bibliography.)

Thompson, J., *Language in Wycherley's Plays* (Univ. of Alabama, 1984). (Studies the semantic/moral contexts of the Restoration.)

Index